THE DICTATOR'S
SHADOW

THE
DICTATOR'S
SHADOW

LIFE UNDER AUGUSTO PINOCHET

HERALDO MUÑOZ

BASIC
BOOKS

Books published by Basic Books are available at special discounts for bulk purchases
in the United States by corporations, institutions, and other organizations. For more
information, please contact the Special Markets Department at the Perseus Books
Group, 2300 Chestnut Street, Suite 200, Philadelphia, PA 19103, or call
(800) 810-4145, ext. 5000, or e-mail special.markets@perseusbooks.com.

Library of Congress Cataloging-in-Publication Data
Muñoz, Heraldo.
The dictator's shadow : life under Augusto Pinochet / Heraldo Muñoz.
p. cm.
ISBN 978-0-465-00250-4
1. Pinochet Ugarte, Augusto. 2. Chile—History—Coup d'état, 1973. 3. Chile—
History—1973-1988. 4. Chile—History—1988- I. Title.
F3100.M863 2008
983.06'5—dc22
2008015654
10 9 8 7 6 5 4 3 2 1

To Pamela

CONTENTS

PREFACE

GENERAL AUGUSTO PINOCHET IS ONE of the world's most recognizable Latin American political figures. Whether Chileans like it or not, the name of their former dictator is remembered from Asia and Africa to the Americas and Europe, by taxi drivers, ambassadors, salesmen, and presidents. Pinochet is in a class with Francisco Franco, Joseph Stalin, Ferdinand Marcos, and the Shah of Iran.

The dictator's name did not recede into obscurity with his death in December 2006. In October 2007, about a hundred students who staged a demonstration at Tehran University against President Mahmoud Ahmadinejad, demanding the release of detained fellow students, chanted, "Ahmadinejad is Pinochet. Iran will not become Chile!" When the former chess champion Gary Kasparov competed in the 2008 Russian presidential elections, he accused Vladimir Putin of being Russia's Pinochet and sought advice from former Chilean dissidents. The former dictator of Chad, Hissene Habré, was widely known as "the African Pinochet."

Many of today's world leaders were inspired to enter politics precisely in order to rally to the cause of Chilean democracy. Chile's struggle against Pinochet became an international cause célèbre. Today's global human rights movement emerged from the worldwide protests and denunciations of the Pinochet dictatorship, spearheaded by Amnesty International and numerous other human rights NGOs.

Pinochet's overthrow of Socialist president Salvador Allende in 1973 led Soviet premier Leonid Brezhnev to reverse a long-standing policy and endorse the principle of armed struggle in third world countries. The lesson of Pinochet's violent coup and the subsequent loss of Communist Party clout in Chile was so important to Moscow that Soviet fear of "another Chile" triggered the USSR's invasion of Afghanistan in 1979, to prop up the Communist regime in Kabul.

The former dictator's arrest in London in 1998, following a warrant issued by a Spanish judge, announced a major change in the administration of international law regarding former heads of government. Henceforth, no former tyrant could be sure of escaping the global justice system.

Yet there is little agreement on Pinochet and his legacy. Margaret Thatcher saw Pinochet as a bulwark against Communism and a leader in privatization of state enterprises, and actively demanded his release. Chile served as a successful laboratory for the Nobel Prize–winning economist Milton Friedman and his monetarist theories, which were pursued by Chilean economists trained at the University of Chicago. Pinochet's Chile would later become the good International Monetary Fund student, the inspiration for the "Washington Consensus," a set of guidelines that showed the road that countries had to follow to "put their economic houses in order" as the IMF wished, and to grow. President George W. Bush's intended reform of the Social Security system drew its inspiration from the pension system imposed by Pinochet in 1980 and later imitated in many countries.

In the 1970s, Pinochet's Chile was the focus of an unprecedented congressional debate on U.S. covert action and human rights policy. Those hearings marked the beginning of Congress's challenge to the executive branch on the conduct of foreign policy. Richard Helms was the first CIA director ever to be indicted, for failing to answer questions before the Senate on the Chilean investigation. The names of Richard Nixon and Henry Kissinger became inextricably linked to Pinochet and Chile. Both dedicated extraordinary time and resources to removing what they perceived as a "red threat" in the Americas and enthusiastically backed Pinochet.

The purpose of this book is to explore Pinochet's impact on contemporary history, and the various meanings and symbols that his figure evokes. This is not a biography but an examination of Pinochet's times and legacy. In a sense, it is my political memoir of Pinochet and his times. Because of him, the course of many of our lives was changed and our earlier plans became subordinated to the priority of fighting the dictatorship. In addition to my own experiences, I have used abundant interviews with pivotal players, confidential documentation, and the vast journalistic coverage of the Pinochet period to narrate events and details of many episodes currently unknown to the general public.

Pinochet did not quite match the caricature of Latin American dictators we see portrayed in American movies or in Gabriel García Márquez's great novel *The Autumn of the Patriarch*. To be sure, he was no Bismarck—but neither was he just another Somoza. He was a man of limited intellect who, placed at a historic crossroad, nonetheless led a process of change in Chile that had a powerful international impact.

Most Latin American dictators ran disastrous economies. Pinochet's was the exception. At first, he leaned toward nationalistic economic policies. It was Admiral José Toribio Merino who pressured him into accepting a new economic model, just as he had once pressured him to join the military coup in the first place. Merino was the true leader of the coup and the leader of the virtual "economic coup." But just as on September 11, 1973, when Pinochet had no choice but to follow although he assumed full control once on board, he accepted the "Chicago Boys'" economic plan and gradually became a true believer in the scheme. Without that revolutionary economic model, Pinochet would be a minor chapter in the history of Latin American military dictators.

As a result of his economic record, though for many the man is the emblem of twentieth-century cruelty, others see Pinochet as the leader who, despite his tyrannical rule, guided the nation to economic recovery and laid the foundation for growth and modernization. The agonizing question is: Was Pinochet necessary? Could Chile have reached its present prosperity without him? This book will address such questions.

Pinochet's ideology was self-interest. In times of passionate commitments and causes, his policy was realpolitik: be pragmatic, appear neutral, and cultivate the trust of those with power and authority. A military man who remained on active duty longer than any other soldier in the world, Pinochet was, above all else, a survivor. For all his ethical and intellectual shortcomings, he possessed a remarkable instinct for power. General Pinochet wasn't an absolute dictator, though he wanted to be one; he accumulated enormous power but recognized its limitations. He knew how to exercise authority and was smart enough to rely on close advisers, whom he generally chose quite well. He was not intelligent—but he was astute. "He did not get where he did by a carefully planned design, but rather by taking advantage of favorable circumstances," former president Patricio Aylwin told me.

Ultimately, Pinochet was the accidental product of a polarization the world experienced in the late sixties and early seventies following the intensification of U.S. anti-Communist policies in response to the Cuban revolution, the national security doctrines espoused by South American military regimes, the 1968 riots in Paris and the extinguished Prague Spring, the Vietnam War, the antiwar protests and the civil rights movement in the United States, Ché Guevara's guerrilla movement in Bolivia, the massacre of students in Tlatelolco Plaza in Mexico City, and even the strongly anticapitalist message of the Vatican. That international reality was mirrored in Chile: homegrown tensions deepened as the Socialist-led left began to advocate revolutionary change, the right defended the status quo with increasing fierceness, and the center, instead of playing a pragmatic role, was caught up in the polarizing tendencies in the country. Hence, political parties were unable to form majority-rule coalitions, and political consensus broke down.

This book begins with the events of 9/11—not 9/11 in 2001 but a different 9/11, the day of the 1973 coup d'état that put an end to the constitutional government of President Salvador Allende of Chile. Having joined the coup at the last minute, Pinochet climbed rapidly toward supreme power, becoming the "primus inter pares" among his colleagues, creating a personal dictatorship, and turning the secret police into an instrument of terror. And he formed a partnership with the Chicago Boys to use dictatorship to lift a ruined economy and attempt to "re-create" the Chilean economy and polity.

At first Pinochet was warmly welcomed by the White House, but the complex relationship between Chile and the United States became entangled when Pinochet's secret police assassinated a former Allende minister, Orlando Letelier, in the streets of Washington, D.C., and later when the Chicago model of economic development began to falter, with inevitable political consequences. Pinochet personified a decades-long U.S. dilemma in the Americas. He embodied the free-market economic policies Washington advocated for the developing nations, but he had ousted a democratically elected government and held power through repression. He remained a committed cold warrior, but he failed to understand that, as the Soviet Union weakened, the United States needed him less—and not at all when the East-West conflict ended.

In the early 1980s the struggle for democracy began to move from clandestine to overt activities, in which I was an active participant. There was much disagreement over the best strategy for fighting Pinochet. The Communist Party opted for armed struggle—its military wing even attempted to kill him—while the rest of the opposition shifted from an initial strategy of protests to controversial participation in a 1988 plebiscite in which Pinochet, under his own 1980 constitution, was the sole candidate in an up-or-down "yes" or "no" vote. The shocking victory of the "no" vote announced the final chapter of Pinochet's rule.

When democracy returned to Chile in 1990, Pinochet did not go away. Some argued that the democratic governments were managing the economy efficiently but that it was a democracy under Pinochet's tutelage, as he continued at the helm of the army and, later, sat in Congress as senator-for-life. In October 1998, to the world's surprise, he was arrested in London, at a clinic where he had sought treatment, on human rights violations charges, at the request of a Spanish judge, Baltasar Garzón. When British authorities allowed Pinochet to return to Chile for health reasons, in March 2000, he was finally charged under Chilean law as a criminal and placed under house arrest. His final fall from grace stemmed, ironically, not from charges of human rights violations but from a terrorism-related U.S. investigation on unreported funds that he had been hiding, under several fictitious names and the names of family members, in accounts in the Riggs Bank and other banks throughout the world.

Pinochet died in December 2006, having watched as, one by one, his closest collaborators were hauled off to jail, some of them placing criminal responsibility squarely in his lap. Although he was under house arrest at the time of his death, he was never actually convicted of any of the crimes of which he stood accused. More than three decades after the first massacres of political opponents, the bodies of many Chileans who disappeared have yet to be found.

Pinochet marked a generation of Chileans and touched countless people throughout the world. For many Chileans he brought a crushing loss of innocence. Once more, Don Quixote had been defeated. We had believed that our country was different from the rest of Latin America and could not fall prey to the horrors of dictatorship. Some of us would surely have pursued quite different lives had Pinochet not existed. Many, like me, decided that the only moral life choice was to fight Pinochet and to contribute to the recovery of our nation's democracy. I am among the fortunate ones for whom this struggle ended happily, though I will forever carry deeply buried emotional scars from the Pinochet era.

—*Heraldo Muñoz*
NEW YORK CITY, 2008

One

A DIFFERENT
9/11

The morning the coup began, I very nearly became the world's first suicide bomber.

By the early hours of September 11, 1973, the military uprising against Chile's constitutional government was well under way. My wife, Pamela, and I were living with my widowed mother in Estación Central, a working-class neighborhood not far from downtown Santiago. I had returned after midnight from Valparaíso, on the Pacific coast, seventy-five miles west of Santiago, where I'd been visiting in my capacity as national supervisor of the People's Stores (Almacenes del Pueblo), an innovative and highly effective government-supported food distribution program that was being established in shantytowns throughout the country. I had planned to sleep late, but I was aroused at about seven-thirty by news on the radio reporting unusual troop movements. Alarmed, I leaped out of bed, showered, and dressed quickly. A thunderous blast—later we realized it was a sonic boom from a jet fighter—rattled the windows of our house while I drank my coffee; the radio informed us that the Chilean navy had rebelled in Valparaíso and that army troops were on the streets of Santiago. Though it wasn't clear yet, Salvador Allende, the world's first and only democratically elected Marxist president, was being deposed.

I took my .32 caliber revolver and rushed to the local Socialist Party headquarters, a late-nineteenth-century house on nearby Grajales Street. None of the senior leadership was there, but a dozen or so young party members were already hard at work destroying files that, if discovered, could put the lives of local militants in danger. On

1

previous occasions we had discussed what to do in the event of a coup; my first task was to retrieve the four sticks of dynamite that I'd cached at my friend Marcos's house. I set out on foot for Toesca Street, where he lived. A long line of military trucks rumbled past, filled with fully armed soldiers in combat fatigues, all of them wearing orange armbands. Were they with us or against us? I could not tell. As it turned out, the troops with orange armbands were rebelling against the government. What about the commander in chief of the army, General Augusto Pinochet? He had behaved like a loyal professional soldier in recent months. I wondered whether he was resisting the coup.

Marcos was politically active only at his workplace; he had kept a low profile in our neighborhood, so his house provided an ideal hiding place for us. He was pale and distraught when he greeted me at the door. We sat together at his dining-room table for a few minutes, listening to the latest news. Nobody had uttered the word "coup" yet, but the pro-government radio station Corporación was broadcasting urgent news bulletins and what I recognized as ominous "coded" messages alerting of a coup in progress. Clearly, this was no repeat of the putsch attempted by a renegade tank regiment in Santiago three months earlier, which had been swiftly put down. We were in serious trouble.

I had given Marcos precise instructions about the dynamite I had entrusted to his care. The sticks had to be rotated every few days or else the nitroglycerine would begin to "sweat," rendering them highly unstable. But when we went to the closet where the explosives were hidden, I was shocked to see that the blue cloth they were wrapped in was totally soaked through. Any abrupt movement could be enough to set them off.

"Why didn't you turn them like I told you to?" I shouted.

Marcos was too agitated to explain; he merely mumbled that he had forgotten. Obviously he had stashed the dynamite in his closet and, perhaps out of fear, never touched it again. I had no choice: I slid the deadly bundle under my coat and said good-bye to him. I wouldn't be returning to party headquarters, which was too obvious a target for the military. Instead we had agreed to regroup at a nearby foundry, Maestranza Jemo, whose workers were all either Socialists or Communists.

A few weak rays of sunlight pierced through the thick clouds as I set off down the street. I did my best to look nonchalant as more military trucks drove by. I was carrying four sticks of highly unstable dynamite and a gun. If I were stopped, I would be arrested for sure—and then, who knew?

As soon as I got to the factory I secured the dynamite inside a large metal drum. By then the young Socialists from party headquarters had made their way across the rooftops to the factory as well. Not counting the workers (who were so intent upon their own discussions that they completely ignored us), there were about ten of us. I was annoyed that our local party security chief, a huge man the size of an American football player, was missing (years later, I learned that he had taken refuge at an embassy), but I was impressed that at least one person I had presumed to be a coward was present and ready to fight and even die.

Somebody said we should destroy our Socialist Party ID cards, so I took mine out of my wallet and tore it up—not an easy task, since it was laminated in thick plastic. Then a bulletin came over the radio announcing what we all knew already—that a coup was in fact occurring. A few stations sympathetic to the government continued transmitting for a while, but one by one they were silenced. Soon only the anti-Allende radio stations remained on the air, broadcasting a steady stream of military songs and marches. Someone asked what we ought to do.

"We have to defend the constitutional government of Allende," I declared. *But with what?* I thought bitterly. Our stockpile of weapons consisted of four sticks of dynamite that posed more of a danger to us than to anybody else, one Mauser rifle that dated back to World War II, and four handguns, including my own. We had hardly any ammunition and our adversaries were heavily armed professional soldiers.

Not that I was a total amateur. Some months earlier I had been selected to receive paramilitary training. Over a six-week period, about a dozen Socialists from different parts of the country had met daily at a beautiful old semi-abandoned mansion on Catedral Street in downtown Santiago. I never learned the names of any of my classmates, because on our first day our teacher had instructed us to adopt aliases. For the same reason, I never knew my teacher's name, although he did tell us that he had been a member of the "Eleno" (from ELN, Ejército de Liberación Nacional, or Army of National Liberation) faction of the Socialist Party that had gone to Bolivia in the mid- to late-sixties to fight alongside Ché Guevara's guerrilla army.

Our teacher taught us how to shoot handguns and how to assemble and disassemble them in the dark. We learned how to survive in hiding, how to follow someone without being observed, and how to detect surveillance. We were also trained in the handling of explosives. One day our instructor explained, perhaps only half jokingly, why it's important to arm a stick of dynamite with your hands behind your back. This way, he said, if the dynamite explodes, "It will blow off part of your ass and not the front of your anatomy." (I thought about his comment that morning, as I pressed the four unstable sticks of dynamite to my chest.)

Aside from target practice, I had used my gun only once, for self-defense. During the March 1973 congressional elections, some Socialist friends and I had driven to a rough neighborhood south of Club Hípico, a Santiago racetrack, to paint political propaganda on the walls of buildings. We had just finished when a group of right-wing thugs insulted and threatened us. As we drove away, an Austin Mini pulled up behind us, guns blazing out of its windows. We threw ourselves onto the floor of our truck among the paint cans, and I and another young man emptied our weapons toward the Mini, striking its windshield, which convinced its driver to abandon the chase. That was the sum of my combat experience.

We all knew what we were supposed to do. In the event of a coup, we had been instructed to report to prearranged safe houses, where official assignments and assault weapons would be distributed. But one member of the group at the factory suggested that we take the initiative right then and there. Ignoring the fact that our dynamite was unusable and our firepower grossly insufficient, he suggested that we undertake a surprise attack on the local police station, the Eighth Precinct, to capture heavier weapons such as machine guns and automatic rifles. As long as we were certain that the police station supported the coup and we knew what security measures they had taken, I had no objection to the plan. I suggested that one of us reconnoiter. A volunteer left immediately and returned ten minutes later.

"Impossible," he said. "The whole block is cordoned off. I couldn't even get near the station, and besides, they have placed heavy machine guns in well-fortified positions."

We were still discussing what to do next when President Allende's voice came over the radio. It was 10:15 A.M. It would be his last speech.

AT THAT MOMENT President Allende was at La Moneda, the presidential palace, preparing to engage in combat with the rebel forces. He was accompanied by his personal security guard, the Group of Friends of the President (Grupo de Amigos del Presidente, GAP). Also with him were a few members of the Investigaciones (the Civilian Police), his personal physicians, and some government officials.

Allende chose to stay at the palace and resist the rebel forces because he thought it was his duty to defend the Republic; also he hoped he could buy some time for loyal troops and political paramilitary forces to come to his rescue. Many witnesses and journalists recorded what transpired at the palace that day.

The night before, President Allende had entertained guests at his residence at Tomás Moro Street 200, in the well-to-do east side of the city. At 9:30 P.M. he'd dined with Carlos Briones, minister of the interior; Orlando Letelier, minister of defense; a journalist friend of his, Augusto Olivares; his political adviser, the Spaniard Joan Garcés; the first lady, Hortensia "Tencha" Bussi; and their daughter Isabel, who had just returned from Mexico. Isabel had brought her father two jackets as a present.

"I hope I am able to wear them," he commented darkly.

"Is the situation so bad?" Isabel asked. Allende did not respond.

The president had arrived late to his own dinner party because he had attended a briefing by Foreign Minister Clodomiro Almeyda, who had just come back from a Non-Aligned Movement meeting in Algeria. For the first time in weeks, Allende felt mildly optimistic. To resolve his differences with the opposition, he had decided to propose a national plebiscite on the impasse regarding the future of the public and private sectors of the economy. He planned to make the announcement the next day.

Allende's economic program was not aimed at achieving an extreme form of socialism. His government had targeted mining conglomerates, large companies, banks, and *latifundia* (very large agricultural estates) for expropriation with the idea of establishing a "social property" sector that would coexist with both a mixed sector and a private property sector of the economy. But as time went by, smaller and smaller factories or farms were seized by workers or activists and placed under the control of the state.

The Socialist Party, to which I belonged, and the Movement of the Revolutionary Left (Movimiento de Izquierda Revolucionaria, MIR) had radicalized the political process in pursuit of socialism, disregarding the fact that Allende had won the presidency by a plurality, and that the governing Popular Unity coalition held a minority of seats in Congress. For their part, the extreme right and the Nixon White House had not given Allende a chance, having launched a destabilization and terror campaign against him and the Chilean economy even before he assumed office. Dialogue promoted by Cardinal Raúl Silva Henríquez between the government and the centrist Christian Democrats, now allied with the right, had failed.

The only option to avoid a military coup or civil war, according to Allende, was a plebiscite in which the voters would be asked, in essence, to reconfirm his presidency of Chile. The president felt he would probably lose the referendum and in that case he was ready to resign to avoid further confrontation.

The dinner was interrupted by news that two trucks filled with soldiers were rushing toward Santiago from the town of Los Andes, about fifty miles to the northeast. Letelier was able to contact General Herman Brady, the army chief for Santiago, who at first responded that he knew nothing about the situation. Later, realizing that the local military commander had imprudently mobilized his troops before the agreed-upon time for the coup, Brady ordered the troops back, claiming that they were normal deployments in anticipation of exercises for the Independence Day military parade on September 19. The dinner ended at 2 A.M. and Allende retired for the night. Just a few hours later, he knew the truth—his government was under attack.

At 6:30 A.M. the president was awakened by a GAP guard, Hugo García, who passed him an urgent phone call from General Jorge Urrutia of the Carabineros, the national military police force, who conveyed to him a message from Valparaíso's police chief: the marines were taking up combat positions in the streets, occupying key sectors, and cutting off the port city from the rest of the country. Dozens of political and labor union leaders had already been arrested. If I had spent that night in Valparaíso, instead of coming home late, I would have been trapped there.

Allende ordered that calls be made immediately to Admiral Raúl Montero, the head of the navy, and to General Augusto Pinochet, the commander in chief of the army, but he could not get through. Montero's phone lines had been severed by his own people during the night; he had been forcibly discharged from his position as commander of the navy because of his reluctance to join the coup. Allende phoned Pinochet at home. He was told that the general was in the shower and would call back in a few minutes. Meanwhile, Alfredo Joignant, the director of Investigaciones, had called the president to confirm the uprising in Valparaíso.

The only military officer President Allende was able to locate was, once again, General Herman Brady. Allende ordered him to send army troops to Valparaíso to quell the uprising. Brady promised to do so, but did not. He was already taking his orders from elsewhere.

A few minutes later, the plotters cut all phone lines at the presidential residence, which was now totally isolated from the outside world. Allende decided to move to La Moneda, the presidential palace, in downtown Santiago. Abandoning his usual formal attire, he dressed in a gray turtleneck sweater patterned with brown figures, dark gray pants, and black shoes. Always elegant, he slipped on a gray tweed jacket; he readied for combat, picking up his automatic AK-47 Kalashnikov rifle, and stepped outside. The inscription on the gunstock read, "To Salvador, from a comrade in arms. Fidel."

Allende's GAP contingent consisted of twenty-three men, armed with two .30 caliber machine guns and three RPG-7s (Russian-made rocket launchers), plus their personal ordnance: AK-47 rifles, P-38 pistols, and Colt Cobra revolvers. Allende ordered part of the team to remain behind to protect his wife. Then, at 7:20 A.M., his motorcade—four blue Fiat 125 cars plus two white armored vehicles—sped downtown. Along with his security guards, the president was accompanied by Dr. Danilo Bartulín, Joan Garcés, and Augusto Olivares. Seven members of the GAP were ordered to remain with the cars in case of an emergency and, in the event of combat, to take positions next door, in the Ministry of Public Works. The rest of the men accompanied Allende inside the palace.

Around the same time that Allende arrived at La Moneda, Minister Orlando Letelier pulled up in front of the Ministry of Defense, just about 330 feet away, accompanied by his driver and his military escort, Lieutenant Colonel Sergio González. As they approached the entrance, González unholstered his pistol and pointed it at Letelier's chest. The minister was informed that he was under arrest, and was taken to the office of Army General Sergio Arellano. Arellano and Admiral Patricio Carvajal had been coordinating the coup from a communications post within the Ministry of Defense. The coup's other leaders were the commander of the air force, General Gustavo Leigh, who was stationed at the Air Force Academy in the Las Condes neighborhood of Santiago; Colonel Nilo Floody, at the Army Military School; and General Augusto Pinochet, who was far away in the foothills of the Andes. Despite its distance from the action, Pinochet's position had been designated Post Number 1.

Allende was pleased to see that General José María Sepúlveda, the head of the Carabineros, was at the presidential palace. He hoped that the 40,000-strong Carabineros force Sepúlveda commanded was on the side of the constitutional government.

At around 7:55 A.M., Allende briefly addressed the nation, confirming that navy officers had rebelled in Valparaíso but asserting that the situation in Santiago was normal. The president encouraged workers "to occupy their places, to go to their factories, and to remain calm and serene."

As Allende finished uttering these words, three Sherman tanks were being positioned on the northern side of La Moneda, their commanders awaiting orders to attack. Four Hawker Hunter jet fighters loaded with Sura rockets had been dispatched to the capital from the city of Concepción, about 325 miles to the south; their pilots' first mission had been to bomb the transmitters of pro-government radio stations.

President Allende issued another order to contact General Pinochet, but the general was incomunicado.

"Poor Pinochet. He must be under arrest," Allende said.

One witness to this episode, the journalist Carlos "Negro" Jorquera, who many years later would work for me at the Foreign Ministry, believed that Allende's concern for Pinochet was sincere. At that point the president still thought that the insurrection was restricted to one sector of the navy.

"Problems with your navy again, captain," Allende said to his navy aide-de-camp, Captain Jorge Grez.

General Sepúlveda of the Carabineros attempted to reach his police commanders by telephone. He managed to contact some of them, but no one seemed to have any information. Another bad sign was that the undersecretary of the army, Colonel Rafael Valenzuela, a government loyalist, had just been prevented from entering the Defense Ministry.

At 8:42 A.M., two radio stations linked to the rebels, Minería and Agricultura, broadcast martial music and the national anthem, followed by a formal armed forces message communicating that a military junta had been constituted by the commanders in chief of the army and the air force, Pinochet and Leigh, and by Admiral José Toribio Merino and General César Mendoza, who had taken over command of the navy and the Carabineros, respectively. They demanded that President Allende resign his post immediately.

There was no hope. The armed forces were not divided; there were no loyal troops to come to the rescue.

Allende responded by addressing the nation once more. "I will *not* resign," he declared defiantly. "I will stay and inform the nation about the preposterous attitude of soldiers who refuse to honor their sworn commitments."

The military responded bluntly.

"If La Moneda is not evacuated before 11 A.M., it will be attacked by land and air."

Nobody in the presidential palace could believe it. Surely the air force would not destroy the historically and symbolically significant building. But the situation continued to deteriorate. One by one, the armored police vehicles parked outside the palace drove away; the Carabineros who had been defensively deployed around its perimeter were now a part of the siege. The country's borders were sealed, all commercial flights were grounded, international communications were cut off. Chile was under military control.

Allende appeared briefly in one of the northern balconies of La Moneda to check what was happening in the street; a few onlookers applauded him and he waved to them. Around 9:15 A.M. Allende phoned the Defense Ministry and talked to General Ernesto Baeza. He suggested that the commanders of the coup meet with him at La Moneda to work out a reasonable solution to the crisis. Baeza consulted with Pinochet, who resolutely rejected Allende's proposition.

"Allende is not a straight shooter, you know," Pinochet told Admiral Carvajal. "If he wants to, he can go to the Ministry of Defense and surrender to the commanders in chief." Carvajal phoned La Moneda to reiterate that Allende had no choice but to resign, and to assure him that a private plane was waiting to transport him and his family to exile in the country of his choice.

Vehemently rejecting the ultimatum, the president chose instead to address the country once more, over Magallanes, the one progovernment radio station that was still on the air. At this point, his only remaining support came from a band of Socialists who were holed up at the Central Bank, one block away from the palace. They had tried to reach La Moneda earlier but had been turned away by ground troops. The head of the GAP presidential security detail had intercepted another armed contingent of eight Socialists and instructed them to return to central party headquarters in San Martin Street, burn all of the party's documents, and then seek refuge until they could reorganize.

The GAP took up their positions inside La Moneda and began to exchange fire with the military forces (the Carabineros inside the palace held their fire). Meanwhile, aides burned the president's private documents, and the Declaration of Chilean Independence, a historic, irreplaceable document dating back to 1818, was securely stored away (though in the end it was consumed by fire).

Allende ordered his military attachés to leave so that they would not have to fight against their own forces. They phoned Admiral Carvajal at the Defense Ministry to inform him that they were abandoning the palace and exited through a side door known as Morandé 80. A third message from the military junta announced that any unauthorized civilians caught carrying weapons or explosives would be executed on the spot; a curfew would begin at 6 P.M. I was at the metal factory when the warning was issued, but it didn't mean much to me. My only concern was how to counter the coup and to die, if necessary.

Meanwhile GAP leaders and the former head of the civilian police, Eduardo "Coco" Paredes, a physician who was a member of the Socialist Party and a staunch Allende supporter, were discussing plans to rescue the president. If Allende could somehow escape the palace, there was a secret underground bunker he could go to, specially built for him beneath a safe house. But there was no way out; the palace was completely surrounded.

At around 10 A.M. Allende received an emissary from the Socialist Party, Hernán del Canto, a former minister in his cabinet. Del Canto asserted that the Socialists were ready to fight and only awaited his word on what they should do; he urged Allende to escape the palace and lead the resistance himself.

"I will not leave La Moneda. I know what I have to do. As regards the Socialist Party, why does it ask my opinion now when it has not cared about my views for quite a while? Tell your comrades that they should *know* what to do at this moment," the president replied sternly.

It was a bitter exchange. Since the 1970 election the president had progressively lost the support of the leadership of his own party, which saw him as excessively prone to compromise with the military and his political opponents. The country had become polarized between Allende supporters and opponents, while the government coalition was fractured between the moderate Communists—to whom Allende felt politically closer—and the more radical Socialists, who nevertheless would side with Allende at such a critical moment.

Across a side street from La Moneda some GAP sharpshooters stationed in the Ministry of Public Works opened fire on troops that were advancing from the south. Troops approaching from the north faced a barrage of gunfire from the rooftops of the Ministry of Finance, the Central Bank, and other nearby buildings. But these were Allende's only defenders. One of the GAP security agents set up a .30 caliber machine gun in one of the second-floor windows of the palace, but within minutes he was seriously wounded and was evacuated to a downtown emergency hospital. Later he was kidnapped from the hospital by the military and was never heard from again.

At 10:10 A.M. President Allende stated that he wished to make another radio address, which turned out to be his last. The Magallanes radio station was standing by. "Shut up, everybody shut up, the president is about to speak to the nation," Jorquera, the journalist, ordered those present in the room. Rising to his feet and leaning on his desk,

Allende picked up the microphone and delivered a speech that those who heard it would never forget:

> Surely, this will be the last time I will be able to speak to you. The Air Force has bombed the transmitters of Portales and the Corporación radio stations. My words do not reflect bitterness, but disappointment. Let them stand as a moral punishment for those who have betrayed their oath. . . .
>
> I say to the workers: I will not resign! Placed on this historic crossroad, I will pay for the people's loyalty with my life. And I say to you that I am certain that the seeds planted in the worthy conscience of thousands upon thousands of Chileans will not be mowed down forever. . . . I speak to the worker, the peasant, the intellectual, and to those who will be persecuted, because in our country fascism has been present for a long time in the form of terrorist attacks, blowing up bridges, cutting off railroads, destroying oil and gas pipelines, in the face of the silence of those who had the duty to take action. History will judge them.
>
> Surely, Radio Magallanes will be silenced and the calm metal of my voice will no longer reach you. It does not matter. You will continue to hear me. I will always be with you.
>
> You should remember me as a noble man, who was loyal to the nation. The people ought to defend themselves, but not commit sacrifices. The people must not permit themselves to be obliterated, demoralized, or humiliated.
>
> Workers of my homeland: I have faith in Chile and its future. Other men will overcome this dark and bitter moment when treason is attempting to prevail. You must continue to believe that, sooner rather than later, the grand avenues will open again through which free men will pass to build a better society.
>
> Long live Chile, long live the people, and long live the workers!

The speech was interrupted just once, when a bullet shattered a window in his office. Allende's last words would inspire the resistance and haunt the military junta for years. Conscious of defeat, he did not call for an armed uprising, because he knew it would result in a bloodbath. At the same time, he resolved that he would not permit himself to be taken alive, lest he appear to have acknowledged the legitimacy of the insurrection.

At Maestranza Jemo my comrades and I, transfixed by emotion approaching despair, were reduced to silence. To millions of Chileans at that moment, all hope appeared to be lost.

"I wonder what General Prats will do?" one of my companions said, referring to the former commander in chief of the army, a known constitutionalist who had resigned his post just a few weeks earlier.

"I don't know," I answered, "but a retired general has zero influence. We are on our own now, and we should go to our safe houses to await instructions."

"What should I do with the Mauser?" asked its owner, a thin young man with a hippie-style beard. He carried the vintage weapon in a guitar case, which did not seem at all suspicious, since he looked so much like a musician.

"Don't take it home," I advised him. "Hide it in the house of a close relative who is politically neutral, in case we need it later."

I knew the weapon was of little use: we had hardly any ammunition for it. The dynamite I had brought here at such risk to myself was useless, too; even so, we stowed it safely away. I considered placing it in the middle of the street as a booby trap for one of the passing army trucks, but I feared that some curious child would pick it up or kick it.

We left the factory at around 11 A.M. I decided to investigate why there was so much military movement in our neighborhood, so I followed the army trucks and armored vehicles to the Alameda, the main avenue that bisects Santiago from east to west. At the intersection of Alameda and Bascuñan Street stood the three-thousand-seat sports arena known as the Chile Stadium. Troops crowded outside its walls. A few buses that were still running were filled with people trying to go home. A couple of stores that had remained open closed their metal shutters while I watched

A truck, packed with factory workers from the south side of Santiago who were guarded by soldiers, approached the arena. Chile Stadium had become a detention camp. My cousin Virginia would shortly be imprisoned within its walls; the folksinger Víctor Jara would be tortured and assassinated there within hours. Later we would learn that most of the junta's prisoners were taken elsewhere, to the much larger National Stadium, an open-air soccer field that seated sixty thousand.

As I walked to my safe house—the home of a Socialist woman whose husband, a taxi driver, was sympathetic to Allende—I wondered what had happened to the party organization, which was supposed to provide us with orders and, more important, firearms. Not far away I could hear explosions and gunfire: the final siege of La Moneda.

Radio Magallanes was silenced at 10:25 A.M., in the middle of a declaration by the Chilean Communist Party (CCP) condemning the coup and calling on all its militants to await instructions—instructions that never came. In the palace, President Allende told all Carabineros of the presidential guard that they could leave, but without their weapons. The head of the guards gave Allende his own helmet, which the president would wear during the ensuing combat. Allende also allowed all service personnel, mostly from the navy, to abandon La Moneda. Then he summoned his remaining aides, ministers, high officials, doctors, and security personnel to the Toesca Room on the second floor, a room normally reserved for formal ceremonies. He spoke with emotion but great composure.

"I will not resign, I will not leave the country, and I will not leave La Moneda. I will fight until the end. I thank all of you for your loyalty, but there must not be pointless victims. Most of you are young, have spouses and children. You have a duty to them and to Chile. This will not be the last battle. . . . From the women, I ask only that you abandon the palace. To the comrades who do not have specific duties to carry out, or who do not know how to use firearms, I ask you to leave now."

When the president finished, there was a profound silence. Not a word was spoken for what seemed like an eternity. Then, his last stalwarts, many of them with tears streaming down their faces, began to sing the national anthem, followed by loud cries of "Viva Allende!"

The president descended to the first floor and headed for an internal patio called the Winter Garden. On a table were laid out the SIG automatic rifles, ammunition, and gas masks left by the Carabineros. Those who knew how to use the weapons picked them up. After the women left (two hid inside the palace until the bitter end), Allende forced his adviser, Joan Garcés, a Spanish national, to leave as well, accompanied by Allende's two daughters, Isabel and Beatriz.

"Go and tell our story to the world," Allende told the Spaniard. In the years to come Garcés would become a full-time activist of the Chilean cause and one of Pinochet's most steadfast enemies. The military had promised a jeep to evacuate the women from La Moneda, but it never came. They had to seek refuge in the nearby offices of the Christian Democratic opposition newspaper *La Prensa*.

Annoyed by the slow pace of the offensive against La Moneda, General Pinochet contacted Admiral Carvajal at the Defense Ministry.

"Are the tanks attacking?" he asked. "What about the infantry? Have they arrived yet?"

Carvajal informed him that the palace was surrounded by soldiers and that the tanks had opened fire. "I believe our forces should soon be able to seize the palace," the admiral concluded.

"Okay. But at eleven A.M. sharp we have to bomb La Moneda from the air because this guy will not surrender," Pinochet told him.

General Leigh of the air force was frustrated. Earlier, he had angrily refused to provide a military escort for the women who wanted to exit the palace. "These are delaying tactics. I am going to attack with my planes right away," he yelled to his men.

But as of eleven fifteen, the fighter jets had yet to appear. After their long flight from southern Chile and the attacks on the radio transmitters, they had had to refuel. This not only added to Leigh's frustration but, more important, embarrassed him in front of his army colleague. Pinochet did not hide his displeasure and ordered General Brady to launch an all-out ground offensive. Artillery shells, mortars, missiles, and high-caliber bullets slammed into the northern side of the palace. Its defenders responded with a hail of gunfire of their own. The president, who had been known as a sharpshooter since his hunting days, joined in the shooting.

José Tohá, a former minister of the interior, considered Pinochet a friend, since the general had often visited Toha's home. He asked Admiral Carvajal to ask the general to suspend the bombardment while he convinced Allende to surrender. Admiral Carvajal called Pinochet to communicate the proposition.

"Unconditional surrender! No negotiations. You hear: unconditional surrender!" Pinochet screamed.

"Okay. Unconditional surrender. And we keep the offer to take Allende and his family out of the country?"

"All these bastards there, Mr. Tohá, that Mr. Almeyda, all these dirty bastards who were about to ruin the nation must be arrested and put on a plane, without any clothes, with whatever they may be wearing," Pinochet replied.

"As far as Allende is concerned, we maintain the offer to fly him out of the country, but the plane falls in midflight. Okay, my old man?"

"Okay, understood," Carvajal replied, unable to contain his laughter. (Years later audiotapes of these exchanges were discovered and made public.)

Still, Allende refused to surrender. He dispatched General Sepúlveda, the loyal head of the Carabineros, to the Ministry of Defense to negotiate a truce. Armored police vehicles picked him up at the palace, but instead of transporting him to the ministry, his subordinates informed him that Carabineros had joined the rebels, persuaded him there was nothing else to do, and took the general to safety at the institutional officers' club.

At around 11:55 A.M., rockets from two British-made Hawker Hunter fighter jets penetrated the second floor of La Moneda. A red-orange ball of fire erupted on the ceiling and the explosion literally lifted several occupants up into the air. In a hallway on the first floor of the palace, President Allende turned to his long time friend, the journalist Carlos "Negro" Jorquera. "We are not afraid, Negro, are we?" he asked.

"Afraid, no; scared shitless, yes!" Jorquera responded.

Fire broke out in the roof structure and in the open "orange trees patio" on the southern side of the palace. (Many years later, this area of La Moneda would house my offices when I was minister secretary-general of the government.) The attacks continued. Four jet fighters passed eight times over the building, firing eighteen twenty-five-pound Matra Sneb rockets. The sharp whistling sound of the incoming rockets and the explosions when they hit their targets could be heard throughout Santiago. The palace was on fire.

Men in helicopters launched tear gas grenades into the building, but they had to withdraw because of the heavy gunfire coming from inside. Sixty-seven people were still with Allende, and most of them continued to fight. A Sherman tank and an armored vehicle also were forced to pull back when they received a bazooka shot and abundant fire from a .30 machine gun handled by one of the GAP guards. Allende, flat on the floor, kept firing his automatic rifle. GAP sharpshooters, encouraged by the resistance from La Moneda, poured down fire from nearby buildings.

Meanwhile, at the presidential residence, Allende's wife, Tencha, and about fifteen GAP security guards took up defensive positions. Attacking troops were greeted by a hail of fire from AK-47 automatic rifles and from a .30 machine gun. Forced to retreat, the attackers called for air strikes.

Air Force Commander Leigh agreed. Because of cloud cover, a helicopter was sent in to "fix the target" for the combat planes. The helicopter withdrew after being struck by dozens of bullets, but two Hawker Hunter fighter jets, guided by the helicopter and aerial photos, flew in. The first pilot fired a rocket at a long structure that resembled the main building of the residence as it appeared in his photos. He'd made a huge mistake—his missile slammed into one of the annexes of the Air Force Hospital, a couple of blocks away. The second jet fighter corrected the error, scoring a direct hit on the residence. Paintings by famous Latin American artists were shredded; antique furniture flew through the air. The first lady survived by hiding under a table. GAP

guards escorted her out of the house and to safety at the Mexican ambassador's residence a few miles away. Grossly outgunned, the remaining defenders loaded their weapons and ammunition in three
cars and a utility truck and sped off to try to join up with paramilitary
resistance groups. Almost immediately, some neighbors began to loot
the smoking ruins of the abandoned mansion.

It was now 1:15 P.M. and the exchange of fire at La Moneda still
hadn't let up. Minister of Finance Fernando Flores phoned General
Baeza and suggested a cease-fire so that a delegation from La Moneda
could walk over to the Ministry of Defense to negotiate surrender.
Three emissaries led by Flores were escorted to the ministry. At that
exact moment, Pinochet telephoned. Carvajal informed him of the
approaching delegation and the terms of surrender they'd offered (Allende's conditions included the formation of a military government
that would respect the rule of law and the social rights of workers and
the immediate cessation of bombing in working-class neighborhoods
and shantytowns). Before Pinochet could protest, the admiral told
him that, of course, the idea was not to negotiate anything—he
would simply arrest the delegation as soon as they arrived. Pinochet
approved: "My view is that we grab all these gentlemen and we send
them out of the country, anywhere they want. And then, in midflight,
we begin throwing them out of the plane," he quipped.

At the palace, "Coco" Paredes, the former head of the civilian police, received a report from civil police headquarters stating that the
military effectively controlled the whole country. It was the last straw;
when he brought him the news, Allende agreed to surrender. The
emissaries at the Defense Ministry were informed of the unconditional surrender and were arrested.

"Order to surrender. The president orders to surrender!" Paredes
yelled, walking quickly through the building. As his supporters lined
up to exit the palace, Allende declared that he would be the last one to
leave. Paredes phoned the Defense Ministry, announced that the president had surrendered, and requested a vehicle.

General Javier Palacios, commissioned to accept the surrender
and to occupy the remains of La Moneda, stormed the palace with a
group of army commandos and intelligence personnel. The soldiers
kicked in the side door on Morandé 80, prompting several doctors,
journalists, and civilian police on the first floor to come out. Unaware
of the order to surrender, a few GAP security men were still firing
their weapons. General Palacios was slightly injured in one hand. After the guards were disarmed, they were severely beaten.

Allende remained on the second floor, in the Independence Room. As the military occupied the lower part of the building, he sent his last remaining companions downstairs.

"Allende will never surrender!" he called after them, and then they heard a muffled noise. Moments later, Dr. Patricio Guijón rushed back into the Independence Room to pick up a gas mask, just in time to see President Allende's body violently contorting on a chair, a consequence of two shots he had fired under his chin with the automatic rifle, which he held between his knees. The sole witness of a suicide that would be kept secret for three decades, Dr. Guijón pulled the rifle away, seated himself next to Allende's body, and waited for the military to arrive, so that in his capacity as medical doctor he could report the president's death.

When he heard that the president was dead, Enrique Huerta, the administrative manager of the palace, picked up his submachine gun and prepared to resume fighting.

"Allende is dead. Long live Chile!" he yelled.

One of the GAP leaders took his weapon away. There was no longer any point to resistance.

BEFORE PROCEEDING TO my safe house, I had rushed back home to check on my wife. Born and raised in a small town in Pennsylvania, she had only traveled outside the United States once before moving to Chile, for a four-day trip to Montreal. Although she had helped me distribute food in the neighborhood, Pamela was no activist. The extreme polarization and violence of Chilean politics struck her as shocking and incomprehensible. Now a military coup was unfolding that could kill us both.

We had met in upstate New York, at the Oswego campus of the State University of New York (SUNY) where I had earned my undergraduate degree thanks to an Institute of International Education scholarship. At eighteen years old I found myself on the shores of Lake Ontario in a town known worldwide for record snowfalls, instead of near New York City as I expected. Since Allende had been elected president, I persuaded Pamela to follow me to Chile. Three days after she arrived in Santiago, Pamela and I were married.

Pamela's shock treatment in revolutionary politics began on our wedding day, November 28, 1972. After a private civil wedding ceremony that she did not understand, as she did not yet speak a word of Spanish, we went for coffee, saw a boring Bulgarian movie, and then attended a massive Allende rally on Alameda Avenue. The president was traveling the next day to New York City, to address the General Assembly of the United Nations.

On September 11, 1973, as gunfire crackled in the distance and I prepared to go underground, I bid farewell to my new wife; I did not know what would happen to me or when I would see her again. I told her to go with my mother to an aunt's house nearby, and I promised to phone her as soon as I could.

Only two people were supposed to be at my safe house. But at around 2 P.M., others began to arrive.

"This is not a safe house if so many of us are here," I protested. Carmen, the owner of the house, insisted that anyone who was not supposed to be there would have to leave. Eventually they did. In the meantime, we wondered what had happened to our promised weapons. Someone said that vehicles would soon pick us up, bring weapons, and take us where we needed to go.

Arnoldo Camú, a member of the Political Commission of the Socialist Party and head of its paramilitary structure, had weapons and was ready for combat. But by 10 A.M., the Political Commission of the Socialist Party, led by the party's secretary-general, Senator Carlos Altamirano, decided that fighting by the party, which actually had a feeble paramilitary structure, would be an act of useless heroism. He ordered a pullback. He and the other leaders then headed to their own safe houses.

At 12:45 P.M., the political and paramilitary heads of the Socialist Party, the Communist Party, and the Movement of the Revolutionary Left—which had not backed Allende's government—met at the Indumet metal foundry. The Communist Party representative announced that his organization had ordered its militants to retreat, because they believed the military's grip on the country was already absolute. Members of MIR had not yet been able to retrieve the group's weapons. The Socialist Party's political commission member, Del Canto, reported that his party had ordered its paramilitary irregulars to retreat.

At 1 P.M. Camú received a desperate call from La Moneda, pleading for help. Disobeying his party's orders, he immediately dispatched two vans to scout the roads between the factory and the presidential palace. Both of them returned with discouraging information: the military had set up roadblocks, totally restricting access to downtown. Camú proposed that they approach the palace from a different direction. But the discussion ended abruptly when someone shouted that buses and armored vehicles carrying about one hundred Carabineros had arrived outside the factory.

The policemen surrounded the factory and opened fire. The plant's workers had received weapons from Camú's team, and they, as well as all participants in the meeting, fired back. The bloody standoff lasted several hours, but by 3:30 P.M. the workers at Indumet surrendered to the now-reinforced police forces.

Meanwhile Camú's forces had escaped the siege and moved on to Sumar textile factory, where another group of Socialists had gathered. A fresh battle broke out, this time with a Puma Army helicopter. The helicopter was forced to retreat when it was hit with more than a dozen bullets, one of which wounded the pilot. The Socialists decided to head for another factory, Madeco-Mademsa; they crossed La Legua, a strongly pro-Allende shantytown. Fighting had already broken out there between a police contingent and some Socialists who had been trapped on their way to join Camú. The reinforced Socialist force, assisted by local residents, overpowered the police. Then another bus loaded with heavily armed Carabineros arrived and a second battle broke out. A college student carrying an RPG-7 was hit in the head by a policeman's bullet and died. Another combatant retrieved the rocket-launcher and fired it. The rocket-propelled grenade crashed through the bus's windshield, severely wounding the driver. Miraculously, however, the grenade did not explode. The policemen jumped out of the bus and ran for cover, while Camú's men and the local militants loosed a barrage of gunfire that left the bus totally destroyed. Several Carabineros died in the gun battle, but all of them would have been killed if that grenade hadn't been a dud.

These few skirmishes were the principal points of armed resistance against the coup, though hundreds of militants like me waited in vain for instructions and arms. Many years later, the secretary-general of the Socialist Party, Altamirano, admitted that the left had failed miserably in its defense of the constitutional government. The leadership of the Socialist Party failed not only to secure a significant supply of arms but also to communicate any coherent instructions to its armed or unarmed irregulars.

Shortly after Allende's death, combined contingents of the army, the Carabineros, and the air force raided La Legua with tanks and planes and commenced a punitive operation aimed at all its residents. More than two hundred people were taken prisoner. Some of them would be tortured to death or made to disappear. Camú was murdered a few days later as he tried to escape arrest near downtown Santiago.

BY LATE AFTERNOON the fighting at La Moneda had long since ended. Allende's followers were lying facedown in a row on the pavement of Morandé Street, on the east side of the still-burning building. There they were repeatedly beaten; a tank was parked only inches away from their bodies and threatened to roll over them at any moment; rounds from machine guns were fired over their heads. Ministers and high government officials were taken to the Defense Ministry; afterward they would be flown to a makeshift prison camp on Dawson Island, an isolated location in Chilean Patagonia. Two navy buses arrived to take the rest of the palace's beaten defenders to the Tacna regiment army barracks, a few miles south. The streets were deserted, and a light rain fell.

At the Tacna, Enrique París, a psychiatrist and close friend of Allende's, was almost immediately separated from the others. He was tortured and assassinated, and his body was made to disappear. (Three decades later, another Enrique París, his son, would serve at La Moneda palace as President Ricardo Lagos's chief administrative aide.)

"All of you are going to be executed," Colonel Joaquín Ramírez yelled at the prisoners as they entered the barracks. Again they were severely beaten. Forty-eight hours later, military trucks arrived, commanded by an officer who bore a list of all those who were inside the palace on 9/11. The professional members of the Investigaciones were placed in the hands of a police inspector, who secured their release from the barracks. The twenty-four men remaining—security guards, lawyers, sociologists, and government officials—were loaded onto the trucks, their hands and feet bound by wire, and transported to a shooting range some twenty miles west of Santiago, where they were murdered in cold blood that same night. "Coco" Paredes, the former head of the Investigaciones, was savagely tortured before he died.

At my safe house, more unexpected guests had arrived, some of them carrying handguns. Their presence was a huge security risk. As evening fell, the overcast skies were further darkened by the news of Allende's death. We remained awake all night. At any moment, we thought, we would be picked up and taken to where we would receive arms and be given orders. But as the night wore on and nobody arrived and no news reports came to us, except propaganda from the coup-controlled media attacking Allende and his supposed luxurious lifestyle, our hopes faded.

At around 7 P.M., the president's body, wrapped in a rug, was transported from La Moneda to the army's military hospital. Admiral Carvajal communicated to Pinochet the news of President Allende's death. Of course, the issue of burial arose immediately.

"Just put him in a pine box, and place him aboard a plane, with his family," Pinochet told Carvajal. "Let the burial take place elsewhere, in Cuba! Otherwise, there will be unrest at the burial ceremony. Even dead this guy is troublesome!"

Finally Pinochet decided to allow a discreet, private burial in Chile. The following day the remains of the president were buried at the Santa Inés Cemetery in Viña del Mar. "Let it be known to all that here lies the constitutional president of Chile," his widow, Tencha, declared bravely over his grave, as the soldiers stood menacingly nearby. In September 1990, when democracy returned to Chile, Allende would be given a proper burial, in the presence of foreign heads of state, intellectuals from all over the world, and the leaders of Chile's reborn democracy. I was present then.

But that reburial would not come for decades; many more were fated to die between Salvador Allende's two funerals. On the day of the coup, thirty-six people, including Carabineros and soldiers, were killed. There had been no war. Pinochet himself later declared, "For all practical purposes, fighting lasted four hours." But by the end of 1973, less than four months later, the number of dead would climb to 1,823—or 119 persons each week.

On the early morning of September 12, I left the safe house and headed toward my aunt's home, taking a long, indirect route through side streets. Many right-wingers in the neighborhood knew me; I could not ignore the necessity of taking such precautions. I found my young American wife in a state of near panic; she had never experienced such a day of upheaval and impotent rage. I hadn't, either, though I had been prepared intellectually for the eventuality. After we had departed from our "unsafe house," a heavily armed military contingent arrived in several trucks to search it. I had escaped arrest this time, but my wife and I would have to go into hiding. Chile had changed, literally overnight. Like thousands of other Allende supporters, I would have to take desperate measures to stay alive.

It would be seventeen years before we would regain the democracy and the freedom that we lost on our 9/11. Pinochet ruled Chile now.

Two

THE TWO
PINOCHETS

Geneeral Augusto Pinochet, the commander in chief of the Chilean army, was full of doubts. Joining a coup d'état could backfire, costing him his career or, worse, his life.

Serious political conflict divided Chile into two antagonistic blocks: the Allende government, composed mainly of the Socialist and Communist parties, versus the opposition, led by the right-wing National Party (Partido Nacional, PN) and the Christian Democracy (Partido Demócrata Cristiano, PDC). Dialogue had broken down as the antagonists had radicalized their postures and, as a spin-off, politicized key actors such as the judiciary and the armed forces. A conviction that the nation now found itself in a total impasse had overcome Chileans of all political persuasions and within the military; Pinochet was feeling the pressure of his subordinates to move against Allende.

On the evening of Saturday, September 8, the army's General Sergio Arellano, nicknamed "the Wolf," had briefed Pinochet at the latter's home in Santiago on the details of the coup plot and warned him that even if all the senior commanders did not participate, the lower-level commanders would. "I am not a Communist," Pinochet growled, banging the table. "Shit!" But for all of his vehemence, Arellano reported to General Gustavo Leigh, the commander in chief of the air force, Pinochet was still reluctant to commit himself one way or the other. Pinochet had promised to call General Leigh, but he hadn't done so that evening.

Leigh shared his concerns with Admiral José Toribio Merino. The next morning, Sunday, September 9, Merino summoned Admiral Sergio Huidobro, commander of the Chilean marines, to his home in the port of Valparaíso, gave him a letter to hand-deliver to Pinochet, and ordered him to use all of his powers of persuasion to bring the general on board. Huidobro hid the letter inside one of his shoes and got into his car, accompanied by Ariel González, an officer in the navy. An hour later—far too soon for them to have made the ninety-minute drive to Santiago, never mind a round trip—the two envoys returned. Admiral Merino felt a lurch of panic when he saw them. But as it turned out, nothing had gone wrong. In a bit of comedy worthy of the Keystone Cops, the officers had realized that they didn't have enough money to pay the highway tolls. When they finally pulled up at Pinochet's residence late that afternoon, the general's youngest daughter, Jacqueline, was celebrating her fifteenth birthday.

That Sunday had been a busy day for Pinochet. Around noon he had been summoned to the presidential residence on Tomás Moro Street. After Pinochet briefed President Allende on public order, Allende informed him of his plans to call for a plebiscite to resolve the national political impasse. Allende's adviser, Joan Garcés, recalls the surprised look on the general's face when he received the news. "That changes everything," Pinochet said. While the general and the president were meeting—the last time they would see each other—Senator Carlos Altamirano, the secretary-general of the Socialist Party, was giving a fiery speech at a rally in which he darkly alluded to military plots being hatched against the government and promised to respond with popular resistance.

When Merino's envoys, accompanied by Admiral Patricio Carvajal, were shown into the general's house, they discovered that Pinochet was already receiving a distinguished visitor: General Gustavo Leigh, the commander in chief of the air force (dressed in jogging clothes rather than his uniform, so as not to attract attention). While the birthday festivities continued in a different part of the house, Leigh bluntly told Pinochet that the time had come to act.

"You have to make up your mind," he declared, "because we and the navy are going ahead, even without the army."

"This could cost us our lives," Pinochet responded. He knew that Merino and Leigh were allies and would support each other. But how much support did they have in the ranks? Besides, Merino was not the commander in chief of the navy.

Admiral Huidobro handed Pinochet Merino's letter, which read as follows: "Gustavo and Augusto: The 'D day' will be 9/11 and the time 6 A.M. Augusto: If you do not commit your troops from the beginning of the movement we will have no possibility of success and we will not live to see the future. Any problem or disagreements, please discuss them with Admiral Huidobro, who is authorized by me. Hoping for your understanding, I send you my regards. José Toribio Merino."

Merino had given instructions that both Pinochet and Leigh sign the letter on the spot as a formal expression of agreement. Pinochet could dither no longer. He would have to declare himself one way or the other, and in the presence of four witnesses, all of them from other branches of the armed forces.

Leigh signed right away. Pinochet nervously offered the excuse that he couldn't find a pen and his personal seal.

While Leigh regarded the army chief disdainfully, Admiral Huidobro offered to lend him his own pen. Pinochet demurred. Finally, when he could procrastinate no longer, he signed the note and stamped his seal on it, but even then he wrote a small message requesting that the coup begin an hour and a half later, so that army divisions spread out across the country would have time to communicate with each other. A tea hosted by his wife for spouses of army generals, to be held on September 11—a few hours earlier the Pinochets had personally ordered cakes and hors d'oeuvres at a pastry shop—would have to be canceled.

The coup was on.

PINOCHET HAD NEVER been officer material. It's doubtful that he ever expected to reach the post of commander in chief of the army. That he would end up ruling the country with an iron hand for seventeen years would have seemed unimaginable to anyone who knew him when he was an unprepossessing young officer. He owed his unlikely success to a studied avoidance of risks, a preternatural ability to keep his own counsel, and above all an attitude of cringing deference and unconditional obedience to his superiors. His strategy was to quietly occupy a secondary role, close to power but in the background and out of danger—but to be ready to move the instant an opportunity presented itself.

When asked what he talked about when he met with President Allende throughout the latter's presidency, Pinochet said, "I never spoke; I only listened. By speaking, one gives up one's ideas." In an interview with María Eugenia Oyarzún, a journalist who would be rewarded for her close friendship with Pinochet with several high posts during his regime, Pinochet confessed, "I knew that if you said something, maybe you would not be promoted. Since I was a child I was taught that a superior is always right. As time went on, I realized that this is not always the case, but I still preferred silence." Pinochet's policy—to keep his mouth shut and to be "always distrustful"—rose to the level of a personal philosophy.

Pinochet never excelled intellectually. Unlike the two commanders in chief of the army who preceded him, Generals Ren Schneider and Carlos Prats, he was not a natural-born leader. But Pinochet had persistence and discipline. Born in the Almendral neighborhood of Valparaíso on November 25, 1915, Augusto José Ramón Pinochet Ugarte always wanted to be a military man. As a child he enjoyed watching military parades because he admired, he would recall, "the uniforms and martial nature" of the military as well as the "way they treated people according to rank." His favorite pastime was to play with toy soldiers. His father, a customs agent, had cherished the hope that his son and namesake would become a medical doctor. But Avelina, his strong-willed mother, supported her son's military vocation.

Pinochet was raised in an upper-middle-class family. The Pinochet children had a governess, María, and Augusto attended private schools in Valparaíso (Seminario San Rafael and Sagrados Corazones) at a time when it was a privilege reserved for the few. They lived in a comfortable two-story house with several bedrooms and a grand salon with a piano.

Pinochet's parents were strict disciplinarians: a severe beating he received from his mother when he disrupted a shopping expedition by whining that he wanted a toy boat was a learning experience that Pinochet never forgot. "I know no other way of life but military discipline," he once declared. Pinochet applied to military school in 1929, but he was too young and was turned down. In December 1931 his mother insisted he apply again, but he was rejected once more, this time because he was judged to be physically weak. Finally, in 1933, when he was sixteen years old, he reapplied for a third time. This time he was admitted.

The Military School (Escuela Militar), was housed then in an imposing classical-style building on Blanco Encalada Avenue. A nearby church on the same thoroughfare, the Virgen del Perpetuo Socorro (Our Lady of Perpetual Help), still has on its wall a marble plaque inscribed "Thanks Holy Mother. Help me always. Second Lieutenant A. Pinochet, 1936." Pinochet thanked the Virgin for his graduation from military school. As a child I passed by that plaque dozens of times on my way to Mass. The house I grew up in was just a few blocks away.

Pinochet had a mystical streak; he was inclined to believe in miracles, spirits, and the supernatural. He recalled his father's death as follows: "I saw my father when his soul left his material body. I was standing in front of his bed when a kind of smoke descended; he got out of bed, came over toward me, stood there for a fraction of a second, and then left." His father's was not the only spirit he'd seen in his house. "One day I was washing my hands and I saw another person right next to me, also washing his hands," Pinochet told the journalist Oyarzún. Fond of consulting fortune-tellers and astrologists, Pinochet confessed that he always wore a gold ring with a square ruby and a Sagittarius symbol as a good luck charm. "The ring brings me luck and I am superstitious," he admitted.

He was never a good military student, and his carelessness got him into trouble. In the early 1950s a pamphlet Pinochet prepared for the Army War Academy (Academia de Guerra del Ejército de Chile) included a map of Chile's borders with Argentina, Bolivia, and Peru that contained such egregious errors that a formal complaint was filed by the navy, on the grounds that it could potentially jeopardize some of Chile's sovereignty claims. Thanks to a sympathetic superior, Pinochet's lapse was overlooked. In 1968, Colonel Pinochet published a book entitled *Geopolítica* (Geopolitics). The text touches on matters ranging from history to economics and geography; it contains a map of the United States showing its main cities and situates its capital in the Pacific Northwest, revealing the author's apparent confusion between the city of Washington, D.C., and the state of Washington.

Following his graduation, in 1936, from the Army War Academy, Pinochet was assigned to the Infantry School in San Bernardo, a suburb south of Santiago. There he shed some of his youthful weaknesses, impressing his contemporaries as a tough young officer and a dapper gentleman, both highly appreciated attributes. Above average in height (just under six feet), he wore a neatly trimmed mustache and cut a dashing figure in uniform. After he was promoted to lieutenant, Pinochet, then twenty-eight, married the younger Lucía Hiriart, just twenty, the daughter of Senator Osvaldo Hiriart, a member of the Radical Party, an antimilitarist, and a leader of the Chilean Freemason movement. In keeping with his emerging philosophy of following the prevailing political winds, Pinochet joined the Masons himself in 1941, a fact his official memoirs don't mention.

The influence of his antimilitarist father-in-law and the turbulent times he was living through all taught Pinochet to keep his mouth shut and to avoid politics. Mónica Madariaga, the general's cousin, recalls that Pinochet's legal guardian at the military school, General Alfredo Portales, counseled him "never to be outstanding in your career because you will be envied by others; also don't be the last. To progress in the military career keep just in the middle, in the anonymous mass." He clearly took the general's advice to heart.

Pinochet's wife, Lucía, did not appreciate the low social status and meager wages of military life and convinced Pinochet to leave the army for a time and work with his father in the private sector. He didn't even last six months. For all its shortcomings, Pinochet decided, the military was where he belonged and where he would stay. It was a mystery why the young Lucía had chosen a military man for a husband. But when she did, she demanded that Pinochet provide her with a superior destiny in life. Like Lady Macbeth, she pushed her husband, fed his ambition for power, and convinced him that he had to cultivate relations with powerful people—and that it might be necessary for him to do evil things to succeed.

He was stationed at the Military School in the 1940s when the Group of Selective Military Officers (Grupo de Oficiales Selectos, GOS), a secret association of military officers dedicated to purging corrupt officers from the ranks of the army and improving the state of military professionalism, was founded. (It was inspired by the Peronist Grupo de Oficiales Unidos, the United Group of Officers, in neighboring Argentina.) Colonel Ramón Alvarez, director of the Military School, was its leader. Despite his personal sympathies with the goals of the GOS movement, the defense minister condemned this secret organization as representing an unacceptable breach in the chain of command and removed Alvarez and his deputy, Lieutenant Colonel Eduardo Yañez, from their respective posts at the school. A large delegation of officers and cadets made their indignation at this move evident by marching to the train station to bid a noisy farewell to Yañez. But Pinochet stayed home, despite the fact that he shared the opinion of his comrades in arms. "We saw the removal of our colonels as an infamy," he would later recall, but for all that, he was careful not to let his feelings lead him to an ill-considered demonstration of his view.

As soon as he was promoted to captain, in 1946, Pinochet requested a transfer to the northern city of Iquique. He preferred to stay away from Santiago and its power struggles. Politics was dangerous and politicians were incapable of acting swiftly and efficiently. The give and take of negotiations, the compromises that were required to form a democratic consensus, did not appeal to Pinochet at all.

Captain Pinochet would grow to love the port of Iquique, in the dry northern desert, and his life there. But in January 1948, he was put in charge of a detention camp situated in the abandoned village of

Pisagua, whose inmates were Communists. The president of Chile at the time, Gabriel González Videla, had been elected in 1946 with decisive Communist support, but in 1948 he had fallen out with his former allies and had enacted the so-called "Law for the Permanent Defense of Democracy"; the party was outlawed, Communist publications were closed down, registered Communist voters were erased from official electoral rolls, and many of their number were jailed or deported.

In his carefully crafted book about the 1973 coup, *El Día Decisivo* (The Crucial Day), which is structured as a long interview with a fictitious journalist, Pinochet reconstructs and embellishes his life history, portraying himself as a consistent anti-Communist and a man of firm ideas. In his telling, one of the prisoners at Pisagua was a former chief administrator (*intendente*) of the Tarapacá region and Communist activist, who, before his detention, had always made sure during a time of shortages that Pinochet's army regiment had enough food and provided him and his officers with unstinting assistance with any problem. Obviously, Pinochet now asserted, "These goodwill gestures by the Communists were oriented to oblige the bourgeois elements; they were a way to help Marxists infiltrate and spread their doctrine."

Pinochet later claimed that his experience in Pisagua had been a seminal one for him, engendering his life long distrust of Communists and providing him with an indelible education in the evils of the left. In his book Pinochet asserted that he underwent a life-changing epiphany at the camp. It was there that he came to understand just how dangerous the Communists were. "The more I knew those prisoners and listened to their thoughts, while, at the same time, I studied Marx and Engels, the more I became convinced that we were mistaken about the Communist Party. It was not just another party. . . . It was a system that turns things on their heads, dismissing any loyalty or any belief," he stated, adding, "I was troubled that these pernicious and contaminating ideas could continue to spread throughout Chile."

Testimonies from former Pisagua prisoners tell quite a different story. Pinochet is fondly remembered as a good-natured officer, easy to talk to, and with democratic convictions. He was not particularly worried about the Communists; he certainly didn't evince any signs of obsession with their political thinking, nor did he seem to hate them.

After a brief transfer to Santiago, Pinochet was again stationed outside the capital, this time in the southern coal-mining towns of Schwager and, later, Coronel, as a delegate of the State of Emergency Authority. The González Videla regime, which had outlawed the Communists, was still in power. There Pinochet supposedly further learned the tactics and doctrines of Communists in the field, since the miners' unions had many party members.

A year later Pinochet returned to Santiago, haunted, he later averred, in his "spirit and mind" by his "concern about where Chile could be led by the Communist movement." But "when I expressed my worries in conversations with my friends," he recounts ruefully, "they would laugh and reply that Chile would never become Communist."

Of course it is highly unlikely that Pinochet would have been so indiscreet as to criticize the Communist Party in public, even among friends. His distaste for political debate and, more important, the proverbial prudence that led him to maintain a low profile and always to carefully guard his tongue probably made him keep to himself all of his critical views on Communism if indeed he had any. There is ample evidence of Pinochet's extreme caution.

During the early 1950s, a former populist dictator of Chile (1927–1931), Carlos Ibáñez del Campo, was democratically elected president on an anti-traditional-politics platform. Governance troubles led Ibáñez to contemplate undertaking an internal coup against his own presidency in order to impose authoritarian rule. His plan was foiled, however, when a group of military officers, from captains up to colonels, organized a movement known as the Straight Line (La Línea Recta), which was staunchly opposed to dictatorial rule. The group had its base in the Army War Academy, where, coincidentally, Pinochet was a teacher.

At first the president tried to co-opt the movement, but later he turned against its leaders and had them arrested and prosecuted; even its rank and file suffered severe career setbacks. Pinochet was in the "eye of the storm," but he managed to escape unscathed. He is absent from every contemporary account of this traumatic episode in the history of the army, and he passes over it in silence in his own memoirs. Shortly afterward he left Santiago again, this time for Ecuador, as a member of a military mission that would take him and his family away from Chile from 1956 to 1960. When he returned to Chile he was stationed in Antofagasta until 1963. From 1964 to 1968 Pinochet was deputy director of the Army's War Academy in Santiago, where he taught his favorite subject, geopolitics.

During the mid-sixties Chilean politics and society polarized as President Eduardo Frei Montalva implemented his "Revolution in Liberty," which, in line with President John Kennedy's "Alliance for Progress," championed agrarian reform, labor union growth, higher education for the poor, and new and ambitious social programs as a way, among other things, to stave off leftist political gains and the appeal of the Cuban revolution. Conservatives, who had supported Frei, now felt betrayed as they strongly opposed agrarian reform and what they judged as radical social policies. The Christian Democratic Party suffered internal turmoil as progressive activists protested what they viewed as the government's inability to effect meaningful social change. The polarization and instability that developed over the decade of the sixties was planting the seeds of Chile's division under the Allende years.

The economic situation of the Chilean military had deteriorated considerably throughout the 1960s. Army officers' salaries were already lower than those of their comrades in other branches of the armed services and budget cuts by the Frei government had exacerbated the situation. In May 1968 about seventy captains and majors resigned en masse from the War Academy in protest. It was a serious breach of discipline, and it provoked the removal of both the commander in chief of the army and the defense minister but the government did authorize a pay raise for the army.

And where was Pinochet—the deputy director of the War Academy—while all this was happening? Once again, he was able to avoid taking a public stand. Pinochet had traveled to the United States on a second honeymoon in early 1968, just as the crisis began to boil over. When he returned he was safely out of the picture and agreed to become the chief of staff of the general commander of the Santiago division. In 1969 Pinochet returned to his beloved Iquique in northern Chile as interim head of the Sixth Army Division. Soon after, he was promoted to brigadier general.

For a brief period Pinochet filled the civil administrative post of regional governor, and it was in that capacity that he was drawn into a conflict with Communists. When radical students seized an industrial school in Iquique, Pinochet refused to negotiate with them. Instead he responded with force, cutting off the school's water, electricity, telephone, and food supplies, and surrounding it with police. Communist members of Congress denounced Pinochet's actions, which, since it was an election season, threatened to spark a full-blown political crisis. The undersecretary of the interior telephoned Pinochet and let him know that the ministry of education was prepared to accept the students' demands.

"I said I was not more papist than the Pope, and that if the authorities in Santiago would solve the crisis their way, they assumed their own responsibility," Pinochet recalled. Once again, he acted pragmatically. When a superior gave him an order—even if he disagreed with it, even if it embarrassed him—he retreated, without becoming emotionally or politically involved in the matter at hand.

The army's economic problems persisted and its officers were becoming restive again. During Independence Day celebrations in 1969, President Frei's military escort intentionally arrived late for the ceremony. Several high officers were prematurely retired as a consequence of this act of insubordination. More seriously, Brigadier General Roberto Viaux, chief of the army division in the northern city of Antofagasta, was accused of conspiring against the government and ordered to resign. A few days later, on October 21, Viaux forcibly seized command of the Tacna Regiment in Santiago. Confusion reigned; it was unclear at first whether the entire army would turn against the Frei government.

Brigadier General Pinochet was in Santiago and his subordinates in Iquique desperately tried to contact him. Nobody knew where he was, and nobody knew which side he was on. After extracting promises from the government to raise officers' salaries and otherwise improve conditions in the army, Viaux surrendered. After it became clear that the putsch had failed, General Pinochet reappeared in Iquique.

Viaux and Pinochet were close friends. Pinochet had visited him in Antofagasta several times and had even stayed at his residence. Viaux had also visited Pinochet in Iquique. Surely Pinochet must have known something about his intentions. *Camino Recorrido* (The Road Traveled), his four-volume official memoir, barely mentions this major rebellion, dedicating only half a page to it, and even those few remarks are characteristically opaque. "Many events took place," Pinochet writes, "some true, others not so." In *The Crucial Day,* Pinochet alleges that he had always criticized the actions taken against General Viaux, though there is no evidence whatsoever of any Pinochet complaint about his friend's removal from active service. But in an interview Pinochet gave to Chilean Finis Terrae University researchers and former aides that was published posthumously, in December 2006, he comes closer to the truth: Viaux "wanted to get me on board [his rebellion] marching southward to take over the government," he admits. "'You are talking nonsense,' I said. . . . 'There are two thousand kilometers to Santiago and on the way they can tear us to pieces. . . . Forget about it.'" Ever the pragmatist, Pinochet refused to stick his neck out for his friend. Following the prevailing winds, he kept quiet, obeyed orders, and thus continued his climb up the ladder of military power.

Considering his long history of caution and judicious fence strad-dling, it is difficult to believe that Pinochet reacted to the September 1970 election of Salvador Allende as he relates in *The Crucial Day*. The night of September 4, 1970, Pinochet asserts, he gathered his officers and the staff of the regional army headquarters together to commu-nicate his bitterness about Allende's election to the presidency. "The country will go down the drain under Marxist domination," he claims he said. "The people of Chile have been fooled; they seemingly don't know where Marxism-Leninism will take us. . . . I am at the end of my career. The challenge of saving Chile will be now in your hands," Pinochet has himself saying. It is almost unthinkable that he would have made such inflammatory comments before such a large group of people. They could easily have leaked out and reached the ears of members of the newly elected government or the army commander in chief, René Schneider, who was a strict constitutionalist.

In fact, far from resisting Allende's rule, Pinochet benefited from it. Commander in Chief Schneider confirmed Pinochet in his post, on Allende's instruction. Schneider, murdered in October 1970 during a frustrated kidnapping attempt promoted by the Richard Nixon ad-ministration, was replaced by another constitutionalist, General Car-los Prats. A couple of years later, before the coup, Pinochet paid fulsome tribute to General Schneider, who had been murdered, he said, "because he defended our democratic institutions . . . and the constitutional and legal principles all men of arms have sworn to re-spect and obey." (During the initial years of his dictatorship, Pinochet would pardon Schneider's assassins.)

With Allende's approval, Commander in Chief Prats named Pinochet commander of the Santiago army garrison. Only a trust-worthy general would have been named to the top position in the capital. In November 1971, as commander of the Santiago garrison, he played host to Fidel Castro during his visit to Chile. Although Pinochet later claimed that he was merely icily courteous to the Cuban leader, witnesses described his manner as warm and admiring. Years later, Castro told a Peruvian high-official, whom I interviewed, that in that 1971 visit Pinochet had presented him with an inscribed book authored by the general.

On Army Day, September 19, 1971, Pinochet led the annual mili-tary parade. President Allende broke protocol and invited the general to the presidential reviewing stand to congratulate him personally for a good exhibition. In late 1971 Pinochet became army chief of staff, the second-highest position in the line of command. Efficiency, discipline, and loyalty were the traits that had allowed Pinochet to gain the president's trust and climb so high in the hierarchy. Though Pinochet was not bright or sophisticated, like his predecessor, Carlos Prats, he made up for it by being trustworthy and loyal, and always acting "according to the book."

Since the success of Allende's Popular Unity coalition in the 1970 election and his ascension to the presidency, Chile had become increasingly polarized. The democratic election of a Socialist Party candidate had stimulated dreams of revolutionary change among workers, peasants, students, and professionals who identified with the left. It had also aroused the fears of the elites, particularly the business class, and was the focus of a growing concern among the armed forces.

Chile became a magnet for intellectuals and artists from all over the world and for progressive politicians who came to see for themselves the "peaceful road to socialism." François Mitterrand and Fidel Castro met for the first time in Chile in 1971. In those days I attended a lecture by Angela Davis and never forgave myself for missing a Duke Ellington concert. Exiles from Latin America's dictatorial regimes—Argentina, Brazil, and Uruguay to name a few—flowed to Chile. Chileans had long forgotten what a dictatorship was, and often referred to any such nation as a "banana republic."

In October 1970, Joan Garcés wrote that President Allende intended to build socialism "within a rule-of-law regime of multipartisanship, pluralism and respect for public, individual and social freedoms." Garcés went on to criticize Régis Debray's "*foco* theory," which advocated exporting the Cuban revolutionary experience to the rest of Latin America, arguing that the French political philosopher and activist did not adequately understand the specific traits of the Chilean political process. Unfortunately, for all of the idealism of Chile's democratic revolution, its management of the nation's economy was unsound.

In line with Allende's economic program to create a "social property" sector," by the 9/11 coup, five hundred companies had been transferred into the social property area, eight of them expropriated and the rest "intervened" (that is, the state officially seized administrative control of the company without transfer of ownership) through executive powers based on a law dating back to a short-lived "Socialist Republic" in 1932. Others had bought out at below-market prices by the state.

A number of foreign and national industrial conglomerates were nationalized, expropriated, or "intervened." Only the copper mines owned by American businesses were nationalized by the consensus of all Chilean political forces, through an act of Congress. At the same time, illegal actions by the International Telephone and Telegraph Company (ITT), which worked with the CIA providing funds to finance a coup to impede Allende's accession to the presidency, prompted further seizures by the state of foreign companies. Members of the right-wing parties believed their property was being systematically looted by the Allende government. Foreign and particularly U.S. multinationals were infuriated by the loss of their investments.

At the outset of Allende's government, salaries rose and prices were kept artificially low. Idle output capacity allowed for an expansion of the economy. Since prices of goods were fixed at low levels, demand grew, investment fell, production plummeted, and businesses went bankrupt.

Nevertheless, until late 1972 most Chileans still believed that they were making history and were willing to endure sacrifices. Many among us thought that inefficiencies in certain sectors of the economy could be compensated for by massive voluntary work campaigns. I can recall working several weekends in a row in early 1973 at a liquefied gas plant in the Cerrillos industrial complex west of Santiago, loading trucks with tanks of propane. We hardly had any lunch or took any breaks, but we all felt we were accomplishing something important. Our perception was that the main problem with the Chilean economy was that the right, in alliance with the U.S. government, was determined to bring about its collapse.

These fears were grounded in reality, not fantasy. Indeed, right-wing paramilitary groups such as Patria y Libertad (Homeland and Liberty) and the Rolando Matus Brigade, sabotaged power lines, railroad tracks, pipelines, and key factories, hurting the economy and adding to the already heightened climate of tension and insecurity. But the ruling coalition's increasing political radicalization and the blatant mismanagement of the economy bear much of the blame for the hyperinflation (260 percent in 1972), the burgeoning black market, and the long lines that consumers were forced to stand on to purchase increasingly scarce fixed-price merchandise. In short, Chile's economy was spiraling out of control.

In early 1973 the Socialist Party chief in my borough urgently ordered me to go to the El As brand jeans factory near my home in the Estación Central neighborhood of Santiago. "Go help those people," he said, referring to the workers. "They have seized the factory. They asked for our guidance, specifically mentioning your name." El As was a modest but well-run jeans factory that employed about thirty-five workers, mostly women.

When I arrived to the factory, the women workers were in a panic. They did not know whether they had done the right thing, because the owner had warned them that "they would pay" for snatching his plant. Moreover, they confessed, its seizure had truly not been their idea. Enrique "Quico" López, a Socialist friend from the neighborhood, had pressured them into action. What scared them the most was that, after they'd already taken the factory, López had arrived with guns to organize their defenses, ordering them to take up positions on the roof, entrance, and back door. The workers did not want any of that. I assured them that they had nothing to fear. I urged them to continue producing jeans and promised to see what I could do to regularize the situation of the factory that was now de facto in state hands. It was an insane situation—a jeans factory with less than forty workers had become a part of the social, or state, sector of the economy! A few months after the coup, the factory reopened under the control of its old owner. But its troubles were far from over. A few years after, it finally disappeared for good when the economy was transformed according to the Chicago model devised by the Nobel laureate economist Milton Friedman and championed by Pinochet, which advocated the primacy of deregulation and comparative advantages; El As went bankrupt in the face of competition from cheap Asian imports.

Either you were for Allende and Socialist changes, or you were radically against them. Families became divided because of political differences. Each sector wanted to carry out its own revolution. Threats of armed violence from both the left and right summoned up the specter of civil war. The growing economic chaos worried the armed forces. Even more ominous, in their view, were the oft-repeated claims by MIR and by my own party that the people would take up arms to defend the government if a military uprising occurred. Though many suspected that the government coalition parties were far from combat-ready, the military nonetheless assumed that they represented a real threat to their monopoly over the control of weapons. Nobody knew how many and what types of arms were in private hands.

In October 1972 the opposition pushed an Arms Control Law through Congress that made it mandatory to report all firearms in private hands to the government and that empowered the armed forces to search for weapons. Tensions rose still higher as factories in state hands and buildings linked to Popular Unity parties or to labor unions became subject to unannounced searches by the military, which were almost always conducted with great violence.

As Chile became increasingly polarized, a few military leaders began to plot a coup. Pinochet was not one of them. On November 2,

1972, Allende appointed Carlos Prats, the commander in chief of the army and minister of the interior, and gave two other high officers of the armed forces cabinet portfolios of their own. We were all surprised by this bold maneuver and were not sure what to make of it. Had Allende stamped out the possibility of a coup by filling his cabinet with members of the military, or had he allowed the military to usurp his power? Was he co-opting the opposition or appeasing it? Whatever interpretation one put on Allende's surprising stratagem, it failed to defuse the growing tensions within the armed forces.

The appointment of the military officers to Allende's cabinet had been preceded by a strike by business associations, truckers, shop owners, and medical doctors that led to some violent confrontations. This so-called "October bosses' strike" was organized and financed by the CIA. One day during the strike, government inspectors were ordered to force owners to reopen their stores in the busy shopping sector of Meiggs Street and Alameda Avenue. Along with about eight other Socialists, I was asked to accompany them, to back them up in the event of trouble. As the inspectors broke the locks and forced open the metal curtains of the stores, a business association lawyer argued furiously with them. Then a small convoy of cars pulled up to the curb and disgorged their passengers—a motley crew of right-wing paramilitary militants wielding chains, numchucks, and wooden bats. Our group, unarmed and overwhelmed by their numbers, retreated to a nearby construction site. A few minutes later we returned with iron bars and about a dozen hard-hat workers; together we beat back the rightists and the stores reopened. The incident was illustrative of the growing sense of anarchy in the country.

Despite the mounting tension, Pinochet remained aligned with the government. When President Allende traveled abroad in late November 1972, Army Commander in Chief Carlos Prats, then serving as minister of the interior, was temporarily named vice president, a constitutionally necessary formality. Pinochet held a celebratory cocktail party where he surprised his superior by draping a presidential sash across his chest. General Prats was embarrassed by his second in command's extravagant display of loyalty.

The prospect of violent confrontation loomed even larger when the Popular Unity coalition of President Allende won eight additional seats in the March 1973 congressional elections, a substantial increase in popular support, but still short of the absolute majority. The opposition hard-liners had aspired to gain two thirds of Congress so they could impeach the president. Instead, they had suffered an electoral setback that left them only one other option: a coup d'état.

On June 29, 1973, Blindados No. 2, a tank regiment based in Santiago, rebelled. Tanks swiftly advanced toward La Moneda palace. General Prats had learned about their plans forty-eight hours earlier and had arrested the regiment's commander. Armed with a Thompson submachine gun, Prats led loyal army troops that overpowered the insurgents.

And where was Deputy Commander Pinochet? Instead of joining his commander in chief in combat, he chose that morning to set off for the Buin regimental barracks, located in a neighborhood to the north of Santiago, which was commanded by a colonel known for his rabid antigovernment positions. Later that day, Pinochet was seen at the head of a column of soldiers from the Buin Regiment, wearing combat fatigues and marching toward La Moneda. But which side was he on? Would he support the rebels or fight them? When he ran across the deputy chief of the civilian police, Pinochet asked him what news he had.

"The loyalist forces have the situation under control," the detective replied.

"I am wearing a combat uniform to defend the constitutional government," Pinochet volunteered and moved on. The policeman said that he would radio La Moneda advising that the deputy army commander was on his way.

At the main gate of La Moneda Pinochet encountered General Prats, whom he embraced, assuring him that he had matters under control. He spoke prematurely.

In the confusion, sharpshooters positioned in nearby buildings opened fire on Orlando Millas, the minister of the economy, just as he was entering the palace to attend a political meeting in support of the president. Only moments before, Pinochet had assured Undersecretary of the Interior Daniel Vergara, just as he had Prats, that order had been restored. Vergara was furious and tried to denounce Pinochet, but nobody there wanted to hear criticism about such a staunchly loyal soldier. In fact, at the political gathering at La Moneda, one of the participants—Enrique Correa, a leftist leader—told me that he recalled someone suddenly asking Commander in Chief Prats "in an exaggeratedly loud voice" for permission to address the president; it was Pinochet, whom Correa recognized because he had met him once. Pinochet delivered a brief but fiery speech before Allende and his guests, demanding tough measures against the rebels.

Allende made a series of cabinet changes the next day, among them removing José Tohá as minister of defense. Tohá, who had also served as interior minister, was a highly competent longtime member of Allende's inner circle. Pinochet had cultivated his friendship for a long time, sending presents to members of his family and visiting him for a companionable drink on many a Sunday afternoon. When he learned of Allende's plans, Pinochet attempted to intercede on Tohá's behalf. When President Allende told Tohá of Pinochet's concern, the ex-minister remarked, "That good old Pinochet. He doesn't realize that his naive impulses could cost him his career someday, if they were ever mistaken for political interference." (Tohá died a political prisoner under Pinochet.)

An anecdote highlighting Pinochet's habit of political ingratiation was recalled by the late senator Volodia Teitelboim, a Communist. "We were at La Moneda during one of the many cabinet changes in 1973. Pinochet and I could not find a seat at the ceremony so we stood together at the end of the room." Teitelboim had never met Pinochet before. The general took the initiative: "How good to get to meet you, Senator," he declared. "You know, I am jealous of you." "Why is that?" asked Teitelboim. "Because whenever we see you on television, my wife, Lucía, elbows me in the ribs and says: 'Why can't you speak as beautifully as he does?'" Teitelboim got the impression that Pinochet was a cunning man who knew how to make useful friends.

In his own account of the June 29 uprising in *Camino Recorrido*, Pinochet rewrites history, claiming that he headed downtown with the Buin Regiment to impede any paramilitary or popular resistance—which Allende had called for—from "attacking our brethren in arms." "We would have reacted violently against such people," he wrote. The uprising, he added, "wiped out the preparations for military action against Mr. Allende that we were carefully planning to execute by late July." But Pinochet was not involved in any conspiracy of the sort, as the historical evidence plainly shows. On June 29 Pinochet was simply registering which way the wind was blowing, and going along with the prevailing course.

After the failed putsch Allende convened a summit meeting at his Tomás Moro Street residence, to which he invited top politicians, senior military officers, Pinochet included, and labor union leaders to discuss the way forward. Pinochet counseled Allende to adopt countermeasures in case of another coup attempt. "I propose that you set up your command at the Tacna Regiment rather than at La Moneda, coordinating your defensive operations with workers," said Pinochet.

On June 30, with the approval of General Prats, a "Committee of 15" was created, consisting of five high-level representatives from each branch of the armed services. The idea was to coordinate efforts to avoid another putsch, but the committee's meetings actually allowed the generals and admirals to openly air their grievances against the Allende government. Pinochet attempted to block any political discussion at the first session of the committee, but he did not succeed, as most members agreed that before they could propose solutions they would have to analyze the national situation.

The evening of the putsch, I attended a rally where marchers brandished low-caliber handguns and sticks in front of La Moneda palace. Looking back, it was a pitiful demonstration of weakness, rather than strength. Clearly, Allende could marshal no significant independent capacity for resistance. The most serious impediment to a coup was General Prats, who was staunch in his defense of the constitutional government. A concerted campaign for his removal began, which climaxed on August 21 when a humiliating demonstration by military officers' wives was held in front of his residence. The women had ostensibly gathered to deliver a letter to Prats's wife that decried their husbands' sufferings as a result of Allende's policies, but things swiftly got out of hand. The protesters, a few of them army officers on active duty, taunted Prats as a coward and scattered chicken feed in his doorway. An army captain in uniform yelled, "General Prats doesn't represent the army. He is a traitor!" When Pinochet arrived to show his solidarity with his commander, with his wife, Lucía, carrying flowers for Prats's spouse, he was booed and insulted. Eventually the police had to be called in.

Prats ordered Pinochet to demand a declaration of support from his generals. Without it, he said, he would be unable to command any longer. If Prats stepped down as commander of the army, it would affect Allende's government, too. Since August 9, a "national security cabinet" had incorporated the three commanders of the armed forces and the head of the national police. Prats's portfolio was now defense.

Pinochet had a meeting with the generals and expressed his ire at the demonstration. It had been "embarrassing and shameful," he said; the women had behaved like "common street vendors [verduleras]. Such an affront to a general," he roared, "can only be cleansed with the blood of generals," a phrase that would be particularly remembered. High officers who had joined their spouses at the rally would be punished, Pinochet said; furthermore, he demanded the resignation of every general whose wife had participated in the demonstration. But for all the bluster, none of the generals resigned and they steadfastly refused to issue a statement of support for Prats. Ratcheting up the tension to an even higher pitch, that same day the lower house of the Chilean congress issued an official political pronouncement against the Allende government, declaring it guilty of unconstitutional actions. Prats had been convinced that a coup was coming since August 3, the day conversations between the government and the Christian Democratic leaders had broken down owing to their demand that a new cabinet be formed with up to two-thirds armed forces representatives and the rest independent personalities. Allende could not accept that, reflected Prats years later; it would have been a "soft coup" (un golpe seco).

Prats resigned on August 23, but not before recommending that Allende appoint Pinochet as his successor. The president promoted Pinochet to the top army post. General Prats later reflected, "I believed that if General Pinochet succeeded me—having shown so much loyalty toward me—there was a possibility that the critical situation of the country would tend to unwind." The new commander in chief of the army was in the hot seat. Allende instructed him to restore order in the army ranks by demanding the immediate resignation of every general suspected of plotting against the constitutional government.

The rightist magazine *PEC* predicted that Pinochet would not last long in his new job. Quoting his remark that an affront to a general "is only cleansed with generals' blood," the publication dryly observed that "so far, Pinochet has not been able to extract even one drop of blood from any of his generals" and added that the new army commander was known as "a man with a loud voice toward those below him, but with zero voice regarding those above him."

Within a matter of days, Pinochet realized that he could not remove any general if he wanted to survive, and communicated the bad news to the president. Allende didn't like it, but was convinced that removing the suspected plotters might only accelerate the feared military coup.

In the meantime, relations between Allende and the other two armed services, the air force and the navy, continued to deteriorate. In early August, Air Force Commander César Ruiz Danyau had resigned his ministerial post. The president forced him to relinquish his air force post as well, prompting his defiance. The crisis was temporarily defused when Allende appointed General Gustavo Leigh air force commander on August 20. Since Leigh refused to serve in Allende's cabinet, the president named a lower-ranking air force general to the ministerial post.

The navy had been plotting against Allende since mid-July. Navy Commander Raúl Montero was a constitutionalist, but Admiral

Merino and other admirals openly challenged the navy chief's authority. Under those circumstances, on Friday, August 24, Montero submitted his resignation to Allende, but it wasn't accepted. The navy
admirals insisted on Montero's removal, and Allende agreed to appoint Merino the new commander on September 7. The navy plotters' move backfired at the last minute when a right-wing newspaper
leaked Merino's impending designation and the president responded
by leaving matters as they stood.

The Popular Unity party chiefs suggested to Allende a bold move:
arrest the coup plotters and use force to defend the government. But
Allende gave the party leaders a lecture on the rule of law, democratic
change, and the constitutional loyalty of the armed forces. What concerned Allende the most at the moment, he said, was the army. He
was suspicious of its internal security plan. He decided to talk to
Pinochet.

As Pinochet recounted in his book *The Crucial Day*, one night in
late August he was summoned to a predawn meeting at Allende's residence. Alarmed, Pinochet awoke his wife and children and took them
to his eldest daughter's home. Pinochet wrote that he was certain
at the time that "someone had betrayed the group of officers [plan-
ning the coup]. . . . Undoubtedly, my life was in danger." When he arrived at Allende's residence at three-thirty in the morning, the
president's living room seemed to have been transformed into a court
of law. Several ministers, including Orlando Letelier, were present, as
well as political leaders from Allende's Popular Unity coalition. "I just
thought that this was the end," Pinochet wrote. Another army general, Orlando Urbina, was also present. Then, a few minutes later,
everyone stood up as the president entered the room. Pinochet recalled that Allende was wearing "a dark suit and a mink hat. He was
wrapped in a blue cape with a fur collar and red lining. It was as if the
Devil himself had joined the meeting."

Allende asked Pinochet about his routine that day, probed him for
his opinions about certain generals, and then complained about terrorist actions being carried out by the right. Pinochet claims he listened without making comments, except to briefly describe his day's
activities, including his presence at a war games session at the War
Academy.

After listening to Allende's complaints about the opposition
Pinochet said, "Mr. President, I would like to sympathize with your
problems and worries because I am also in favor of order. But I must
make it clear to you that I am not a General Rojo"—referring to Vicente Rojo, the general who, during the Spanish Civil War, sided

with the Republicans although he was not a leftist. Around the break of dawn Pinochet left the presidential residence, giving General Urbina a ride. Urbina confided before his death that both he and Pinochet had gone together in the same car to and from Allende's house, a fact that Pinochet omits in his memoir. Apparently, Pinochet wanted to dramatize that solely he was the target of the president's supposed suspicion.

In Pinochet's highly revised version of events, he was already secretly planning the military coup long before this meeting, and was only pretending to be loyal. Actually, he did not even know that the real coup plotters had been meeting regularly for months at the residence of a conservative lawyer in Santiago's exclusive neighborhood of Lo Curro. Gonzalo Vial, a historian who was minister of education during the Pinochet regime, wrote a biography of Pinochet in which he concluded that "there is not a word, not even an insinuation that [Pinochet] favored or accepted, not even hypothetically, in any perspective, let alone prepared, a military coup or anything similar." Vial adds categorically that "Pinochet never conspired with anybody against Allende, until well into September 1973." That is, until that Sunday, September 9, 1973, when General Leigh and Admiral Merino forced him to join an unfolding coup.

THE DAY BEFORE the coup, Pinochet took his wife and his youngest children to the Mountain Training School in Río Blanco, Los Andes, an army camp close to the border with Argentina. Pinochet once had said, referring to the world's generals he most admired, that "all of them shared a common factor: they left open a retreat option, just in case things would go wrong; when they had no assurance of success." If the coup failed, the Pinochet family could flee to Argentina. The Mountain Training School commander, Colonel Gustavo Cantuarias, offered his distinguished guests the best rooms in the officers' quarters. Colonel Cantuarias was both a close friend of Carlos Prats and a constitutionalist. The next day he would resist orders to arrest copper workers; on September 12, accused of being an Allende sympathizer, he would be arrested and transferred to the Army Military School in Santiago. He died there three weeks later, allegedly after shooting himself. Pinochet did nothing to help him.

On September 11, Pinochet arose early. At 7 A.M. his car picked him up, but instead of proceeding directly to his command post at the Telecommunications Center in Peñalolen, he made a brief detour and stopped at the house of one of his adult children. When Pinochet didn't show up on time, the other plotters were worried. General Oscar Bonilla was about to take Pinochet's place.

As soon as he did arrive, he informed his military aide de camp that a military coup was in the making. "Excuse me, General, but I cannot go along with this," said his assistant. "Okay," Pinochet responded. "Then, you are under arrest." Pinochet's period of vacillation was over and his stance had hardened into ruthless determination. It was time for the army commander to take charge. As Pinochet had so often observed, to be truly useful, an individual must be able to obey orders, but he also must know how to give them. Pinochet was about to show a very different side of himself to the world.

In the late afternoon of 9/11, once the coup was fully consummated, Pinochet received a telephone call from Admiral Patricio Carvajal. "We have scheduled a meeting of commanders in chief here at the Defense Ministry, understood?"

"No," replied Pinochet. "You must come up here to Peñalolen."

Already, the army general was assuming ownership of the coup. When it proved logistically impossible to transport the other commanders to the foothills of the Andes—rainy weather made it too dangerous for the helicopters to land—Pinochet agreed to meet on middle ground. At around 7 P.M. the commanders gathered at the Army Military School. Admiral Merino and César Mendoza, the new chief of Carabineros, had never met before and were duly introduced to each other. Pinochet, who knew how marginal a role he'd played in the coup compared to the others, was nervous. He saw a potential rival for power in General Leigh and he did not fully trust Admiral Merino.

In the course of the long, disorganized meeting that ensued, the four leaders decided to extend the stage of siege, possibly to break relations with the Soviet Bloc countries and Cuba, and to communicate the news of President Allende's death by means of a written statement. A military junta had to be formally constituted. But who would preside over it? General Leigh argued that the question should be settled on the basis of seniority. Since he had assumed his post as air force commander three days before Pinochet had been elevated to commander in chief of the army, he declared himself the rightful head of the junta. Pinochet disagreed, arguing that what mattered was not the seniority of the commanders but the respective ages of the institutions they led. Since the army was created before the navy, and the air force was created before the Carabineros, he should head the junta.

According to Pinochet's *The Crucial Day,* this discussion had already taken place on Sunday, September 9, when General Leigh and

Admiral Huidobro had pressured Pinochet into joining the coup, one of many dubious contentions in Pinochet's writings. Years later Merino asserted that Pinochet had offered the leadership to him, but that he had refused it. Instead, he said, the four officers had adopted an unwritten gentleman's agreement that Pinochet would preside on behalf of the army at first, but that the presidency of the junta would rotate among the services. That never happened.

Finally the four leaders had themselves sworn in as members of the junta. Etched in my memory is General Leigh, practically screaming on TV that the military would "eradicate the Marxist cancer from Chile." I have no particular memory of Pinochet or what he said.

The junta immediately named a cabinet, which, with the exception of the justice and education portfolios, consisted entirely of members of the armed forces and the Carabineros. The choice of minister of education was difficult. Nobody could think of anyone to nominate, until Pinochet remembered that he had had a good teacher, many years back, at the military school. Within a matter of hours seventy-year-old José Navarro was located and sworn in (a few weeks later he was removed, having proved himself a total disaster as minister).

THE MORNING AFTER the coup I left my "unsafe safe house" and visited Pamela and the rest of my family at my aunt's house, where I knew they would be safe for the time being. As for me, I didn't know what to do. I had no party contacts or instructions; there were only a few hours left in the day before the early evening curfew began. I called my cousin Guillermo Valenzuela, a Socialist sympathizer who, though more dedicated to his parents' bar-restaurant business than politics, was a veteran of street fights with right-wing gangs. Maybe together we could figure out what our next step should be. We decided to meet at my mother's house. Hours before curfew the neighborhood streets were already eerily empty. Guillermo arrived on schedule, armed with a handgun.

Although we were getting most of our information from the military junta-controlled media, both of us had already heard rumors of killings of left-wing militants. The embassies in Santiago were filling up with asylum seekers; Socialist and Communist leaders had vanished. We locked the doors and set about destroying any documents that could have linked us to a Popular Unity party. We burned leaflets and letters and notes; the smoke was so thick we worried that a neighbor would call the fire department and attract the military to our door. But ours was not the only bonfire burning in Chile that night; many of our neighbors were doing the same thing. Any books that could be construed as suspicious had to be hidden as well. We agreed that it didn't make sense to keep waiting for instructions that would never come; the next morning we went our separate ways, simply trying to survive.

Leftist leaders were summoned to present themselves immediately at the Defense Ministry. Most of them did, because they felt that they had nothing to fear. Many of them were summarily arrested and tortured; some of them disappeared forever. Rightist magazine *Qué Pasa* asserted in an editorial that "to open a new door, the country must pay its share of blood."

A strong strain of xenophobia emerged in the military regime. The day following the coup, the junta issued an ultimatum to all foreign residents, ordering them to present themselves at the Defense Ministry or at a local police precinct. Three days later, a new official communiqué warned, "We will have no compassion with foreigners who have come to kill Chileans. Citizens: be alert to discover them and to denounce them to the nearest military authority." More than six hundred foreigners were arrested, many tortured, and some of them killed after the coup. The brilliant writer Roberto Bolaño, born in Chile but raised in Mexico, was arrested during a road check and imprisoned for several days on suspicion of being a "Mexican terrorist," because of his foreign accent. He got out thanks to the help of two detectives who had been his classmates in high school.

A local Christian Democratic leader, Juan Alucema, sent me a disquieting message. Pamela, being a foreigner, should present herself to the Defense Ministry, he said. The person who delivered the message to me, his next-door neighbor, was afraid that Alucema might denounce my wife to the military. She didn't have her passport because it was with her application for a permanent visa, which was being processed at the Ministry of the Interior. Later we learned that it had been destroyed during the bombing of La Moneda.

I asked the messenger, whom I knew, only one favor. "Tell Alucema," I said, "that if anything happens to Pamela, I will track him down and put a bullet in his head, if it's the last thing I do." That was the last we ever heard from Mr. Alucema.

With each passing day, more and more stories circulated through informal channels about detentions, torture, and killings. On September 18, Chile's national Independence Day, Pinochet forced the Catholic Church into offering a Te Deum to thank God for "national liberation" through the military coup. Cardinal Raúl Silva Henríquez had refused to conduct the Mass at the Military School but settled for the Gratitud Nacional church on Alameda Avenue. All living former presidents plus the four junta members attended, as did the members of the Supreme Court, which had welcomed the military coup. Following protocol, Pinochet was placed in a visible and privileged position. A photograph of his stern bull dog face, his eyes hidden by sunglasses, a deferential military aide behind his back, was published the next day in newspapers all over the world. Pinochet's was the public face of the dictatorship in Chile. When asked why he almost always wore dark glasses during the early years of the junta, he gave a surprisingly candid response: "Because it is a way of hiding things. . . . Lies can be discovered through the eyes, and I lied a lot."

The next day, September 19, the bodies of eleven former Allende officials were found floating in the Mapocho River, a few blocks away from the Gratitud Nacional. The day before, the newspaper *La Tercera* had headlined with a Pinochet quote on its front page: "There will be no mercy for extremists." Throughout the city, the military searched houses and apartment buildings and confiscated thousands of books, posters, journals, and records suspected of being "subversive," dumped them into huge piles in the streets, and set them on fire, then arrested their owners. Outside a progressive bookstore on MacIver Street I saw hundreds of books piled up on the sidewalk, vigilantly guarded by two army soldiers with automatic rifles.

On September 21 Pinochet gave his first press conference in front of national and foreign journalists. The general offered reassuring words to a foreign correspondent who wondered when Chile would return to democratic rule. "As soon as the country recuperates and overcomes chaos, I am sure that the junta will hand power back [to an elected government]." Answering another question, Pinochet declared, "Marxist resistance has not ended. . . . Chile continues in a state of internal war. And those who deviate will have to assume the costs of law under a state of war." It was a war against all those who refused to follow Pinochet's diktats.

Labor union chiefs, peasant activists, student leaders, Allende sympathizers were systematically arrested, tortured, and often assassinated. Pinochet's repressive arm was the soon-to-be-feared DINA (Dirección de Inteligencia Nacional), a secret police unit led by an obscure army colonel named Manuel Contreras. The seal of the DINA, a fist wrapped in an iron glove, read: "Republic of Chile Presidency of the Republic—DINA." Ghastly torture techniques, unheard of in

Chile before, became commonplace. One of the most notorious DINA torturers, Osvaldo Romo, offered shocking details in a jail-house interview after the end of the Pinochet period. There was, for example, "the submarine," when a prisoner was submerged in a tank of water mixed with excrement and ammonia until the victim began to drown; the *parrilla* (the electric grill), in which a nude, soaking-wet victim was tied to a set of metal bedsprings while electrical shocks were administered to the mouth, ears, and sexual organs; "the perch," in which a prisoner was hung from a wooden rod by his or her ex-tremities until bones fractured and the victim passed out from the pain. Finger and toe nails were extracted with pliers; rats were intro-duced into women's vaginas. Many women were brutally raped (more than a dozen female prisoners were impregnated by their cap-tors); pregnant women were tortured and killed; other prisoners were forced to play Russian roulette, to endure sleep and food deprivation, to undergo mock executions, and much more. Judicial investigations determined that prisoners were injected with toxic substances and, after death, their fingerprints were burned and obliterated with blow-torches and their bodies dumped in the ocean. Extrajudicial execu-tions and disappearances of prisoners became the hallmark of the Pinochet regime.

Hundreds died, particularly during the first weeks and months af-ter the coup. Concentration camps were set up throughout Chile: Chacabuco, Pisagua, Quiriquinas, Dawson Island, Ritoque, Tejas Verdes, Londres 38, Villa Grimaldi, José Domingo Cañas, Academia de Guerra Aérea, Escuela de Caballería de Quillota were but some of the places where Chileans were detained and systematically tortured and killed. Asked once by a foreign journalist about the torture of po-litical prisoners, Pinochet responded, "No, sir. [The prisoners] hit themselves to claim they have been tortured in the detention places." Writs of habeas corpus were dismissed by the courts with form letters sent to lawyers and families of the victims.

At the National Stadium, the site of the 1962 World Soccer Cup, thousands of prisoners were tortured and at least one hundred were assassinated on the spot. Major Mario Lavandero of the army, who was in charge of the foreign prisoners section of the stadium, was murdered on October 18, 1973, presumably because he delivered a group of Uruguayan prisoners to the care of the Swedish embassy. Major Lavandero's father had been Pinochet's fencing instructor dur-ing the 1930s, but his repeated appeals to Pinochet to authorize a formal investigation into his son's death fell on deaf ears. Major

Lavandero's parents died without ever having been granted the interview they requested with their old friend Pinochet. The stadium, once a place for life, entertainment, and the joy of sports, had turned into a charnel house.

Many years later, in 2003, while visiting Afghanistan as the chairman of the Al Qaeda and Taliban Sanctions Committee of the UN Security Council, I asked to see the local stadium where the Taliban shot in the head women suspected of being unfaithful, and men accused of Western proclivities were hanged from soccer-field goal posts. My heavily armed security escort did not like the idea, but we wound up visiting the Kabul stadium. In 2003 it was once again a peaceful place for the celebration of life—children were training for a soccer game. For a brief moment, that shining morning in Kabul, I remembered Chile's National Stadium in 1973.

I had worked for several months in 1973 as national supervisor of the People's Stores (Almacenes del Pueblo). The store infrastructure was made available by the expropriated national supermarket chain Montserrat, which ran the Almacenes del Pueblo program, while the sale of the goods, provided at cost, was managed by the *pobladores* (shantytown dwellers) themselves. Among other things, it was my job to make sure that the program was not abused, that only very poor neighborhoods without proper commercial infrastructure would participate.

Several days after the coup I was ordered to report to Montserrat, which was now being headed by an army colonel appointed by the junta; and formally resign my post. "It's better to go and sign whatever they ask you," a colleague told me. I thought I had nothing to fear, since I had done my best to administer a social project that was both legal and highly worthwhile. I was given an appointment to see the colonel the following day at 8:30 A.M. I arrived a half hour early and waited for three hours. Not having had breakfast, I decided to go to a corner café for five minutes to grab a cup of coffee. Of course, that was just the moment that my name was called. When I returned, his secretary said nervously, "The colonel is too angry to see you in person. He asks that you submit your resignation in writing." I responded that in that case I would not resign; he would have to fire me. The secretary feared she would be blamed, so I signed a letter, which stated that I was being let go against my will. Then I left the premises, taking a copy of the letter for my files.

Some two weeks later, a friend told me to be careful because the DINA secret police were looking for Alejandro "Mickey" Villalobos,

an MIR militant who had been active in the People's Stores movement (he was later arrested and his name is on the long list of disappeared prisoners); People's Stores staff could become targets of
repression.

I was urged to seek asylum at an embassy. Practically the only
diplomatic mission not accepting refugees at that point was that of the
United States. I refused, because I thought it would be an act of cow-
ardice. Moreover, diplomatic residences and offices throughout Santiago were already packed with thousands of people who feared for
their lives; the junta was not letting them leave the country.

Around this time I received a desperate call from my friend Jaime
Fernández, an accomplished guitarist who had performed with the
musical group Peter, Paul, and Mary, and who had until recently
served as the assistant cultural attaché of the Chilean embassy in
Washington. Jaime had returned to Chile just before the coup; he had
sought asylum in the Venezuelan embassy but nobody there knew
him. I managed to convince a midlevel Socialist leader to intervene on
Jaime's behalf with the Venezuelans. I next saw Jaime about eight
years later, in Caracas.

Jaime was one of the lucky ones. Lumi Videla, a philosophy student at the University of Chile and an MIR militant, was twenty-six
years old and had one son when she was arrested by the DINA on
September 21, 1974. She was tortured to death at a detention house
located on José Domingo Cañas Street on November 3 (her husband,
Sergio Pérez, was also arrested by the DINA; he is still among the
"disappeared"). The next night, during the curfew, Lumi's body was
thrown over the high walls of the Italian embassy, a brutal threat to
the 202 Chileans who were inside the compound waiting for safe-
conduct papers. It was also an act of payback against the Italians for
granting asylum to Humberto Sotomayor, an MIR leader who had
narrowly escaped a raid on a safe house in southern Santiago where
the MIR chief, Miguel Enriquez, had been gunned down. The
Pinochet government issued a communiqué stating that Lumi Videla
had been murdered inside the Italian embassy while asylum seekers
were holding an orgy, a lie that El Mercurio duly reported. Needless to
say, this crude fabrication was easily discredited by the judge who
eventually investigated Videla's assassination.

On October 19, 1973, twenty-six people were executed by army
troops in the mining town of Calama and were buried on the road to
nearby San Pedro de Atacama. Among the prisoners were mine workers, engineers, union leaders, teachers, students, and the journalist

Carlos Berger, the husband of my friend Carmen Hertz, a human rights lawyer who became Chile's ambassador to Hungary under President Michelle Bachelet. Most of the twenty-six men had been arrested on or around the 9/11 coup and were in Calama's public jail, some of them serving sentences that had been passed by war tribunals. Berger, a Communist Party member who was the director of El Loa radio station, had been arrested at the station during the coup, released, and rearrested the next day. He was sentenced to sixty days in jail for keeping his station on the air the day of the coup. Carmen assumed Carlos's defense and by October 17 had succeeded in having his remaining jail sentence commuted in exchange for a fine. Carmen had already bought two tickets to Santiago. But on October 19, a Puma helicopter carrying General Sergio Arellano and some other army personnel landed at the local army base. What would later be known as the "Caravan of Death"—a squad of Pinochet army officers that toured several cities throughout Chile and ultimately executed almost one hundred political prisoners—had arrived. On General Arellano's orders, all twenty-six prisoners were transported to a desolate place known as Topater, where they were savagely murdered with daggers and gunfire.

Carmen had gone to the army base that same morning but had been unable to get the documents she needed. At 5 P.M. she visited Carlos in the public jail. At 8 P.M., during curfew hours, he and the other twenty-five prisoners were taken to their deaths. Carmen was told that her husband had been transferred to a prison in Santiago. She searched for him—and was lied to—for years.

Two years after their murders, the prisoners' remains were disinterred with heavy machinery and, under the supervision of Captain Carlos Minoletti, placed in bags and transported to the Calama airport, where they were loaded onto a DC-6 air force plane, from which they were dumped into the ocean. More than thirty years later, a judicial process determined that high-ranking military officers, including the army general in charge of the region, not only knew about the illegal removal of the bodies but ordered it. Still, the truth eventually came out. Enough forensic evidence was left behind at the original burial place to allow for identification of thirteen of the victims, but no trace of Carlos Berger was ever found. In 1984, his father, Julio Berger, committed suicide. In June 1988, Carlos's mother, Dora Guralnik, also took her life, never knowing what had happened to her son. Entire families were murdered, like Sergio Maureira and his four sons, whose remains were dumped in a lime oven in the rural community of Lonquén. The list of atrocities goes on and on.

What role did Pinochet play in this wave of repression and violence? Of course he didn't always know about particular crimes, but he and the other members of the junta had sent out unambiguous signals from the very first day of the coup: the military government was "at war" with Marxists, union leaders, Allende supporters, rabble rousers, and dissidents. Pinochet gave the green light for systematic repression in his first press conference, when he warned that the war was not over, despite the overwhelming victory that the junta had won against Allende, despite the almost complete absence of organized armed resistance. Pinochet became a "hands-on" ruler who was on top of every major political and military decision, as in the case of the Caravan of Death executions implemented by General Arellano but ordered by Pinochet.

In a regime as hierarchical as Pinochet's it would have been unthinkable that his direct subordinates were torturing and killing thousands of people without his approval. But Pinochet denied knowing anything about the repression and atrocities. In a long series of interviews with two leading Chilean journalists, Raquel Correa and Elizabeth Subercaseaux, conducted in 1989, he was asked about the many documented atrocities.

"That, I never knew about," Pinochet claimed.

"But at some point you must have learned about the summary executions," the journalists pressed on.

"Never. How could you imagine that I'm some kind of connoisseur of violence? I am not an SS trooper."

The reporters inquired about the torture and death of the folksinger Víctor Jara and the disappearance of Eduardo "Coco" Paredes, who had been arrested on the day of the coup at La Moneda.

"Those are just tales," Pinochet responded angrily. "No bodies were ever found! The bodies all disappeared."

"I saw bodies in the Mapocho River," countered one of the journalists.

"You must have very sharp eyesight," Pinochet replied sarcastically. "Leftist combatants probably threw their comrades' bodies in the river," he added.

When asked about repression by the DINA and about their secret torture camps, Pinochet responded, "I cannot say yes or no."

In the same interview, Pinochet denied knowing that the Nazis murdered millions of Jews. When asked about Hitler's culpability for the Holocaust, Pinochet answered: "Maybe he was guilty, maybe not."

"But Hitler was perfectly aware of the existence of the concentration camps and the killing machines, the ovens, the forced labor, the gas chambers. It would be unthinkable to imagine that all of that was done behind Hitler's back," the two journalists said.

Pinochet was adamant. "I repeat," he answered. "Maybe it happened as you say, or maybe not. . . . I do not defend Hitler and his system because I have many good friends of Israelite origin. And I cannot accept what happened during the World War II years."

"But the whole of humanity believes Hitler was an assassin," the frustrated journalists insisted.

"Maybe he was. Or maybe he was a person who was unaware of what was happening; or perhaps he authorized everything. I do not have much information about him." Pinochet's stubborn neutrality about Hitler's role in the Holocaust was reflective of his denial of his own role during the dictatorship.

Pinochet's direct knowledge of crimes of torture and the murder of particular individuals is illustrated by an episode of November 1974, when representatives of the ecumenical Committee Pro-Peace requested that the Spanish Catholic priest Antonio Llidó be released from prison. Pinochet got angry when they showed him a picture of Llidó and responded, "This guy is no priest; he is a member of the MIR!" Llidó had been arrested by DINA agents in October 1974 and is still missing today.

Pinochet used exactly the same words as the DINA torturer Romo to justify torture. Romo is on the record as saying, "*You had to squeeze,* some more than others . . . but under torture everyone talks, everyone." Similarly, when Pinochet was under arrest in London and an interviewer asked him whether naming Colonel Manuel Contreras as head of the DINA might have been a mistake because of all the tortures and murders he perpetrated, Pinochet answered, "At that moment [Contreras] was the right man because *we had to squeeze.*" It seems reasonable to assume that Romo had been paraphrasing his bosses.

Leftists and other opponents of the military coup were fired from public and private enterprises, some fifty thousand from public administration services alone. Thousands of professors and students were expelled from universities; whole social sciences departments were shut down. My younger brother, an MIR student leader, was expelled from the State Technical University. Leftist political parties were banned outright and all other political parties were declared "in recess." The National Congress was closed down, elections were put off indefinitely, and voter rolls were eventually destroyed. By January 1974, 50 percent of all Chilean journalists were out of work. Of the eleven national newspapers that had existed at the time of the coup only four survived; leftist weekly magazines disappeared, and the handful of left-wing radio stations that weren't bombed into silence during the coup were simply shut down.

Censorship by the dictatorship reached ridiculous levels. In 1975, when the Russian chess masters Anatoly Karpov and Viktor Korchnoi competed for the world title, the Chilean censors kept the news off the air because the Soviets and the Pinochet government did not have diplomatic relations. Even the pro-government newspaper *La Segunda* was closed for one day as a sanction for having announced an increase in the price of cigarettes on its front page. Such news "had altered people's tranquillity," the censor declared.

During a soccer game between Santiago Morning and Aviación (at the time, the air force team in Chile's professional soccer league), Santiago Morning's coach became so irate at the referee's calls that he shouted at Aviación's manager, "You are going to become champions thanks to governmental decree!" Two days after the story was printed in *El Mercurio*, its author, the sportswriter René Durney, was fired and jailed.

The Pinochet dictatorship particularly distrusted books and authors. Gustavo Olave, who had written a novel six months before the coup entitled *Los Asesinos del Suicida* (The Murderers of the Suicide Man), was arrested and imprisoned for three months when his book was published, despite the fact that it had nothing to do with politics. When the confusion was cleared up, he was told that the ban on his book would continue unless he changed its title.

The late Erich Rosenrauch, an Austrian by birth who had lived in Chile since an early age, published a novel in 1973 entitled *Muertos Útiles* (The Useful Dead). Every copy of his book was impounded, and Rosenrauch, whose parents had emigrated to Chile to escape Nazi persecution, was arrested. He was released when the military discovered that the title of the novel had no topical significance, but his books were never released and his original manuscript was lost following its seizure when his house was searched.

In January 1975, a University of Chile at Valparaíso official issued a list of books to be purged from the university's inventory. Among the texts to be destroyed were all of the works of Marx, Engels, and Lenin, and also books by John Kenneth Galbraith and Gunnar Myrdal.

Many of those arrested saw their home libraries disappear. In December 1975 the journalist Hernán Millas's house was searched by the military. Not only did the army troops help themselves to his family silver, they carried away several boxes filled with books. Millas was told he would get them back once they were inspected by the proper authorities but he never did. Years later, one of Millas's nephews stumbled on some of his most valuable volumes (his name was in them) in an antique shop in Paris. Stealing first editions and rare books from dissidents and selling them in Europe was such a widespread practice by the secret polices of Chile, Argentina, and Uruguay that it apparently became a practice to help finance their operations.

Not just books were censored. Between 1973 and 1990, when democracy returned to Chile, about one thousand movies were forbidden, 66 percent of them during the first seven years of the dictatorship. Among the prohibited films were *Casanova*, directed by Federico Fellini; Liliana Cavani's *The Night Porter;* Norman Jewison's *Fiddler on the Roof;* Wes Craven's *The Last House on the Left;* Peter Medak's *The Ruling Class;* and Martin Scorsese's *The Last Temptation of Christ.*

During a dinner I hosted for Sidney Pollack in New York in 2004, we speculated about what Pinochet might have had against his *Three Days of the Condor*, which was also banned. Pollack suspected it was the plot, which revolved around a CIA hit team eliminating a team of analysts who had discovered a secret invasion plan and chasing its sole survivor. I suggested that what the government found most objectionable about the movie was its title. The movie was released while Pinochet's DINA was covertly assassinating dissident leaders abroad under the code name Operation Condor. When I became minister secretary-general of the government under President Ricardo Lagos, one of my achievements was to make it possible for Chileans to watch whatever movies they wished. On December 9, 2002, the Chilean Congress passed the legislation that made film censorship a thing of the past. A few weeks later Scorsese's *The Last Temptation of Christ* was screened for a SRO crowd in downtown Santiago.

In those first frightening days and weeks after the coup, I had few contacts with my Socialist comrades. We simply tried to survive. I had one very close call in October. Pamela and I had returned to live at my mother's house in Estación Central, after moving around from house to house. One Saturday afternoon I looked out the window and saw army trucks and dozens of troops in combat gear. I realized they were coming for me when I saw the two prisoners they'd taken already in the back of a military Jeep across the street. I knew them both well:

Mario Zamorano, a fifty-year-old tailor, and Villalobos, the secretary of organization of the Socialist Party for the Ninth commune (borough), where we lived.

I told my wife that I was about to be arrested, put on a jacket, and sat down to wait. Resistance was pointless—I was hopelessly outnumbered and outgunned. Right outside our door a soldier held a .30 caliber machine gun. For a brief moment I considered fleeing across the rooftops, but that might put Pamela in jeopardy. I told her to get in touch with her congressman, to contact Senator Ted Kennedy, and to use any other influence she could muster on my behalf. The priority was to find out where I would be taken. When several minutes went by and the army troops had still not entered our house, I wondered what was going on. Ten more minutes passed, which felt like an eternity. Suddenly, to our astonishment, the troops, the military trucks, and the Jeep all sped away. We couldn't believe it.

Much later, when calm had returned to the street, someone knocked softly on our door. It was Doña Alicia, our next-door neighbor—we'd known her for decades, she'd seen me and my brothers grow up. The soldiers had mistakenly gone to her house instead of ours, she said, and demanded that she give me up. When she explained that she only had two daughters and a young boy, they'd turned her house upside down. Even so, she had refused to betray me.

About four years later, in Mexico, I ran into Mario Zamorano, one of the prisoners I'd seen in the Jeep. We embraced and he shed tears as he told me his side of the story. The military had a list of names, mine among them. When the caravan pulled up in front of my house the prisoners knew it was my turn. They couldn't believe it when the soldiers went to the wrong door; they were ecstatic when they gave up the search and left without me. "The military bastard was really mad," Zamorano told me. For the two prisoners it had been a small parenthesis of satisfaction in the midst of their own miseries. Had the officer had the right address, had our neighbor been any less stalwart, my destiny would have been the same as theirs—detention and torture in the National Stadium for many months, followed by forced exile.

During a 2005 dinner in my honor given by Barbara Walters at her Fifth Avenue apartment in Manhattan, she proposed during dessert to discuss a topic suggested by a recent movie, *Match Point*, where the main character's life is altered by a stroke of luck. As the charming hostess with an inquisitive mind that she is, Barbara asked all guests at her round dining table to tell a personal story where chance had changed one's life, excluding moments such as the meeting of a spouse or similar family milestones. There were top journalists, businessmen, academics, and diplomats present, including Kofi Annan. His story was good: when he emerged as a strong contender for the post of UN secretary-general, Boutros Boutros Ghali, who was fighting to continue at the helm of the organization, sent Annan off to the former Yugoslavia to make him vanish as a potential candidate to his post. But chance would have it that Annan's skillful performance as UN envoy in that crisis region impressed many world leaders and actually propelled him to the front-runner position and, eventually, to the secretary-general berth. But when the guests at Barbara Walters's home heard my story of escaping arrest, torture, and exile because a military patrol had mistakenly entered the house next door to where I lived, everyone agreed it was by far the best story of luck altering the course of one's life.

After that close escape, Pamela and I decided to leave my mother's residence. It occurred to me that we could rent a house on the Pacific coast. Nobody would think of looking for us there, since beach towns are desolate in the off-season. We consulted the want ads in the newspaper and found a reasonably priced house in El Quisco, about seventy miles west of Santiago. The owner lived in the wealthy part of the capital, in Pedro de Valdivia Street, near Providencia Avenue, a stylish tree-shaded boulevard. I still remember his last name: Mr. Lea-Plaza, a distinguished name of the local "aristocracy." As we signed the rental contract, both Pamela and I noticed a big ashtray with the inscription *Partido Nacional*. It was the right-wing party that had bitterly opposed Allende and now wholeheartedly supported the junta. Perhaps it would be to our advantage to have a right-wing landlord.

A nice feature of the rented house was the large short-wave radio that was included among its furnishings. Radio Moscow broadcast a daily program called *Escucha, Chile* (Listen, Chile), which offered uncensored news about what was going on in our country as well as information about the emerging activities of Chilean dissident leaders in exile. The radio also picked up a late-night program from the Kingdom of Tonga, an island in the South Pacific Ocean that I associated with the legendary Captain Cook. I would learn a lot more about Tonga in the time we spent in El Quisco.

One night, during curfew hours, we were startled by a loud banging on our back door. The previous day we'd run into Mario Felmer, a Central Committee member of the Socialist Party, and his wife, Margarita, whom we knew well from Santiago and who, coincidentally, were also hiding out on the coast. When we saw each other in a bus, we just exchanged nods; we didn't speak a word. Neither of us knew if the other was being followed, or if they were involved in an underground operation. But despite our caution, perhaps someone had noticed that we knew each other. There was another possibility, too, which I shared with Pamela. I had forgotten to throw away the newspaper where I'd seen the ad for the rental place we were living in; it was still in my mother's house with the listing circled in ink. It had been an unforgivable security slippage on my part. We turned off the radio and I went to open the door. The next thing I knew I was looking down the muzzles of two submachine guns. Two policemen and a civilian were standing on the back steps.

"What are you doing here?" asked one of the policemen.

"I am on vacation with my wife," I responded. "We rented this place from Mr. Lea-Plaza and came in the off-season to avoid the summer crowds. You can come in if you want," I added, trying to be as cool as possible though my heart was racing.

The three men exchanged glances. *Had they been able to hear Radio Moscow before we turned it off?* I wondered. "There is no need to," the civilian said. "I am a neighbor who lives here all year round and I know the owners of this house never come until the summer. When I saw the lights burning and sounds I thought that thieves had broken in."

"Sorry to disturb you," said the policeman who had done most of the talking. "Have a good vacation." We closed the door and hugged. That night we did not sleep well.

Pamela tried to convince me that we should move to the United States, but I was not ready yet. I resented the U.S. government's role in the coup; moreover, I had secured a job as a research assistant at the Institute of International Studies of the University of Chile. In a rare case of open competition for faculty and researcher positions, the institute had advertised for applications in order to fill the positions. I made it to the short list and was hired. After months of unemployment, I finally had a paying job. At the same time I enrolled in a graduate program in international studies at the Political Science Department of the Catholic University of Chile. Things seemed to be moving in a more positive direction.

I became close with a small group of graduate students at the Catholic University, all of them relatively active in dissident organizations. Soon we were exchanging resistance publications and information. One of them did not like the fact that I and others often brought underground pamphlets to class. Once we were all in a car looking at contraband and he demanded that the driver pull over. "You are going to get us all arrested!" he yelled, as he climbed out of the car. When he decided to move to Mexico we organized a modest farewell party at a restaurant in the Portada de Vitacura, a well-to-do neighborhood on the eastern side of Santiago. The dinner was attended by Pamela and me; Jorge Vera and his friend Marcia Scantlebury; Juan Pablo Lira and his Ecuadorian wife, María Correa; plus, of course, our departing honored guest, Luis Díaz and his companion, Elvira. We had a good time, particularly when Juan Pablo read some anti-Pinochet verses that he had brought along with him. We were about to leave when, without warning, we were surrounded by uniformed army troops with automatic weapons. "Hands up!" a noncommissioned officer yelled. "Everyone out!"

Had somebody heard the anti-Pinochet verses and denounced us? We soon realized that it wasn't just us—everyone in the restaurant was being marched with their hands up to an army truck half a block away, where still more people were being held. As we walked toward the truck with rifles pointed at our backs, I saw Juan Pablo out of the corner of my eye, swallowing something he had taken from his shirt pocket. The military did not search us but demanded that all the men produce their ID cards. It was a random search and control operation; it reminded me of films about the Nazis in occupied France. After a couple of hours they returned our IDs and let us go. As we walked to a nearby parking lot, still shaking, I turned to Juan Pablo and asked him what he'd done with the incriminating poems.

"I thought I had eaten them," he said with a nervous laugh. "But I just discovered that what I ate was some water or electricity bill I was carrying!" The verses were still in his pockets. After the return of democracy Juan Pablo went on to become ambassador of Chile to Colombia and Peru. In 2008 he held a high position in the Ministry of Foreign Relations.

The prevailing sense of insecurity was intensified by occasional news of more killings, arrests, or disappearances. One day the DINA secret police came to the Catholic University campus and arrested Professor Juan Avalos, who was never seen again. The Political Science Department, where I studied international affairs, was shut down in mid-1975 because its director, Edmundo López, had invited the former president Eduardo Frei Montalva to give a lecture. López was expelled, along with many other professors.

In 1975 Pamela insisted that we move back to the United States, at least until things in Chile calmed down. John McCamant, a professor at the Graduate School of International Studies of the University of Denver, was then a visiting scholar in the Political Science Department of the Catholic University. He also urged me to go to the States.

"Take advantage now to get away, do a Ph.D., and then evaluate whether you want to return," he insisted. "Any day now you are going to be jailed," he warned.

Three

THE POWER
TO DICTATE

Pinochet knew that he would have to act quickly to consolidate his power. Getting himself named president of the junta was only the beginning. He would have to deal decisively with the true coup leaders and potential rivals—particularly Generals Sergio Arellano, Augusto Lutz, Oscar Bonilla, and Manuel Torres de la Cruz.

Pinochet's key ally would be Colonel Manuel Contreras, who at the time of the coup was the director of the Military Engineers School in Tejas Verdes, near the central coast of Chile. A chunky, round-headed individual of medium height, Colonel Contreras had studied intelligence and counterintelligence with the U.S. Army in Fort Belovoir, Virginia, and Fort Benning, Georgia. Under Contreras's command, the Tejas Verdes camp soon became known as the place where the most brutal tortures took place. Contreras was named chief of Pinochet's secret police, the DINA.

The DINA, also known as the "DINA Committee," was composed of officers and troops drawn from all the armed forces. There were other intelligence services in Chile that did their own repressive work, including the Air Force Intelligence Service (Servicio de Inteligencia de la Fuerza Aérea, SIFA), led by Colonel Edgar Ceballos, and its so-called Comando Conjunto (Joint Command), but they never offered any serious competition to the all-powerful DINA. The reason for its extraordinary power was its direct connection to Pinochet, who was its chief mentor, defender, and client. Through the DINA, Pinochet would hunt down dissidents all over the world; just as important, its resources allowed him to keep a tight rein on his rivals within the army.

Another way to eliminate his rivals was to force them into retirement or to place them in positions where their power was diminished. After the coup the junta dictated numerous "decree laws" (juridical norms dictated by a de facto regime, having the force of a law enacted by a legislature). A key one, issued in late September 1973, eliminated the Army Evaluation Board, a move that transferred to Pinochet supreme power over its highest-ranking officers' careers. In December 1973 Pinochet announced changes in the army hierarchy. General Augusto Lutz, a potential rival, had been director of the Military Intelligence Service (Servicio de Inteligencia Militar, SIM); he was removed from that post and named secretary of the military junta. Another rival, General Manuel Torres, who had been head of the powerful military region of Punta Arenas, the southernmost region of Chile, was named inspector general of the army. But that posting turned out to be a temporary one—only a few weeks later, in mid-February 1974, Pinochet forced Torres into retirement, ostensibly because of an accidental explosion of a munitions deposit under his care. Another coup plotter, General Sergio Nuño, also left the military.

General Oscar Bonilla had been named minister of the interior and he took his job seriously. He visited poor neighborhoods, constantly toured the country, and insisted on maintaining full control over public order at the national level. Informed of the tortures that went on at the Tejas Verdes regiment, led by Colonel Contreras, Bonilla made a surprise visit in May 1974 and verified its gross human rights violations. He ordered Contreras to be arrested and replaced by his deputy. Contreras refused to surrender himself or to leave his job, claiming he answered only to Pinochet.

Sometime later, during a cabinet session, Contreras was invited to make a presentation to the ministers about the need to improve security in the government offices. "There is leftist infiltration in government," he declared.

"What evidence do you have?" inquired Bonilla.

Contreras looked at Pinochet for his cue. "My general," he said to the minister of the interior. "There are some matters that cannot be discussed publicly."

Bonilla was so furious he almost vaulted over his desk to hit Contreras, but Pinochet put an immediate end to the discussion.

General Lutz also had a run-in with Colonel Contreras. One of his son's teachers had contacted him in desperation to inquire about her husband, who had been arrested by the fearsome DINA. Lutz phoned Contreras, hoping at least to get some information about the case.

"I cannot grant you access to the information you request," responded Contreras. "Only the president is authorized."

"Who the hell do you think you are?" fired back General Lutz. "How dare you say that to a general of the Republic! We'll see about this!"

In June 1974, at an army generals meeting, Generals Bonilla and Lutz complained that a colonel could not overrule a superior officer. Their complaints extended to the DINA as well, whose lack of accountability violated the chain of command. Pinochet cut off the discussion. "I am the DINA, gentlemen," he said. That was all.

Colonel Contreras and Pinochet met daily at 7:30 A.M.; Contreras was the only DINA official Pinochet spoke to. Within a short time the other branches of the military withdrew from the DINA; it was almost entirely staffed by members of the army. With the DINA on his side, Pinochet strengthened his position within the junta.

In March 1974, the Advisory Committee of the Junta, created in late 1973 and staffed mostly by army officers, managed to discard the idea of a rotating presidency of the junta, arguing that such an arrangement stifled executive agility and clarity in command. Also, the military government would be guided by "goals," not "datelines." In short, the junta was no longer a transitional regime.

The field was open for another bold move by Pinochet. On June 17, 1974, he presented the other members of the junta with Decree Law 527, called the Estatuto de la Junta Militar (Statute of the Military Junta), which transformed its president into the "Supreme Chief of the Nation" (Jefe Supremo de la Nación) and the sole possessor of executive powers, and reduced the junta to the "legislative branch" of the government. A few days later Pinochet ordered a ceremony to enact the decree law. None of the other members of the junta even knew about the ceremony until the last minute. A presidential sash was specially designed for Pinochet; the plan was for the Supreme Court president to hand it over to the new "Supreme Chief of the Nation" as the climax of the ceremony. Hundreds of guests and the press were invited. While the guests arrived at the Diego Portales Building, the junta's headquarters, a furious discussion was taking place inside.

"Who do you think you are, God?" snapped General Leigh.

Pinochet banged his fist on a glass-topped coffee table with so much force that it shattered. "Let's cut out this crap," he roared. "If you insist on making a big deal out of this we'll suspend the ceremony and work out a solution!"

"You have summoned just about everyone in Santiago. Suspend the ceremony? . . . My ass! Go ahead!" Leigh said, throwing up his arms.

The traditional title for a chief executive in Chile had always been "President of the Republic." To Leigh and some of Pinochet's fellow officers, "Supreme Chief of the Nation" bordered on the ridiculous. Dissident voices within the regime did not keep quiet. Pinochet resolved their disagreement in his own inimitable fashion.

A few days after the ceremony, the cabinet was reshuffled. General Bonilla was removed from his Ministry of the Interior post and moved to the much less significant position of defense minister; General Lutz was relieved of his duties as secretary of the junta and transferred to the Punta Arenas command post at the Strait of Magellan. Fifty-one years old and in good health at the time of his transfer, General Lutz fell ill during a cocktail party six months later. He was rushed to a local hospital, where he was found to be suffering from internal bleeding. His condition began to stabilize after surgery; but, just to be safe, his sons decided he should be transferred to the bigger and better equipped Military Hospital in Santiago. Almost immediately, strange things began to happen. First, a report was broadcast over the radio that the general had died but was later withdrawn—an unusual error for the media to make in a period of such robust censorship. Then a DINA colonel was assigned to "protect" Lutz. Even his family members were not permitted to see him alone. Then the general received a second surgery for what had now been diagnosed as an ulcer. Though he had reportedly been recuperating well, two days later his bleeding recurred. After that, there were a series of inexplicable accidents: a catheter that had been draining blood from the patient's stomach was removed, provoking a pulmonary crisis that was so serious he had to be connected to a ventilator; there were further setbacks when he was accidentally administered a double dose of antibiotics. The desperate general slipped his wife a piece of paper on which he had scrawled an urgent message: "Please, get me out of here." When Lutz learned that he would be honored with a visit from his old comrade in arms, the "Supreme Chief of the Nation," he told her, "Please, do not let that man come visit me." Pinochet came anyway.

On November 28, 1974, General Lutz died of septicemia. Distraught, the Lutz family went to Pinochet and demanded a summary investigation. "Fine," said Pinochet. "Contact General Eduardo Díaz. He will conduct a forensic investigation." General Díaz told the widow that he would keep her apprised of his progress. A month and a half later, she ran across General Díaz and asked about the investigation. "What investigation?" he replied. "Your husband's death was due to an illness that became aggravated, you know that!"

Off the record, a general confided in Lutz's daughter Patricia, "Your father was led to his death." Some fifteen years later, Augusto Lutz Jr. recalled that when his brother Alejandro was doing his medical internship at the Military Hospital, "we told him to search for our dad's file. He did, but it had disappeared."

In 2006, a judge revisited General Lutz's case in connection with the suspicious death of former president Eduardo Frei Montalva, a Pinochet opponent who died in 1982 from an infection he contracted during an operation. A military surgeon who had operated on General Lutz had also participated in Frei's operation, along with, among others, a doctor who worked at a clandestine DINA clinic.

By late 1974, as Pinochet removed rivals and forced several generals into retirement, he began surrounding himself with close supporters. One of them was Colonel Sergio Covarrubias, a former student of Pinochet's at the War Academy, who was elevated to the rank of general and organized the presidential general staff. Covarrubias exercised great influence over his boss and helped the so-called Chicago Boys (the neoliberal Chilean economists who had studied under Milton Friedman at the University of Chicago) and the *gremialistas* get close to Pinochet. The *gremialistas*—conservatives who admired the corporate state ideology of Franco's Spain—were led by Jaime Guzmán, who wrote speeches for Pinochet, elaborated decree laws, and became a key drafter of the 1980 constitution. Both Colonel Covarrubias and Guzmán ultimately fell out of favor with Pinochet when both insistently complained about the excessive powers of Contreras and the DINA.

General Bonilla practically disappeared from public view after his transfer from Interior to Defense. On March 4, 1975, only three months after General Lutz's death, General Bonilla was returning from vacation near Curicó, about 120 miles south of Santiago, when his Puma helicopter crashed, killing him. The French manufacturer of the helicopter sent two technicians to Chile to investigate the accident along with the air force, but the investigation was handed over to the army and classified as "secret." Frustrated by the obstacles they faced, the two French experts made plans to return home. They never got there. On March 22, they were both killed in another helicopter accident, this one a crash into Santiago's San Cristóbal Hill. One by one,

Pinochet's potential rivals in the army died or left their jobs, and no-body dared ask too many questions.

By October 1975, the only Pinochet army colleague who had been active in the 9/11 coup plot and who remained standing was General Sergio Arellano, "the Wolf." Square-faced, green-eyed, and mustachioed, Arellano was a charismatic leader. He had also clashed openly with Colonel Contreras and the DINA. "Some are talking about the emergence of a Gestapo, with all the macabre connotations that such a word brings to memory," he told Pinochet. In early 1975 Arellano had been transferred from the powerful Second Army Division and kicked upstairs to the Joint Chiefs of Staff; in October Pinochet asked him to become ambassador to Spain, while remaining on active duty. Arellano flatly refused and in a tense meeting with Pinochet he submitted his resignation and went into retirement

On Sunday, September 30, 1974, the DINA eliminated one of the most important potential obstacles to Pinochet's rule. The former army commander Carlos Prats—to whom Pinochet had once been so steadfastly loyal—and his wife, Sofía, had been granted safe-conduct out of the country in the early days of the coup after Prats read a state-ment on television in which he stated that he would not oppose the junta. Now living as exiles in Argentina, Prats and his wife were return-ing to their residence in Buenos Aires; Prats was about to pull his car into the garage when a bomb placed under the gearshift exploded, blowing the couple to pieces. A DINA agent, Michael Townley, a U.S.-born and Chilean-raised operative, had planted the radio-controlled device two days earlier. Pinochet denied any involvement in the assas-sination of his former superior, but he made no effort whatsoever to cooperate in the investigation of the crime, perhaps because of the ru-mors that the memoir that Prats was writing included damaging infor-mation about him. General Prats was denied military honors at his funeral in Santiago and police agents harassed the few people who dared attend. In his voluminous memoirs Pinochet dedicated one quarter of a page to Prats's assassination, which he suggested had been committed by the left, and referred to the murder as "sad news."

Pinochet had remarked once that it was impossible to have per-manent allies or friends. "Why, Pedro de Valdivia [Chile's Spanish con-queror in 1541] was in this country only a short time when he had to hang his partner Pedro Sánchez de la Hoz, because he had rebelled against him," Pinochet reflected philosophically.

When asked how he had become the country's ruler, Pinochet modestly declared that "God put me there. Providence or destiny, or whatever you want to call it, put me there." In fact, his quick rise to supreme power was ruthlessly executed. In December 1974, he finally had himself named president of the Republic through another decree law. With the army firmly under his thumb and the unwavering support of Colonel Contreras and the DINA, he was strong enough to take on whatever resistance might arise in the other armed branches or in the country at large. In June 1975 Pinochet declared: "I will die, my successor will die, but there will never be elections again!"

PINOCHET'S BIGGEST PROBLEM was the Chilean economy. When the military junta named its first cabinet, it designated Army General Rolando González as minister of the economy, Admiral Lorenzo Gotuzzo as minister of finance, and General Eduardo Cano as president of the Central Bank. None of them was notably effective or competent. By October 1973 it was already clear that General González would have to be removed. General Leigh retained Raúl Sáez, a Chilean civil engineer residing in Venezuela, to act as economic adviser to the junta. Sáez turned down the junta's invitation to become economy minister, but agreed to advise them on González's replacement. A few days later, in a waiting room outside General Leigh's office, Saéz ran into Fernando Léniz, the top executive of the *El Mercurio* newspaper chain. Léniz was there to ask Leigh to intervene in a censorship matter affecting one of his newspapers; Sáez was waiting to present his list of candidates for the economy post to the junta. When his meeting began, Sáez recommended three names. "Actually," he observed, "one of them is sitting right outside your door at this very minute."

"Who is that?" asked Leigh.

"Fernando Léniz, manager of *El Mercurio*. He is technically competent and I am sure he wants to help."

The next thing Léniz knew, he was being ushered into a much more luxurious waiting room than the one he had been in before. Léniz's friend Admiral José Toribio Merino stepped out of the junta meeting and joined him. "Do you want to be economy minister?" he asked.

"I didn't have much choice," Léniz told me many years later.

The next day General González was named ambassador to Paraguay and Léniz became economy minister. Léniz brought in a group of his friends—young, politically conservative economists who had trained at the University of Chicago—and they set to work transforming the Chilean economy.

Actually, much of the groundwork for the economic plan that Léniz's team would produce had been laid *before* the coup, and Admiral Merino had been involved. In early 1973, Admiral Merino had asked a businessman named Roberto Kelly, a close friend and former navy comrade of his, to prepare an economic program for post-Allende Chile. Kelly, along with another businessman, Hernán Cubillos, had recruited two graduates of the University of Chicago, Emilio Sanfuentes and Sergio de Castro, dean of the Catholic University's economics department, to lead the task force that created the document that would become known as *el ladrillo*—"the brick"—because of its length of over five hundred manuscript pages. Kelly and the economists met in Viña del Mar to put the final touches on the plan in May 1973, and then they handed it over to Admiral Merino. Interestingly, the 1975 U.S. Senate report *Covert Action in Chile: 1963-1973* states, in an often disregarded passage: "CIA collaborators were involved in preparing an initial economic plan which served as the basis for the Junta's most important economic decisions."

The day after the 9/11 coup, Kelly had gone to see a former navy classmate, Admiral Lorenzo Gotuzzo, who had just been named finance minister, and handed him a copy of "the brick." A few days later, during one of the junta's first cabinet meetings, Pinochet addressed Minister Gotuzzo: "There is some economic document circulating around. I don't know where it came from, or who authored it. Inform me, please."

"Well," Gotuzzo replied, "I had not bothered to tell you about it, my general, because it is the most free-market and Manchesterian capitalism plan that has ever been written." Kelly, who was present at the meeting as the designated director of national planning, and Admiral Merino immediately began to lobby for the plan. Admiral Merino spearheaded the market-oriented reforms, pushing Pinochet into accepting the Chicago-inspired reforms in what amounted to a virtual second coup led by the admiral.

The Chicago graduates followed the monetarist school of economics thinking propounded by the Nobel Prize laureate Milton Friedman and his university colleague Arnold Harberger, who was married to a Chilean woman. Harberger's wife was not the only connection between Chicago and Chile. The University of Chicago and the Catholic University of Chile had an exchange program dating back to 1956. When the Chileans returned home, they had been thoroughly inoculated against welfare thinking and fully indoctrinated in the gospel of free markets, careful control of the money supply, and the elimination of subsidies and protective tariffs. A number of these Chicago Boys, as they became known, organized a think tank called Center for Socio-Economic Studies (Centro de Estudios Socio-Económicos, CESEC). *El Mercurio* opened up its editorial pages to them and they wrote essays on their economic theories. The Chicago Boys tried to put those theories into practice when they drafted an economic plan for a Conservative candidate, Jorge Alessandri, in the 1970 presidential race. Alessandri's advisers in the business community rejected it as too liberal, however, and made sure that it never saw the light.

Their next big opportunity came in October 1973, when the Chicago economist Sergio de Castro was summoned to a meeting with the junta. The issue was what to do with price controls and currency devaluation. De Castro of course argued in favor of devaluation, so prices would return to their natural levels and the free market could sort out issues of supply. Hugo Araneda, a lawyer specializing in finance law who was a Pinochet military school buddy and former cavalry officer, took the opposite stance, arguing that price increases would hurt the poor. Undecided, the junta froze the debate.

The Chilean military was traditionally "statist." This is not surprising, considering that the Chilean army was shaped in 1885 by a Prussian army captain and professor of military science, Emil Körner, who inculcated in his officers the identification with the interests of the state that characterized the military under Bismarck. Though most military men had opposed Allende's economic policies, they still favored robust state action in support of industrialization and economic development. They deplored Allende's expropriations, but were not prepared to privatize everything; they firmly believed that state ownership of major natural assets and resources would assure national strength and security.

Many of the coup leaders from the army, particularly Generals Bonilla, Nuño, and Arellano, began to complain about the negative social impact of the junta's economic policies. Pinochet took Minister Léniz along with him to military garrisons throughout the country. "Here in the barracks is my power," Pinochet would tell him when they met with assemblies of soldiers, noncommissioned officers, and military officers. "Now explain to them why the price of bread is going up."

The Advisory Committee of the Junta, led by Colonel Julio Canessa of the army, served as Pinochet's inner circle and helped him formulate economic policy. Always distrustful, Pinochet wanted a counterweight to the neoliberal economists.

The army advisers distrusted Léniz at first because he had been recommended by Admiral Merino. Their relations were icy until one day Colonel Canessa greeted Léniz with a broad smile. "Why didn't you tell me that you were married to Raquelita!" he exclaimed. "It is a pleasure to work with the son-in-law of my former army commander in chief, General Carlos Mezzano. You are one of us, after all. I thought you were a navy guy!" From then on, Minister Léniz never had a problem with Pinochet's army advisers.

Jorge Cauas, a Chicago Boys ally, was named the new finance minister, and Raúl Sáez was finally convinced to take a seat in the cabinet as the minister of economic coordination. The three men's politics tended to cancel each other out: Cauas was the more ideological free-market liberal; Saéz was a "gradualist"; and Léniz, though pro-market, was a pragmatic man who occupied the middle of the road.

Pinochet took copious notes during meetings with his economic ministers and advisers. He carried pencils of different colors with which he underlined and annotated his observations; he would interrogate his ministers repeatedly until he was certain he understood whatever subject was at hand. He also kept his ministers on their toes, asking them about promises or assertions made in cabinet meetings that he had carefully recorded in his notebook.

Pinochet often boasted that he was an avid reader of history, but he also admitted that he only spent about fifteen minutes a day reading, just before he went to sleep. His favorite subjects were Napoleon's life and times, the Roman Empire, Chilean military history, and the history of famous battles. One of his most admired figures in world history was Louis XIV (the Sun King), the French monarch who had proclaimed himself and the state to be synonymous ("L'état, c'est moi"). But if Pinochet's intellectual capacities were limited, he had as shrewd a sense of self-preservation as anyone; he knew how to choose skillful advisers (from whom he demanded absolute loyalty) and he almost never failed to recognize looming threats. By the spring of 1975 he could see that inflation was out of hand and unemployment was at record highs. Chile's economy was spiraling into a full-blown crisis.

In April 1975, Roberto Kelly, director of the National Planning Office (Oficina Nacional de Planificación, Odeplan), had just returned from a conference in Lima, where some of the Chicago economists who worked under him told him that they wanted to resign, lest they be blamed for a crisis that was not at all of their making.

Kelly requested an urgent meeting with the junta president. Pinochet received him as he was changing into a formal white military jacket for a ceremony. He gave Kelly two minutes to make his point.

"The economic situation is extremely serious. Nobody is taking tough decisions and the Central Bank is printing so much money that inflation is sky high. I am worried that you may not be thought of as Chile's savior for much longer. You could become our funeral director instead," said Kelly.

Pinochet did not like Kelly's metaphor, but understood that he had a major problem. He gave Kelly and his team just forty-eight hours to come up with a full-blown plan of action. A meeting was set for Sunday, April 6, at 9 A.M. at the presidential summer residence in Viña del Mar. This was the opportunity that Kelly and the Chicago Boys had been waiting for. If they could get Pinochet fully in their camp, then all of the lesser army generals' resistance to their plans would crumble. They had already made strong inroads. The month before, Milton Friedman had been in Chile. He'd given a lecture at the junta building headquarters entitled "Gradualism or Shock Treatment?" in which he attributed the causes of inflation to deficit spending and argued that the only solution to Chile's problems was a set of drastically restrictive measures. Friedman and Rolf Lüders, one of his former students, had sat down with Pinochet for a private meeting on March 21.

Friedman explained to Pinochet the benefits of economic freedom and fiscal rigor. He advocated a whole roster of radical measures. "Otherwise, the patient could die," he said. Pinochet asked him to put his ideas in writing, and he did.

Friedman recommended an economic shock policy: the replacement of the escudo with pesos, as an anti-inflation measure; massive cuts in government spending; movement toward a free exchange rate; and flexibility in the labor market. The ideas that Kelly presented that Sunday drew heavily on Friedman's paper and also followed ideas outlined in "the brick." Finance Minister Cauas translated Kelly's, Friedman's, and the Chicago Boys' proposals into a "Plan for National Recovery."

Pinochet backed the plan and granted Finance Minister Cauas special powers to implement it. Without conferring with the junta, he reshuffled the cabinet, replacing the moderately reformist economy minister, Léniz, with an ardent Friedmanite, Sergio de Castro. Then Pinochet wrote to Friedman, thanking him for his recommendations and informing him that they were already being "put fully into practice."

The Chicago Boys were now in complete control of the economy. Sáez had serious reservations about the Chicago plan (which was why he was demoted from minister of economic coordination to

minister for external coordination—a nonexistent post). General
Leigh was also against it. The "shock treatment" struck them as dan-
gerously likely to provoke a deep recession. Witnesses recall Pinochet
and Leigh leaving the cabinet room together and yelling at each other
in the next room.

At least two top Pinochet economic advisers have told me that
the general had at best an incomplete understanding of the economic
policies that he was staking his—and the country's—future on. But
Pinochet bought into Friedman's notion that he had to cure the dis-
ease of "statism," not just its symptoms; that he needed to strive for
macroeconomic equilibrium and take radical action against inflation.
Shock treatment was the only way. "If you want to cut a dog's tail you
don't do it gradually; you do it in one single chop," Friedman had said.

I am convinced that Pinochet was not a full convert to the gospel
of the free market yet. He was too deeply embedded in the army culture for that. But just as in his days of indecision prior to the coup, he
did not have much choice. The bitter medicine the Chicago Boys pre-
scribed appealed to Pinochet's authoritarian bent: Who had ever been
harmed by a dose of tough discipline? The Chicago Boys were young,
self-confident technocrats. Moreover, Pinochet had never truly liked
the big businessmen who historically had lived high on the hog off
state subsidies while looking down their noses at the military and
their families.

Arturo Fontaine, the former editor of *El Mercurio* and an enthusiastic Pinochet partisan, argued in his book *Los Economistas y el Presidente Pinochet* (The Economists and President Pinochet) that Pinochet
saw the Chicago Boys as "a battalion of commandos in the political
and economic fields, with capacity to innovate and destroy old-fashioned
routines and norms." They might have had a tendency to "exaggerate
and reach extremes in their actions," Fontaine admitted, but they
were "the vanguard of a national revolution"; "a neo-right that resur-
rected the principles inherent to liberalism, as well as a revival of authoritarian tradition."

Finance Minister Cauas announced the shock treatment blueprint
to halt inflation and renew growth on April 24, 1975. People had to
"tighten their belts," announced the government. Public spending
would be slashed much more deeply than it had been already, more
employees would be kicked off the public payrolls. Taxes would be increased and the inflation-indexed national housing assistance program would be terminated. Prices and interest rates were allowed to
rise, tariffs were reduced, and the process of privatization began

apace. Most public enterprises were sold for a minimal portion of their true value, and many were actually purchased through state financing. The immediate effects of the plan were disastrous. Unemployment rose, production fell, GDP collapsed by 12.5 percent, and foreign reserves vanished.

Economy Minister Sergio de Castro, a bluff, no-nonsense rugby enthusiast, had expected a rough transition; he was prepared to ride out the storm. Although he was close to Admiral Merino, de Castro would establish a close relationship with Pinochet as well. De Castro justified the need of a dictatorial regime, which was music to Pinochet's ears. But their friendship did not begin auspiciously. During a long cabinet debate about what to do with state-owned textile factories, Pinochet cut in to close the discussion. "Gentlemen," he said. "I am the one who holds the pot by the handle."

De Castro, then an adviser to Minister Léniz, could not contain himself. "Well, Mr. President," he said. "You might be left just holding the handle." A deep silence fell over the room for about fifteen seconds, but to the economic adviser it seemed an eternity. At last the debate ended and the meeting was adjourned.

As de Castro was leaving, a military aide approached him and told him that General Pinochet wanted to see him. "You were very insolent there in that meeting," Pinochet said angrily. The economist apologized and explained that he hadn't meant to be disrespectful. Then Pinochet burst into laughter. "Civilians just don't understand the military," he said. De Castro's boldness delighted him.

By the end of 1976 the Chilean economy was showing definite signs of improvement. On December 28, 1976, Sergio de Castro was named finance minister. Not only would de Castro be the most important minister in the economics portfolio; he was well on the way to becoming the most powerful minister in the entire cabinet.

But before de Castro could ratchet up the shock treatment to an even higher level, there were still obstacles to be overcome—namely General Leigh, who continued to question the social costs of the Chicago experiment. The air force was the branch of the junta in charge of the social area; it continued to issue proposals that harked back to the welfare state, such as a labor code. Needless to say, they were systematically rejected. In March 1976, Air Force General Nicanor Díaz Estrada was replaced as minister of labor by a strong Chicago Boys ally. But General Leigh continued to be a thorn in Pinochet's flesh.

Leigh, the commander in chief of the air force, was perhaps Pinochet's most formidable adversary. Square-jawed and serious-minded, the fifty-three-year-old aviator was a man of strong personality and sharp intelligence. He had never considered Pinochet to be his intellectual or political equal and had clashed with him on numerous occasions. But by 1977, the two were engaged in an all-out war.

The night of July 9, 1977, thousands of young conservatives gathered on "Chacarillas," a hillside in Santiago, to commemorate the battle of "La Concepción," a memorable combat in Chile's late-nineteenth-century war against Peru and Bolivia in which seventy-seven Chilean soldiers chose death over surrender when they were pinned down by a larger force in the Peruvian highlands. The event was reminiscent of one of Mussolini's spectaculars. Amid torches and patriotic symbols, medals were awarded to seventy-seven distinguished young Chileans; at its climax Pinochet gave a speech denouncing liberal democracy as "naïve and spineless" and hailing the emergence of a "new democracy" that would be "authoritarian, protected, integrating, technical." Beginning in 1980, he announced, Chile would undertake a five-year program to transform itself into a "controlled democracy." Elections would be held in 1985 to fill two thirds of the seats of a unicameral Congress (the government would name the other third). This Congress would in turn elect a president of the Republic. General Leigh and other members of the junta publicly protested that they had not known about the transition timetable and had barely conferred on the constitutional changes. (Not that it ultimately mattered—Pinochet discarded the plans for the transition as he assumed absolute power.)

Then, on December 16, 1977, the United Nations General Assembly in New York condemned the Chilean regime for human rights violations by the widest margin in its history: ninety-six voted for condemnation of the government and only fourteen voted against. Pinochet was furious; after considering several "courses of action" proposed by his advisers, he decided to call for a national plebiscite on whether Chileans supported his rule or not. General Leigh and Admiral Merino were stunned by the idea, particularly when they found out about it less than two days before it was officially announced on December 22. The junta met privately and the debate turned ugly.

Both Leigh and Merino wrote formal letters opposing the plebiscite, which, for constitutional considerations, was modified to a "consultation." They worried that the prestige of the armed forces could be affected. Worst of all, wrote General Leigh, it projected an image of a "personalistic regime." Pinochet steadfastly argued that his decision to call for a referendum was his "exclusive prerogative" as the chief of state and sole holder of executive power. Eventually Pinochet pressured Admiral Merino to change his mind and withdraw his letter of protest; Leigh, however, remained intransigent.

An unexpected complication arose when the state comptroller general, Héctor Humeres, declared that he could not certify the "consultation" as legal without a law decree, which Leigh refused to endorse. Pinochet demanded Humeres's resignation—he had been scheduled to retire soon anyway—and replaced him by nightfall with Sergio Fernández, one of his most trusted civilian advisers, who was much more amenable to cutting red tape. The referendum was held on January 4, 1978, under state-of-siege conditions, without voter rolls, without poll watchers, without any public debate or critical press coverage. The ballot consisted of the following statement: "Faced with international aggression launched against our Fatherland, I support President Pinochet in his defense of the dignity of Chile and reaffirm the legitimacy of the government." Voters were instructed to put their marks next to a Chilean flag for "Yes" and a black box for "No." Needless to say, Pinochet received the ringing endorsement he had sought. "Politicians, this is the end for you," he declared at his victory rally that night. General Leigh did not attend.

The air force chief began to put as many obstacles as he could in the way of executive projects. In March 1978, Pinochet, reasserting his own presidential power, proposed to take the "insurmountable differences about the powers of the state and their exercise" to state council arbitration. The tension reached new heights when murmurings of a coup began to emanate from air force circles.

In July Leigh gave an interview to the Italian newspaper *Il Corriere de la Sera* in which he proposed his own timetable for the political normalization of Chile, the drafting of a constitution, a political parties statute, an elections law, and new electoral rolls. Worse yet, Leigh declared that he would resign from the junta in the event that credible evidence emerged that implicated Chile's military government in the assassination on September 21, 1976, of the exiled diplomat and politician Orlando Letelier in Washington, D.C. The interview set off a political firestorm. Pinochet summoned some of his most trusted ministers and told them he planned to remove General Leigh from the junta and from the air force.

On Saturday, July 22, an ominous want ad appeared in *El Mercurio:* "Due to ill health and cancellation of my pilot license, I need to sell my plane, which is in good condition. Those interested bring cash only. Málaga No. 195." It was General Leigh's home address. A similarly eerie ad, mentioning a "faulty plane compass," was published in the daily newspaper *La Tercera.*

The events of Monday July 24, 1978, resembled the early hours of the 9/11 coup. Army combat troops encircled the Defense Ministry and the junta headquarters and every air force base in Chile. When General Leigh arrived at his office at the Defense Ministry around 8:30 A.M. he found that the doors to the building were shut. He eventually got in, but soon discovered that he was virtually a prisoner in his own office. Leigh went up to the fifth floor and sat down with Pinochet and the other members of the junta. He suggested that if they could reach a consensus on a timetable for normalization, they could probably resolve their other disagreements as well. But Pinochet was in no mood to negotiate. He held up a sheet of paper.

"Here is a list of every occasion when you have diverged from the government line," he said. "Besides, you must resign anyhow, because you said you would want to leave when the Letelier judicial process begins."

"I will not resign," Leigh responded.

"Then I am going to remove you."

"On what basis?"

"Don't worry; we have the prerogatives to do it. Here is the law decree so you can sign it," replied Pinochet, sliding the document across the table.

"Do what you want!" General Leigh answered furiously. "If you want to violate the law, go ahead; but I will sign nothing."

"No problem, we have another law decree ready," Pinochet said with a smile. He had ordered the preparation of an executive decree declaring General Leigh "incompetent" to continue serving in the junta, due to "mental incapacity."

"I am leaving to meet with my generals," announced Leigh.

"You will do no such thing," Pinochet declared. "I am asking for the resignation of every air force general who is senior to Fernando Matthei." Except for the air force attaché in Washington, D.C., Matthei, the minister of health (and a Pinochet loyalist), was the only air force general who had not gone to Leigh's office that morning. In fact, he was sitting nervously in an office next door waiting for Leigh to make his exit so he could be sworn in to his new duties.

Leigh left the room without signing the law decree. When Leigh went to inform his generals of the situation they were prepared to offer up armed resistance. Leigh cut the discussion short; he did not want a bloodbath. He tried to call a press conference, but the media were sternly warned away. So he went home.

Fernando Matthei was now the senior general and commander in chief of the air force and a member of the junta. Eight of his superiors

had been removed to clear the way for his ascension; ten generals below him resigned in solidarity with Leigh. The air force hierarchy was
devastated, leaving Pinochet much freer reign to do as he pleased. In
his memoirs Pinochet refers to this crisis under the mordant subtitle
"General Leigh Goes into Retirement."

BY THE END of 1977, the recovery was proceeding apace; Chile's rate
of economic growth had reached a robust 8.7 percent. But in 1978
Chile almost went to war with Argentina. The crisis began in February 1978, when the Argentine military government, led by General
Jorge Rafael Videla, formally announced that it rejected the arbitration verdict handed down in May of the previous year by H.M. Queen
Elizabeth II of England, which awarded to Chile three islands (Nueva,
Picton, and Lennox) and adjacent islets south of the Beagle Channel
up to Cape Horn, a zone that had long been disputed by Chile and Argentina. Instead of accepting the verdict, the Argentine military government invited its Chilean counterpart to a direct dialogue to
negotiate a "reasonable and equitable" delimitation of the Beagle
Channel area. In the ten months since the verdict, jurists and diplomats from Chile and Argentina met irregularly but made no progress
toward a negotiated settlement; in the meantime, troops, fighter
planes, and warships from both countries moved toward Patagonia
and Tierra del Fuego.

Perhaps the only moment of genuine national unity during the
Pinochet regime occurred as the Beagle Channel dispute deepened. In
Chile, the opposition Christian Democratic leader and former president, Eduardo Frei Montalva, declared his "unrestricted support for
the permanent interests of Chile, which prevail over governments that
are transitory." From exile, Carlos Altamirano, the secretary-general of
the Socialist Party, and Clodomiro Almeyda, a former foreign minister
under Allende, both issued statements supporting Chile's sovereign
rights over the disputed zone. (When, several years later, the dispute
was finally resolved, I drafted and read a public statement on behalf of
the Socialist Party that supported its peaceful outcome.)

By early January 1978 the Chilean Foreign Ministry knew that Argentina would declare "irremediably null" the Queen's panel ruling
on the Beagle Channel zone. Mocking the professional diplomats,
whom he called "talc faces" (empolvados), Pinochet decided to take
matters in his own hands. Manuel Contreras was by then a general
and still Pinochet's most trusted subordinate (though he was no
longer the head of the DINA because of the Letelier assassination and
its repercussions for Chilean-U.S. relations). Pinochet dispatched him

to Argentina to speak directly to General Videla, the president of the Argentine junta, and try to arrange a personal tête-à-tête between the two military dictators. By the next day the time and place for the summit had been set: the two leaders would meet in Mendoza, Argentina, at El Plumerillo Air Base, on January 19, 1978.

The Mendoza meeting did not yield a concrete solution to the Beagle dispute, but at least it opened the door to further direct negotiations. As their agreement to continue talks was being drafted, Pinochet offered his Argentine counterpart some friendly counsel. "You have to take full charge and impart orders, my friend," Pinochet told him. "Look, General, three persons [in a junta] cannot lead; nowhere in the world can there be a collegiate command. Take charge, you give the orders; you cannot continue as you are! With full command you can control those who want war."

General Videla nodded his head in polite agreement. "The history of Argentina is different than Chile's, you must understand," he said. "We cannot govern Argentina if the three branches of the armed forces do not rule together." A week later the Buenos Aires government, as expected, formally declared null the Queen's decision.

The two military leaders met again in the southern Chilean city of Puerto Montt on February 20, where an accord was formally signed to engage in direct talks with a six-month deadline to reach an agreement. Pinochet named a businessman, Hernán Cubillos, a man with good contacts in the United States, as foreign minister, replacing Admiral Carvajal. Six months later, the negotiations had not produced any progress; Chile declared them "exhausted" on November 2, 1978. In expectation of air raids, red crosses were painted onto hospital roofs and schools in Chile; Buenos Aires imposed blackouts on its cities at night. The European Community urged a peaceful outcome to the growing crisis, the White House offered its good offices, Chilean and Argentine Catholic bishops sought the assistance of the Vatican. Despite all these efforts, on Thursday, December 21, 1978, a declaration of war against Chile, ready to be signed, lay on the Argentine leader General Jorge Videla's desk.

Pinochet, according to many accounts, remained unrattled throughout the crisis. While he recognized that Argentina could inflict serious damage on Chile, he was certain that the Chilean infantry would ultimately prevail. Even so, he had no desire to preside over a bloodbath and continued to press for a negotiated solution. The navy had an aggressive confidence in its tactical superiority vis á vis the Argentines, though, like the air force, it was having troubles securing supplies: the Kennedy Amendment, which prohibited American security assistance and arms sales to Chile, was exacting a toll. The pressure on Finance Minister de Castro to make money available to stockpile arms was immense. Yet de Castro held firm and Pinochet backed him up. So long as there was even a remote possibility of a negotiated solution, he refused to modify his budgetary plans. Discussions in Pinochet's ministerial cabinet reached a fever pitch.

"Mr. Minister, you will be the first one to face a firing squad when war breaks out with Argentina," Defense Minister Carlos Forestier threatened de Castro on one occasion. De Castro recalls that his army cabinet colleague was in deadly earnest. Finally, in January 1979, Pope John Paul II proposed a mediation process that both sides endorsed. Though diplomats wouldn't sign off on a final agreement for another six years, war had been averted; Pinochet's and de Castro's brinksmanship had paid off.

As the war clouds dissipated, the Chicago Boys forged ahead with their economic plans. Pinochet's vigorous support of their efforts didn't stop him from ordering the development of a domestic arms industry sector that by 1983 had already begun to show an export capacity. Pinochet also continued to appoint trusted military advisers to key economic posts, seemingly as a counterbalance to the Chicago civilians. Pinochet, ever cautious, liked to hedge his bets. Army Colonel Gastón Frez had been named undersecretary under Economy Minister de Castro. The friction between Frez, a statist, and the liberal-minded de Castro got so severe that de Castro demanded that Pinochet choose between him and the undersecretary. But when Frez asked to be returned to a regular army post, Pinochet instead placed him in the key position of executive vice president of the National Copper Corporation (Corporación Nacional del Cobre, CODELCO), the largest Chilean state copper mining corporation. No matter how much pressure the Chicago Boys put on him, Pinochet never considered privatizing CODELCO—because of Frez's staunch resistance, for one thing, but also because the Chilean defense budget was historically linked by law to export earnings from copper.

Pinochet carried out a delicate balancing act between the statists and the Chicagoans. In December 1978 Roberto Kelly, then director of the National Planning Office, expressed his dissatisfaction with Pinochet's advisory committee, whose staff of military officers rotated as their postings changed. Economy Minister Pablo Baraona had offered to resign his post for the same reason. Pinochet counseled Kelly not to do anything rash. A few days later, Kelly was sworn in as the new economy minister.

Pinochet's first choice for the job, in late December 1978, had not been Kelly. A young new star, a Harvard-educated economist named José Piñera, had so impressed the general with a briefing on the prospects of the Chilean economy that he had asked him to repeat it for the benefit of the junta members. But when Pinochet wanted to name him economy minister, de Castro and the Chicago Boys had vetoed him, because he wasn't a member of their circle. Piñera was named labor minister instead.

Vasco Costa, José Piñera's predecessor in the Labor Ministry, had been ousted from his post because he had provoked a labor dispute that was beginning to have international repercussions. A notorious hard-liner, Costa had sponsored a number of pieces of legislation that further threatened workers' rights, which had already been drastically curtailed since the coup. The tipping point came when he called for union elections within forty-eight hours—and insisted that every candidate sign a sworn statement that he or she hadn't belonged to a political party during the last decade. Most of the Socialist and Communist unionists had already been killed, arrested, or forced into exile. This new measure eliminated the centrist Christian Democrats, as well.

This provoked the AFL-CIO to propose a world ports boycott against Chile, to begin on January 8, 1979. The Pinochet government could ill afford a boycott, especially with the Beagle Channel crisis so near the boiling point. Pinochet sent Finance Minister Sergio de Castro on a secret mission to Washington, D.C., where he met with the AFL-CIO president, George Meany, and his main advisers. From the outset Meany made it clear who had the upper hand. Pointing toward the White House through a window in his office, he said, "Over there in that building I have seen about ten presidents come and go; but I am still here."

The minister explained that Pinochet had important new plans for the labor sector, including the restoration of the right to strike.

"Mr. Minister," Meany responded, "you must return to Chile. The key for averting the boycott is not here in Washington; it is in Santiago."

De Castro took Pinochet a clear message. Absent a new labor policy, the boycott would go ahead. Pinochet, always willing to accept reality, showed Vasco Costa the door. The new labor minister got to work immediately on a package of new labor laws; he also invited labor leaders to meet with him. Tucapel Jiménez, president of the National Public Workers Association (Asociación Nacional de Empleados Fiscales, ANEF), was the first to accept.

A few weeks later, Pinochet approved a package of decrees that canceled most of the previous minister's measures against labor. It wasn't a total victory for workers, however. Collective bargaining was only permitted within each company, rather than across whole industrial sectors; the package also included freedom-of-affiliation and voluntary payment of dues measures that were hardly appealing to unionists. There was much to complain about, but after some vigorous lobbying the AFL-CIO agreed that there had been enough of an advance in Chilean workers' rights to head off the boycott.

Having cut the Gordian knot of labor reform, Piñera's next project was the creation of a new pension system, something that the Chicago Boys had been trying in vain to do for five years. The economist Miguel Kast, who would become a trusted Pinochet adviser, had been sent to the Wharton School to study an alternative to the broken pensions system; he returned with an individual capitalization funds project, which was energetically opposed by the anti-Chicago sectors in the government every time he presented it. But in 1980 Piñera accomplished what had seemed all but impossible: the old pay-as-you-go pension system, which was based on a common fund financed by workers, employees, and the government, was replaced by a system of private savings accounts in which workers deposited 10 percent of their salaries. Employers were released from contributing to the new system at all, and the state's contributions were drastically reduced.

There was beginning to be talk of an "economic miracle" in Chile, which the Chicago Boys were glad to take credit for. With rare exceptions, the economists were untroubled by repression, torture, or the disappearances of dissidents. They were seeing good fiscal results, and that was all that mattered. It was ironic. Milton Friedman believed his economic system provided the foundation for freedom in every walk of life; in Chile, his ideas had proved themselves to be compatible with one of the worst dictatorships on the globe.

During his second visit to Chile, in November 1981, when he was a guest of the Mont Pelerin Society, Milton Friedman gave a press conference in which he voiced his reservations about Pinochet's regime, warning that "a free economy will be difficult to sustain unless it is accompanied by a politically free society." The Nobel laureate also dismissed the notion that the market economy model could only be applied by a "strong regime." Few paid him any heed.

Pinochet felt triumphant, at long last. But the seemingly successful Chicago economic model would soon come tumbling down, threatening his hold on power.

Four

PINOCHET'S
GLOBAL REACH

K issinger wasn't sure whether he should go to Chile to meet
Pinochet during the spring of 1976. It wasn't an ethical issue.
Secretaries of state rarely attended Organization of American
States (OAS) general assemblies unless there was a real crisis in the region. But Pinochet was a loyal anti-Communist and he was facing increasing opposition in the U.S. Congress, which was seeking to cut off
military sales to his regime.

An antileftist leader who had overthrown a "Communist-leaning
president" could not be permitted to fail, since the repercussions
would be felt around the world. And there was another effect Kissinger
worried about as well: if Pinochet did not buy his weapons and military hardware from the United States, he would buy them elsewhere.
Plus, there was the war at home to worry about—that is, the turf war
that went on in Washington, between the White House and the Congress over the conduct of foreign policy. Nixon and Kissinger could
not allow Congress to set limits on their policy toward Pinochet's
government. If it was Chile today, it might be a bigger country tomorrow (like South Korea, Kissinger believed). Chile might have just been
a pawn in the global realpolitik chess game that the secretary of state
was constantly waging against his domestic and foreign adversaries;
but for Pinochet Kissinger's visit marked a great personal victory.

In his 1979 memoirs, Kissinger asserted that human rights were
the "underlying theme" of the conversations he held with Pinochet
in the course of his visit. In his 1999 *Years of Renewal*, Kissinger returned
to the subject, dedicating a whole section of the book to that same
1976 trip. Challenging even the most minimally balanced evaluations

of President Allende, Kissinger alleged that the democratically elected government was characterized by "incompetence, corruption and violation of democratic rights." Allende represented "a danger [of] a Communist state on the mainland" of the Americas, he contended.

Absurdly, Kissinger asserted, "After Allende entered office in November 3, 1970, the covert programs seeking to block his inauguration were terminated [sic]." Indeed. Why would U.S. covert activities to impede Allende's *inauguration* have continued once he was *already in office*? Moreover, contrary to every serious historical account of the era, Kissinger declares that "human rights abuses [under Pinochet] subsided" after the dissolution of the DINA secret police in 1977. Not a word is said about the Letelier assassination. The 1999 volume reiterates his earlier claim that in his meetings with Pinochet he had "made it clear as to where we stood on human rights," selectively quoting phrases from his speech to the OAS General Assembly to buttress his point.

But the declassified transcripts of the talks between Kissinger and Pinochet, released in 2000, reveal a starkly different picture than the one presented by the former U.S. secretary of state. Kissinger, accompanied by Assistant Secretary William D. Rogers, visited Pinochet at his office at noon on June 8, 1976.

"I want to tell you that we are grateful that you have come to the conference," Pinochet said as their meeting began.

"It is an honor," Kissinger responded diplomatically, knowing full well that the presence in Chile of the U.S. secretary of state was an invaluable image booster for the internationally isolated dictator.

"I have always been against Communism," Pinochet declared, getting straight to the point. "During the Vietnam War, I met with some of your military and made my anti-Communism clear to them. I told them I hoped they would defeat it."

"We defeated ourselves in Vietnam because our country was so divided," Kissinger responded. "In the United States, as you know, we are sympathetic with what you are trying to do here. . . . We wish your government well. At the same time," he continued, "a lot of pressure is being exerted on our government, especially Congress, but also the executive branch, over the issue of human rights." Kissinger assured Pinochet that the White House opposed further constraints on aid to Chile. Almost apologetically, Kissinger explained that while he would inevitably have to address the issue of human rights at the OAS General Assembly, he would be sure to do so in the most general way. "The speech is not aimed at Chile," Kissinger explained. "I wanted to tell you about this. My evaluation is that you are a victim of left-wing groups around the world, and that your greatest sin was that you overthrew a government that was going Communist." Nevertheless, human rights posed a "practical problem" that had to be addressed, if for no other reason than to mollify the U.S. Congress. Of course, he added, "none of this is said with the hope of undermining your government."

"We are returning to institutionalization step by step," Pinochet replied, obviously unenthusiastic about the subject. "But we are constantly under attack by the Christian Democrats. They have a strong voice in Washington. . . . Gabriel Valdés has access. Also Letelier," Pinochet complained.

Kissinger was surprised. "I have not seen a Christian Democrat in years," he said.

"Letelier has access to the Congress," Pinochet insisted. "We know they are giving false information."

Kissinger reiterated that while his statement in the OAS General Assembly would be designed to please Congress, it would not be "offensive to Chile."

"We are behind you. You are the leader," Pinochet said. "But you have a punitive system for your friends."

"It is unfortunate," Kissinger reflected. "We welcomed the overthrow of the Communist-inclined government here. . . . I want to see our relations and friendship improve. We want to help, not undermine you," Kissinger concluded.

Pinochet had held his first press conference not long after the coup, on September 21, 1973. A CBS reporter asked him about the rumors of American involvement in the coup and whether the White House had had advance knowledge of it. Pinochet insisted that the coup had been "a national movement."

"Not even my wife knew about what I was about to do on 9/11," he said. "The U.S. had nothing to do with it, nor any other country."

Of course Pinochet was being disingenuous. He knew that the Nixon administration had not merely sought, as apologists of intervention have argued, to preserve free media and opposition political parties (which were never truly threatened and actually flourished under Allende), but had funded paramilitary groups that perpetrated terrorist acts, financed the crippling October 1972 "bosses' strike," and engaged in a secret destabilization war against Allende's Chile. The Socialist-led government committed serious mistakes in a vibrant democratic period, but even before it had adopted a single measure, the CIA and Chilean right-wing groups were already attempting a coup d'état against President-elect Allende. Though the coup was indeed Chilean-made, it was undoubtedly U.S.-sponsored.

In private transcripts of Kissinger's conversations with Nixon—which were made public only in 2004, in the midst of a new controversy about the U.S. role in the breakdown of Chilean democracy—the two men exchange words about the coup.

"Our hand doesn't show on this one," Nixon states.

"We didn't do it," Kissinger replies. "I mean we helped them . . . created the conditions as great as possible," he adds.

Kissinger and Nixon became obsessed with Chile. Although the U.S. ambassador to Chile, Edward Korry, had cabled Washington in 1970 hailing Chile's democracy and defining the country as "one of the more decent places on earth," Nixon and Kissinger believed that Allende's election "was a challenge to our national interests." Kissinger feared that Chile's influence could spread throughout the rest of the hemisphere, and even to countries such as France or Italy, where it was not unthinkable that a Socialist-Communist coalition could win a presidential election.

Despite the Nixon administration's blatant hostility to his presidency, Allende had sought to cultivate a pragmatic relationship with it.

Only three months after Allende was inaugurated, in February 1971, Admiral Elmo Zumwalt, the U.S. chief of naval operations, visited Chile and met with Allende and the chief of the Chilean Navy. Informed that the aircraft carrier *Enterprise* was in Rio de Janeiro, preparing to round Cape Horn and cross to the Pacific, Allende suggested that Admiral Zumwalt bring it to Valparaíso.

Zumwalt was personally very enthusiastic about the idea and cabled the Pentagon the same day. Allende made his invitation public. But Nixon and Kissinger, backed by the CIA, strongly opposed the idea, and the invitation was officially declined. Despite that rebuff, the Chilean president declared that Chile would "never provide a military base that might be used against the United States."

Ironically, precisely in February 1971—at the same time that he was snubbing Allende—Nixon, in his annual foreign policy report to Congress, declared that his policy toward Chile was "to keep open the lines of communication" and that the White House was "prepared to have the kind of relationship with the Chilean government that it is prepared to have with us." What Allende didn't know, though he sensed it, was that the Nixon administration had made up its mind about him a long time before.

On September 15, 1970, ten days after Allende's election, a meeting was held at the Oval Office, chaired by Nixon, in which he issued the famous order to move against the president-elect. CIA Director Richard Helms's handwritten notes read: "1 in 10 chances perhaps, but save Chile! . . . Not concerned risks involved. . . . $10,000,000 available, more if necessary. Full-time job, best men we have." Years later, in testimony before the Senate Intelligence Committee, Helms remarked, "If I ever carried a martial baton in my knapsack out of the Oval Office, it was that day." Kissinger had set the policy tone when he pronounced his infamous dictum: "I don't see why we need to stand by and watch a country go Communist due to the irresponsibility of its people."

Ambassador Edward Korry had warned the outgoing Eduardo Frei administration that "not a nut or bolt [would] be allowed to reach Chile under Allende." The idea was to pressure President Frei into joining a plot to foil the ratification of Allende's election by the Chilean Congress, which was scheduled for October 24, 1970.

On October 6 Kissinger summoned Richard Helms to the White House so that a clear message would be sent to the local CIA station: "Contact the military and let them know that the U.S government wants a military solution, and that we will support them *now and later*" (author's emphasis). When Frei and the Christian Democrats did not back what became known as the "Rube Goldberg" gambit to impede congressional ratification, the White House decided to pursue a secret track 2 approach: the violent option to get rid of Allende.

The CIA contacted Chilean military officers to provoke them to stage a coup in advance of Allende's inauguration on November 4, 1970. Money and weapons were supplied to two terrorist groups, one led by a retired general, Roberto Viaux, and one commanded by General Camilo Valenzuela of the army. The idea was to kidnap General René Schneider, the commander in chief of the army, and blame the action on the left, creating a chaotic situation that would derail Allende's inauguration. In the early-morning hours of October 22, General Viaux and other right-wing extremists cut off General Schneider's car and shot him to death. Schneider's assassination backfired, as the nation rallied behind constitutional rule.

On November 6, 1970, only days after Allende's inauguration, Nixon presided over a National Security Council meeting on Chile in the White House cabinet room. Kissinger opened the meeting.

"All of the agencies are agreed that Allende will try to create a socialist state," he said. A modus vivendi might be possible, but at the "risk that he will consolidate his position and then move ahead against us."

"If we have to be hostile, we want to do it right," Secretary of State William P. Rogers suggested. "We can put an economic squeeze on him."

"Our main concern in Chile is the prospect that [Allende] can consolidate himself, and the picture projected to the world will be his success," affirmed Nixon. "If we let . . . leaders in South America think that they can move like Chile and have it both ways, we will be in trouble. Latin America is not gone, and we want to keep it," he concluded.

Following this meeting, the White House issued National Security Decision Memorandum 93, "Policy Towards Chile," which outlined the ensuing economic warfare against Allende's government. Henceforth no new federal loan guarantees would be extended to Chile and existing subsidies would be terminated. Private investment by American businesses would be actively discouraged; maximum pressure would be brought to bear on foreign financial institutions to discourage them from making loans to Chile as well. On Nixon's explicit order, the United States would sell off part of its copper holdings, flooding the market and depressing worldwide prices—a harmful measure, indeed, since copper was Chile's chief export.

Allende in his speech at the UN General Assembly on December 4 had denounced an "invisible blockade" and hostile actions toward Chile on the part of multinational corporations such as ITT and Kennecott Copper Company. Charles Bray, the spokesperson for the State Department, vehemently denied that the United States was blockading Chile and attributed the country's difficulties to its lack of "credit worthiness."

In fact Chile had suspended its debt service payments by late 1971, but in February 1972 it initiated talks with its principal creditor nations to renegotiate the terms of its loans. Deals were reached with European creditors, but Washington opposed the renegotiation of the Chilean external debt so long as Allende refused to pay for American copper companies that Chile had nationalized.

Robert Dallek, in his book *Nixon and Kissinger,* based on declassified documents on the Richard Nixon presidency, concludes that "Kissinger became Nixon's point man in managing the CIA's Chilean operations." Looking back it is truly amazing that Chile occupied so much of the time of the U.S. president and his secretary of state in the midst of an expanding Vietnam War, the Middle East conflict, the opening toward China, and the SALT negotiations with Moscow. In fact, in his memoirs Richard Nixon identifies Allende's Chile as a top challenge of his foreign policy agenda: "America was being tested in the fall of 1970 by war in Vietnam; by the threat of war in the Middle East; by the introduction of threatening nuclear capabilities in Cuba. In Chile the test was just as real, although much subtler." Henry Kissinger advised Nixon in late 1971 that "Chile could end up being the worst failure of our administration—our Cuba."

"Truman had lost China, Kennedy had lost Cuba. Nixon was not about to lose Chile," commented Richard Helms. Four years after the coup, in the famous interviews of Richard Nixon with David Frost, the former president insisted that if he hadn't acted against Allende, Chile and Cuba would have formed a "red sandwich" that eventually could have turned "all Latin America red." The web of illegal actions, secret payments, distortions, and cover-ups to destabilize Allende would become a kind of foreign policy Watergate of the Nixon administration. The rest of the story is well known.

In contrast to its public tepidness and covert hostility toward Allende's administration, Washington's posture toward Pinochet was publicly cool and privately ardent. Pinochet had not had a particularly close relationship with the American embassy in Santiago. After all, until forty-eight hours before the military action, he was not a part of the coup; though nobody knew for certain where he stood, ostensibly he was loyal to the Allende government. The United States had regarded Pinochet at best as a potentially lukewarm ally; he still had a lot of catching up to do.

On September 12, 1973, less than twenty-four hours after the coup, Pinochet held a secret rendezvous with the U.S. military attaché, Colonel Carlos Urrutia. Pinochet explained the junta's plans and broached the issue of official diplomatic recognition of his regime. A cable by Ambassador Nathaniel Davis about the conversation indicated that Pinochet "showed understanding and was relaxed about the matter of recognition and volunteered that obviously [the United States] should not be the first to recognize." Two weeks later, on September 24, Nixon extended the desired diplomatic recognition.

A classified cable from the White House Situation Room dated September 13, 1973, stated: "The U.S. government wishes to make clear its desire to cooperate with the military Junta and to assist in any appropriate way. . . . We welcome General Pinochet's expression of Junta desire for strengthening ties between Chile and the US." The cable added that it would be "best initially to avoid too much public identification between us." Ambassador Davis was also instructed to convey this position to Pinochet quickly. Davis responded the next day with the news that "Pinochet expressed most sincere appreciation and said he would like to keep privately in touch." Kissinger lied during his September 27 confirmation hearing for secretary of state when he declared that Washington had decided "not to say anything that indicated either support or opposition" to the Pinochet-led junta. In fact, the signals the U.S. administration had been sending could not have been clearer.

On September 14, the U.S. Mission to the United Nations recommended to Washington that the military government send "a representative of stature, presence and alertness to New York without delay" to counter the rising criticisms of the junta for its human rights violations. Ambassador Davis lobbied Santiago to send a delegation of Christian Democratic politicians to foreign capitals to defend the junta, an idea that later materialized with the aid of CIA financing.

CIA collaborators were actively involved in the preparation of the "White Book of the Change of Government in Chile," a propaganda publication issued by the junta to justify the coup that was distributed in Washington and other foreign capitals. Before the coup, the CIA prepared "arrest lists" of key civilian leaders and "other operational data." Though the U.S. Senate report *Covert Action in Chile* asserts that this information was not passed on to the Chilean military, it seems difficult to believe that such concrete "contingency plans" remained solely within the walls of the CIA station in Chile.

In the days following the coup, the Chilean Air Force requested that the U.S. provide, urgently, one thousand flares "for illumination purposes in military operations against extremist groups" plus other military gear, a request recommended for approval by Ambassador Davis as a key signal of support for the junta. A subsequent request for an American "detention center adviser" was nixed by the ambassador as too likely to present eventual "political problems."

An afternoon meeting on Chile held at the White House Situation Room on September 20, 1973, presided over by Kissinger and attended by Treasury Secretary William Simon, NSC adviser Brent Scowcroft, and officials from the CIA, the Pentagon, the Joint Chiefs of Staff, Office of Management and the Budget, and the State Department, gave the green light to the military government. In addition to agreeing on formal diplomatic recognition of the regime, the high-level group also decided to deliver medical and food supplies and, more important, authorized Ambassador Davis to discuss with Pinochet "Chile's middle and long term economic needs." The "invisible blockade" was lifted; abundant U.S. economic and military assistance began to flow to Chile.

By that time, the American media, members of Congress, and spokespersons of NGOs were denouncing the killing fields of Chile. On October 1, 1973, Kissinger, now secretary of state, responded to Deputy Assistant Jack Kubisch's concerns about the United States' appearing too close to Pinochet with his realpolitik line, "I think we should understand our policy that however unpleasant they act, the [Pinochet] government is better for us than Allende was. So, we shouldn't support moves against them by seemingly disassociating."

But, to Kissinger's frustration, the U.S. Congress, led by Senator Edward Kennedy, soon began to move to cut off arms sales and assistance to Pinochet. In a meeting held on December 3, 1974, Kissinger took issue with the critical views of Pinochet conveyed by his assistant secretary for inter-American affairs, William D. Rogers, asking, "I'd like to know whether the human rights problem in Chile is that much worse than in other countries in Latin America, or whether their primary crime is to have replaced Allende and whether people are now getting penalized, having gotten rid of an anti-American government. Is it worse than in other Latin American countries?"

"Yes," Assistant Secretary Rogers responded bluntly.

Kissinger tried a different approach. "The worst crime of this [Pinochet] government is that it's pro-American," he declared. "Is this government worse than the Allende government? Is human rights more severely threatened by this government than Allende?"

"Well, I can't say that, Mr. Secretary," Rogers demurred cautiously. "In terms of freedom of association, Allende didn't close down the opposition parties. In terms of freedom of the press, Allende didn't close down all the newspapers."

Washington's policy toward Pinochet, which at first consisted of a cool public attitude that masked a warm private embrace, soon evolved into openly friendly relations. Financial support was indispensable for Pinochet, since the country's domestic situation was not solid enough to attract foreign capital. Between 1974 and 1976, the Nixon and Ford administrations endorsed the renegotiation of Chile's foreign debt at the Paris Club (the informal group of creditor nations that deals with debt-related issues of indebted countries). Total U.S. economic aid during that period rose to $183.6 million, as opposed to the meager $19.8 million that Allende received. Export-Import Bank credits and other loans, not included in the preceding figures, reached $141.8 million during those years, as compared to only $4.7 million during the Allende administration. The Pinochet government received $66.5 million in World Bank credits during its first three years, whereas the Allende government received no credits whatsoever from that institution, and $237.8 million from the Inter-American Development Bank, as opposed to only $11.6 million lent during the Allende years.

As a means of strengthening its ties with the United States even further, the Pinochet regime signed agreements during the second half of 1974 with the American companies that had been expropriated during the Allende years. Anaconda, Kennecott, and even ITT would all receive compensation.

Chilean foreign policy aligned itself with that of the United States. One of the few controversies between Santiago and Washington during this period erupted when Chile voted in favor of a draft resolution declaring Zionism to be a form of racism at the United Nations General Assembly. The State Department sent a note to Pinochet expressing its profound disappointment over the Chilean vote, which, according to an American diplomat, "reciprocated an Arab promise not to promote accusations against Chile on the issue of human rights." A few days later, General Pinochet announced that Chile would change its vote, since it did not reflect his thinking on the matter.

President Gerald Ford had been in office just six weeks when the CIA admitted to having run an undercover campaign against Allende from 1970 to 1973—a revelation that set off a firestorm in the media.

Reflecting the growing concern in Congress, President Ford sent Secretary of the Treasury William Simon to Chile in May 1976 to explain to Pinochet that economic assistance to Chile could not continue unless he loosened "restrictions on human rights." Simon declared that Pinochet had assured him that he would do so and that, therefore, "it would be unjust to impose limitations on American aid to Chile while the problems were being corrected." In October 1976, the U.S. Congress finally suspended arms sales to Chile and limited economic aid to $27.5 million. But by then, private loans were much easier for Chile to come by in the world financial markets.

ON JULY 13, 2001, while I was serving as deputy foreign minister of Chile, Joyce Horman requested an audience with me in Santiago. I granted it immediately. Joyce, who later became a close friend in New York, was the widow of the American citizen Charles Horman, who had been arrested and then murdered in the days following the coup. The Academy Award–winning movie *Missing,* starring Sissy Spacek as Joyce and Jack Lemmon as Charles's father, Edmund, had made her famous.

I had recently received boxes containing thousands of American government documents regarding U.S. policies and actions in Chile between 1970 and 1990, released by the Clinton administration. Most of the documents were stamped "Top Secret," "Sensitive," or "Eyes Only." (The files had been declassified simultaneously in Washington, D.C., and Santiago, in the context of the Pinochet detention process in London, thanks in large part to the determination of a group of national security archives researchers, led by Peter Kornbluh, at George Washington University. I have drawn on many of those documents in writing this book.)

Joyce came to my office, accompanied by her friend Terry Simon, on a bright and sunny Southern Hemisphere winter day. She wanted to know if any of the 24,000 documents contained any new information about her young husband's disappearance and if they did, she wondered whether that information would be made available to the Chilean tribunals so that those involved could be prosecuted.

At the Foreign Ministry, the director of human rights had the task of analyzing the boxes of documents with a team of trusted English-speaking diplomats. I was briefed almost daily about their progress; at times, I was surprised by what I learned.

On September 17, 1973, a few days after the coup, neighbors of the Hormans had seen Charles taken away by a military patrol that also confiscated boxes full of books, film tapes, and other objects from their house. The Pinochet regime came up with the ludicrous story that leftist extremists impersonating army personnel had kidnapped and murdered Horman to embarrass the military government. At first, the American administration actually credited the junta's fantastical account. By early October 1973, even after credible information from a former detainee was available to U.S. embassy officials in Santiago about Horman's likely death in the National Stadium detention camp, Ambassador Nathaniel Davis and the consul claimed that they had information that suggested that Horman was "alive and well," probably in hiding or making his way out of the country through an underground "escape pipeline."

Charles's father, Ed Horman, had arrived from New York on October 5, to join Joyce in the search for Charles in hospitals, morgues, foreign embassies, and known detention centers. The American ambassador refused to accompany them in their desperate search. On October 18, after Ed and Joyce Horman had been told by embassy officials that Charles might be "alive and well," Ambassador Davis reported that the previously unidentified body of Charles Horman had been delivered to the morgue on September 18 and buried in the Santiago General Cemetery on October 3. The cause of death was "bullet wound."

Soon thereafter, Ed and Joyce returned to New York, distraught and angry about the embassy's role in casting doubts over Charles's forced disappearance and the covering up of the full circumstances surrounding his death. But there was more. In the preparation of this book I was privileged, thanks to Joyce Horman, to read the private notes and correspondence of Ed Horman in his search for his missing son and, later, in his fruitless efforts to gain justice after Charles's assassination was confirmed by the Chilean military. From the voluminous handwritten notes and documents emerges the picture of a man who recorded every conversation, every little detail in official documents and statements that could get him closer to truth and justice.

Among the documents in Ed Horman's archive there is a heavily censored State Department cable, dated August 25, 1976, released pursuant to a Horman family lawsuit against American officials that the family initiated in 1982. Seventeen years later, in October 1999, during the Clinton declassification process, the document was disclosed in full, revealing that "U.S. intelligence may have played an unfortunate part in Horman's death. At best, it was limited to providing or confirming information that helped motivate his murder by the government of Chile. At worst, U.S. intelligence was aware the government of Chile saw Horman in a rather serious light and U.S. officials did nothing to discourage the logical outcome of the government of Chile's paranoia." The unclassified report went on to confirm that Rafael González was the Chilean intelligence officer who acted as liaison with the American embassy on the Horman case. This is the same Rafael González who, on June 8, 1976, told *CBS News* and the *Washington Post* that Horman had been executed after he was questioned by the Chilean Army's intelligence service because he "knew too much."

I assured Joyce that any new information that could serve justice would be sent to the Chilean courts. In fact, I informed her that we had already officially transmitted a first set of translated documents to the Chilean Supreme Court. We exchanged views on the possibility that a special judge be designated to consider the case (we explained that the government did not have that authority) and on the hypothetical participation in the case of the Chilean State Defense Council. The next day President Ricardo Lagos received Joyce at La Moneda palace in what I recall as a frank and emotionally charged conversation.

I was outraged but not surprised to learn how unhelpful the American embassy in Santiago had been to persecuted dissidents. By contrast, during those days, Sweden's ambassador, Harald Edelstam, had turned into a sort of a folk hero in Chile after he personally rescued dozens of prisoners from the hands of the military forces, which led the junta to declare him persona non grata in early December 1973.

I witnessed firsthand the U.S. embassy's indifference to the Pinochet regime's human rights violations. Some time after the coup, my cousin Judith Troncoso Valenzuela was arrested in Puerto Montt, a city in southern Chile, where she was a nutritionist at the local hospital. Nobody seemed to know who had detained her and where she had been taken; permanent disappearance was a real possibility in those days.

Pamela called the American embassy. She told them that she was an American citizen married to a Chilean, gave my name, and explained the situation in general terms. A few days later I was contacted at the political science department of the Catholic University, where I was a graduate student, by someone from the U.S. mission, who instructed me to go at night to the residence of a U.S. diplomat whose name, if I ever knew it, I have long since forgotten. "Come alone," I was told.

The diplomat lived on Pedro de Valdivia Norte Street, steps from San Cristóbal Hill. It was a brief meeting. Though he was sympathetic about my cousin's situation, he cautioned me that a foreign mission was limited in what it could do. "Do not call us again," he said.

Some days later a friend who had good personal ties at the French embassy got me an interview with its deputy head of mission. He received me at the old but distinguished French-style embassy mansion on Condell Street, in the well-to-do borough of Providencia. The French diplomat listened carefully and took notes. As we spoke, I remembered that Pinochet's ancestors came from Saint Malo, in France.

"We have some contacts with the Pinochet government," he told me. "We will make our best efforts." Shortly thereafter my cousin was released from an air force detention center outside Puerto Montt. She was never charged with any crime and she never received an apology or an explanation. Judith never spoke about her time in jail, except to tell us that one day her captors told her she would be released because many people in Santiago, including a foreign embassy, were asking about her. I never found out which embassy it was, but I had a good guess.

PINOCHET REGARDED HIMSELF as more than a staunch ally of the U.S.; he fancied himself a global anti-Communist crusader. The positive signals he received from Washington led him to overstep his bounds, taking his terrorist campaign abroad, even to the streets of Washington, D.C. Pinochet worked closely with the other anti-Communist dictatorships that ruled South America during the mid-seventies. Brazilian military officers were frequently seen at the National Stadium detention center, advising their Chilean counterparts on torture techniques and interrogating their countrymen. On October 16, 1973, a group of Brazilian prisoners in Santiago's National Stadium recognized a compatriot, Alfredo Poeck, a known torturer.

I gained firsthand knowledge of the international reach of Pinochet's repression and persecution. One day my close cousin Francisco "Pancho" Sepúlveda, whom I had not seen since the coup, informed me, his face livid with outrage, "They arrested Robby 'Pelao' Robotham and they killed his cousin Jaime." The Robothams were a tight-knit middle-class family with the usual dreams of progress and higher education for their happy and intelligent children. Robby had been a classmate of ours in high school at Liceo de Aplicación. The coup turned the Robothams' dreams into nightmares. Jaime had studied sociology at the University of Chile, from which he had been expelled because of his Socialist activities. He was twenty-three years old when, on New Year's Eve, 1974, he and a friend were arrested by the DINA on a Santiago street in Ñuñoa borough, near his home.

Brutally beaten and subjected to torture by electric shocks at the secret Villa Grimaldi detention house near the foothills of the Andes, Jaime became a part of a shameful intelligence operation that was orchestrated by the secret polices of Chile, Argentina, and Brazil, to cover up the DINA's murderous activities.

In July 1975, the Chilean press published a list of 119 Chileans, all of whom had been seen in DINA custody and had supposedly died in Argentina "in armed confrontations between extremists." The list had been reprinted from two obscure publications in Argentina and Brazil that subsequently ceased to circulate. Then, on July 24, 1975, the front page of the Chilean daily *La Segunda* ran a lurid headline: "MIR Members Exterminated Like Rats." The story was that two charred, bullet-riddled bodies had been found inside a car north of Buenos Aires. A note on the corpses read, "Executed by the MIR." One of the bodies was identified as that of Jaime Robotham. The pro-Pinochet press presented the story as though it provided definitive proof that many of the individuals portrayed as "disappeared" had in fact left the country clandestinely.

But relatives who traveled to Argentina to identify the two bodies discovered that they were not their loved ones at all, and that the documents found in their clothes were forgeries. In the case of Jaime, the ID photo dated back to his high school days; Jaime's mother had given it to Investigaciones policemen who'd claimed to be probing her son's disappearance. The Robothams had been dragged into a DINA disinformation ploy that became known as "Operation Colombo," the first example of the internationalization of repression by Pinochet's secret police.

It was only natural that the South American dictatorships would want to pool their efforts to combat their leftist enemies. In late November 1975, Pinochet invited the intelligence chiefs from Argentina, Brazil, Uruguay, Paraguay, and Bolivia to Chile to agree on an ambitious new plan: to work together on transnational operations to eliminate their enemies. The plan was called Operation Condor in honor of Chile's national bird. An unwritten premise of the operation was that it could count on the support of the leader of the anti-Communist bloc: the United States.

John Dinges, an American journalist and friend of many years, thoroughly researched Operation Condor, drawing on declassified U.S. documents, secret correspondence of the DINA, and a valuable cache of files from Paraguay's intelligence police that were discovered accidentally in 1992. He concluded that its targets were not only "terrorists," but any dissidents worldwide who were perceived to pose a political threat.

The regimes were not merely paranoid. The 9/11 coup had reaffirmed a belief among progressives in Latin America (and elsewhere) that Allende's peaceful road to socialism was not possible and that solidarity actions across borders were a necessity. In August 1973 four radical left organizations, from Chile, Argentina, Uruguay, and Bolivia, had established the Revolutionary Coordinating Junta. After the coup, the revolutionary transnational organization intensified its actions, particularly in Argentina. These groups became a priority target of Operation Condor. But Condor also cast its net much wider, in terms of both geography and targets.

When Pinochet convened the intelligence chiefs in Santiago in 1975, he chaired the conference's opening session. After he greeted the participants, he turned the platform over to Colonel Contreras of the DINA, who outlined the purpose of the gathering. "Subversion no longer recognizes formal national borders," he said. "It has become coordinated internationally." Although the security agencies had met before, most recently in Buenos Aires in early 1974, and had worked together to make a few arrests and to kidnap and make disappear a handful of leftist leaders, they could do much more. Contreras's proposal, based on a detailed discussion paper and agenda dated October 29, 1975, that each of the participants had received (a photocopy of which I have read), laid out a three-stage process: first, to establish in Chile a Coordination Center that would be a clearinghouse for information, backed by the latest technology; second, to engage in operational activities within the six member countries that would be totally secret and deniable, with no records kept about them; and third, to extend operations—particularly assassinations—beyond South America. Operation Condor's stage would be the whole world.

Colonel Contreras's proposal was approved by the other five intelligence chiefs and a formal document was signed, committing each signatory to participation in the plan. Brazil had attended as an observer; it formally joined the consortium in 1976. The CIA found out about the Condor plan very quickly, less than two months after its creation. Dinges's investigation convincingly suggests that the United States government had detailed knowledge of Condor assassination plans, long before Orlando Letelier was murdered on September 21, 1976, and that Kissinger, in fact, had begun to exert some efforts to stop the conspirators' plans—efforts that were called off, strangely enough, on September 20, the day before Letelier was killed.

Up until the Letelier assassination, Contreras and Pinochet were satisfied that they had the United States' official support. Colonel Contreras had traveled to the United States to meet with Deputy CIA Director General Vernon Walters in March 1974, after which the CIA provided trainers for the DINA secret police. CIA documents show that Contreras received a single payment from the agency as a regular asset in mid-1975, though the CIA later decided that, given the appalling human rights record of the DINA, Contreras should not be a regularly paid asset.

Walters and Contreras met again in Washington, in January 1975, just four months after the DINA assassinated General Carlos Prats in Argentina. In August 1975, Contreras went to Washington for a third get-together with Walters. This time, he also met with members of the U.S. Congress. Pinochet personally arranged this last trip so that Contreras could explain Chile's position "on the human rights issue" to senior Washington officials. It was unbelievable: the executive head of the bloodiest repression machine in South America traveled to Washington to explain Pinochet's human rights policy. Despite a CIA evaluation that judged Contreras's visit to be "counterproductive,"

Vernon Walters welcomed him with a formal luncheon at CIA head-quarters in Langley.

An experienced spy, General Walters played the "good cop, bad cop" routine with Pinochet. But on balance he was one of the regime's closest and most reliable friends, regarding any favors that he did for Pinochet as sound investments in an anti-Communist ally.

Manuel Contreras, who liked to be referred to as "Condor One," set up a team to carry out DINA's international operations: among others, Colonel Pedro Espinoza, in charge of operations; Colonel Raúl Iturriaga, head of the external department; Michael Townley, an Iowa-born agent who had moved to Chile as a boy when his father was put in charge of Ford Motor Company's Chilean division; and Captain Armando Fernández Larios. While Operation Condor was active, Chile became a safe haven for right-wing terrorists. The Cubans who participated in Orlando Letelier's assassination received training in making remote control bombs. Relations between the Pinochet regime and the extremist Nationalist Cuban Movement were so positive that many Cuban fugitives from U.S. justice went to Chile as well. Some, like Virgilio Paz, even received free medical treatment. A coded message I discovered in my research, sent from the Chilean embassy in Washington to the Chilean foreign minister in August 1975, reveals that a former Cuban army general, Oscar Pino, identified as "President of the Central Committee of the Government of the Republic of Cuba in Arms," based in New York City, had received a letter signed by Foreign Minister Admiral Patricio Carvajal, informing him that he would be received in Chile by Pinochet and members of the junta. Apparently Señor Pino had been in Chile before, for meetings with security personnel. These Cubans, many of them veterans of the botched 1961 Bay of Pigs invasion, became a sort of reservoir for terrorist operations worldwide. Ties with the Cuban exiles became strained when the Chilean military government expelled Rolando Otero, a Cuban terrorist sought by American authorities for a bombing he committed on U.S. soil. However, relations with the Cuban radicals had been smoothed over by the time of the Letelier operation.

The Italian neo-fascist leader, Stefano delle Chiaie—alias Alfredo di Stefano, alias Topogigio—of the terrorist group Avanguardia Nazionale, was a guest of Pinochet in Chile in May 1974. He was accompanied by Commander Junio Valerio Borghese, known as "the Black Prince," who had been a naval officer in Mussolini's fascist regime and was the founder of right-wing terrorist groups. The Cuban and Italian terrorists' first collaboration with the DINA took place in Rome.

On October 6, 1975, the Christian Democratic leader, Bernardo Leighton, a man who had opposed the Allende government but who favored a broad coalition of forces against the dictatorship, was shot in the head on a street near the Vatican with a Beretta 9 mm by Pierluigi Concutelli and Salvatore Falabella, two of delle Chiaie's most trusted operatives. Leighton's wife, Anita Fresno, was shot as well. Miraculously, both of them survived. Townley, along with Virgilio Paz, a Cuban exile, and delle Chiaie had been in Rome a few days earlier.

Pinochet's close relations with foreign terrorists became evident when he traveled to Madrid with his wife and children, Colonel Contreras, and a large security contingent, to attend the funeral of the Spanish dictator, Francisco Franco. Franco had died on November 20, 1975, and Pinochet had decreed three days of official mourning in honor of the "Caudillo," whom he so admired. Pinochet and his entourage checked into the Ritz, where Contreras arranged for a brief meeting with a group of Spanish and Croatian ultranationalists, as well as with a contingent of Italian neo-fascists led by Stefano delle Chiaie. Between photographs, delle Chiaie introduced himself to Pinochet.

Pinochet instantly remembered their previous meeting. "I heard that Commander Borghese died. I am very sorry," he remarked. Vicenzo Vinciguerra, one of delle Chiaie's followers, later testified before an Italian judge that Pinochet, referring to the botched Leighton assassination, offhandedly remarked that it was too bad "the old man doesn't want to die." Pinochet's press chief, Federico Willoughby, belatedly concluded that this wasn't the sort of meeting that should be conducted in public and cut the proceedings short. Nevertheless, Colonel Contreras took advantage of the opportunity to present delle Chiaie with his $5,000 payment for the Rome job.

The U.S. government's representative to Franco's funeral was Vice President Nelson Rockefeller. In a conversation I had with Admiral Jonathan Howe, Rockefeller's assistant for national security affairs, he recalled that Rockefeller was annoyed by the presence of noisy Franco followers outside the *Valle de los Caídos* (Valley of the Fallen), the Spanish Civil War–era cemetery that Franco had had built. As the foreign dignitaries departed after the graveside ceremony, the fascists cheered Pinochet, greeting him with a Nazi salute.

"Let's get out of here fast," Rockefeller said. Then he pointed to Pinochet. "That man is very dangerous," he said. He was right.

In Madrid the Chilean dictator was not treated anywhere near as well as he would have liked. Several heads of state warned that they would not attend the Te Deum Mass for Franco on November 27 if Pinochet was present. The Spaniards took due note and diplomatically recommended that he return home. Pinochet was furious, since he had intended to celebrate his sixtieth birthday with his family in Spain. He returned to Santiago on November 24, 1975, one day before his birthday.

Pinochet and the DINA felt so confident about their relationship with Washington after Kissinger's visit to Chile in June 1976 that two weeks later the DINA international operations team got the order to assassinate Orlando Letelier. Later, all those directly involved in the plot, from Contreras to Townley, pointed their fingers at Pinochet as having either directly ordered or at least approved the murder of the former Allende foreign minister and ambassador to the United States.

On Tuesday morning, September 21, Letelier was driving down Massachusetts Avenue on his way to work at the Institute for Policy Studies. His Chevy Chevette had just entered Sheridan Circle when a bomb exploded under it. Letelier's legs were blown off and he died instantly; Ronni Karpen Moffit, a young colleague at the institute, was sitting in the front seat. She was also killed when a piece of shrapnel severed her carotid artery and windpipe. Her husband, Michael Moffit, who was riding in the backseat of the car, survived with minor injuries. The radio-controlled bomb had been placed by Michael Townley and detonated by two Cubans, Virgilio Paz and Dionisio Suárez. Armando Fernández Larios, a Chilean army captain, and Mónica Lagos, a DINA agent, had been in charge of the surveillance of Letelier in the days leading up to the assassination.

Washington had had several warnings about the plot. At the outset of the operation, Townley and Fernández Larios traveled to Paraguay to obtain false passports and U.S. visas. Colonel Benito Guanes, the director of Paraguay's military intelligence, who had been present at the founding meeting of Operation Condor in Santiago, issued the passports under the names Williams and Romeral. The Paraguayan protocol chief presented the passports to the U.S. consulate, which stamped the visitors' visas. But as often happens in the shady world of intelligence, where favors can be repaid, a Paraguayan source tipped off the U.S. ambassador, George Landau, about the real identities of the passport holders. Landau photocopied the documents, photographs, and visas and sent them on to the CIA and the State Department. Once it became known that the two men were clandestine operatives, the ambassador demanded the visas back.

As a decoy, two other DINA agents, using the same names, Williams and Romeral, got U.S. visas in Santiago using a different set of false passports, this time Chilean ones, and bought round-trip tickets to New York. Later, Townley and Fernández Larios used still another set of phony passports, this time under the last names Petersen and Faúndez, to obtain yet another set of visas. This time it worked.

After Letelier's assassination, the CIA director, George H. W. Bush, recalled the Paraguayan incident and started to connect the dots. As the investigation started to point to Pinochet, Guillermo Osorio, the Chilean diplomat who had issued the passports for the DINA team, was found dead of a gunshot wound at his home in Santiago in October 1977.

It was a strange case, whose contours were revealed in a conversation I had with Osorio's son Carlos. Guillermo Osorio, a career diplomat of conservative leanings, was the consular director at the Foreign Ministry at the time of Letelier's murder; he regularly signed the passports that the secret police demanded. His relatives knew that, as a precaution, he kept a notebook with the data on all the passports he issued to the DINA. In 1977, when as chief of protocol he traveled to Washington to prepare for Pinochet's visit to attend the Panama Canal treaties ceremony, Osorio was approached during a cocktail party by FBI agents who showed him copies of the false passports issued to the DINA operatives involved in the Letelier assassination. "Is this your signature?" the FBI agents inquired. "Yes, it is," Osorio responded, nervous and surprised about the awkward situation.

As soon as Guillermo Osorio returned to Chile he told Foreign Minister Admiral Patricio Carvajal about the incident with the FBI in Washington. "I suppose you denied everything," the admiral said. "Well, no, I just told the truth," Osorio replied. Not long after that, Osorio turned up dead, of what was officially branded as a suicide. Osorio's notebook had disappeared. When his son Carlos arrived at his parents' residence after learning the news of his father's death, about a dozen policemen were there who impeded access of family members to the bedroom of the deceased. Among those present was Army General Carlos Forestier, a friend of Osorio's, who stated, "To the media we declare that the cause of death was a heart attack." Standing in the garden and looking through a window, Carlos Osorio was able to see his father's corpse between two beds, but when the family was finally allowed to view the body, it had been placed on a bed and a gun was on his father's chest. An autopsy was denied and a summary investigation concluded that he had shot himself with his right hand —though Osorio, an accomplished hunter, was left-handed. The suicide version did not make sense to family members, since Guillermo

It was clear that there was a certain amount of mutual distrust between us, but over the course of the many conversations that followed, Korbel and I developed a natural sympathy that turned into friendship. Although I did not take any of his courses, I ended up spending more time at his office talking politics than most of his Soviet studies students. When he asked me about the Chilean Socialist Party and the Marxist president, Salvador Allende, I explained that, although Allende had called himself a Marxist, most of his political career had been in Congress, where he had led the Senate, and that he had been a candidate in three presidential contests before he was finally elected in 1970. I expounded that the Chilean Socialist Party had emerged in the early 1930s as a strong competitor of the local Communist Party, and that it rejected the Communists' unswerving allegiance to Moscow. Korbel was surprised to learn that, during World War II, then Senator Allende and the Socialists had strongly championed the Allied cause, unlike Chilean Communists, who assumed a neutrality stance influenced by the 1939 Soviet-German Nonaggression Pact, and that Allende had even hosted a meeting with the special U.S. envoy, Nelson Rockefeller, during a 1942 visit to Santiago to discus common efforts to press the Chilean government to break diplomatic ties with the Axis powers. Though the Socialists regarded Marxist thought as an important ideological source, I informed Korbel, we were also influenced by the nationalist Latin Americanist thinking of the nineteenth-century Peruvian leader Juan Carlos Mariátegui, and by a myriad of other progressive philosophers and political leaders, from José Martí to Antonio Gramsci. "Then in the end you are just like me," Korbel concluded one day. "You are a Social Democrat."

With time, I came to agree with him. Korbel was a fascinating man. A man of culture, he had a crisp sense of humor that his friends enjoyed. Korbel's favorite student was a classmate who also became a good friend of mine. Her name was Condoleezza Rice.

Condi, as we knew her then, was one of Korbel's top students, a serious scholar of Russian history and language and a bright student of contemporary Soviet affairs. Condi, as I recall, attended some of the academic and political Chilean solidarity activities I organized at the university. I particularly remember a long talk we had at the faculty lounge of GSIS, where she inquired in detail about the root causes of the breakdown of democracy and the current situation in Chile. It never occurred to me that my enthusiastic briefing might have an influence on the future U.S. secretary of state. Our paths crossed many more times in later years, as we served our respective countries in various foreign policy posts.

Gradually I contacted friends and fellow Socialists in other American cities and Europe. Denver became a stopover for leading Chilean exiles, such as Laura Allende, a former senator who was the sister of President Allende and who stayed at our apartment in Denver and lectured at GSIS. Also the folksingers Angel and Isabel Parra came to Denver. As the Chilean community grew with the arrival of former political prisoners, we were able to organize larger events such as concerts with Chilean musical groups such as Inti-Illimani and Quilapayún. We sent the money we collected to Mexico, where the Socialist Party had a strong base, or, when we had a safe courier, directly to Chile, where it was used for underground resistance activities.

Amnesty International and the Quakers helped us find housing and jobs for the political prisoners who arrived in Denver and Boulder in early 1976. Most of them came from jails in the north of Chile, from Antofagasta or Calama, the copper-mining town. One of these exiles came from the lake region in southern Chile. Renato Invernizze had been sentenced to death by a war tribunal but had been saved, he confided to me years later, because he was the illegitimate son of the most powerful businessman in the region. Another incoming refugee was Enrique Guerra, a former union leader in a flour-mill factory. An Allende sympathizer but not a party member, he had been spared the fate of his fellow prisoners, who were taken out of jail and assassinated one night by the Caravan of Death led by General Arellano. Enrique, a man of humble origins and limited formal education, was wise and tough. Every October 19 he would take the day off from his job at a supermarket in Denver to remember and shed a few quiet tears for his fellow prisoners who disappeared that night in 1973.

We became strong friends with these exiles, most of whom had never been abroad and who were coming directly from jail to an unknown land. Unlike Vietnamese refugees who arrived in the United States about the same time, Chileans received absolutely no federal or state government assistance—no language courses, no housing, food stamps, or guaranteed jobs. The Chileans were helped at first by the goodwill of Americans such as the Quakers; and they were left to struggle on their own, which they did very well. In time many of them saved enough money to buy their own houses and send their children to college.

Practically all of the Chilean exiles who were allowed into the United States were Socialists. Most ended up in Los Angeles, Chicago, and New York, though a few settled in northern Texas. At a national conference in Chicago I was elected member of a troika that loosely coordinated Chilean Socialists in the United States. In Denver we organized a local Socialist Party and assembled a team to play soccer in the Colorado amateur league, where we became vice champions. To promote our cause we put together a musical folk group, directed by José Cornejo, a Chilean who was attending college in Denver. I volunteered to learn how to play the *quena*, a pre-Columbian wooden flute, and the *charango*, a small mandolin-like instrument with a set of five double strings that is used in Andean music. Pamela stoically put up with my musical learning process, for the sake of democracy.

One day we were in a soccer scrimmage, training for the Colorado state tournament, when one of the few Chileans who was not on our team came running onto the field at the University of Denver yelling, *"Mataron a Letelier, mataron a Letelier!"* ("They have killed Letelier!") We stopped our practice and gathered on the sidelines. One of the Chilean players said, "It was Pinochet and the DINA. It can't be any other way." We all agreed, as a feeling of anger mixed with profound sadness set in among us.

I was particularly shocked and distraught, since I was scheduled to go to Washington in a few days to begin writing my Ph.D. dissertation and to work with Letelier. I had won a grant from Resources for the Future to finance my stay in the capital, plus I had been awarded a guest fellow position at the Brookings Institution, the leading academic institution on economic issues and foreign policy. Brookings was only a couple of blocks away from the Institute for Policy Studies, where Letelier worked—ironically, right across the street from the Chilean embassy. What sense did it make to go to Washington now that Letelier was dead?

I had met Letelier in the summer of 1972, when I had just completed my B.A. at the State University of New York in Oswego and was about to return to Chile. At the time I was leading a social program called Oswego County Opportunities, which focused on assisting Puerto Rican and Mexican migrant workers who came to the area each summer to pick lettuce; they lived in conditions that bordered on slavery. I had contacted César Chávez and his United Farm Workers' Union on their behalf; an envoy from the union visited me secretly in Oswego and explained what the process of organizing a union would entail.

My intense but entirely legal presence at the farms to meet with migrant workers alerted the owners, who soon learned of the unionization plan. Shortly thereafter I received a written death threat signed by the John Birch Society. Suspicious cars drove slowly by the house where I rented a room, and my landlord became very agitated. I informed the Oswego Police Department, which ordered patrols of the neighborhood.

I called a friend at the Chilean embassy in Washington, D.C., who in turn informed Ambassador Orlando Letelier. Immediately Letelier sent me a message: I had to get out of Oswego right away and move to Washington, D.C. There, the embassy would facilitate my intended return to Chile.

"What is he doing with this migrant worker business? Does he want the Nixon administration to accuse Allende of sending activists to interfere in U.S. internal affairs? That's all we need now," Letelier had said about my activities, not altogether angrily.

A few days later I was a house guest of the Chilean press attaché in Washington, Andrés Rojas. I stayed for about a month, and worked as a busboy at the restaurant of the Hotel Washington, located around the corner from the White House. I had the privilege of attending at least one informal meeting with Letelier and his closest colleagues at his office and social gatherings at the apartment of the writer Fernando Alegría, who was the cultural attaché at the embassy, and at the homes of leading academics close to Chile. Letelier, a charismatic man who loved to play the guitar for his friends, was critical of Allende's policy of extending state ownership to small enterprises. "One day we will learn that Minister Vuskovic"—the economy minister—"has taken over roasted peanuts carts on street corners!" he grumbled.

In his memoirs Pinochet does not even mention Letelier's assassination when he refers to events that occurred in 1976, but he touches on it later, when he discusses U.S.-Chilean relations. In one of those passages Pinochet asks: What reason could the DINA have had to murder Letelier? Ten days before the bombing, Letelier's Chilean nationality had been revoked by a decree signed by Pinochet. Letelier was considered a traitor because he had successfully lobbied against the granting of some international loans to the junta and because he was viewed, like the Christian Democratic leader, Bernardo Leighton, as someone who could potentially form and lead a government in exile. Kissinger must have recalled that Pinochet had insistently complained about Letelier's influence in Washington when they met in Santiago on June 8, 1976. Three months later, Letelier was dead.

In my research I discovered that Pinochet's envoy to Washington, Ambassador Manuel Trucco, had sent a series of coded messages to the Chilean Foreign Ministry inquiring about Letelier's travel documents. On August 28, 1975, Trucco demanded to know "with which type of document did Orlando Letelier leave Chile?" A few days later, on September 2, the Chilean ambassador stated that he had "indications that Orlando Letelier might be traveling with a Chilean diplomatic passport" and requested that he be informed "if there is evidence of the actual return of the diplomatic passport that Letelier held as ambassador or minister of State," as well as the exact serial numbers of those documents so as to declare them null and void. Clearly, Letelier was the subject of both extraordinary vigilance and extreme hostility throughout all levels of the Pinochet government.

Inside the U.S. government there was a growing conviction that Letelier was a victim of the DINA's Operation Condor. In a meeting with Justice Department officials on October 4, 1976, CIA Director Bush was told that the murder most likely had been planned by DINA. Two days later, a CIA field officer reported that his sources believed that the "Chilean government" was "directly involved in Letelier's death." The blunder with the Paraguayan passports led the FBI and the Justice Department investigations directly to the DINA agents Michael Townley and Armando Fernández Larios. With the election of Jimmy Carter to the U.S. presidency, Condor operations, at least those beyond Latin America, began to fall apart.

I did not cancel my move to Washington; besides, I could still work with those who were pressing to bring Letelier's assassins to justice. I arrived in mid-October 1976, only weeks after the murder, and rented an apartment about four blocks from Brookings. I went to IPS and met with Letelier's widow, Isabel Margarita, and with some of Letelier's colleagues, including Saul Landau—who would become a dear friend—and my Chilean compatriot and friend, Juan Gabriel Valdés, an IPS researcher and graduate student who, when democracy returned to Chile, would hold several top government posts.

At Brookings I was given a small office on the fifth floor. Ironically, my window looked out on the Chilean embassy. Every day I saw the routine of diplomats arriving, going out to lunch, and returning home. It pained me to see the Chilean flag; it no longer represented the democratic, law-abiding, culturally sophisticated nation I loved.

I knew that DINA agents were embedded at the embassy, as they were at all major Chilean diplomatic missions. Police Major Héctor Vilches headed a new Department of Security at the Foreign Ministry in Santiago, from which he issued orders directly to DINA agents abroad to spy on ambassadors, diplomats, and local exile groups. These operations were known as MIS/1–1976.

I began writing my doctoral dissertation on foreign policy and raw materials, as the U.S. presidential elections entered their decisive phase. The economist C. Fred Bergsten was assigned to be my dissertation adviser. I attended the Friday luncheons at Brookings, where senior economists and foreign policy experts such as Charlie Schultz, Arthur Okun, Lawrence Krause, Barry Blechman, Henry Owen, and of course my adviser, most of them linked to the Democratic Party, would sit around a large round table and discuss everything from presidential politics to domestic economic policy, nuclear politics, and the situation in the Middle East. We young Ph.D. candidates and guest scholars sat on chairs behind them with our brown bag lunches on our laps.

Jimmy Carter's candidacy seemed stronger since in the debates he was generally agreed to have bested President Gerald Ford. I had paid special attention to the second debate, on October 6, 1976, in which one of the panelists asked President Ford if he would consider liberalizing his foreign policy to end "bloodshed in Chile, Chilean prisons, and throw our weight around for the values we hold dear in the world." Ford's long response focused first on South Africa and the Middle East and then on South Korea and China. When Carter's turn came he said, "I notice that Mr. Ford didn't comment on the prisons in Chile. This is a typical example, maybe one of many others, where this administration overthrew an elected government and helped to establish a military dictatorship." Then Carter noted that 85 percent of all Food for Peace aid to South America was being directed to Pinochet's Chile. Foreign policy, usually a tangential issue in American presidential elections, had become a key topic.

Ford never responded to Carter's comments about Chile during the debate. He also committed blunders when he said that there was no "Soviet domination of Eastern Europe" and that he believed Poles did not consider themselves dominated by Moscow.

On election night, November 2, 1976, I was invited to a party at the home of Jacqueline Martin, the administrative secretary of the foreign policy program at the Brookings Institution, to watch the returns on TV. Almost everyone attending was a Brookings Democrat. I well recall the prevailing sense of jubilation when Carter was declared the winner, with 297 electoral votes, having won also the majority of the popular vote, the first time a Democrat had done so since 1964. It seemed to me that night that Pinochet's situation had just grown worse.

Carter's election as president was the beginning of a new era in relations between Chile and the United States. Pinochet immediately adopted a defensive stance. On November 17 and 18, 1976, only a few days after Carter's election, the military government released 304 political prisoners. This occurred amid a growing debate within Chilean government circles about how to respond to international pressure and to the new Washington administration. *Blandos* (moderates) argued for a gradual lifting of the most repressive measures of Pinochet's regime, while the *duros* (hard-liners) defended the dictatorship, rejecting any political opening, even if symbolic.

Carter's commitment to a robust human rights policy inevitably resulted in the deterioration of official ties between the United States and Chile. In March 1977, Brady Tyson, the American delegate to the UN Human Rights Commission in Geneva, expressed the "profoundest regrets" of the U.S. delegation "for the despicable acts of subversion of the democratic institutions of Chile, taken by certain U.S. officials, agencies and private groups." Tyson added that "the policies and persons responsible for those acts [had] been rejected by the American people." That sincere apology was later criticized as "inappropriate" by President Carter. Even so, the administration's friendliness toward the opposition continued as former president Eduardo Frei Montalva and Allende's former foreign minister, Clodomiro Almeyda, were received in Washington by, respectively, Vice President Walter Mondale and Undersecretary of State Warren Christopher. When Pinochet called for a national plebiscite on January 4, 1978, in which Chileans had to vote in favor of either the military regime or a United Nations resolution condemning the regime, the U.S. State Department strongly criticized the regime's procedures on the grounds that they did not meet the minimum "freedom of expression guarantees."

But there were some contradictory signals from the Carter administration as well. In September 1977 President Carter extended an invitation to all heads of state in the region to attend the signing of the Panama Canal treaties. Augusto Pinochet never expected to be invited to Washington and he jumped at the opportunity to meet with Carter and other presidents of the nations of the Americas.

On September 6, 1977, at 6 P.M., Pinochet, dressed in a light-color business suit, arrived at the White House for what he feared could be a tense meeting. But he had already won points merely by being allowed to enter the White House for a face-to-face meeting with the American president. Outside, five hundred demonstrators, led by Isabel Margarita, Orlando Letelier's widow, and the Colombian writer Gabriel García Marquez, protested Pinochet's presence in Washington.

Carter expressed that his human rights concerns extended worldwide and invited Pinochet to help him understand the situation in Chile.

"My country is the victim of a vast and successful Marxist propaganda campaign," Pinochet replied with a straight face, dismissing completely the notion that there could be any serious human rights problems in Chile. "Everyone should come to Chile to see," Pinochet added. "What is going on inside is not what they say."

The president seized on the point and cornered Pinochet into accepting UN observers to visit Chile, which the dictator had refused to authorize in the past. International observation could be a "way to clear up the allegations," Carter asserted. Pinochet came out of the meeting smiling and saying that he and the U.S. president had "entirely agreed" on the human rights issue. "It was a conversation, not an interrogation," Pinochet described the interview to the press. Later, he acknowledged that Carter had asked for the release of some political prisoners.

Asked about the Letelier assassination in a press conference, Pinochet swore that his "government had nothing to do with it," nor that it had any previous knowledge about it. The cunning general might have been splitting hairs, reasoning that his DINA force was not, strictly speaking, a component of the government. Lawrence Barcella, a U.S. attorney, would declare some time later, "Either avenging angels were killing Pinochet's opponents year after year, or he was well aware that his secret police arm was out there directing the annual assassinations of his enemies. It was inconceivable that Pinochet did not know."

Carter had not said anything to Pinochet about the Letelier assassination. There were several reasons for his reticence. Aware of Pinochet's intransigence when challenged, he did not want to lose all remaining influence with the dictator, particularly when his own administration was still divided on the question of whether Pinochet was personally involved. Besides, Carter wanted to discuss other issues, such as nuclear proliferation, arms purchases in the region, and the bilateral situation between Chile and Bolivia.

In the meantime, Assistant U.S. Attorney Eugene Propper, the head prosecutor in the Letelier case, moved steadily to gather evidence proving that Letelier's murder had been planned and executed by Pinochet's DINA. A formal extradition request for the perpetrators of the crime was sent to Chile. Meanwhile, the Pinochet regime hired the Washington firm of Anderson, Pendleton & McMahon to conduct a public relations campaign in the U.S. media, the business world, and Congress.

When Terence Todman, the assistant secretary of state for inter-American affairs, visited Santiago in August 1977, he found that the military government had responded to the growing pressure for human rights reform by dissolving the DINA security police, replacing it with the Central Nacional de Informaciones (CNI). DINA activity had become a specific area of U.S. human rights concern in Chile. Contreras had become a liability, but he remained a trusted member of Pinochet's inner circle. Though relieved of his duties, he had been elevated to the rank of general. Of course, replacing DINA with CNI was largely a cosmetic change. The CNI would become as repressive as its predecessor, as Contreras operated in the shadows to erode the authority of CNI's director, General Odlanier Mena. For example, Contreras held him responsible for the killing by the Movement of the Revolutionary Left of Colonel Roger Vergara, the chief of the army's intelligence school. Contreras also pushed for tougher action by the new intelligence agency until Mena was finally fired. But in 1977 the dissolution of the DINA sent an important signal to the United States.

Always the pragmatist, a year later Pinochet decided that he had to give up the DINA agent Michael Townley. The pressure within his own regime from moderates and from his economic policy team had left him little choice. Pinochet ordered the undersecretary of the interior, Air Force Colonel Enrique Montero, to travel to Washington to lay the groundwork for Townley's surrender. On April 7 he signed the so-called Montero-Silbert accord with Earl J. Gilbert, the U.S. attorney for the District of Columbia, which stipulated the terms through which the Pinochet government would hand over Townley to American authorities. But the hard-liners in Chile balked. The minister of the interior, Army General César Benavides, phoned Undersecretary Montero in Washington, D.C., to inform him that Townley could not be handed over after all, because he was being processed by the Chilean courts.

Montero told him, "My general, I cannot go back to Chile as undersecretary of the interior if I am forced to look like a fool before the Americans."

The following morning Minister Benavides called again to say that the matter had been revisited. Townley would be delivered to the Americans. Many years later, in an interview, Montero admitted that Washington had put together a formidable case against the Pinochet government. "What was done with Letelier in Sheridan Circle was equivalent to stepping on Uncle Sam's toes," he said.

On April 8, 1978, Townley, escorted by two FBI agents, boarded a Miami-bound Ecuatoriana Airlines passenger plane. Under a plea bargain agreement, he confessed his participation in Letelier's assassination and testified that he had committed the crime under the direct orders of the DINA director, Manuel Contreras. Townley's wife, Mariana Callejas, also a DINA agent, publicly accused Pinochet of betraying a loyal foot soldier. After initially refusing to cooperate with U.S. authorities, Townley testified that he had "no regrets" about killing Letelier because he had acted "as a soldier" on Pinochet's behalf.

In June 1978 Pinochet's power was at its weakest ebb since he'd taken over. During a reception with the diplomatic corps in Santiago on June 23, he spoke privately to U.S. ambassador George Landau. In his report on the conversation Landau observed that Pinochet, "who normally drinks very little, had two scotch and sodas. His face grew redder and redder as he spoke to me. He appeared a deeply troubled man and his concern that he might be replaced by other military officers seems to be foremost in his mind."

The moderates inside Pinochet's government were of the view that all of those implicated in the Letelier assassination had to be extradited to the United States; otherwise, the survival of the regime would be in jeopardy. The hard-liners argued that no government could give up its intelligence chief to a foreign power and that Pinochet should not yield to pressure to extradite the military officers accused in the Letelier murder either. Pinochet opted for a pragmatic, middle-of-the-road solution. He asked for General Contreras's resignation from the army. Contreras blamed the moderate members of Pinochet's cabinet for his problems and announced he would file a complaint against three of them. Pinochet ordered Contreras to drop the accusation, and the former secret service chief responded that "once more" he would follow the orders of his superior. Observers wondered whether "once more" was a not-so-veiled insinuation that Letelier had been assassinated on Pinochet's orders.

The U.S. Justice Department presented a petition for the extradition of Contreras and the other military officers to the Chilean authorities. Assuming that they would rule against the petition, Pinochet asked the Supreme Court judges to rule on the question of extradition. In October 1979, the Supreme Court of Chile rejected the petition and ordered the officers' immediate release. As a consequence, the United States temporarily withdrew its envoy to Santiago, Ambassador Landau, and announced a series of economic and diplomatic sanctions against the Chilean government, including the total suspension of credits and military supplies, reduction of military and diplomatic personnel accredited in Santiago, and a ban on future financing and guarantees for U.S. projects in Chile from the Export-Import Bank (the official export credit agency of the U.S. federal government) and the Overseas Private Investment Corporation (an independent agency of the U.S. government that supports American investment in emerging markets). In June 1980, as an additional reprisal against the military government, the Carter administration excluded Chile from the inter-American UNITAS XXI naval maneuvers.

Pinochet saw Washington, whose support had been crucial during the installation of his regime, become a formidable adversary. He complained that some in the U.S. government apparently considered Chile "an overseas colony."

Pinochet blamed the Carter administration for the most embarrassing moment suffered by the dictatorship's foreign policy, and perhaps one of the most notable fiascos in the history of diplomacy: Pinochet's abortive "opening to Asia and the Pacific." The general liked to travel and constantly sought opportunities to counter Chile's isolation through high-level presidential visits abroad. In early 1979, Deputy Foreign Minister General Enrique Valdés transmitted an oral invitation he had received in Manila for his chief to visit the ASEAN (Association of South East Asian Nations) countries. The invitation was never formalized in writing, and Foreign Minister Hernán Cubillos avoided getting involved in the preparations for the tour, leaving all arrangements in the hands of the *casa militar,* Pinochet's military staff. The grand tour of Southeast Asia was gradually reduced to a state visit to the Philippines. Even so, it would be of historical importance.

The Chilean ambassador in Manila, Charles Le May, a retired admiral, made detailed preparations with Philippine officials. Pinochet and his wife, Lucía, would stay in the east wing of the Malacañang palace; the streets of the capital would be adorned with Philippine and Chilean flags. Pinochet would receive a doctoral degree *honoris causa* from a local university; a banquet in his honor would be held at the historical Hotel Manila, where MacArthur had lived during World War II.

Pinochet was radiant when the airplane took off toward the Pacific from Santiago with a large delegation aboard. The aircraft made a stopover at Easter Island and another at Pape'ete, Tahiti; afterward it flew in the direction of the Fiji Islands. On Saturday, March 22, at 2:30 P.M., while Chilean diplomats finalized the arrangements for a dinner at Manila's La Tasca restaurant, the Philippine foreign minister, Carlos Rómulo, urgently phoned the Chilean ambassador in Manila.

"Your president's visit has been canceled," Rómulo said gravely.

"What are you saying?" gasped Le May.

"I am saying that the visit has been canceled. I cannot explain why because I do not know."

Le May pleaded for an audience with Marcos, but the foreign minister said it would be impossible. Instead, he agreed to meet with him at his own residence for half an hour. When Le May arrived, Rómulo couldn't tell the distraught ambassador much more than he had on the telephone. He dropped hints that the Philippine government could not guarantee Pinochet's security, and added that Marcos had traveled south to see to an urgent matter.

"But is it a cancellation or a postponement?" Le May inquired anxiously.

"It is a cancellation."

"This will have grave consequences for our bilateral relations."

"I understand," said Rómulo, cutting the conversation short. "I would not like to be in your shoes."

Pinochet's plane was approaching Fiji when Ambassador Le May phoned the aircraft through a connection facilitated by General Odlanier Mena, head of the CNI, who had remained in Santiago. Le May gave the bad news directly to Pinochet, who remained silent for so long that Le May thought their connection was failing.

The news spread like wildfire throughout the plane, filled as it was with Pinochet's family members, four ministers and their wives, high military officers, senior officers of the armed forces and Carabineros, presidential aides, protocol and foreign ministry officials, numerous journalists, secretaries, and the security guard.

Surprisingly for many, Pinochet did not seem particularly angry. He was silent and he was worried. I interviewed passengers who told me that for the first few hours Pinochet apparently feared he had been overthrown.

The plane landed on Nandi, Fiji, on Sunday, March 23, at 12:30 A.M. As the plane taxied to a halt, more bad news came. The airport workers refused to place a stair for the passengers to descend; later, Fijian security forces surrounded the plane, raising the tension to the boiling point. Finally a stairway appeared on the tarmac and an insouciant airport worker climbed aboard the plane to fumigate it. It was stifling inside the cabin; the captain had turned the plane's motors off and the air-conditioning did not work.

After tense negotiations, the passengers were given permission to deplane, but Pinochet was no longer allowed to lodge at the governor's mansion in Suva. Although Fiji was only a stopover, Pinochet's entourage had demanded a reception befitting a head of state, angering Fiji's leader, Ratu Sir Kamisese Mara. Now that the visit to Manila had been canceled, the Fijians decided to cancel their official reception, too. To add insult to injury, the Chileans' luggage was searched and they were subjected to slow bureaucratic procedures. Finally, Pinochet's delegation moved on to the Regents Hotel, but on the way demonstrators pelted his car with eggs and tomatoes. It would be hard to imagine a more humiliating set of circumstances for a dictator.

Pinochet was supposed to make stops in Papua New Guinea and Hong Kong as well. These plans were immediately scratched. Foreign Minister Cubillos had been invited to Japan after the Philippine visit, and he told Pinochet that perhaps he should go directly to Tokyo from Fiji.

"No, my friend," Pinochet said. "You will go back to Chile with me."

Pinochet's intimate circle still believed they were the victims of a plot. General César Benavides, the minister of defense, phoned aides and friends in Santiago to make sure there had not been a military movement against Pinochet. Minister Benavides was told that everything was calm and in order in Chile; there was no saber rattling at all.

After paying extortionate prices for fuel and food, Pinochet's plane took off from Fiji at ten the next morning. Now Pinochet really was furious, since he knew his position in Chile was as solid as ever. He placed the blame for the debacle squarely in Foreign Minister Cubillos's lap. Pinochet's daughter Lucía told journalists on the plane that her father had been betrayed. People at the Foreign Ministry knew there would be problems with the visit and they ignored them, she claimed.

But it was Pinochet's entourage that had ignored what in retrospect seem like unmistakable signals that began emanating from Manila on the eve of the visit. Philippine officials had eliminated any welcome speeches at the airport and Pinochet had been strongly advised not to wear a uniform on arrival—a suggestion that Pinochet had angrily rejected.

Chilean diplomats explained to journalists that Ferdinand Marcos had had to travel unexpectedly to Mindanão because of clashes between government forces and the Muslim guerrillas of the Moro Liberation Front, but an anonymous Philippine official revealed that Marcos was in fact annoyed with Pinochet for pushing so hard for the invitation. Chilean journalists who were in Manila awaiting Pinochet's arrival saw that a big party was being held on one of the yachts owned by Marcos. According to witnesses, the Philippine dictator was on board.

When Pinochet arrived back in Santiago, a huge reception had been arranged for him at the airport and, later, at the Diego Portales government building.

"I cannot accept a slap in the face of my country, and therefore I will cut relations with the Philippines!" Pinochet announced before several thousand followers who were clamoring for blood. None of the junta members knew that Pinochet would sever diplomatic ties with Manila.

The next day, at a meeting with ministers and advisers, Pinochet demanded the resignation of Foreign Minister Cubillos. No further details were given about the cancellation of the visit, because Ambassador Le May, who had arrived in Santiago after a strenuous trip across half the globe, was too sick to attend the meeting.

The hard-liners demanded Cubillos's head. Pablo Rodríguez, the former chief of Patria y Libertad, the right-wing paramilitary group, wrote that Chile had to cultivate relations with its "natural allies of anti-Communist orientation," like Saudi Arabia, Taiwan, and South Africa. Domestic authoritarian measures should not be relaxed to please President Carter and other Western democracies, the hard-liners argued. They reasoned that Pinochet's regime was already so isolated internationally that the costs of greater domestic repression would be minimal.

About one week later, the Philippine ambassador to the United States, a cousin of Imelda Marcos named Eduardo Romualdez, traveled to Santiago carrying an apologetic letter from Marcos and an official explanation: Eight alleged terrorists from Libya had been arrested a few days before the visit; they had been plotting to assassinate Pinochet and Marcos. Marcos had been whisked to an isolated safe location as a precautionary measure, which was why he had not been available immediately after the trip's cancellation. Pinochet accepted his fellow dictator's excuses and diplomatic relations with Manila were duly restored.

Pinochet's willingness to swallow his pride to resolve a foreign policy crisis was evidenced in another episode a few years later. In 1983, the French foreign minister made some strong ad hominem comments about Pinochet. The Chilean foreign minister, Miguel Schweitzer, requested and was granted an immediate audience with Pinochet first thing the next morning to decide on a course of diplo-

matic action. Minister Schweitzer opined that the Chilean ambassador in Paris should be recalled immediately. Pinochet looked at his
minister and said, "And how do we manage to send him back?" The
meeting lasted fifty seconds.

Pinochet blamed Jimmy Carter for the whole embarrassing
episode. Carter, he reasoned, had pressured Marcos and the ASEAN
leaders to suspend Pinochet's visit. Marcos, the old fox, knew that he
had to stay on friendly terms with the American president, because
he had human rights issues of his own to worry about. Years later, in
an interview with the trusted journalist María Eugenia Oyarzún,
Pinochet confessed that he never believed the story about the assassination attempt. "Carter gave the order not to receive me," Pinochet
said. "If you receive Pinochet, we will cut everything we give you, and
Marcos liked his little money, you know," Pinochet concluded.

THE NOVEMBER 4, 1980, American presidential election was followed
in Chile with as much anticipation as in the United States. Early in the
evening it became clear that Ronald Reagan was bound for a great victory. Indeed, Reagan won by a landslide. Pro-Pinochet Chileans were
joyous—not so much about Reagan's victory as about Jimmy Carter's
defeat. The hated U.S. president had bitten the dust. Good times were
coming for Pinochet, they assumed.

The Republican candidate had severely criticized Carter's human
rights policy, especially as it had been applied to regimes friendly to
the United States such as Pinochet's Chile. Reagan's criticism was
based upon a distinction between authoritarian and totalitarian governments made popular by Jeane Kirkpatrick, who became the new
administration's ambassador to the United Nations. According to
Kirkpatrick, authoritarian governments in Latin America—right-wing
dictatorships—occur in traditional societies that lack sufficient development for democratic systems to function. Applying excessive pressure on such governments does not generate democracies, but instead
smoothes the way for totalitarian regimes, defined as Marxist-Leninist.
For that reason, the best way to convey the U.S. government's criticism on human rights would be by using "quiet diplomacy"—direct,
private, government-to-government communication—and not by
public accusations.

The conservative orientation of the new administration led the
Pinochet regime to expect decisive changes in U.S. policy. They were
not disappointed. In February 1981, one of Reagan's first moves with
respect to Chile was to lift the ban imposed by the Carter government

on Export-Import Bank–subsidized credits to finance American exports to Chile, followed by an invitation to the Chilean Navy to participate in the UNITAS hemispheric naval exercises. The U.S. government later modified its negative vote on World Bank and Inter-American Development Bank credits for Chile.

In June the Chilean foreign minister, René Rojas, went to Washington, where he was received by Vice President George H. W. Bush and Secretary of State Alexander Haig. Rojas expressed his hope that the White House would ask Congress to lift the Kennedy Amendment banning arms sales to Chile, as it had done in the cases of El Salvador, Argentina, and Angola.

Rojas also discussed repealing the amendment with the Republican senator Howard Baker and the conservative Republican senator Jesse Helms. Senator Helms and his colleague Strom Thurmond of South Carolina had earlier drafted a letter to Henry Kissinger supporting the resumption of military aid to Chile, in which they asserted that the Pinochet regime was "a government which provides more freedom than exists in most of the countries of the world at the present time."

Helms and Thurmond had been in Chile in August 1975 to meet with Pinochet and to bolster his regime. Senator Helms, who became a strong personal friend of Pinochet's, proposed the outright abolition of the Kennedy Amendment. However, the Democrats, headed by Senator Edward Kennedy, negotiated a compromise agreement with moderate Republicans that made the resumption of military aid dependent on President Reagan's certification that there had been "significant improvement in human rights." This congressional agreement also specified that the Chilean government had to cooperate in the investigation of the Letelier case and display an attitude of clear opposition to international terrorism.

Reagan wasted no time in sending positive signals to Pinochet. The U.S. ambassador to Chile, George Landau, a career diplomat who in his Paraguay posting had uncovered the false passports scheme that pointed to the DINA as the culprit in Letelier's murder, was replaced by the reliably right-wing James Theberge, a former colleague of Kirkpatrick's at Georgetown University. A pro-Pinochet Washington lobbying group, the American-Chilean Council, had in 1975 published an essay by Theberge entitled "Chile: Key Target of Soviet Diplomacy" as the first in a series of propaganda pamphlets.

Everyone believed that the certification concerning human rights would soon be forthcoming. But as it turned out, Reagan did not provide it and by 1983 there were discernible tensions between Santiago and Washington. Given Reagan's campaign for democracy, aimed primarily at the Soviet Union, the White House wanted to see at least some signs of political tolerance on the part of the Pinochet regime so that it could justify Chile's certification before Congress and U.S. public opinion. But human rights in Chile suffered a setback during these years instead of an improvement.

Kirkpatrick visited Santiago in August 1981 for a meeting with Pinochet that she described as "most pleasant." Only three days after her visit, Pinochet expelled four opposition leaders from the country, including Jaime Castillo, chairman of the Chilean Committee of Human Rights, for having signed a declaration of solidarity with labor union leaders who had been put on trial for submitting a labor rights petition to Pinochet. Castillo and other human rights attorneys had unsuccessfully sought an interview with Kirkpatrick during her visit to Chile. In April 1982, the *New York Times* ran an editorial under the headline "Quiet Diplomacy, Deaf Chile," which criticized President Reagan's low-keyed human rights policy, noting Pinochet's continuing human rights crimes and his government's manifest lack of cooperation on the Letelier case.

Not surprisingly, when the U.S. Senate Republican majority leader, Howard Baker, visited Chile in January 1982, along with his colleagues Paul Laxalt and Ernest Hollings, he was cautious in his statements. After meeting with Pinochet, Baker declared, "There are still problems which complicate our relations. In the course of this visit we have discussed such problems in detail and with frankness." On the subject of "quiet diplomacy" Senator Baker added that "the success or failure of this new technique depends largely upon how the other countries, including Chile, will react to it."

Secretary of State George Shultz stated in mid-1982 that, in order for the White House to grant certification to Chile, "We would have to find evidence of an improvement of the human rights situation," as well as "some clarification concerning the investigations of the Letelier case." Authorities in the White House wished to give Chile the desired certification—but Chile would have to meet them halfway.

Five

REGIME ON
THE ROPES

Iwas sitting in an unmarked police bus with an automatic rifle pointed at my head when Pablo Neruda's widow, Matilde Urrutia, shouted, *"Compañero,* yell your name! Tell us your name!" It was February 1979, when dissidents in Chile were still disappearing. Knowing a political prisoner's name and tracing his or her detention place could make the difference between life and death.

None of the academic seminars I had attended in Washington, D.C., and Europe during my period abroad, between September 1975 and September 1978, had prepared me for the brute reality of the Chilean police state. I had rejected several attractive job opportunities in the United States to be a researcher at the Institute of International Studies of the University of Chile, an oasis of relative freedom within the Pinochet-controlled state universities. Pamela remained in Denver to wrap up her job at a medical human resources company while I returned to Santiago to look for a place to live. I had promised her that I wouldn't get involved in underground activities. But soon after arriving, in September, 1978, I contacted Socialist Party activists.

By early February 1979, I was deeply involved in the Socialist efforts to demand public respect for labor rights. My brother Carlos and I went to a demonstration at Diego de Almagro Square, close to downtown. The atmosphere seemed a little strange when we got there. There were fifty or sixty demonstrators in the middle of the square and many more civilians observing—not all of whom seemed to be our supporters. We felt reassured by the presence of Matilde Urrutia, the respected and well-known widow of the poet Pablo Neruda. But our forebodings were swiftly borne out; no sooner had a couple of union leaders climbed onto an improvised platform to speak than police vehicles appeared out of nowhere and all hell broke loose.

Two Carabineros grabbed me and tried to drag me away. They were smaller than me and I put up a good fight at first, but when other policemen came to their aid I went limp. I was violently thrown inside a bus, which already held a half dozen or so detainees, and ordered to sit. A few minutes later my captors pushed an obviously pregnant woman onto the bus with such violence that she practically flew across the narrow bus corridor. I strongly protested, using some choice language. A Carabinero struck at my head with the butt of his automatic rifle. I covered my head just in time and the blow landed on the fingers and palm on my right hand. The pain was excruciating (two fingers were fractured, as it turned out), but I saved my skull. While another young detainee who had also protested the woman's treatment was severely beaten in the back of the bus, the policeman who hit me pointed his gun at my head.

"If you don't stay in your seat I will put a bullet in your head," he screamed. "Just try to move!" he challenged me.

Not only was he completely out of control, he seemed more a criminal than a law enforcer. It was at that moment that Neruda's widow approached the bus and demanded the release of the prisoners. When her appeal failed, she approached the window of the bus where I was sitting with a gun at my head, and asked my name. I decided not to risk testing the policeman's will. I could not believe that the same person who had enjoyed intellectually stimulating lunches at the Brookings Institution a few months before had now landed in the back of a dirty Carabineros bus with a gun to his head.

All of the detainees, about fifteen of us, were taken to a nearby precinct on San Francisco Street. There, we were forced to kneel on a cement patio. "So you were insulting my General Pinochet," one of the policemen said, just before they began to beat us. When they had finished, we were ordered to remain on our knees. As time passed and we no longer saw the Carabineros around, several of us tried to lift a knee off the floor, to relieve the pain. To our surprise, one of our fellow "prisoners" summoned the policemen, shouting, "This one, that one, and that other one," as he pointed at me and other detainees who were not fully kneeling. The supposed prisoner was an undercover cop who was there to watch us and ascertain any other dangerous plans we had besides peaceful protests.

As I was identified as one of those violating the order to remain on my knees, two Carabineros struck me with their sticks and kicked me with their heavy-duty boots. My back hurt—later it turned black and blue—but the pain in my fractured fingers far eclipsed the new beating. After a few more hours of kneeling—the cold cement alleviated the pain in my fingers—we were ordered to stand and hand over our identification papers. From then on, we were no longer subjected to torture or ill treatment.

It was sometime past midnight when we were released. My family had been beside themselves with worry; they'd already contacted a Catholic priest they knew to try to find me. I made them promise not to tell Pamela, who was still in Denver, that I had been arrested.

A week later I was supposed to appear before a local police court, along with my fellow detainees. We arrived around 8 A.M., only to discover that, since we were accused of provoking public disorders and "insulting the President of the Republic," our case had been elevated to a major crimes tribunal (*Quinto Tribunal de Mayor Cuantía*). One of my university colleagues, Raymundo Barros, offered to be my defense lawyer. Though criminal law was not his forte (he was a well-known expert in international law), I trusted him with my criminal case. Together, we prepared my defense. I would declare that I hadn't been involved in the demonstration at all, that I had been browsing for old books in a nearby used bookstore when I heard the uproar from the square and had gone over to see what was happening. A jazz musician who knew me through a cousin offered to attest that he had seen me in the bookstore.

When we finally appeared in the criminal court, everything went fine. The magistrate accepted my defense and my witness and, actually, seemed annoyed with the case. I was "temporarily acquitted" of the charges, meaning that the case could be reopened at some future date. Nothing ever happened again, and except for one of my fractured fingers, which never healed properly, I soon forgot about the arrest and beating I suffered that February 1979.

Attending demonstrations was only a small part of my political activities. Shortly before moving back to Chile, I went to Europe and met in East Berlin with a former Socialist congressman, Víctor Barberis, who was based in Mexico and was in charge of the North America office of the party. Our rendezvous was at the East Berlin home of the Socialist leader, Clodomiro Almeyda.

The East German government of President Erich Honecker had been generous with Chileans, welcoming thousands of refugees such as Almeyda. In the German Democratic Republic (GDR) most Chilean refugees had jobs, a chance to study, schooling for their children, and other benefits. So it was not surprising that when the Berlin Wall fell and the GDR dissolved, Honecker sought refuge at the Chilean embassy in Moscow, where Almeyda was chief of mission; he eventually traveled to live in Santiago, where he died in May 1994. But life in East Germany became unbearable for many, particularly for Socialists accustomed to the freedom, critical debate, and nonconformism we had known in pre-coup Chile. The discipline and control exercised by the East German Communist Party made Chilean Socialists uneasy. Permissions to travel outside the GDR were often delayed or denied. The Stasi secret police and its informants spied on Chilean exiles (as well as their own citizens).

Víctor Barberis explained that the Socialist Party was going through difficult times. I thought he was referring to the challenges of surviving in exile, but he was actually talking about a brewing division within the Socialists that rank-and-file activists like me did not yet perceive. Once I returned to Chile, I should contact Ricardo Lagos, a Socialist economist, he instructed me. "You're a scholar and we need detailed proposals that are in touch with day-to-day Chilean reality."

I went to see Lagos about a month after I returned to Chile. We had a good conversation. Lagos told me that leftist scholars and activists were analyzing the Chilean reality at some social science centers and he invited me to attend those meetings. Lagos also suggested we get together socially as soon as Pamela arrived from the United States.

At Vector Center of Economic and Social Studies, directed then by the labor expert Manuel Barrera and located in downtown Miraflores Street, we discussed politics and society from a Socialist perspective. At the time academic institutions were difficult to maintain financially, but we struggled to keep them afloat because they became vital instruments for dissidents to regroup. They also provided a framework for opposition political convergence; for example, the left's Vector Center and the Latin American Social Sciences Faculty (Facultad Latinoamericana de Ciencias Sociales, FLACSO) coordinated some activities with the Christian Democratic–leaning Corporation for Latin American Studies (Corporación de Estudios para Latinoamérica, CIEPLAN). I got to know several colleagues at these institutions who eventually became good friends.

Things took a more practical turn when the brilliant sociologist Enzo Faletto decided to invite a small group of Socialists to meet every Thursday at Vector. The idea was to diagnose what had gone wrong with the Allende government and from there to develop an effective strategy to confront the dictatorship, rooted in hard-nosed analyses of present reality and not in preconceived ideological schemes.

The meetings were attended by Lagos, Faletto, Ricardo Nuñez, Luis Alvarado, Rodrigo Alvayay, Eduardo Ortiz (who became director of Vector at a new, more affordable location), Eduardo Trabucco, me, and a few others. We became known as "the Thursday group." Our discussions were honest and self-critical; it became clear to all of us that the radicalized Socialist Party bore a significant share of the responsibility for Allende's downfall. Moreover, we perceived that Chile was changing. For example, the growth of the services sector of the economy, combined with the repression of labor leaders, was causing union membership to drop dramatically, which naturally led to a decline in the political power of industrial workers.

Also, death, repression, and exile had made Socialists reappraise the paramount value of the rule of law, which some had criticized in the past by opposing "formal" to "real" democracy. Many Socialists began to read the work of the Italian philosopher Norberto Bobbio, who had written that those committed to social change "must defend above all the rule of law. Providing it, certainly, with new content," as he said, "but never forgetting that the new content, if not inserted in the structures of the rule of law, will end up becoming new instruments of inequality and oppression." In addition, some Socialists began to advocate different, more open party structures, capable of incorporating new challenges besides the class struggle, such as gender equality, environmental protection, and decentralization of power. Such Socialists began to be called "renovated."

After our 9/11, the Socialist Party had fallen apart. Its internal tensions, reflected in a 1967 party Congress vote endorsing "revolutionary violence" while, at the same time, electing the most moderate secretary general, Senator Aniceto Rodríguez, had intensified with repression. Some leaders had sought asylum in embassies and others had been jailed or killed. In 1975 the "Internal Secretariat," composed of Ricardo Lagos Salinas (no relation to the Socialist economist Ricardo Lagos Escobar), Carlos Lorca, and Exequiel Ponce, had been made to disappear by Pinochet's DINA. Abroad, the "External Secretariat" was led by Carlos Altamirano. In 1978, during a Socialist conference that was called the Algiers meeting but was held in Berlin for security reasons, Altamirano abandoned his view that Allende's overthrow was due to the lack of "a military policy to face up to a conflict that was inevitable and that ultimately needed a military-type resolution." In addition, instead of advocating the classical alliance of the left with the Communist Party, Altamirano now believed that the Socialists had to seek a long-term understanding with the centrist Christian Democrats.

The new leaders of the Internal Secretariat disagreed with Altamirano's diagnosis and rejected the idea of an alliance with Christian Democrats at the expense of the Communists. In April 1979, the Internal Secretariat removed Altamirano as secretary-general and replaced him with Clodomiro Almeyda.

The Altamirano group responded by holding a conference of its own in Paris that became known as the Twenty-fourth Congress of the Socialist Party. The Internal Secretariat's decisions were disavowed; Almeyda was accused of attempting to impose on the party a "supposedly Marxist-Leninist, ahistorical, outmoded and antidemocratic orthodoxy." Ricardo Nuñez, the former secretary-general of the State Technical University, who had lived in East Berlin but who could enter Chile legally, was named party chief. In short, the Socialist Party, the party of Allende, had experienced a schism, just when unity was most needed to confront Pinochet.

We could not believe the news when we heard it. "This is a gift for Pinochet," Ricardo Lagos said.

Behind the Socialist split was a deep disagreement over how to confront Pinochet and, eventually, about the future of democratic politics in Chile. The "renovated Socialists" shared the diagnosis made by Enrico Berlinguer, secretary-general of the Italian Communist Party, who, reflecting on the Allende experience, had called for a "historical compromise" between the left and Christian Democracy as the only sensible option to ensure a democratic road to socialism. A new social bloc for change had to be created based on mass struggle and political consensus; what was needed was "not a leftist alternative, but a democratic alternative," argued Berlinguer. The European debate on Chile led to what later would become widely known as "Euro-Communism."

In the short term, an alliance with the Christian Democratic Party was essential to confront the dictatorship in Chile. But later, too, a coalition with Christian Democracy—a historic compromise, in Berlinguer's words—would also be needed to break the three-thirds logjam of Chilean presidentialism, in which a strong left, a strong center, and a relatively strong right canceled one another out, and in the end just one sector tended to govern alone, as a minority, an inherently unstable arrangement. An alliance of Socialists and Christian Democrats would ensure a majority coalition for future democratic stability and social change, we thought.

Also behind the Socialist rupture and the intraleft polarization was a deep disagreement about the importance of democracy. When the Solidarity labor movement led by Lech Walesa rose against Communist rule in Poland, the Chilean Communist Party secretary-general, Luis Corvalán, blamed the problems on "the abandonment by Polish Communists of Leninist principles and internal party norms." In January 1982 Corvalán praised the repressive measures taken by General Woijciech Jaruzelski "to impede a bloodbath similar to that of Chile." In contrast, the Socialist leader, Carlos Altamirano, had visited Warsaw in 1981 to meet with Walesa in order to convey to him and to the Solidarity movement the full support of the Chilean Socialist Party, or at least of its "renovated" wing.

Lagos and I decided not to take sides on the Socialist division, though we felt closer to the Altamirano-Nuñez group. Instead, Lagos decided to launch a campaign for reunification. The major division within the Socialist Party had been preceded by the emergence of other, smaller, splinter groups. This would be the chance to bring them all back together. Since many in the Thursday group had opted to remain neutral, we began to be invited to the reunification conversations as "honest brokers."

During a visit to Mexico, Ricardo Lagos met with Hortensia "Tencha" Bussi, President Allende's widow, who asked about his stand on the Almeyda-Altamirano rupture. Lagos explained our position. "Then you are the Swiss. You are neutral like the Swiss," Tencha said. The name stuck.

"How can we join the Swiss?" many Socialists asked us. I responded that we were not another faction. "We simply will not take sides on the division and we believe that most rank-and-file Socialists want a united party to fight Pinochet," I repeated.

Socialist groups and factions mushroomed during this period of division. They all claimed to represent the party. As if "the Swiss" were referees in the conflict, the leaders of those groups began to meet with us to argue their respective cases. In the meantime, a movement of "Socialist Convergence" began to develop in the early eighties, involving mainly small leftists groups and parties that were splinter groups from the Christian Democratic Party in the late sixties and early seventies, as well as independents. The "Socialist Convergence" movement saw the vacuum caused by the atomization of the historic Socialist Party as an opportunity to supersede it through the creation of a broader force of all progressive and Socialist-leaning forces. But Ricardo Lagos, I, and a few other Socialists, although we attended those meetings, never abandoned our efforts at encouraging Socialist Party reunification. The Socialist Party, being firmly rooted in Chilean society, seemed to us indispensable for fighting the Pinochet dictatorship. The Convergence movement gradually dissolved as the Socialist Party regained its unity.

By 1980 Pinochet had overcome serious challenges to his power. He had expelled Air Force General Gustavo Leigh from the junta in 1978; he had avoided war with Argentina over the Beagle Channel dispute, which was now in a mediation process in the hands of Pope John Paul II; he had offset U.S. pressures over the Letelier case by handing over the DINA agent Michael Townley and dissolving the DINA secret police; and he had dictated an amnesty for all who had committed crimes between September 1973 and March 10, 1978, except for the pending investigation of the Letelier case.

But if he had kept his foes at bay, he was subject to pressures from within his own coalition, on both sides of the political spectrum. The moderates within his government, especially the Chicago Boys, felt that the free-market economic model could only be validated internationally and sustained domestically if there was at least a semblance of democracy. Jorge Alessandri, a former conservative president (1958–1964), and his allies on the traditional right were embarrassed by Chile's pariah status. Perhaps a "protected democracy," embodied in a new constitution, would be an option that Pinochet could accept. Besides, Chile's long and cherished legal tradition demanded a constitutional legitimation of the Pinochet regime. Pinochet's base, his hard-line supporters, of course did not want any constitution.

A constitutional commission, headed by Enrique Ortúzar, who had been a minister in the conservative Alessandri administration, had been created in 1973, but five years went by before Pinochet asked them to present a draft constitution for his consideration. The Council of State, a ghost institution created strictly for cosmetic reasons, headed by Alessandri, was to consider the draft constitution. The former president took his role seriously; to Pinochet's annoyance, he introduced temporary articles to the document that established concrete dates and mechanisms for the transition to a "protected democracy." Pinochet would stay on as president until 1985, but his powers would decline progressively. The military junta would cease to be the "legislative power," and would retain only an advisory function.

Pinochet did not like the proposition. He wanted to remain in power for at least another sixteen years after 1980; probably Pinochet calculated that by 1997 he would be eighty-one years old, a good age to begin thinking about retirement. Ortúzar diplomatically suggested that sixteen years might be too long. "Fine," Pinochet said, walking to a blackboard where he drew a vertical line. "Eight years and we cut." Pinochet drew another line. "Then another eight years. In the middle we hold a ratification plebiscite." The issue was settled.

The constitution established an eight-year "transition period" toward, at best, a protected democracy, punctuated by a plebiscite in 1988 that would "approve" (or "disapprove") a single candidate as president of the Republic. A transitory article in the constitution spelled out that the commanders in chief of the armed forces and the general director of Carabineros would "unanimously propose to the country," at least ninety days before the end of Pinochet's eight-year transition mandate, the person to occupy the presidency for the following eight years. No specific date was fixed for the plebiscite; no specific candidate name was mentioned in the transitory section of the constitution. Pinochet naturally assumed that he would be the official candidate and would continue in power to complete the full sixteen years. In the unlikely event that the person proposed by the armed forces lost the plebiscite, the constitution determined that Pinochet would continue for one more year and presidential and congressional elections would take place in 1989. Otherwise, the earliest date for elections would be 1997. Alessandri protested Pinochet's decision and quietly resigned his post.

Besides being tailored to accommodate Pinochet's personal rule, the new constitution was overwhelmingly antidemocratic. The Senate it established was non elected to a significant extent; it created a military-controlled National Security Council; it impeded the president of the Republic's power to remove the commanders in chief of the armed forces; and it was virtually impossible to amend.

Nevertheless, in August 1980 Pinochet cynically called for a referendum to ratify the constitution—a national election that would be held just one month after he announced it. Not only did the opposition have almost no time to prepare its campaign, but also it was denied access to the pro-government newspapers and television. All public demonstrations against the constitution were forbidden; with my own eyes I saw people being dragged off a public bus and beaten for shouting, "Vote 'no' on the charter!" The dictatorship authorized just one opposition rally—the first since the coup—on August 27. It was held in an indoor arena, the Teatro Caupolicán on San Diego Street. Press access was denied, except for a couple of radio stations close to the Catholic church. The perimeter of the theater was cordoned off by Carabineros, and hundreds of police were deployed right outside. The arena was packed to the rafters, with about ten thousand people. Crowds of people were unable to get in. I was inside; the atmosphere of courage and contained energy was electric.

The main speaker was former president Eduardo Frei Montalva, the distinguished Christian Democratic politician who had opposed President Allende's Popular Unity government. Frei minced no words. He denounced the constitution as illegitimate in its origins and antidemocratic in its substance; it was "illegal, science fiction, and a fraud," he added for good measure. A "no" vote would at least be a testimonial gesture by the people.

As we exited the arena, melées broke out between the police and the participants. Since there were so many of us, we fought back—throwing and landing punches and kicks on our attackers. That night the TV anchorman Patricio Bañados of the University of Chile's Channel 11 refused to read several paragraphs of a news report that viciously attacked Frei and the rally. His contract stipulated that he was not obligated to read insults or lies against persons or institutions. When Bañados stepped off the set, the director of the channel was waiting to fire him.

The plebiscite was held on September 11, 1980. The "yes" vote got 67 percent, against a 30.1 percent "no." In some boroughs and towns more people voted than actually lived there. Pinochet was jubilant. At a rally in front of the junta headquarters on the night of September 11, 1980, he gave a speech celebrating his victory. He promised jobs, new housing projects, cars, telephones and television sets, and the creation of a great "military-civilian movement for Chile" during the next eight years. The following day Pinochet gave a press conference. When asked why he had said one day before the constitutional referendum that he would not be a candidate if elections took place in 1989—a startling statement that would come back to haunt him years later—he seemed to confirm it: "I have never said that I will not be a candidate. I said that I would not be here. I have said hundreds of times that I do not aspire to reelection, because a man over seventy years old does not perform adequately in a post like this."

On March 11, 1981, Pinochet was sworn in as president of the Republic according to the provisions of the new constitution. He moved the presidency to a rebuilt La Moneda palace, away from his former junta colleagues. Some time later, Pinochet had himself promoted to captain general of the army, a rank that only the national hero and liberator, Bernardo O'Higgins, had held before. Pinochet added a few inches to his military cap to make him look taller than his army comrades. Admiral Merino complained privately that he now had to request an audience with Pinochet through his Army Advisory Committee.

PINOCHET FELT STRONGER than ever. Not only had he overcome the problems that plagued him during 1978 and 1979, but he had won the plebiscite. To top things off, Ronald Reagan had been elected president of the United States. The opposition would feel the impact. Human rights leaders were kicked out of the country, and Frei Montalva died mysteriously after undergoing surgery.

On Thursday, February 25, 1982, Tucapel Jiménez, president of the National Association of Public Employees (Agrupación Nacional de Empleados Fiscales, ANEF), was declared missing after he failed to appear at any of the labor union meetings that he was scheduled to attend that day. One week earlier Jiménez had made a public appeal for the unity of all workers and their organizations to fight for democracy and against the government's economic policy. The official newspaper, La Nación, had denounced his statement as echoing the "phraseology of international Communism," and had attacked the ANEF, calling it "the best bastion of Marxists, though their leaders disguise themselves as Social Democrats." Pinochet himself had issued oblique threats against Jiménez, though he was careful not to name him specifically.

Jiménez's body was found that same evening, in the rural borough of Lampa, north of Santiago, inside the taxi he drove for a living. The Datsun 150Y was found on a dirt road; strangely, it was surprisingly clean, particularly the door handle on the driver's side. He had been shot in the head and his throat was slashed. Juan Alegría, a poor carpenter from Valparaíso, confessed in writing to the murder before committing suicide by slashing his wrists and hanging himself. Supposedly he had simply wanted to rob Jiménez, but when he learned of the union leader's identity he was overcome with remorse. Later, it was discovered that Jiménez had been assassinated by the CNI and Alegría was murdered as part of the cover-up; his confession was a complete fabrication.

Just when everything seemed to be going right for Pinochet, the Chicago economic model tumbled and came crashing down.

By 1981 Chile was in the midst of an economic boom. Fixing the price of the peso at a low rate of thirty-nine to the U.S. dollar had stimulated massive imports of goods that were either new to local consumers or that Chile had manufactured in the past. A formerly discreet bourgeoisie now flaunted its prosperity with luxury cars, mansions, and shopping sprees abroad, while the poorer sectors attempted to participate in the consumption boom by taking on debt to purchase portable radios or television sets. Unemployment, though, remained stubbornly high, at about 17 percent, as factories went broke as a result of the inflow of cheap imports.

Chilean businesses borrowed heavily in the international financial markets that were replete with "petrodollars." Consumers also borrowed in fixed-rate dollars in the local market. In 1982, 50 percent of the loans granted by the Chilean banking system were in dollars. Getting indebted in dollars was good business, because banks extended loans denominated in cheap dollars at lower interest rates than loans denominated in pesos.

But in May 1981 there was an unexpected alarm signal. The old and prestigious Sugar Refinery Company of Viña del Mar went broke. Furthermore, in 1981, the price of Chilean exports began dropping, while international interest rates increased and the dollar became more expensive.

The rise in the dollar was a result of the Reagan administration's efforts to bring inflation below 10 percent. Paul Volker, head of the Federal Reserve, had increased interest rates, contracting the growth of the money supply, which led to a recession of the American economy beginning in 1982. In parallel, the prices of Chilean commodities, including copper, plunged because of the world economy's downturn. The Chilean economy exhibited a huge balance-of-payments current-account deficit of 15 percent of GDP by the end of 1981.

The Chicago Boys believed that there would be an "automatic correction," that is, high interest rates would attract foreign capital as savings, which would beef up the reserves of the Central Bank. The increase in the availability of money would make interest rates fall. That was the theory, anyway. But reality dictated otherwise. The Central Bank began losing reserves and money became scarce.

Finance Minister Sergio de Castro went on national television on July 24, 1981, to calm things down. He offered an optimistic assessment of the regime's economic achievements, though he warned that difficult times were ahead due to the changing external environment. No radical measures were announced. Though Chilean businesses pleaded for a currency devaluation, Minister de Castro stuck to the Chicago orthodoxy to combat inflation and the value of the peso remained fixed at thirty-nine to the dollar. Instead, he asked Pinochet to decrease spending by restricting consumption. This would be accomplished through a decree lowering public-sector wages, and indicating to the private sector the need to reduce salaries by about 12 to 13 percent to reach a new equilibrium. Wages would fall anyhow through inflation, de Castro argued. He added that devaluating the fixed dollar-peso exchange rate would erode confidence in the regime. Pinochet accepted his minister's position, but the junta disagreed, at least on the wages issue.

At a very tense cabinet meeting presided over by Pinochet, de Castro and Labor Minister Miguel Kast went on the offensive again, this time trying to get an agreement to eliminate the minimum wage as the first step in a gradual approach to adjust the economy. If the minimum wage was not eliminated, Kast and de Castro argued, unemployment would increase, since businesses would prefer to lay off workers than to pay them excessive wages. Kast had requested solidarity from fellow ministers before entering the cabinet meeting room. Almost nobody argued against him, except José Piñera, minister of mining, who insisted that there was no causal relationship between minimum wage and unemployment. Furthermore, he argued, the state had a social responsibility to protect the weak—even a market economy needed regulations that favored the poor. Pinochet agreed with Piñera. The minimum wage would not be scratched. A furious de Castro insulted Piñera as they left the conference room.

On November 2, 1981, the state seized four private banks and four finance companies that were on the brink of collapse. A full-blown crisis had broken out, confirming growing fears about weaknesses in the Chilean banking system. By year's end over half of the capital and reserves of local banks and financial companies had been compromised by bad loans. The economic groups that had grown under the shade of economic liberalism had lent money to their offshoots and sibling companies, and many of them were now defaulting, producing a domino effect in the capital markets. The Banco de Chile, for example, had at least eleven major debtor companies that belonged to its parent conglomerate, the BHC group, headed by the businessman Javier Vial. Several other economic conglomerates were at risk. To avoid total chaos, the Central Bank announced that the state would guarantee the savings deposits in the banks and financial companies that it had taken over—a promise that cost the government some $300 million within the following sixty days.

In April 1982 Pinochet summoned his economic team to La Moneda once again. De Castro insisted that devaluation was not an option. Pinochet gave a hint of things to come when, clearly annoyed, he said, "Why don't we just admit it? This situation, as it stands, is already a failure."

On Friday April 16, 1982, Pinochet summoned de Castro to his office at La Moneda and asked for his resignation. In protest, the whole cabinet resigned en masse. A noticeably shaken Pinochet appeared on television on April 19, 1982, to announce that his cabinet of ministers had resigned and that he would designate a new team shortly. Surprisingly, he still did not immediately announce the currency devaluation, but the removal of the powerful finance minister, de Castro, until then the top Chicago Boy within the Pinochet regime, was a political earthquake.

The Chicago Boys were not a monolithic bloc—some were more fundamentalist in their beliefs than others. The more orthodox Chicago group was led by de Castro. This group, which included Pablo Baraona, Jorge Cauas, Alvaro Bardón, Roberto Kelly, and Miguel Kast, believed that the market was a sphere of automatic exchanges ruled by immutable laws. Following the precepts of philosophers such as Friedrich von Hayek, these economists believed in unlimited economic freedom and saw the role of government as being confined to creating and defending markets and facilitating private initiative; naturally they dismissed Karl Popper's warning about the "paradox of freedom," that unrestrained economic freedom could be as unjust as the exercise of unlimited physical freedom by strong individuals over weak ones, depriving the latter of their freedom. They prioritized reducing inflation and stimulating growth by controlling the money supply, freeing prices, reducing the size of the state (and limiting it to a "subsidiary" role), creating private capital markets, eliminating subsidies, and opening the country to foreign trade. Pinochet felt particularly close to this fundamentalist group because it believed that democracy had to be suspended until the long-term transformations needed in the economy were fully implemented. But Pinochet's alliance with this orthodox circle was, as usual, conditioned by the general's pragmatism in the face of hard reality. That's why at a moment of crisis he veered in the direction of populist economic policies, only to eventually rely on a more pragmatic group of Chicago Boys like Hernán Büchi, José Piñera, and the businessman Carlos Cáceres, who shared the basic orientations of Chicago but were willing to introduce state regulations, subsidize sectors of the economy, and even show some political flexibility to save the market system.

In the midst of the 1982 crisis, Pinochet intended to name military men to the key economic posts. The Chicago Boys launched a counteroffensive when Pinochet floated the name of General Gastón Frez—who had blocked the privatization of copper and had been hostile to the Chicago orthodoxy all along—as a replacement for de Castro. As usual, Pinochet opted for the middle ground. An unimpressive

Chicago economist, Sergio de la Cuadra, was named to Finance, Army General Luis Danús to the economy post, and General Frez was designated minister of planning.

Pinochet's indecisiveness aggravated the problem. The new finance minister, backed by an advisory team of Chicago Boys, clashed with Economy Minister Danús, and cabinet sessions devolved into endless debates, which only confused and irritated the dictator. At one of those meetings, General Frez said to Pinochet, "My general, I would not like it that you should become the first president in recorded history to officially lower wages."

One Sunday in June 1982, Pinochet's military staff ordered the three cabinet members de la Cuadra, Danús, and Frez to report to the Defense Ministry early the next morning for a meeting. Pinochet, who continued as army commander in chief, never lost sight of where his power emanated from: his position as both head of state and head of the army. Hence, on Mondays he worked out of his office at the Defense Ministry, where he would review army matters or phone military attachés in key foreign embassies to be updated on their duties. Naturally, the three ministers assumed that Pinochet wished to address a military problem when they gathered there. They were taken aback by his announcement.

"Gentlemen, we will devaluate," Pinochet abruptly declared.

De la Cuadra was given the responsibility of determining how large the devaluation should be. Economy Minister Danús would announce the measure on national television. Planning Minister Frez would be responsible for taking control of the dollar deposits to avoid a run on the foreign currency. That night General Danús, dressed in military uniform, announced to the nation that the value of the dollar would rise from thirty-nine to forty-six pesos, an 18 percent devaluation of the peso. Furthermore, the peso would continue to slide progressively in relation to a basket of foreign currencies. "Only fools save dollars," I remember the Chicago economist Alvaro Bardón saying just a few days before the devaluation.

Devaluation was a disaster for those who'd borrowed in dollars; overnight their debts multiplied. Businesses went broke, foreclosures shot up, and layoffs skyrocketed. By the end of 1982 unemployment had risen well above 20 percent and the GDP had fallen 13.2 percent. Unemployment was in fact much higher than this, for emergency employment projects, which paid low wages for street sweeping and other menial tasks, disguised the extent of joblessness.

I saw the devaluation from a different perspective. In 1979 Pamela and I had taken out a loan to purchase a modest new apartment on

Vicuña Mackenna Avenue at the end of Florida borough, a semirural sector that was almost an hour from downtown Santiago during rush-hour traffic. Though it was ridiculously overpriced, it was the only place we could afford to buy with our limited dollar savings. One Sunday in 1982, as we were driving around the upper-middle-class borough of La Reina, near the mountains on the eastern side of Santiago, we saw an "open house" sign on Reina Victoria Street, a pleasant tree-lined neighborhood. We decided to stop and take a look. Six Mediterranean-style townhouses were for sale. The townhouses were still under construction but they were beautiful and only minor finishing work was left to be done. Pamela and I were sure that they would be out of our reach, but to our surprise a salesman told us that their prices had been reduced because they belonged to a woman who had borrowed in dollars before the devaluation. Now she was in a hurry to wrap up the construction, sell the houses, and pay off her debts before the dollar went any higher. "She may well accept an offer below her reduced price," the man said. She did. Within two weeks we signed a contract and a few weeks later we sold our apartment in La Florida—at a loss—and transferred our mortgage to the buyer, made a down payment for the La Reina townhouse, and secured a new home loan. Thanks to the devaluation, we had raised our standard of living.

In the meantime, Pinochet turned to his inner circle of military advisers. He instructed his military chief of staff, General Santiago Sinclair, to follow closely the economic discussions going on in his administration and to gather information about the different cliques and alliances that were forming. His new cabinet consisted of ten military officers and only six civilians.

The shock waves from the devaluation were still spreading. The Central Bank decreed restrictions on the purchase of dollars for Chileans traveling abroad, and a "black market" for dollars emerged. The banks' portfolios of unpaid debt climbed to about $1.5 billion, equivalent to 54 percent of the financial system's capital and reserves. Outstanding debts mushroomed as companies continued to go bankrupt. The government devised a formula to bail out the troubled banks: the Central Bank would purchase the banks' bad-debt portfolios in exchange for nontransferable bonds that would be paid back over the course of a decade. But there was one basic condition: lending to affiliated companies would have to be brought under control. Henceforth, "related portfolios" would account for no more than 2.5 percent of a bank's total loan portfolios. One key businessman, Javier Vial of the BHC conglomerate, which controlled 130 companies through its powerful Banco de Chile, resisted the plan.

Vial, a self-confident and aggressive entrepreneur from the Chilean aristocracy, whose business empire had been made possible by the Chicago Boys' privatization policies, did not want to sell off his banks' bad-debt portfolio. Moreover, he had the temerity to criticize Pinochet's economic policy decisions in public.

Pinochet angrily blamed the crisis on Chile's new plutocracy and their Chicago-trained enablers. "I have been too soft," he said. "I should have kicked out of the country one hundred or maybe two hundred people who raised paper empires." Rightly fearing that Pinochet was referring to him, Vial sent more cooperative signals to La Moneda. Still, he refused to relinquish control of his empire. Taking matters into his own hands, he defied both the Pinochet government and the disgraced but still influential Chicago Boys. Using Banco Andino, a Panama-based financial institution owned by his conglomerate, Vial began to illegally channel funds to his BHC companies. Vial's partner, BHC's executive vice president, Rolf Lüders, who had been one of Milton Friedman's favorite Chilean acolytes, resigned from BHC when he saw how few of the measures he had recommended to resolve the crisis were adopted.

Finance Minister Sergio de la Cuadra lasted only four months in his post. In August 1982 Pinochet named Lüders, now an ex-BHC executive, as "bi-minister" of the economy, giving him control of both the finance and economy posts. The idea was to achieve greater coherence in economic policy by putting it in the hands of a well-respected "pragmatist." By then $1 billion in reserves had evaporated. Every day another $22 million escaped the Central Bank through over-the-counter operations.

Lüders focused on reaching a standby agreement with the IMF, which he did in January 1983. Following that agreement, on January 13, 1983, he decreed the administrative seizure of five more banks—including the Banco de Chile and Banco de Santiago—and the liquidation of three other banks. A World Bank expert calculated that by then the Chilean banking system's unpaid loans had reached $4 billion. These new interventions sparked a panic, as Chileans rushed to their banks to withdraw their savings, exacerbating the crisis. In response, the Finance Ministry announced a new set of emergency measures, including the renegotiation of debts, a 20 percent increase in import duties, and a sharp increase in the gas tax.

The cost to the state and the Chilean taxpayer of the Pinochet regime's subsidies to local private banks (since foreign banks would not agree to write off their losses) and purchases of bad loans was about $7 billion. Ironically, after years of enforced privatization, the Pinochet regime now controlled 80 percent of Chile's financial sector; because of the tight connections between the banks and their affiliate companies, Pinochet exercised a greater degree of control over Chile's economy than Allende had ever dreamed of.

Javier Vial was not expelled from the country, but he ended up in prison for illegally funneling funds to BHC companies from the Banco Andino. "Bi-minister" Lüders resigned from Pinochet's cabinet in February 1983 after he was stripped of his post at the Economy Ministry; he joined Vial in jail for his previous involvement in Vial's illegal activities.

THE CLIMATE OF economic crisis—and the reemergence of Socialist leadership—encouraged people to become politically active again, and accelerated political dialogue. The message of Socialist Party re-unification championed by "the Swiss" began to bear fruit and talks to that effect commenced among the principal factions. Surprisingly, we, "the Swiss," were invited to participate in the deliberations. I represented our group in conversations that took place at clandestine locations. Strict security measures were always in place, since many of the participants were prime targets of the secret police. I was pleased to see Almeyda followers at the talks, led by Julio Stuardo and Akin Soto.

A first step toward reunification was reached in early 1983 with the creation of a Permanent Committee for Socialist Unity (Comité Permanente de Unidad Socialista, CPU). One day Ricardo Lagos contacted me as the reunification negotiations advanced toward a formal reunification agreement.

"Both the Almeyda and Altamirano leadership trust us and want the Swiss to be represented in the new organization. They want us to join the Central Committee of the reunified Socialist Party," he said. "Who do you think should be in the Central Committee, aside from you and me?"

We did a quick count of the most active of "the Swiss," all members of the Thursday group. And we agreed on six names, including ourselves. The other four would be Eduardo Ortiz, Jaime Ahumada, Eduardo Trabucco, and Rodrigo Alvayay. Enzo Faletto, our Thursday discussions leader, was an anarchist at heart; he did not want to be considered. So we presented six names. Following our lead, each of the six groups coming together to form the new Central Committee put up six names, for a total of thirty-six. Lagos quipped, "If 'the Swiss' had

had seven names to give them, the new Central Committee of the Socialist Party would have had forty-two instead of thirty-six members!"

As we closed the agreement, though, the Almeyda group balked. Those in Berlin and some of the local leaders disagreed with the "renovation" ideas that the majority of the pro-unity Socialists held. But in the end some Almeyda militants, led by Julio Stuardo and Akin Soto, decided to stay with the reunification process, which culminated on September 4, 1983, as the CPU transformed itself into the Socialist Party of Chile. Though the result wasn't quite what he'd hoped for, it was much better than the rupture experienced in April 1979.

Our next task was to seek common ground with the Christian Democrats so that we could present a united front against Pinochet. The Christian Democratic Party had been illegal since 1977. By 1982 their leader, Eduardo Frei Montalva, had died under suspicious circumstances; Andrés Zaldívar, another important leader, had been exiled. In late 1982, Gabriel Valdés, a former foreign minister, was chosen president of the Christian Democrats, along with a new directorate composed of leaders such as Patricio Aylwin and Sergio Molina. They were ready for an alliance with the Socialists.

I began to travel throughout Chile to meet with activists, sometimes in groups of no more than a dozen people, to recruit them back into the organization and rebuild our old networks. I remember a round-faced old man in Osorno, a town in the southern lakes region, who shed tears when we invited him and others to become active again in the party. "I thought I would die with the sorrow of Allende's downfall and without ever seeing my Socialist Party rise. Thank you for renewing my hopes," he said.

On March 15, 1983, an important step had been taken toward the creation of a powerful, concerted opposition to Pinochet when a "Democratic Manifesto" was signed by leaders of the Christian Democratic Party, the Radical Party, a small social democratic group, and even an anti-Pinochet contingent of the right. Two Socialists signed as well, as individuals. Six months later, on August 16, 1983, the signatories of the Democratic Manifesto established a new coalition that became known as the Democratic Alliance (Alianza Democrática, AD); its members shared basic democratic principles and a commitment to peaceful methods of struggle against the dictatorship. Our Socialist Party in process of final reunification, led then by the former Allende interior minister, Carlos Briones, joined the coalition. I attended the constitution of the AD at a gathering with hundreds of participants in a private club, the Spanish Circle, where a jovial and optimistic atmosphere could be felt. We did not realize it then, but that was the end of the Popular Unity coalition that had taken Allende to the presidency more than a decade before.

The decision to join our efforts with the Christian Democrats and other anti-Pinochet groups who did not share our overall ideology had been heatedly debated within our ranks. We had concluded that all the democratic forces in Chile had to unite in peaceful struggle against Pinochet. In contrast, the Almeyda wing of the Socialist Party, which did not join the AD, along with the MIR (Movimiento de Izquierda Revolucionaria) and the Communist Party, advocated "all forms of struggle," including violent insurrection.

The AD issued a document that we had previously discussed within the Socialist Party entitled "Bases for Dialogue Toward a Grand National Agreement," which outlined the steps that we needed to take to regain democracy, including, first and foremost, a truly democratic constitution that would emanate from a genuinely representative constitutional assembly. Pinochet had to resign and a social pact would need to be negotiated to sustain a provisional government. It was a daring platform, but Pinochet was too distracted by the economic crisis to try to quash us.

In fact, in mid-1983, the leadership of the Socialist Party had come out from underground. We convened a press conference to announce that, ten years after the coup, the Socialist Party was once again a vital part of the national political landscape. "Either we are all going to jail, or we will open a space for tolerated political discourse," a member of our political commission declared. The next day, a newspaper published a news report headlined "Socialist Party: 'It Is Time to Abandon Clandestine Activities.'" Nobody went to jail, although the security forces began to follow us and at times hit us with repressive actions.

We Socialists still hadn't given up on the Communist Party. We visualized the AD as an embryonic foundation of a future government of national unity integrated by all opposition parties, from the Christian Democrats to the Communists. The model we had in mind was the Provisional Government of the French Republic toward the end of World War II (1944–1946), led by Charles de Gaulle and based on a tripartite alliance of the Christian Democratic, Socialist, and Communist parties. But the differences regarding methods of struggle against Pinochet made an agreement with the Communists virtually impossible. Nevertheless, our Socialist Party attempted to create an informal coordination mechanism through the "Socialist

Bloc," a small coalition of leftist parties, which would serve as a bridge between the Democratic Alliance and the Communist Party. The Communists refused the offer, demanding "to sit at the main table" of the Democratic Alliance, an unrealistic aspiration in view of their insurrectional policy. The Communists and the Almeyda Socialists opted instead to create their own leftist alliance, the MDP (Movimiento Democrático Popular).

The economic crisis had aroused Chilean workers. Chile's most powerful union, the 23,000-member Confederation of Copper Workers (Confederación de Trabajadores del Cobre, CTC), which was led at the time by Rodolfo Seguel, a dynamic twenty-nine-year-old, contacted Democratic Alliance leaders to propose a national strike against Pinochet's economic policies and dictatorial regime. A national strike struck us as an excessively ambitious goal. Instead, a national day of protest was set for May 11, 1983.

The political climate was dangerous. Just a few months before, in December 1982, two labor union leaders, Manuel Bustos and Héctor Cuevas, had been arrested and expelled from the country for attempting a street rally like the one in which I had been arrested a couple of years earlier. Moreover, Pinochet had reacted strongly against the protests of farmers, many of whom were seeing their land auctioned out from under them to satisfy debts. Their leader, a wheat producer named Carlos Podlech, a right-wing former army captain who had served with Pinochet, was also expelled from the country.

During the national day of protest, workers and employees would slow down their usual rate of production and leave work early, children would be kept home from school, nonessential purchases would be avoided, and, most important, all citizens would bang on pots and pans as an audible sign of defiance against the regime at precisely 8 P.M. The Cooperativa radio station, owned by opposition figures, would keep the public informed about the protest plans.

There was a strange mood in the air that May 11. There was less traffic than usual on the streets, absenteeism in schools was high, and incidents occurred in several universities by midday. The national copper company acknowledged that copper-mine workers had paralyzed production. Most shops downtown closed very early and public transportation was scarce by late afternoon. There was an air of nervous anticipation in the desolate streets of Santiago by 6 P.M., usually the height of rush hour. I went out to see for myself what was happening. I sensed that Chileans were quietly preparing for the protest at 8 P.M., though I knew that it might simply be fear that I saw in my compatriots' faces as they rushed homeward.

At eight o'clock, Pamela and I stood expectantly on the patio of our townhouse in Reina Victoria Street. We heard nothing—no protest, no noise. Suddenly there was a banging of pots several blocks away, then more noise from different spots north, east, and south of our neighborhood. Pamela and I began to bang on our own pots and pans. Our neighbors to the left and to the right joined in. Everybody seemed to be protesting; beneath the anonymity of the clear night sky it was a cacophonous symphony of defiance. It was a huge victory for the opposition.

The noise continued; soon, automobiles added to the clamor as their drivers honked their horns, as they did when the Chilean national team won a big soccer match or qualified for the World Cup.

Armed with Uzi submachine guns and dogs, the Carabineros at first did not know how to react. Then, as was their fashion, they perpetrated indiscriminate acts of violence: in Tomás Moro and Bilbao streets and in La Reina borough, they fired their tear-gas canisters randomly at large apartment buildings; they smashed the windshields of honking cars and dragged their drivers out and beat them. But there were too many cars for them to make a difference, as I saw for myself when I took to the streets, triumphantly honking my horn. In some shantytowns, dwellers put up barricades and set tires and debris on fire.

Over six hundred people were arrested that night. Rodolfo Seguel and other union leaders were charged with violating state security laws and were removed from their trade union posts. A furious Pinochet suspended Cooperativa radio station's press privileges; the transmitters of other dissident radio stations were destroyed. At daybreak on Saturday, May 14, army troops cordoned off five of Santiago's largest slums, ordered all the men and teenagers into soccer fields, and made house-to-house searches for weapons and opposition propaganda material. But Seguel and the AD were not intimidated or discouraged. We dared to hope that with a few more protests, Pinochet might be forced to resign. A second protest was called for June 14, 1983.

My friends Arturo and Samuel Valenzuela, Chilean-American academics who taught in the States—Arturo at Georgetown University and Samuel at Yale—were in Chile at the time, so I invited them to observe the action with me. As the banging of pots and pans began, we climbed into my VW Amazon and drove through the upper-class streets of Providencia.

"Do you want to go to a more dangerous neighborhood?" I asked imprudently. "Of course," the Valenzuela brothers responded.

We headed toward the Grecia Circle as the protest heightened, only to find ourselves in the midst of a violent demonstration. Barricades of boulders and burning tires blocked the street, manned by protesters wearing ski masks. I honked the horn, signaling that we were on their side. Then, since there was no traffic around, I violently drove the car over the curb and along the sidewalk to get past the barriers. The clamor of banging pots was deafening as I steered along the narrow sidewalk. All the while Samuel Valenzuela, apparently unfazed by our immediate situation, yelled, "There is a civil society in Chile! By God, there is civil society!"

There was tear gas mixed with the smoke; the fumes were almost unbearable. Even so, the car did not bottom out in a ditch or get jammed between a burning barrier and a wall. Once we were back on the pavement, I drove down Grecia Avenue and turned onto Pedro de Valdivia Street toward Providencia borough. People were out in the streets banging pots and waving Chilean flags. After we'd driven about ten blocks, there was a loud noise from under the car. It was a blowout. When we got out of the car, we discovered a *"miguelito"* sticking out of one of the tires, a twisted nail sharpened on both ends to stop vehicles.

The June 14 protest was far more successful than the first one because it spread to provincial cities. Pinochet fairly sputtered with rage: "To the *señores* politicians I tell them: very soon we will send them to their dirty caves!" Three protesters were killed by stray bullets fired by police forces and undercover CNI agents who patrolled working-class neighborhoods in unmarked vehicles. At about 1:30 A.M. a dozen security agents surrounded the house where the union leader, Seguel, was staying that night and took him away. Seguel's arrest and that of other union leaders prompted a call by a dissident group called Project for National Development (Proyecto de Desarrollo Nacional, PRODEN) for a national strike on July 12, which, though it again did not succeed as a work stoppage, turned into another protest. Instead, we centered our efforts on the fourth national protest, scheduled for August 11, 1983.

The day before the fourth protest, Pinochet reshuffled his cabinet once again, this time bringing in as interior minister an experienced politician, Chile's ambassador to Argentina, Sergio Onofre Jarpa, the old right-wing opponent of President Allende and the former leader of the National Party. Jarpa's mission was to seek some sort of understanding with the opposition. Jarpa did not like the Chicago Boys and he blamed them for the economic crisis. But Pinochet had not entirely abandoned the liberal economic line—he had replaced the fallen finance minister, Lüders, with Carlos Cáceres, a pro-free-market lawyer. As usual, Pinochet was covering all his bases.

Encouraged by the newly appointed Catholic archbishop of Santiago, Cardinal Juan Francisco Fresno, and the U.S. State Department, Jarpa, acting as a virtual prime minister, sought a dialogue with the Democratic Alliance. The Reagan administration had favored a peaceful transition to democracy with economic stability all along; with the birth of the Democratic Alliance, Washington had someone else to talk to besides Pinochet.

As the fourth protest began, on August 11, Pinochet ordered army troops into the streets of Santiago. Twenty-eight people died in the bloodiest protest yet, some inside their homes in shantytowns. Pinochet had given a tough warning before the protest: "Be very careful, because I will not give up an inch. Security in Santiago will be taken care of by eighteen thousand men and their orders are to act very harshly!"

Minister Jarpa scheduled his first meeting with representatives of the Democratic Alliance on August 25, 1983, at the residence of Cardinal Fresno. The Socialist Party decided not to attend the dialogue with Jarpa, given the brutal repression of the protests. We felt that for any dialogue to be meaningful, it had to be preceded by the elimination of the state of emergency and the legal recognition of political parties. We Socialists were open to negotiation and compromise, but would not give up on the essential objectives of the Democratic Alliance.

Even without us, the representatives of the Democratic Alliance were forceful in their demands. They insisted on the restoration of essential freedoms, the return of exiles, the rehiring of fired copper-mine workers' union leaders, the rescission of repressive temporary articles of the constitution, an immediate end to the state of emergency, and a proper investigation of the killings during the August 11 protest. No settlement was reached, of course, but Jarpa agreed to continue talking. A few concessions followed. A list of Chilean exiles who could return home was published, night curfew was ended, and there was greater tolerance toward dissident media and political parties—an opportunity that others besides those on the left took advantage of. Ultranationalists and CNI security agents created a movement called Avanzada Nacional, while followers of Pinochet's adviser,

Jaime Guzmán, closely linked to the orthodox wing of the Chicago Boys, founded the Unión Demócrata Independiente (UDI) Party.

A second dialogue between Minister Jarpa and the Democratic Alliance, again minus Socialist representatives, took place on September 5, 1983, also at the home of Cardinal Fresno. The atmosphere was tense in the wake of the MIR's assassination of Army General Carol Urzúa, the chief administrator of Santiago. Jarpa invited the opposition to participate in the drafting of a new agenda of political laws: the Political Parties' Law, the Electoral Tribunal Law, the Statute of the Parliament, and others. The laws would be put to a plebiscite in 1986; if approved, parliamentary elections would be held that same year so a new Congress could be installed as early as 1987. To accomplish this, the itinerary fixed in the 1980 constitution would have to be altered. The Democratic Alliance leaders offered to send comments on the political laws through the group of opposition jurists known as the Group of 24.

A fourth protest was held on September 8, 1983, which again was marred by arbitrary, unprovoked attacks on opposition leaders. I was a part of a peaceful noontime sit-in that was violently disrupted by the police. Some of us fought back, setting off a street battle that lasted for hours. Gabriel Valdés, the Christian Democratic president, was hit by a water cannon and, later, by a tear-gas canister. Genaro Arriagada, a Christian Democrat, was similarly mistreated. I remember seeing a pair of distinguished opposition economists dressed in tweed jackets joining us in throwing rocks at the police. Pinochet, typically mean-spirited, made fun of Valdés's soaking by the water cannon.

Despite the fracas, a third dialogue was scheduled between Jarpa and the opposition, which for us Socialists seemed more useless than ever, since Pinochet had now declared that "whatever the costs," the constitution would not be modified, though "politicians could continue talking." Air Force General Fernando Matthei, a junta member, had argued in favor of shortening the constitutional itinerary, but, once again, Pinochet prevailed.

To make matters worse, Rodolfo Seguel, who had already spent thirty-four days in jail for organizing what Pinochet considered an "illegal strike," had been imprisoned again in early September, after he called Pinochet an "absurd and fanatic dictator." On October 2, Pinochet reiterated that the government had already chosen "a goal, a road, and it will comply with that." At a rare breakfast meeting with foreign correspondents, Pinochet ruled out stepping down before 1989. "The citizenry gave me a mission, and when a soldier receives a mission, he completes it," he said, adding that the protests signified "nothing." Economic recovery was the key to regaining support for the government and nothing else mattered. The dialogue was over.

The Democratic Alliance called for every chapter of the organization throughout the country to organize "open town meetings" (*cabildos abiertos*) that would challenge the dictatorship with demands for employment, debt renegotiation for small business and homeowners, student loans, and basic freedoms. On October 20, 1983, the Democratic Alliance established an executive committee with a monthly rotating presidency, comprising Gabriel Valdés representing the Christian Democrats (September 1983), Enrique Silva Cimma for the Radical Party (November 1983), and Ricardo Lagos, on behalf of the Socialists (December 1983). A giant AD rally was held in November, the first outdoor public gathering since the coup, which congregated about half a million people.

When Ricardo Lagos became president of the AD in December, one of his first duties was to lead a delegation to Argentina to attend the inauguration of President Raúl Alfonsín, the Radical Civic Union Party (Unión Cívica Radical, UCR) leader who had won the presidential elections after the collapse of the military junta in the wake of the disastrous Malvinas War (also referred to as the Falkland Islands War). Lagos asked me to organize the mission; the members would be Gabriel Valdés for the Christian Democrats, Enrique Silva Cimma for the Radical Party, Mario Sharpe for the Social Democrats, Armando Jaramillo for the Republican right, and Lagos himself for the Socialist Party.

Around this time I had been named international secretary of the Socialist Party. I maintained regular contact with embassies based in Santiago (with a few notable exceptions—I did not make any efforts to contact U.S. diplomats, nor was I sought out by them, at least until 1986) and liaison with Socialists in exile, providing them with information on the national situation and party matters through a bulletin and direct communications. Leading a team of foreign policy experts, I drafted press releases on international political issues, briefed our leaders on technical aspects of foreign affairs, and participated in press conferences.

Somewhat later I also became a member of the editorial board and a columnist for *Convergencia,* a Socialist journal published in Mexico. Since I lived in Chile, for security reasons I used a pseudonym, Bernardo Valenzuela. More than one friend in Chile asked me if I knew who "Bernardo Valenzuela" was.

Mixing academics with politics, whenever I lectured in the United States, Europe, or Mexico, I would spend a good part of my time meeting with refugees and exiled Socialist leaders.

A couple of days in advance of our trip to Argentina I traveled to Buenos Aires to make sure things went smoothly in this first trip abroad of the AD. Buenos Aires exuded excitement and joy as it welcomed its democratically elected president. I had only one huge problem as I endeavored to prepare our program for the visit: when I arrived in Buenos Aires nobody at the Argentine Foreign Ministry knew anything about the Chilean opposition delegation.

After spending two days in a row in a waiting room of a protocol office in charge of the presidential inauguration, and buttonholing every official I could, I obtained four invitations for the presidential inauguration ceremony and one for that of Vice President–elect Víctor Martínez. "You should be more than satisfied," said an annoyed protocol chief I had pestered constantly.

I communicated the good news to Lagos and asked him who he thought should go to the vice presidential ceremony. "Let's send the right-winger Jaramillo," I suggested. Lagos was not fully convinced, but he agreed. That night I went to the delegation's hotel and placed the invitations under the doors of the four other leaders and contacted the reception desk to make sure that all of them would be called so that they could attend the ceremony the next morning.

Everything went perfectly. The Pinochet delegation was furious when Lagos, Valdés, and the other two dissident leaders arrived; they were even angrier when they saw that the dissidents were seated seven rows ahead of them. When the opposition delegation gathered a couple of hours later, Armando Jaramillo, not knowing yet that the others had been at the presidential ceremony, proudly said, "Hey, fellows, I just came back from attending the inauguration of Vice President Martínez, and I saw none of you there. You missed something beautiful." During the following hours we met with President Alfonsín at his suite in the Hotel Panamericano, with President Felipe González of Spain and France's prime minister Pierre Mauroy, among others. The Chilean democratic coalition was gaining international recognition.

In the meantime, the economic crisis continued to worsen in Chile. Pinochet had had to accept strict IMF terms to obtain so-called standby loans, which were subject to yearly evaluations of agreed goals. Moreover, to regain investor confidence he had had to assume all the domestic banks' debts with foreign lenders. Critics of the Chicago Boys argued

Pinochet speaking to the nation from La Moneda Palace. CREDIT: *La Nación*

General Augusto Pinochet and President Salvador Allende during the ceremony when Allende named him commander in chief of the Army on August 23, 1973. Eighteen days later Pinochet overthrew the president in a coup. CREDIT: *El Mercurio*

Marriage ceremony of Heraldo Muñoz and Pamela Quick, on November 28, 1972, before a civil judge and witnesses. After the ceremony the couple went to an Allende rally. COURTESY OF THE AUTHOR

Allende's Interior Minister, Jose Tohá, flanked by Army Commander, Carlos Prats, and General Augusto Pinochet in combat gear and dark glasses during the failed "putsch" known as "Tanquetazo" about three months before the coup. Pinochet arrived on the scene when Prats had the rebellion under control. CREDIT: *EL MERCURIO*

The Military Junta, constituted on 9/11/73. From left to right: General César Mendoza (Carabineros), Admiral Jose Toribio Merino (Navy), General Augusto Pinochet, and General Gustavo Leigh (Air Force). That same day Pinochet was named president of the Junta after he argued the primacy of the Army over the other armed branches CREDIT: *EL MERCURIO*

September 11, 1973. La Moneda presidential palace in Santiago is bombed by Chilean Air Force Hawker Hunter fighter jets during the coup d'état against constitutional President Salvador Allende.
CREDIT: *EL MERCURIO*

Security guards, government officials, doctors, and aides of President Salvador Allende taken prisoner outside La Moneda palace, after being beaten and threatened to be run over by a tank. Most of them were tortured and summarily executed less than 48 hours later.
CREDIT: *EL MERCURIO*

Fidel Castro and Augusto Pinochet, at a ceremony during Castro's visit to Chile in 1971. Pinochet later said he was cold and distant with the Cuban leader.
CREDIT: *EL MERCURIO*

Policemen and army troops detaining Allende supporters in Santiago.
CREDIT: *EL MERCURIO*

Thousands of political prisoners were detained at the National Stadium in Santiago after the 1973 coup. There, scores were tortured and murdered. American journalist Charles Horman's father, Ed Horman, visited this stadium in search of his son, as portrayed in the Academy Award–winning movie *Missing*. CREDIT: *LA NACIÓN*

Economy Minister Pablo Baraona and Finance Minister Sergio de Castro, two of the leading "Chicago Boys" whom Pinochet put in charge of the economy to stabilize and reform it.
CREDIT: *EL MERCURIO*

Secretary of State Henry Kissinger and General Augusto Pinochet, in June 1976, during Kissinger's visit to attend the General Assembly of the Organization of American States. Kissinger told Pinochet he would speak about human rights but that the U.S. government supported him. Pinochet complained about Orlando Letelier's activities abroad, who was killed three months later in Washington, D.C.
CREDIT: *EL MERCURIO*

Allende's former minister and ambassador to the United States Orlando Letelier, speaking at a Chilean solidarity rally at New York's Madison Square Garden on September 10, 1976, less than two weeks before his assassination in the streets of Washington, D.C., by Pinochet's secret police. This was Letelier's last photograph alive. CREDIT: MARCELO MONTECINOS

The car of Orlando Letelier, after a bomb placed by terrorists directed by Pinochet's secret police exploded, killing him and his academic colleague Ronnie Karpen Moffit. CREDIT: EL MERCURIO

Hortensia "Tencha" Bussi de Allende, President Salvador Allende's widow, and the author in Mexico City, 1983. "Tencha," exiled in Mexico from 1973 to 1988, became a widely-respected moral leader of the Chilean democratic movement in exile. COURTESY OF THE AUTHOR

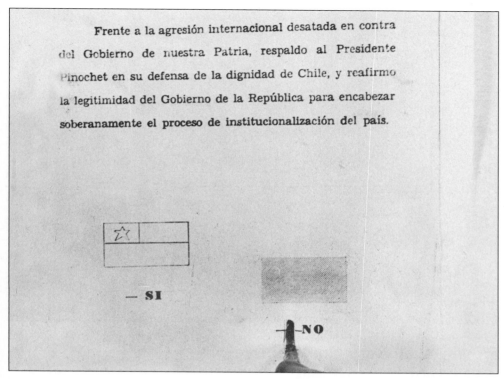

Frente a la agresión internacional desatada en contra del Gobierno de nuestra Patria, respaldo al Presidente Pinochet en su defensa de la dignidad de Chile, y reafirmo la legitimidad del Gobierno de la República para encabezar soberanamente el proceso de institucionalización del país.

— SI

—NO

On January 4, 1978, a referendum *(consulta)* was ordered by Pinochet after the United Nations condemned Chile on human rights violations. The ballot had a Chilean flag next to the "Yes" (for supporting Pinochet) and a black flag next to the "No." Not surprisingly, without voting rolls and under state of siege, results showed that 75 percent supported Pinochet and 20 percent voted against. CREDIT: *EL MERCURIO*

Augusto Pinochet and his wife saluting a crowd of supporters at a celebration of the victory of the "Yes" vote in the 1978 referendum. CREDIT: *EL MERCURIO*

Former President Eduardo Frei Montalva addressing an indoor rally to oppose the 1980 plebiscite on a new constitution. The author was present inside the arena. CREDIT: *EL MERCURIO*

A burnt bus is used as a barricade by *pobladores* during protests against the Pinochet dictatorship in a popular Santiago neighborhood on July 12, 1983. CREDIT: *EL MERCURIO*

General Oscar Bonilla, one of the original 1973 coup plotters who fell out of favor with Pinochet and his secret police. He died in what was presented as a helicopter accident. Two French experts of the helicopter manufacturer investigating the accident curiously also perished in another helicopter accident. CREDIT: *La Nación*

General Augusto Lutz, who had frequent run-ins with secret police chief Manuel Contreras, died at the Military Hospital under strange circumstances. CREDIT: *La Nación*

Former Army Commander in Chief Carlos Prats. Prats trusted Pinochet's loyalty to the constitutional government and recommended him to Allende for the top Army post. Prats and his wife were assassinated in a terrorist bombing in Buenos Aires, perpetrated by Pinochet's secret police. CREDIT: *La Nación*

Air Force General Alberto Bachelet, father of Chilean President Michelle Bachelet, was brutally tortured and died in captivity on March 12, 1974. CREDIT: *La Nación*

Carlos Berger, journalist and lawyer, director of radio station "El Loa" in the northern town of Chuquicamata, was arrested on the day of the coup and later condemned to 60 days in prison by a "war tribunal"; while serving his sentence Berger was kidnapped and assassinated by an Army contingent. COURTESY OF CARMEN HERTZ

Tucapel Jiménez, labor leader, director of the National Association of Public Employees. He was shot in the head and his throat slashed by the CNI secret police on February 25, 1982. The secret police mounted a failed concealment ploy killing an innocent carpenter who left a "suicide note" blaming himself as the culprit of the labor leader's assassination.
COURTESY OF TUCAPEL JIMÉNEZ FUENTES

Charles Horman and his father, Ed. Charles was living in Chile at the time of the coup with his wife, Joyce; he was arrested by the military and disappeared. Ed traveled from New York and he and Joyce searched desperately for Charles, until his body was found in the Santiago morgue; he was killed by several gunshot wounds.
COURTESY OF JOYCE HORMAN

Lumi Videla, MIR activist. She was arrested by secret police agents on September 21, 1974. Tortured to death, her body was thrown inside the Italian embassy which housed numerous refugees, during the curfew hours. CREDIT: LA NACIÓN

In Madrid, in November 1975, Pinochet stands by Francisco Franco's casket, which is covered by a Spanish flag and is flanked by military officials and security guards. CREDIT: *La Nación*

Patricio Aylwin, spokesman of the democratic opposition to Pinochet and Christian Democratic leader, speaking at a press conference in 1989 to launch a publication by Heraldo Muñoz (center), flanked (on the left) by Ricardo Lagos, president of the Party for Democracy (PPD). COURTESY OF THE AUTHOR

On March 11, 1990, Pinochet takes off the presidential sash at the ceremony at the Chilean Congress to hand it over to Senate president Gabriel Valdés, who, in turn, placed it across the chest of democratically elected President Patricio Aylwin (in the middle). CREDIT: *La Nación*

The oldest military man in active duty in the world, Pinochet leaves the Army commander post in March 10, 1998, at an emotional ceremony led by President Eduardo Frei Ruiz-Tagle. CREDIT: *La Nación*

Pinochet, then a Senator-for-life, talks to the President of the Chilean Senate, Andrés Zaldívar, after an agreement was reached, with Pinochet's support, to eliminate 9/11/73 (the day of the coup) as a national holiday. Zaldívar had been exiled by Pinochet during the dictatorship. CREDIT: *EL MERCURIO*

Former British Prime Minister Margaret Thatcher visits her friend former dictator Augusto Pinochet and his wife on March 26, 1999, while Pinochet was under house arrest in Virginia Water, Surrey, fighting extradition to Spain. Thatcher was a long-time Pinochet supporter. CREDIT: *EL MERCURIO*

After his detention in London, Augusto Pinochet arrives at the Santiago International Airport, freed for health reasons, and suddenly gets up and walks normally. CREDIT: *EL MERCURIO*

Augusto Pinochet smiles receiving supporters from Congress at the entrance of his house in the outskirts of Santiago, on August 9, 2000. Pinochet had just been stripped of his immunity to face trial for human right abuses. CREDIT: *EL MERCURIO*

President-elect Michelle Bachelet swears-in as President of Chile as out-going President Ricardo Lagos (center) looks on, and Senate President and former President of Chile Eduardo Frei Ruiz-Tagle conducts the oath in Valparaíso, March 11, 2006. Frei's father, Eduardo Frei Montalva, died under suspicious circumstances during the Pinochet regime; Bachelet's father, General Alberto Bachelet, was imprisoned, tortured and died in captivity in Pinochet's period, and Lagos spent time in jail under Pinochet. CREDIT: *EL MERCURIO*

Three unidentified mourners render homage with the Nazi salute to Pinochet at his funeral in December 2006. CREDIT: EFE NEWS AGENCY

that the IMF's terms made it virtually impossible to reactivate the economy. Pinochet acknowledged the criticism when, in April 1984, he removed Finance Minister Carlos Cáceres, who had negotiated the IMF loans, and replaced him with the neo-Keynesian economist Luis Eduardo Escobar. Earlier Pinochet had substituted Economy Minister Andrés Passicot with the engineer and businessman Modesto Collados. Once again, the general had displayed his pragmatic streak—he was not wed to the Chicago doctrine; he was willing to try whatever worked.

The former finance minister Sergio de Castro declared in a 2007 interview, "Even in the most prosperous years the [economic] model didn't feel like a one-way street. I always had the feeling that someone could convince [Pinochet] to reverse course." In fact, General Carlos Molina told me that when he was a young army officer at the War Academy, around 1980, Pinochet had discussed with them the government's economic policies, and that those policies had been severely criticized by the officers. Pinochet had reacted annoyed, and had stuck to the rigid Chicago strategy. Many years later, when Pinochet had retired, General Molina recalled that episode with Pinochet and the ex-dictator confessed that he should have introduced substantial modifications to the Chicago model. In 1984 Pinochet was in that doubtful mood.

Minister Escobar did not have it easy in his post at finance. Many of the midlevel economists and bureaucrats in his department adhered to the Chicago creed, resisting Escobar's more protectionist stand. In addition, he began to clash with his new colleague, Economy Minister Collados, who was more sympathetic to the Chicago Boys than Escobar was. The Chicago rearguard found they still had an unconditional ally in the junta member Admiral José Toribio Merino. When an attempt was made by the new minister of labor to redraft the Chicago-style Labor Code, Admiral Merino stopped it cold.

Escobar argued that the state had to play a forceful role in a "stable economic reactivation." A general refinancing of debts was key to alleviating the sufferings of the middle class; import duties had to be raised to help domestic producers; short-term credits needed to be secured from commercial banks. All this would require deficit spending. Escobar devaluated the peso again and the outflow of reserves stopped, but, well into 1984, he continued to be attacked by Collados and the pro-free-market advocates within the government.

By mid-1984, after additional protests, we began wondering about how much further we could go with this strategy of staging protests. Still, another protest was called for September 4, 1984.

Pinochet, who was already annoyed at Jarpa's insistence on a political opening and dialogue with the opposition, decided to kill two birds with one stone by resuming hard repression. Over nine hundred protesters were arrested, one hundred fifty were injured, and ten were killed. One of the fatalities was a French Catholic priest, André Jarlan, who was struck in the head by a 9 mm bullet from an Uzi submachine gun from Carabineros while he was inside the wooden rectory of a church in La Victoria, a poor *población* south of Santiago. The French ambassador arrived in the *población* demanding an investigation (a cover-up was attempted as Carabineros officers provided false information on the case to the investigating judge). It was the first time since the days immediately following the coup that we saw an ambassador in action in favor of human rights.

A few weeks later massive search operations in poor neighborhoods and slums yielded almost four hundred more arrests. One hundred forty of the detainees were "relegated" into forced internal exile to Pisagua, the old prison camp in northern Chile that Captain Pinochet had commanded in the 1940s. The most radical dissidents did not take this lying down—bombings in Santiago and four provincial capitals damaged banks, government offices, and telephone lines. Blackouts and attacks on police stations increased.

On Sunday, November 4, Pinochet announced that he was reimposing a state of siege. A week of political unrest led to fourteen more deaths. Lagos, as president of the Democratic Alliance, declared that the crisis reflected a government that had "nothing to offer to the country, except the will of Pinochet to stay in power under a constitution most Chileans do not accept." Lagos also called for a another protest. The next day, Minister Jarpa submitted his resignation, which Pinochet decided to keep on hold.

As in George Orwell's novel, in Chile "1984" became a watchword for state brutality. In October, a bomb destroyed a Catholic church in Punta Arenas in Chile's Patagonia. It was officially determined to be a leftist terrorist operation, but the body and the identity card of an army intelligence operative, Lieutenant Patricio Contreras, were found in the rubble. The government's explanation was that perhaps Lieutenant Contreras had died while trying to deactivate a bomb that had been placed by leftist extremists. Nobody bought that story.

Also in October 1984, Mario Fernández López, a local Christian Democratic leader in Ovalle, in northern Chile, who was a truck driver, died after being arrested by CNI personnel from Santiago. Blows to his abdomen had ruptured his internal organs; he'd died from hypobolemic shock. A military tribunal absolved the murderers, accepting instead the theory that Fernández, while trying to escape, had accidentally struck his thorax against the sharp edge of a table. Eventually, an appeals court, backed by a Supreme Court decision, reversed the military tribunal's ruling, concluding that the detainee could not have possibly suffered the alleged fatal accident, and condemning the CNI agents involved to several years in jail.

The Roman Catholic Church, which reported that 1,655 people had been detained for political activity and protests in the first six months of 1984, also felt the heavy hand of repression. Ignacio Gutiérrez, a Spanish priest in charge of the Vicariate of Solidarity, was forced to leave the country when the government canceled his residence visa, despite the Church's protests. Not much later, Father Dennis O'Hara, an American priest who had lived in Chile for six years and had sent cards to his parishioners expressing his wish to see an end to torture, was also arrested and deported.

Francisco Javier Cuadra, the new head of the Ministry Secretary General of Government (Ministerio Secretaría General de Gobierno), who quickly became a young Pinochet favorite, orchestrated a new hard-line offensive (created in 1976, this ministry is the government's principal organ of communication with the public). Radio stations were closed, and independent magazines and newspapers that had emerged in recent times were prohibited. It was tough times again.

I was a foreign affairs columnist at *APSI,* one of the weekly magazines that were closed. Already struggling to make their publication break even, the editors, Marcelo Contreras and Sergio Marras, called me into an emergency meeting, where we brainstormed how we might survive. Pinochet's problem with *APSI* concerned domestic news. How about if we printed a sharp international politics edition that was still relevant to local matters? It was exactly what we had done in 1981 when *APSI* was forbidden from covering national news and received a nine-month suspension as a punishment after producing a successful issue on the CNI secret police. Now I put together an issue of the magazine on international affairs that dealt with repression and democratic struggles around the world and Reagan's policy toward Chile, and even included comic strips and caricatures dealing with external affairs that nonetheless spoke to the local public. It worked. The magazine began circulating again and, little by little, it shifted its focus back to Chilean politics.

On June 29, 1984, the Socialist Party had held a semiclandestine meeting at the Audax Italiano Club on Carmen Street, south of downtown Santiago. It was a plenary meeting to which we had invited leaders of other parties, including the Christian Democratic representative

Patricio Aylwin, as well as delegates of the Communist Party and other groups. About a hundred people came. That night my car, which had been parked across the street from the club, was robbed. A briefcase was torn open but the only things missing from it were political documents. A couple of valuable items, including a portable short-wave radio, had not been stolen. The cars of a few other participants in the meeting had also been broken into, and their valuables were also untouched. It was an unmistakable message from the CNI: we are following you and can hit you whenever we want.

Not long after the imposition of the state of siege, CNI personnel—an army officer commanding a group of armed men wearing ski masks—arrived at our party headquarters, located in an apartment on Serrano Street, and smashed down the doors. "It's over. Mr. Lagos is finished. You understand!" the officer yelled at the people inside.

Ricardo Lagos was not there at the time, but he arrived while the CNI agents were still searching the premises. Unfazed, he demanded an explanation.

"Mr. Lagos, we know you and your comrades very well," one of the agents said. "In fact, we belong to a unit that specializes in the Socialist Party."

"If you know what we do, then you should be cognizant of the fact that we only exercise our right to peaceful dissent," Lagos responded angrily.

The agents departed soon after.

Not long after that episode, on January 3, 1985, the CNI invaded our Socialist think tank, Vector, arresting its director, Eduardo Ortiz, and other researchers and political leaders who were on the premises, including Marcelo Schilling. That night, Minister Cuadra announced that a fake institution, a front for subversive activities, had been successfully neutralized.

Ricardo Lagos and I set to work besieging human rights officials and organizations with phone calls, and the government was quickly flooded with protests—including one from the U.S. State Department. The Vector officials were quickly released, but we were horrified, upon returning to the premises, to discover that the CNI had stolen everything that wasn't nailed down: furniture, documents, fax machines, even wastepaper baskets.

Jarpa finally left the cabinet on February 16, 1985, and Finance Minister Escobar quit along with him. Pinochet sarcastically stated that he had allowed Jarpa's dialogue with the opposition to proceed just as "fancy footwork to gain time." Jarpa was replaced by an unimpressive businessman, Ricardo García, while Escobar's place was taken by Hernán Büchi, a young economist trained at Columbia University but sympathetic to the Chicago doctrine. It seemed that Pinochet's instinct was now leaning back toward the side of liberal economic policy. Yet Pinochet, as usual, covered all bases. He named Army Colonel Enrique Seguel as Central Bank president and gave greater authority to his military staff, which had been transformed into the Ministry Secretary General of the Presidency (Ministerio Secretaría General de la Presidencia) under the direction of his trusted adviser, General Santiago Sinclair.

Pinochet had neutralized the protests through repression. Through Jarpa, he had cunningly bought time while he waited for an economic recovery to take hold. Protests no longer seemed the way to get rid of Pinochet. A sense of frustration began to grow among us, but we were not ready to give up.

MARCH IS WHEN the school year begins in Chile. At 8:40 A.M. on March 29, 1985, under state-of-siege conditions, security forces kidnapped the teacher Manuel Guerrero from Colegio Latino Americano High School. Another teacher who interfered was shot. Almost simultaneously, Manuel Parada, a sociologist working with the Vicariate of Solidarity, was also kidnapped. Parada had been taking testimony from an air force deserter about security operations. The following day, Santiago Natino, a retired publicist and painter, was forced at gunpoint into a car. The three men, all members of the Communist Party, were assassinated and their bodies dumped near the town of Quilicura. Their throats had been slit and their hands, arms, and abdomens had been slashed.

The case, which became known as the *degollados* ("the slit-throated"), shocked a country inured to repression and horror. I was particularly saddened by the crimes, as Manuel Parada was the son of my friend María Maluenda, an actress and the former Allende envoy to Hanoi. As usual, the Pinochet regime blamed the killings on the left, possibly foreigners. "Chileans do not kill by slashing throats," Pinochet declared. But a brave judge, José Cánovas, working with abundant witnesses who were willing to testify, identified fourteen commandos from a secret police group known as Dicomcar (Dirección de Comunicaciones de Carabineros) as the culprits. Because of long-standing rivalries between the CNI and the Carabineros, the CNI provided abundant evidence against Dicomcar.

The public outcry was so strong that Pinochet decided that General Rodolfo Stange, the deputy director of the Carabineros and the operative head of the institution, should be removed from his job. But it wasn't enough. General César Mendoza, the Carabineros' director, a junta member and an unconditional ally of Pinochet, was less respected within the police corps than Stange, plus he had become a lightning rod for the public's outrage. Loyal friend or not, Pinochet finally told Mendoza that he would have to be thrown to the wolves. Mendoza understood.

Pinochet suggested to Mendoza that his replacement be an army general rather than a member of the Carabineros. Mendoza responded that such an alternative was preposterous. Then, bizarrely, Pinochet said, "Let's bring back Stange." The problem was that Stange's retirement decree had already been processed. But as a Pinochet justice minister, Mónica Madariaga, said once, "In a dictatorship you can do everything," and so it was that the comptroller general was forced to remove with a razor blade the stamp with which Pinochet had approved Stange's retirement.

On August 2, 1985, General Mendoza formally resigned because of the crimes that had been committed by the secret Carabineros unit. (Pinochet had never even considered resigning when similar DINA and CNI crimes were revealed and proven.) General Stange took Mendoza's place in the junta and consolidated his control over the Carabineros. Stange was smarter than Mendoza and independent-minded. Of German descent, Stange would often speak in German with Air Force General Fernando Matthei, also a son of German immigrants, during junta meetings, which irritated Pinochet.

Beginning in 1985, as Finance Minister Büchi backed away from the dogmas of the Chicago Boys, the economy began to show signs of recovery. Macroeconomic indicators improved, particularly economic growth, while inflation came under control. Further devaluations, along with policies that favored export-oriented productive sectors, improved the balance of trade. More important, Pinochet gave Büchi the green light to privatize several state-owned firms and to reprivatize companies belonging to what was called the "strange area of the economy" businesses that had fallen under state control as a result of the 1982 crisis. The sale of those companies helped offset the decline in fiscal revenues caused by the devaluations, enabling Chile to comply with IMF conditions.

Büchi did not eliminate in one fell swoop the 35 percent import duties that his predecessor had imposed, but, pragmatically, reduced them gradually; interest rates were not left to the market but were fixed, or "guided," by the Central Bank. Büchi agreed to provide special "protection," or subsidies, to politically sensitive sectors of the economy such as wheat, sugar, and oil. The Chicago doctrine had been watered down, but out-and-out "statism" had also been ruled out. Büchi's variations on the Chicago creed not only seemed to be working, they accommodated Pinochet's pragmatic personality.

By the end of 1984 Cardinal Fresno had asked three trusted advisers to draft a National Accord for the Transition to Democracy, the so-called *Acuerdo Nacional*. The Catholic Church had shifted from directly challenging the dictatorship on its human rights violations to mediating between the government and the opposition.

The real aim of the National Accord was to create a bargaining partner whose strength and legitimacy were such that Pinochet could not possibly ignore it. The cardinal's advisers contacted not only the Democratic Alliance parties but also the right-wing National Union Party and the remnants of the old conservative National Party. The radical left MDP alliance was formally excluded from the discussions because the groups that formed it had not renounced armed struggle, but an informal liaison with the Communists was set up through Luis Maira, the leader of the Christian Left. The more extreme pro-Pinochet Unión Demócrata Independiente party did not participate in the discussions either, because they were opposed in principle to negotiating with the opposition at all. The discussions concluded on August 25, 1985. The National Accord document brought together the widest spectrum of voices yet in favor of democratic reconstruction.

But Pinochet simply ignored it, as many had feared he would. When General Matthei publicly opined that the agreement was "interesting," Pinochet reprimanded him. Matthei was not the only member of the junta who viewed the accord in a positive light, which greatly annoyed Pinochet. At one of their meetings, Pinochet had an assistant read out loud transcripts from Admiral Emilio Massera's trial in Argentina, where he defended himself against the charges stemming from the "dirty war" perpetrated against the Argentine opposition. Pinochet was implicitly warning his generals that they, too, could find themselves on trial if they did not remain strongly united against reform. He issued orders that no one in the government should even acknowledge that they had received a copy of the National Accord.

Cardinal Fresno made a last appeal to convince Pinochet about the merits of the agreement. "You should dedicate yourself to pastoral matters," Pinochet rebuked him. "All politicians are pests and they are using you," added Pinochet.

The cardinal insisted that dialogue should be given a chance, touching on the social crisis. "There is misery in the streets; people are begging," said Fresno.

"There is also misery in the United States."

"No, there is poverty there; here there is misery that touches the soul," Fresno responded.

"The National Accord is over! Let's turn the page," snapped Pinochet. And that was that.

After a heated debate, the Central Committee of the Socialist Party voted on the wording of a statement that I helped to draft. In it we valued the National Accord as a legitimate agreement about the future of Chile's political system; we added that social mobilization against the dictatorship should continue. Pinochet immediately set about poisoning the well, by preparing a critique of the National Accord and circulating it to all military units and military academies. Despite a desultory campaign to gather signatures in support of the National Accord, it received over eight hundred thousand endorsements—but inevitably it withered.

Yet informal contacts prospered between opposition forces and moderate pro-government sectors to exchange views on the factors that hampered or helped a broad-based strategy for transition to democracy. The Center for Development Studies (Centro de Estudios para el Desarrollo, CED), founded by Gabriel Valdés and led by Edgardo Boeninger (later a minister in President Aylwin's cabinet), began a low-profile series of academic meetings among social scientists and political leaders, including former Pinochet ministers and informal representatives of the Communist Party. I was a regular participant in those meetings, which lasted about one year, from early 1985 to the beginning of 1986. It was the first occasion that many of us had to dialogue with pro-regime actors and for them to listen to the wide spectrum of the opposition. At times there were tough discussions but these were never leaked to the press; slowly, a sense of "civic friendship" began to emerge among the members of the group. We also realized it would not be easy to replicate this effort at the national political level.

After the failure of the National Accord, a group called the National Civic Assembly sprung up in April 1986 and drafted a document called "The Demand of Chile." I had meanwhile moved the axis of my academic work to the Academy of Christian Humanism, a nongovernmental institution under the aegis of the Archbishop of Santiago, so I was an NGO delegate at the civic society conference that produced this document. (My job transfer had been precipitated by an act of censorship at the university's Institute of International Studies, when its new director had forbidden the circulation of the manuscript of a book I had written about the military government's foreign policy.)

The National Civic Assembly called for a protest on July 2, 1986. A ghastly event occurred during that July 2 protest. Nineteen-year-old Rodrigo Rojas, the son of exiles and a resident of Washington, D.C., was covering the protest as a freelance photographer working for *APSI*. He met eighteen-year-old Carmen Gloria Quintana, an engineering student, at a barricade in General Velasquez Street, on Santiago's west side, where protesters were igniting gasoline cans and Molotov cocktails. A truckload of army soldiers, led by Lieutenant Pedro Fernández Dittus, detained Rojas and Quintana, beat them up, and then proceeded to pour gasoline all over both teenagers and set them on fire. When the two youngsters attempted to put out the flames, they were beaten unconscious. Fernández Dittus ordered the soldiers to wrap the bodies in blankets and load them onto the truck. Then they drove to the outskirts of Santiago and dumped the bodies near the international airport. Unbelievably, they were still alive. They managed to crawl to the roadside, where a passing motorist saw them and took them to a hospital. When the scandal broke, the army denied any involvement, claiming that the youngsters had burned themselves accidentally. An eyewitness who'd blamed the soldiers was kidnapped at gunpoint by the CNI and threatened with death unless he recanted his testimony. He and his family sought and received protection from the Catholic Church.

Rodrigo Rojas only lived for a few days after he was found; Carmen Gloria Quintana survived but her face and body were severely disfigured. Rodrigo Rojas's death worsened the already declining relations between the Pinochet regime and the Reagan administration. Pinochet's refusal even to talk to his moderate opposition, combined with his continuing repression of demonstrations, convinced Washington that its "quiet diplomacy" was not working. As early as December 1983 the White House had granted human rights certification to Argentina, in recognition of its advancement toward democracy, but continued to deny it to Chile. Washington made it increasingly clear to Pinochet that he could no longer count on its unconditional support. In February 1984, Secretary of State George Shultz delivered a speech in Boston in which he declared that Chile "was not in tune with the democratic spirit which could be felt from one end to the other of Latin America."

Following the reimposition of martial law, which brought to a close the political opening attempted by Interior Minister Jarpa, Secretary of State Shultz let it be known that the Reagan administration "was very disappointed" with Pinochet. A month later, President Reagan himself, during the celebration of International Human Rights Day, issued a proclamation in which he specifically deplored "the lack of progress toward democratic government in Chile."

But if Washington was increasingly critical of Pinochet, the American embassy in Santiago was an ally. The right-wing ambassador, James Theberge, maintained that pressuring Chileans through vetoes on loan applications at international financial institutions would be "counterproductive" because "the Chilean Government will do no more favors for the United States," read an internal memo by Theberge dated November 1984.

Assistant Secretary of State Langhorne Motley felt that so long as Pinochet could not be persuaded to initiate a transition to democracy, Washington should be satisfied by the eventual removal of martial law and the softening of press censorship. Elliot Abrams, the assistant secretary of state for human rights, disagreed.

In June 1985, when a vote for a World Bank loan to Chile was approaching, Pinochet hastily lifted the state of siege. The United States reciprocated by opposing a resolution condemning the military government at the UN Human Rights Commission. They also voted in favor of the loan.

Secretary of State George Shultz was consolidating his control of American foreign policy vis-à-vis the neoconservatives, and Chile policy shifted accordingly. The change could be noticed in the replacement of the political appointee James Theberge (remembered fondly by Pinochet in his memoirs as "one of the few true friends" of his regime) by a career diplomat, Harry Barnes. Elliott Abrams assumed Langhorne Motley's post as assistant secretary of state for inter-American affairs. Abrams had been the architect of Reagan's human rights policy, which, though mainly designed as a tool to be used against Communist regimes, also became an element of persuasion for influencing authoritarian regimes to advance toward democracy.

Democracy had returned to several South American countries that had previously been under dictatorial rule, and dictators had fallen in Haiti and the Philippines. These events provided a basis for the development of the "third force" thesis, which envisioned an alternative to the two-sided, either-or conflict of the cold war. Instead of tolerating authoritarian governments because they were lined up against Communism, the "third force" theory proposed supporting emerging democratic movements that would oppose the authoritarian regimes in their own countries and provide a bulwark against Communism.

Support for transition through dialogue was reiterated during Ambassador Harry Barnes's presentation-of-credentials ceremony on November 18, 1985, when he remarked to General Pinochet, "I am happy to know that I will have the opportunity to witness directly the installation of stable and permanent democratic institutions in Chile, a process which the people of my country warmly welcome and support." Pinochet was furious with Barnes's declarations and with his observation during a private session that "the shortcomings of democracy are cured with more democracy." A participant in the ceremony told me that Pinochet warned the ambassador, "Do not attempt to influence things here!"

Pinochet slammed the door shut and never met the American envoy again, except once a year when he visited an international trade fair where he and Barnes would exchange a few polite words. After one of those brief encounters a local newspaper published a picture of Pinochet and Ambassador Barnes with the caption "Until next year!"

All of the agencies in the U.S. government had arrived at the conclusion that Pinochet did not want to reestablish democracy, and that his obstinacy fostered polarization and instability, which served in turn to strengthen the Communist Party. According to this analysis, Pinochet himself was laying the groundwork for armed insurrection against his own regime.

Thanks to the influence of Vernon Walters and Jeane Kirkpatrick, Washington had systematically opposed UN resolutions critical of the Pinochet regime. But by 1986, with the policy change in Washington, Pinochet could no longer rely on a blank check from the U.S. delegation. In March, when the UN Human Rights Commission discussed the critical report submitted by the special rapporteur on human rights in Chile, Fernando Volio of Costa Rica, whose appointment had been promoted by the United States, Washington voted in favor of a draft resolution that made specific recommendations to the Chilean government. Pinochet angrily repudiated the American position. The tension was exacerbated two days later when White House Chief of Staff Donald Regan said on television that the United States was not "at the moment" attempting to destabilize the Pinochet regime, but that "there were means through which that government could be induced into a more democratic way of life."

In May 1986 I visited Washington, D.C., as an officially invited guest, to meet with U.S. authorities in my capacity as international secretary of the Socialist Party. It was a clear sign of the new American attitude toward Socialists. I held conversations with Robert Gelbard, deputy assistant secretary of state for inter-American affairs, Néstor Sánchez, deputy assistant secretary of defense, and other officials and senior aides to senators and congressmen. I recall that most of the talks focused on whether the United States should use economic sanctions against Pinochet to pressure him into initiating a democratic transition. The notes I kept from those conversations reveal that there was a vibrant internal discussion within the administration about the issue. "Sanctions are like a gun with one bullet; if you fire it then you don't have anything else to use," said Gelbard. "They would hurt the Chilean people," I was told at the Pentagon. My interlocutors did not dismiss the sanctions option, particularly since Senators Edward Kennedy and Tom Harkin were working on a bill calling for specific economic sanctions against the Pinochet regime. I recall telling my interlocutors that, in the end, it would be we Chileans who would recuperate democracy in Chile, though the United States and other countries could play a critical supporting role.

In 1986 Senator Edward Kennedy visited Chile. Human rights lawyers and opposition leaders who met with him at the airport were violently attacked by organized pro-Pinochet demonstrators (some of whom would become leading congressmen and senators of right-wing parties after the return of democracy) while the police simply looked on. Since Ambassador Barnes, unlike his predecessor, had regular meetings with the democratic opposition, including the Socialists, I had the chance to talk safely with Kennedy at a reception at Barnes's residence. The day before, I had drafted and cosigned with Secretary-General Carlos Briones a Socialist Party declaration welcoming Kennedy to Chile and praising him for his consistent support for democracy and human rights. Some time later, when the playwright Arthur Miller visited Chile, I had the opportunity to talk with him at Barnes's official residence as well.

The bilateral relationship reached a new low in July 1986 after the murder of Rodrigo Rojas, a U.S. resident. The American government demanded an immediate and thorough investigation, and the punishment of those responsible. Ambassador Barnes attended his funeral, which ended in violent police repression. American media supported the proactive stand taken by Barnes on behalf of human rights.

However, the ambassador's behavior was severely criticized by Jesse Helms, of South Carolina, who visited Chile a few days later. After meeting with Pinochet for two full hours, on July 11, Helms attacked the American press for its "critical views" on Pinochet and accused Ambassador Barnes of "planting the flag of the United States at a Communist activity" (referring to his presence at the funeral of the teenaged Rojas, who had been burned alive by soldiers). Senator Helms blasted the State Department bureaucracy for "leading President Reagan into error and distorting his policies." Helms was silenced when the White House upheld Barnes's conduct. "Today . . . we had a meeting of the NSC [National Security Council] about Chile and about how we can persuade Pinochet to move towards a democratic form of government," Reagan wrote in his personal diary on the evening of November 18, 1986. "We have agreed we must try."

To my surprise, in his extensive memoirs *Camino Recorrido* Pinochet quoted my book *Una Amistad Esquiva* (Elusive Friendship: A Survey of U.S.-Chilean Relations), which I wrote with the political scientist Carlos Portales, to explain the policy changes by the Reagan administration toward his regime. Pinochet shared my assessment that the growing militarization of some left-wing sectors of the opposition and the exhaustion of the protests had activated—unfortunately, in his view—the East-West red light in Washington, leading it to support moderate forces seeking a peaceful transition. Pinochet quotes me in other passages of his memoirs, although his intelligence advisers erred once again; he labels me and my coauthor, both of us Socialists, as "Christian Democratic specialists."

Indeed, the Reagan administration had distanced itself considerably from Pinochet. Yet the U.S. accompanied its public criticism of the Pinochet regime with pragmatic attempts to gain leverage through a rapprochement with the Chilean armed forces, and by America's official endorsement of multilateral lending to Chile, an example of compliance with IMF requirements. The Reagan administration did not want to push the Pinochet regime over the edge. It was a policy of "carrots and sticks," favoring moderates and excluding radicals, with a peaceful transition to democracy as the goal.

Six

TO KILL PINOCHET OR
DEFEAT HIM WITH A PENCIL

They waited in silence, hidden behind bushes at a bend in the narrow and winding road into Cajón del Maipo, a canyon outside Santiago formed by the Maipo River. It was sundown on Sunday, September 7, 1986, one of the first weekends of the approaching Southern Hemisphere spring. From their hilltop vantage, twenty-four young combatants, members of the Manuel Rodríguez Patriotic Front (Frente Patriótico Manuel Rodríguez, FPMR), the military wing of the Communist Party, looked out across the tree-covered slopes of the Andes Mountains and down the steep precipice to the river that flowed through the canyon. But they weren't there to enjoy the scenery. They carried grenades, LAW (light antitank weapon) rocket launchers, RPGs (rocket-propelled grenades), M-16 and SIG automatic rifles, and plenty of ammunition. They were there to kill Pinochet.

The FPMR had been considering plans to assassinate Pinochet since 1984. Some of them had been dismissed because of the risk to innocent civilians. But Pinochet was vulnerable when he left Santiago on weekends to visit his mountain retreat in El Melocotón, on the G-25 road along the Cajón del Maipo. He always returned to Santiago with his security entourage on Sunday evening, right about sunset. A plan to dig a tunnel filled with explosives under that road was discarded in its initial phases, because Pinochet's convoy traveled so fast that it would be easy to blow up the wrong vehicle. A commando attack would have more certainty of success.

The Communists had said that 1986 would be a "decisive" year. We Socialists assumed that it was because the Communists would attempt to assume a greater leadership role in the protest movement.

We never suspected what would happen on that Sunday, September 7, 1986.

The fighters had assembled at a five-bedroom rented house in the small village of La Obra at 5:45 P.M. Both the house and the vehicles for the operation had been rented by César Bunster, son of Allende's ambassador to London, and Cecilia Magni (a.k.a. Commander Tamara), a blonde sociologist who had studied at The Grange, an exclusive high school in Santiago.

César Bunster had returned legally to Chile in 1986. A member of the Communist Youth, he wanted to assume a frontline role in the struggle against Pinochet. One day Commander Tamara had made contact with Bunster at an agreed-upon spot downtown in the Paseo Ahumada, and had put him to work on administrative chores for the FPMR. Some weeks later Bunster complained that he wanted "action."

"We have plenty of fighters. We need people like you, who know how to drive a car, who have a distinguished last name, tall and clean-cut, a man who can mingle in various social settings without raising suspicion," Commander Tamara lectured Bunster. But shortly thereafter she made contact again to notify him that he would participate in "a historic operation." "There are few possibilities of coming out alive," she warned. "Then it can only be to kill Pinochet," Bunster guessed. Tamara smiled without responding.

The mission was called "Operation Twentieth Century." The FPMR combatants' ages ranged from seventeen to twenty-eight. They were led by José Valenzuela Levy (Commander Ernesto), twenty-eight, who had attended the exclusive bilingual Nido de Aguilas high school in Santiago and also had studied in the United States. Only a few of them had formal military training and just a handful had real combat experience (Ernesto had received formal military training and had actually become an officer of the Bulgarian Popular Army). They had been recruited carefully by the FPMR leadership for their political reliability and their fearlessness, not their military prowess. Some of them had never held an M–16 automatic rifle. Though they'd rehearsed many times, all their practices had been "dry," that is, they'd simulated shooting but hadn't used live ammunition so as to avoid calling attention to themselves.

The commandos reviewed their plans one last time, cleaned their rifles, and checked their rocket launchers. Each of them knew what he or she had to do; the operation had been planned and rehearsed to the last detail. The group was divided into four combat units. Unit 501 was the containment and clash unit, which would stop Pinochet's motorcade with a Peugeot station wagon pulling a home trailer and cut off the forward security section of the convoy; Unit 502 was the assault unit, which would fire on the second and third vehicles of the caravan, one of them Pinochet's bullet-proof Mercedes Benz; Unit 503, also an assault unit, would destroy the fourth car in the convoy; Unit 504 was the rearguard unit, in charge of eliminating the last vehicle in the motorcade and cutting off any possible escape from the scene of the ambush.

Exactly one week earlier the combatants had made the same preparations for the action, but the sudden death of Jorge Alessandri, the conservative former president, on Saturday, August 30, had caused Pinochet to change his routine, and he returned to Santiago at three o'clock Sunday morning instead of in the evening.

It was risky to keep the rented house an extra week, but they had no choice. The leases on the trailer and other items that would be used in the operation were extended via phone calls, and the fighters continued to maintain their low-key presence in the area. Most of them were staying at the Carrió hostel in San Alfonso, pretending to be seminary students on a spiritual retreat. The tension mounted when a woman from the car rental agency showed up unexpectedly at the La Obra house to find out about the Peugeot and trailer. The cash deposit they had left was insufficient for the extra week, plus she was suspicious and wanted to make sure that the address César Bunster had given her was genuine. Satisfied to learn that the people at the house knew who Bunster was and that the vehicles were safely parked in a locked area, she left without further ado.

Now—Sunday, September 7—there would be no more surprises. On Saturday night, most of the combatants were unable to sleep. After a good breakfast and a final review of their plans, they were ordered into their rooms in the rented house, where they were to remain for the rest of the day. Someone played Allende's last speech in La Moneda on a cassette recorder.

At El Melocotón, a compound on a large estate that had been purchased by Pinochet from the government at a suspiciously low price, Pinochet, his wife, Lucía; his mother-in-law; his eleven-year-old grandson, Rodrigo García; a navy attaché, Pedro Arrieta; Dr. Domingo Videla; and several security guards, including "black berets" from the army's special forces, prepared for their return to Santiago. Army Corporal Oscar Carvajal, Pinochet's driver, inspected his car, a brand-new blue armor-plated Mercedes. It was still unfamiliar to him; he'd spent the weekend practicing maneuvers so he could get used to its feel. Unlike the Mercedes that Pinochet had just stopped using, this one had bullet-proof tires. Inside, the backseats were separated from the driver by a glass window that could be raised or lowered by either the driver or the passengers. The windows were tinted and hung with curtains.

The FPMR combatants' Peugeot was also armored, but in a much more ad hoc way—they'd leaned a marble table top against its side. The fighters had covered their fingertips with glue to avoid leaving fingerprints. That afternoon Juan Moreno Ávila, a.k.a. Sacha, had lost one of his fingertip glue attachments when he was picking up a soft-drink bottle, but he'd tried to wipe the bottle clean. At the last minute Ernesto decided that Commander Tamara would not participate in the attack. She and César Bunster would have to move out on Sunday. She protested, but he explained that she would be needed to direct the retreat operation of all those who might survive the ambush. Ernesto decided that Héctor Maturana, a.k.a. Patricio, should dress as a woman when he rode in the Peugeot station wagon, to avoid any suspicion that they might not be a vacationing couple.

At 6 P.M. Pinochet and his entourage were ready to leave. Pinochet's advance security vehicles, two 360 GLS Volvos and a Nissan Stanza, driven and manned by members of the CNI, had checked the route twice already that Sunday afternoon. They reported no problems. The passengers in the main vehicle were Pinochet and his grandson in the back and Commander Arrieta, the navy attaché, and Corporal Carvajal, the driver, in front. Pinochet's wife had made an appeal for her husband to stay an extra night, but the general was as stubborn as he always was once he'd made a decision. The convoy left just a few minutes past 6 P.M.

A couple of minutes later, an FPMR militant named Nadia and Isabelle Mayorez, a Swiss girl, who were posing as tourists in the town of San José de Maipo, phoned the combatants' house in La Obra from their hostel to report that the convoy was on its way. The commandos had measured exactly how long it would take the caravan to drive from the hostel to the ambush zone. Commander Ernesto could hear the police sirens through the phone.

"Okay. He is coming. Everybody to your posts," he ordered.

The combatants got into a Toyota Land Cruiser, a Toyota Hi-Lux pickup, the Peugeot station wagon with the trailer, and a Nissan Bluebird and departed in the direction of the nearby bend of the road known as Cuesta Achupallas. Most of them took up positions on the hill on the north side of the road. On the other side of the road was a steep slope—in places a sheer drop—to the river. Two men remained inside the Peugeot, ready to pull out and block the road at just the right moment. The combatant known as Tarzan for his weightlifter physique stood by the side of the road with a backpack and a football, as if he were a soccer player waiting for a ride. The biggest and most daring operation the FPMR had ever undertaken was about to begin. It was a watershed moment for the Chilean Communist Party, which had been gradually changing its tactics from peaceful resistance to "all forms of struggle," including armed combat.

THE GROUNDWORK FOR the operation had been laid some six months before. Two hundred miles off the Chilean coast, two fishing boats, the *Chompalhue* and the *Astrid Sue,* owned by a fictitious company, Cultivos Marinos Chungungo, had rendezvoused with a Cuban ship and offloaded crates containing about 170 LAW M72 A2 rocket launchers, 115 RPG-7 rocket launchers, about three thousand M-16 rifles, and tons of explosives and ammunition. The operation had netted the FPMR an arsenal that could equip a veritable army. The weapons were unloaded in a small cove in Carrizal Bajo, near the town of Vallenar. Most of the arms were carefully buried in Carrizal Bajo for later distribution and use.

But the CIA got wind of the operation and alerted the Chilean military. On August 6, 1986, a joint CNI, army, and Carabineros raid captured two dozen members of the Patriotic Front and most of the weapons. But a number of arms were already in the hands of combatants.

Why had the Communist Party resorted to armed struggle? The answer was in its recent history. While the Western European Communists and Chilean Socialists concluded that the failed Allende experience made it imperative to seek "historical compromises" with progressive centrist forces, the Soviets and the Chilean Communist Party (CCP) had drawn the opposite lesson.

Chilean Communists had historically favored a peaceful road to Socialism—Nikita Khrushchev's doctrine—through the formation of broad alliances of progressive forces. In the 1950s, in fact, the leadership of the CCP had expelled the Luis Reinoso group, which advocated armed struggle to gain power. Fidel Castro's endorsement of guerrilla warfare in the 1960s had been indirectly attacked by Luis Corvalán, the secretary-general of the Chilean Communist Party, in an article in *Pravda*. Corvalán had also bitterly criticized the Chinese Communist Party for its "anti-Sovietism" and for not sharing "the thesis that the peaceful road is, in contemporary times, a real possibility in many countries."

Allende's presidential victory in 1970 had been hailed in Moscow as "second only to the victory of the Cuban revolution," a fact reflected in the appointment as head of the Soviet mission in Santiago of Aleksandr Vasilyevich Basov, a member of the Central Committee. The Soviet leadership considered the CCP so important, and they were so affected by the setback of the coup to their influence in Latin America, that Moscow paid the huge political price of exchanging Secretary-General Corvalán, who was in jail in Chile, for the Russian dissident Vladimir Bukovsky, who was locked up in a psychiatric ward in the USSR. Corvalán had been in prison for two years, first on Dawson Island, by the Strait of Magellan, and then in Santiago. (The KGB had devised a plan to rescue him from Dawson Island in a commando raid that would use a cargo vessel, helicopters, and a submarine, but the plan was never approved by the leadership of the Soviet Communist Party.)

Not only the coup but also signals from Moscow caused the big shift in the CCP line. In 1974 Boris Ponomarev, an alternate member of the Politburo and the International Department chief of the Soviet Communist Party, wrote an influential article affirming that every revolutionary process had to be ready "to change quickly the forms of struggle, peaceful and nonpeaceful" and to "respond with revolutionary violence to the reactionary violence of the bourgeoisie." In addition to this, the Soviet leader, Leonid Brezhnev, referring to Chile in a speech before the Twenty-fifth Congress of the Communist Party of the Soviet Union, roundly declared that "a revolution must learn how to defend itself." Chileans had been naïve not to prepare for the coup militarily, he implied, or, worse yet, had lacked fighting spirit. In April 1980, Stephan Chernovenko, the Soviet ambassador to France, warned the United States that Moscow was determined to sustain the Communist regime of Mohammed Najibullah in Afghanistan by declaring that it "would not permit another Chile" (the Chilean Communists supported the Soviet invasion of Afghanistan, the Socialists led by Altamirano rejected it). The Brezhnev regime had abandoned the Krushchev doctrine.

The new armed component of the Communist strategy was influenced as well by the views of the so-called Leipzig group, a CCP research team that focused on the armed forces and alternative political scenarios, and by those of an East Berlin Chilean group that pushed Secretary-General Corvalán into the direction of armed insurrection. The experiences of Nicaragua and El Salvador were also a persuasive factor, as Secretary-General Corvalán remarked in October 1982. The Soviets began to urge Latin American Communists to coordinate with guerrilla groups in "political-military fronts," following the Sandinista model.

The FPMR wing of the CCP had been founded in 1983 under the technical leadership of twelve commanders who had received military training in Cuba. Its top leader, Raúl Pellegrin, also known as Rodrigo and José Miguel, had actual combat experience in Nicaragua. The Communists were not so audacious as to attempt a military defeat of the professional Chilean armed forces. Their hope was that escalating social mobilization, supported by armed struggle, could lead to a countrywide insurrection that, they believed, had the potential to divide the armed forces, as had happened in Iran when massive street protests prompted the Shah's army to turn against him in 1979. The Pinochet operation was seen as a key catalyst for national insurrection.

PINOCHET'S FIVE-CAR MOTORCADE was preceded by two motorcycles driven by armed Carabineros, which cleared the route with their sirens. The first car was a gray Chevrolet Opala carrying four policemen; Pinochet's Mercedes was the second car; behind Pinochet's Mercedes was a Ford LTD in which rode three army guards and Captain Juan McLean, the head of the security team; the fourth vehicle was a Mercedes-Benz identical to Pinochet's with two army sergeants on board, plus Pinochet's doctor; bringing up the rear, the fifth vehicle, a second Ford LTD, carried four "black berets" dressed in combat gear. Three other "advance security" vehicles of the CNI were not far from the convoy, two of them on the lookout several miles ahead of the motorcade, and a white Volvo a few miles behind. In total, there were twenty-seven armed men, twenty-three of whom were expert combat troops.

As on every Sunday evening, traffic was heavy as weekend vacationers and day-trippers returned to Santiago—even more so after soldiers of a nearby army regiment, Engineers No. 2, received an order to keep the road clear for the motorcade on the El Manzano Bridge, which was under repair. The soldiers aggressively stopped all traffic in both directions, causing a massive tie-up. After Pinochet crossed the bridge, Navy Attaché Arrieta ordered the CNI Volvo that was following a few miles behind to stop and make sure that traffic on the bridge was quickly restored, lest legions of inconvenienced drivers turn against Pinochet. With that, one of the CNI vehicles was separated from the impending combat.

The ambush site was at the top of a steep slope that forced traffic to slow down. As the convoy drew near, Unit 501, containment and clash, moved the station wagon with the camper trailer from its parked position, drove it across the road, and halted, as if it were in the middle of making a U-turn. As the first security vehicle in the convoy switched on its siren, the driver pretended to be arguing with his female companion over a road map. Tarzan kicked away the football he was carrying and prepared to fire a LAW rocket.

Commander Ernesto had decided that the motorcycles should pass before he gave the order to fire at will. One of the motorcyclists steered around the Peugeot; the second barely avoided crashing into the trailer and radioed Lieutenant Yordan Tavra in the Chevrolet Opala to warn him about the obstacle just ahead. At that moment, Ernesto opened fire; the rest of the combatants began shooting, too. Tarzan's rocket launcher jammed and after a few seconds misfired, hitting the ground between the caravan vehicles; he then began firing with his M-16. Víctor Díaz, the son of a disappeared political prisoner, had the second motorcyclist in the sights of his M-16, but he did not shoot because a small car suddenly stopped, obstructing the line of fire; a man had climbed out of the car with two kids who apparently needed to relieve themselves right then and there, on the side of the road, at the worst possible moment. The motorcyclist drove his bike into an eatery across the road.

The ensuing scene was one of total confusion, with cars slamming on their brakes, clouds of smoke, explosions, bullets flying, and sirens screaming. In the car behind Pinochet's, Captain McLean, microphone in hand, ordered, "Back, go back!" but a bullet had already shattered the windshield and torn through the left femoral artery of the car's driver, who collapsed over the wheel. Lieutenant Tavra jumped out of his car and aimed his Uzi toward the hill where he had seen one assailant. Nervous, he was unable to replace the clip once he'd emptied it; he tried to fire a shotgun but it jammed. Bullets ripped into his shoulder and his groin. He and Corporal Miguel del Río played dead to save their lives.

The Ford vehicles attempted to clear the way for Pinochet's Mercedes-Benz to retreat. Mauricio Hernández, a.k.a. Ramiro, was positioned on the hillside toward the rear of the motorcade. He fired a LAW rocket that partly destroyed Captain McLean's Ford. McLean ordered his men to abandon the burning vehicle; the driver, Cardemio

Hernández, tried, but he died when a bullet perforated his chest. While McLean and an army corporal ran for cover on the hillside, the fourth occupant of the car died, still in the backseat. The combatants lobbed hand grenades and raked the convoy with their M-16s. The siren on the Opala went mute as a LAW rocket tore open its roof.

Tarzan continued firing from the side of the road where he was standing. "Surrender, sons of bitches! Surrender!" he yelled.

One of his companions asked, "Why surrender when we are winning?"

"No, shithead, I mean *they* should surrender," Tarzan said as he focused again on the battle.

Inside Pinochet's Mercedes, Commander Arrieta ordered Carvajal to drive in reverse and accelerate. Several bullets struck the windshield and side windows, showering glass on its occupants, but its armor held fast. The car pulled up onto the shoulder to avoid the vehicles behind it; Pinochet didn't say a word as it crashed against the embankment. A moment later, Carvajal had to stop because he couldn't see; the windows were shattered and his side mirror was splashed with blood. He asked his passengers to open the curtains over the back window so he could use the rearview mirror. Pinochet did not move, but his grandson did as he was asked.

Two of the "black berets," Corporals Pinilla and Guerrero, had sought cover on the hillside. Another, Juan Fernández Lobos, wisely avoiding the fight, jumped over a small stone fence on the river side of the road and plunged sixty feet straight down. Corporal Roberto Rosales was torn to pieces when a LAW rocket exploded next to him. Pinilla and Guerrero returned fire, joined by Captain McLean. Then, a LAW rocket hit the trunk of the second Ford LTD, setting it on fire.

McLean saw one of the attackers, whom he later described as a dark-haired young man dressed in a blue sports jacket and blue pants, firing in his direction. One of the bullets struck his left leg. McLean had lost his Cobra revolver and asked Pinilla, who also had a Galil 5.56 rifle, to give him his Beretta 9 mm pistol. At that moment Corporal Guerrero was shot and killed.

"Let's cross. Let's run across the road!" yelled the captain.

Pinilla and McLean crawled and then ran with their heads down and jumped over the stone fence, tumbling over 120 feet down a steep slope. Pinilla lost his rifle.

Meanwhile, Pinochet's driver continued to back up, guided by Commander Arrieta, who had opened his door slightly so he could see. The car was now full of dust. Despite the barrage of M-16 fire, both Carvajal and the driver of the alternate Mercedes were able to turn their cars around. Both of them accelerated to sixty miles an hour.

But there was still the rearguard group, Unit 504, to contend with. Marcos, one of the combatants on the hill, fired his LAW rocket launcher directly at Pinochet's vehicle. The rocket slammed into the frame of one of its doors but skidded off without exploding. The distance between the launcher and the car had been less than fifteen feet, the minimum necessary for the rocket to arm itself. Then Pinochet's Mercedes had to get past the Toyota pickup truck, which was blocking the road. Combatants on the truck aimed their automatic rifles at the tinted glass windshield of the approaching car. Juan Moreno Ávila (Sacha), standing on the road, fired his rifle from about twelve feet away, right in front of the approaching Mercedes. He fired his weapon until the last possible second, when he jumped aside to avoid being run over. Pinochet's car and the alternate Mercedes squeezed past the pickup, half-climbing the steep embankment, out of the war zone and speeding down the road at eighty miles an hour. Pinochet finally recovered his powers of speech.

"We escaped a big one, Grandson," he said.

When Pinochet submitted his written account of the incident for the judicial investigation that followed, he declared that his first impulse when the ambush started was "to get out of the car to confront the attackers, but the driver violently stopped the car and began backing up." The available testimonies reveal nothing but a passive attitude on the part of Pinochet, except when he covered his grandson with his body when glass was flying inside the vehicle. It was the grandson who helped the driver regain visibility by opening up the back curtains.

No more than six or seven minutes had passed when Commander Ernesto blew a whistle twice, signaling retreat. The combatants had been wearing running suits over their street clothes and they got rid of them. Then, leaving Pinochet's wounded where they lay, they rushed to their getaway cars, which were parked a few hundred feet away. "We could have killed them all, but we did not because they were defenseless and we were not murderers," one of the attackers stated twenty years later.

When they climbed into the cars, they realized they were all still alive. The only casualty was one combatant's minor leg wound from a grenade fragment of their own. As they sped off someone in the lead car, carrying the combatants from the containment and attack groups, yelled, "Long live Chile, *mierda!*" They were surprised how little return fire they'd received; the humiliating image of Pinochet's tough security troops jumping off the cliff to save their lives was a spectacle they especially relished. "Maybe the tyrant jumped over also," one of the combatants joked. But in one of the following vehicles the rearguard group combatants were silent because they knew Pinochet had escaped.

Pinochet's Mercedes-Benz sped back toward the El Melocotón farm, followed by the second Mercedes. Commander Arrieta radioed the car behind.

"Yes, we are following, over," responded the driver of the second Mercedes-Benz.

"Do you have any casualties?" inquired Arrieta.

"Negative, negative. What about my general. Does he need the doctor?"

Arrieta looked toward the backseat and asked: "My general, are you feeling okay?"

Pinochet hardly responded: "All right, all right," he croaked.

"Where the hell are the CNI!" Commander Arrieta exploded when he realized that the white Volvo was not at El Manzano Bridge.

Then the doubts began to creep in. Who had perpetrated the ambush? The firepower they'd brought to bear suggested that they might be renegade members of the military; perhaps another coup was under way. The soldiers of the Engineers No. 2 Regiment were still on the bridge. The alternate Mercedes moved in front, in case they opened fire. When they didn't, Sergeant Carpio, the driver of the alternate car, ordered two of the soldiers to get into his car with their weapons. "Quick, this is an emergency and this is an order," he said, as the surprised soldiers climbed in. He quickly filled them in on the situation, then stopped again just past the bridge, where another small group of soldiers kept guard, and let one of the soldiers out of the car. "Tell them what happened and pass on the information," he said. Then he sped off, with Pinochet's car right behind. It was already dark when the two battered Mercedes passed through the gates of Pinochet's mountain estate.

Although they'd assumed that most of their number would die in the operation, the FPMR fighters had prepared a detailed escape plan. They placed removable police dome lights on top of their cars and pretended to be security agents, shoving their guns out the windows, turning on the Land Cruiser's siren and honking their horns aggressively, and otherwise demanding an open road as Pinochet's guard normally did. As they careened toward Santiago they saw no sign of either of the two CNI advance vehicles nor of the police motorcyclist —who had eluded the ambush and reached a Carabineros post a few miles down the road. The first CNI car had turned around and driven toward the ambush site after shots were reported, but it was apparently delayed by heavy traffic. But even so, they must have seen the three combatants' cars passing by in the opposite direction with their dome lights and guns thrust out the windows, knowing perfectly well that they were not a part of the motorcade. The second CNI advance vehicle must also have crossed paths with the escaping combatants as it drove to the battle site from a nearby Carabineros post in the village of Las Vizcachas, where it had been stopped when the shooting began. The CNI agents knew they were outgunned; clearly they decided that discretion was the better part of valor.

Approaching the police post at Las Vizcachas, the combatants readied for another firefight as they saw barriers and sandbags, as well as Carabineros wearing helmets. Though they kept their M-16s at the ready, they decided to wave their hands, demanding quick passage. Amazingly, their ruse worked: the barriers were lifted and the three vehicles sped through without a problem—this despite the fact that the first motorcyclist who had dodged the ambush was on the scene (the FPMR fighters spotted him). He would have known which vehicles belonged to Pinochet's caravan and which didn't. Just like his colleagues in the CNI forces, he clearly was not in the mood for more shooting.

Though the combatants were long gone and Pinochet was resting safely at El Melocotón, an imaginary battle broke out at the ambush site. When the reinforcements arrived, they heard ammunition detonating in the burning vehicles and returned fire. The "battle" lasted for more than twenty minutes—much longer than the original ambush. The scene was horrific. Body parts were everywhere: on the hillside was the left leg of a special forces soldier who'd been blown to pieces; twenty feet away, a severed hand lay on the pavement. A charred, headless body sat inside a burned-out vehicle.

Five security troops and police were killed; twelve other members of the motorcade were wounded. The confusion only worsened as more troops and Investigaciones police arrived. Different groups obeyed the orders of different chiefs belonging to different armed branches. A detective combing the cliff's edge for clues slipped and fell a few dozen feet, violently striking his head on a rock. By a strange coincidence, his last name was McLean—the same as the army captain's—a very uncommon name in Chile. When an ambulance was requested to transport him to Santiago, the rescue personnel argued that McLean had already been evacuated. How could two McLeans be hurt? Chaos reigned.

Pinochet and his people at El Melocotón were deeply shaken. Some thought that "Carlos the Jackal," the Venezuelan terrorist, might be involved, since there had been rumors of his presence in Chile. But most of them, including Pinochet, suspected that hidden forces within the military were to blame. Contributing to the suspicions concerning an attempted coup was the fact that one of the attackers' vehicles, the Toyota Land Cruiser, belonged to the navy. Was the navy behind the operation? But the explanation was simpler: Bunster had rented the Land Cruiser, which even had a functioning siren, from a small entrepreneur, who had purchased it from the navy, but the transfer of ownership had not been completed.

General Guillermo Garín, Pinochet's military chief of staff, ordered reinforcements to the ambush zone. Then, in coordination with Interior Minister Ricardo García, he convened an emergency meeting at La Moneda, attended, among others, by Minister Secretary-General of the Government Francisco Javier Cuadra; the CNI chief, General Humberto Gordon; and other notables. The switchboard operators at La Moneda attempted, unsuccessfully, to contact Pinochet at El Melocotón. Communications inside the canyon were always difficult. (According to an interview I conducted with the deputy chief of Pinochet's security detail, after the 1986 discovery of caches of weapons at Carrizal Bajo, Pinochet's security staff had requested that an antenna be installed within the canyon to facilitate communications, that travel routines for the presidential convoy be changed, and that a helicopter be deployed at the general's weekend retreat, but none of these measures had been adopted.)

If Pinochet was dead, General Garín reflected, Admiral Merino had to be called to assume command of the nation. But Pinochet finally got through to La Moneda. "I am going to Santiago," he said.

"My general, by no means," Garín replied. "There are still clashes in the area and we do not know if there are other ambushes prepared along the way." Pinochet accepted his chief of staff's advice and decided to stay put. But, always distrustful, he worked the phones, calling all his army regiment commanders, to make sure that the attack was not linked to some secretly planned military uprising.

The FPMR militants abandoned their vehicles and weapons in various points of La Florida borough, mainly along Vicuña Mackenna Avenue, and separated. Alternately walking and riding on buses, they made their way by deliberately circuitous routes to their homes and safe houses. One of them stopped at a neighborhood bar to have a drink—to make himself look less suspicious and perhaps also to celebrate. The one wounded combatant went to a prearranged "medical contact point," where, after meeting a man with a specific journal under his arm and giving him the password "Operation Twentieth Century," he was taken blindfolded to an underground clinic, where the grenade fragments were surgically removed from his leg.

It must have been around 9:30 P.M. when I learned of the attack on Pinochet. I immediately turned on the television to watch the news, and then I phoned a few friends. Some expressed doubts about the veracity of the ambush. "This could be just a sham, an excuse for Pinochet to come down strong on the opposition," one of them said.

There was no question that this would be a dangerous time for us dissidents. A state of siege and a curfew were decreed that same night. Six opposition magazines were shut down and an international news agency was placed under censorship. But when Pinochet appeared on TV to demonstrate that he was still alive, standing next to his bullet-riddled Mercedes-Benz, dressed in a parka with his hand bandaged because of some scratches caused by flying glass, I was convinced that the attack had been real. Pinochet was pale and his face was distorted by a rictus of fear or shock. I had never seen him looking so shaken and insecure. At that moment all FPMR combatants saw the evidence of their failure to kill Pinochet.

Pinochet still only fully trusted his immediate companions and his La Moneda contacts, a perception that was conveyed to me by a high military officer who was involved in the post-ambush events. The next day, Monday, September 8, the old general returned to Santiago by helicopter. According to witnesses I interviewed years later, he was in "a terribly aggressive temper" when he arrived at La Moneda. Now that he felt safe, he would take measures. "This is war with all its letters," he said. "It is a war without limits and without quarter." In an interview with journalists Raquel Correa and Elizabeth Subercaseaux Pinochet said, "I am no saint or Mahomet. If they give me a slap in the face, I strike back with two."

But if he wasn't a saint or Mahomet, he still enjoyed special access to the Almighty. Pinochet attributed his lucky escape to Our Lady of Perpetual Help, whom he had revered since he was a military cadet. Perhaps advised by communications experts, or guided by his own good political acumen, Pinochet said that after looking at the bullet-riddled back window of his car, "I perceived the image of the Holy Mother. At first I thought it was a result of the strong emotions I had experienced, but then other people shared the same thought." Two days later, the wrecked cars from the convoy were exhibited outside

La Moneda. Everyone agreed that the outline of Our Lady of Perpetual Help could be perfectly discerned in the Mercedes' shattered back window. Clearly Pinochet had been saved by a higher power.

But back to the war "with all its letters." The first night of the curfew, September 8 at around two in the morning, barely seven hours after the attack on Pinochet, a secret police group surrounded the house of the electrician Felipe Rivera in Pudahuel borough and forced him into one of their cars. Two hours later the same group arrived at the house of Gastón Vidaurrázaga, a teacher and MIR member whose mother was a judge in a Santiago tribunal. He was shot twenty times as, only half-dressed, he attempted to escape. Then the night raiders went to the Bellavista neighborhood, where they violently kidnapped José Carrasco, an MIR militant and journalist who covered international affairs for the biweekly magazine *Análisis*. Carrasco's fifteen-year-old stepson yelled desperately, demanding to know where they were taking his stepfather. A decade earlier, in 1976, the DINA secret police had kidnapped his biological father, who had then joined the ranks of the disappeared. I knew José Carrasco; he often used the documentation center that I had created at the Academy of Christian Humanism. At dawn of the ninth, the bullet-riddled bodies of all three men were found at different locations around Santiago. All of them bore signs of torture. The following night, the CNI abducted the publicist Abraham Muskatblit, a Communist Party member. His body was found in a ditch in a rural area outside Santiago.

Minister Francisco J. Cuadra, the government spokesman, offered the usual Pinochet regime cynical explanation in such cases: the killings had been committed by the left: the deaths were attributable to "an internal purge among Marxist groups due to the failure of the ambush against General Pinochet," said Cuadra.

The CNI, which had failed to protect Pinochet, had in cowardly fashion wanted to assassinate five people, one for each of the five Pinochet security guards killed at Cajón del Maipo, but the fifth abduction failed. Luis Toro, a Vicariate of Solidarity lawyer who, years later, worked with me at the Foreign Ministry, had taken precautions. When CNI thugs arrived at his home, he opened his second-floor window, shouted a password, and rang a bell. His neighbors all turned their lights on and the brave agents of the CNI swiftly retreated.

Within twenty-four hours after the ambush, Pinochet ordered search operations to commence in the main shantytowns and poor neighborhoods of Santiago. Death threats were received in labor union offices, student associations, and in the homes of human rights lawyers and activists. The French priests Pierre Dubois, Daniel Caruette, and Jaime Lacelot were expelled from the country.

That night of the ambush and of the assassination of the leftist militants, the lives of other political leaders hung in the balance. Around the same time that the kidnappings were beginning, a civil police contingent arrived at a house in a gated community in La Reina borough. Exactly at 2:15 A.M. the policemen burst into the bedroom of Ricardo Lagos and his wife, Luisa Durán, with submachine guns in their hands.

"Don't worry, Mr. Ricardo, we are from the Investigaciones," one of the policemen said when Lagos demanded to know their identities.

"What do you want and by what right do you invade my bedroom? Show me an arrest warrant," Lagos demanded.

"Don't worry," the detective repeated. "We have to take you with us. Lucky for you we arrived first."

Lagos got dressed and was taken away to the Investigaciones headquarters, without any warrant or justification and despite the protests of family members and neighbors.

Perhaps he *was* lucky. When one of Lagos's sons opened the door to the detectives, one of them had asked, "Have they come yet; has anybody come already?" Several other leftist political leaders from different groups were also arrested that night. "Yes, there are politicians involved [in the ambush]. I do not know which ones, but there are," Pinochet told a confidant.

At the police headquarters a prosecutor interrogated Lagos, reading from a dossier: "June 1974, he [Lagos] participates in the clandestine political commission of the Socialist Party with the false name 'Guillermo.'"

"You are wrong," Lagos responded angrily. "Your information refers to Ricardo Lagos Salinas, a twenty-four-year-old Socialist arrested in 1974 and made to disappear. I am Ricardo Lagos Escobar." The rest of the dossier referred to the correct Lagos. One item in it, included to illustrate Lagos's alleged "advocacy of violence," was an interview he'd given to *Newsweek* a few weeks before the ambush, in which he expressed the opinion that violence in Chile would worsen with Pinochet's continued repression.

I and other friends of Lagos and his family began a campaign to free him. I wrote to scholars in the United States who knew him to urge them to write letters to their congressmen, publish op-eds in major newspapers, and so forth. At the University of North Carolina at

Chapel Hill, where Lagos had taught, and at Duke University, where he had obtained his Ph.D., his friends organized committees demanding his release.

I went to visit him in jail. He and the other opposition politicians were being held at the Carabineros prison facility on San Martin Street, which, ironically, used to be the address of the headquarters of the Central Committee of the Socialist Party. After the building had burned to the ground on the day of the coup, the parcel had been seized and occupied by the Carabineros. Lagos seemed to be in good spirits. His major concern was that he could be expelled from the country and sent into permanent exile. He asked me to go to the embassies of all the countries where regular flights from Chile landed and get their authorities to promise not to accept him in case he was expelled. The priority was Argentina. My conversation with the Argentine chargé d'affaires, Raúl Estrada, was reassuring. "I can assure you that President Alfonsín's government will send Ricardo Lagos back in case he arrives by plane," he said. "And if he is left on our border, we will not let him in." Peru was a harder nut to crack. The ambassador was quite reticent, but the foreign minister did not want to be dragged into a neighbor's problem by accepting a deported opposition leader. The Brazilians expressed a similar view.

Lagos's wife and I arranged meetings and visited with several other ambassadors. The American ambassador, Harry Barnes, not only agreed with our petition but also immediately sent one of his diplomats, Counselor Donald Tomking, to visit Lagos at the police headquarters. The State Department had already issued a communiqué on September 9 strongly condemning the attack on Pinochet, welcoming the release of two American priests who had been interrogated about the ambush, and expressing "continued concern about the detention of certain opposition leaders . . . without any evidence before a court of law of some connection of these individuals to the Sunday attack."

One day Lagos told me, "We need a political heavyweight to ask for my release."

"How about former president Carter?" I suggested. "He is very active, well respected, and influential. Even Pinochet would have to pay attention, and I know Bob Pastor, his Latin American adviser."

Lagos liked the idea. I contacted Pastor and he delivered. Within a couple of days, I received the following telegram from Jimmy Carter: "I have just learned that Ricardo Lagos, a former President of the Democratic Alliance, a coalition of democratic parties in Chile, was recently arrested and imprisoned without charges in Chile. All people interested in democracy and human rights in the Hemisphere must be concerned with the illegal arrest of such an important leader. I hope the Chilean government will either issue formal charges, or release Mr. Lagos from prison immediately."

The declaration was distributed to all the international wire services on September 18, 1986. The next day, every major Chilean newspaper and radio station carried the news of former president Carter's appeal. Lagos sent a thank-you note to Carter; many years later, during a seminar, he personally reminded him of his opportune message. "Carter was truly moved by my thankful reminiscence," Lagos told me. He was also helped by an unrelated circumstance: Pinochet's foreign minister, Jaime Del Valle, had managed to get a meeting at the UN General Assembly with a group of European counterparts; but the Spanish foreign minister, Francisco Fernández-Ordoñez, opposed going ahead with the interview if Lagos wasn't released. The Pinochet regime needed to mitigate its international isolation. After twenty-one days in prison, Lagos was released. No charges were ever lodged against him.

Eventually he learned that a police inspector who had been his student at the University of Chile had been on night shift after the ambush and saw the arrest warrants, which included his former professor. Realizing that Lagos was in danger, the inspector ordered a group of detectives to pick up Lagos immediately; they also went to José Carrasco's house but got there too late to save him. This explains why Carrasco's name appears along with Ricardo Lagos's in the initial list of people arrested by the police that appeared in the September 9 edition of the government newspaper, *La Nación*.

The failed attack on Pinochet, and its repressive consequences, drove an even bigger wedge between the Communists on the one hand and the Socialists and the rest of the moderate opposition on the other. I helped draft a declaration of the Socialist Party released on September 8, which rejected "once more the strategy of armed struggle against the military regime, since, in the end, it only means more pain and death for the people of Chile."

Among other post-ambush actions taken against the opposition, the CNI pressured a prosecutor to interrogate several people, including me, who had participated in a meeting on external debt in Havana, Cuba, in August 1985. The conference had been attended by a large number of Chilean exiles and about a dozen of us from inside. According to a report prepared by Pinochet's secret police, the external debt conference was a "disguise" under which "plans were elaborated for the overthrow of the Supreme Government, through various strategies imposed by the Marxist Government of Cuba." That couldn't have been further from the truth. In reality, a violent argument had taken place between five of us delegates of the Socialist Party, led by Ricardo Nuñez, known as the "renovated" Socialists, and "Humberto," one of the men in charge of the Chile desk in the America Department of the Cuban Communist Party.

The Cuban Communists distrusted us, disagreed with our views on democracy, and, most important, arrogantly dismissed our strategy of peaceful social mobilization. They favored and supported the armed-insurrection strategy of the Communist Party through the FPMR, and the violent road traditionally advocated by the MIR. The Chilean Socialists the Cubans talked to were the group led by former foreign minister Clodomiro Almeyda. They preferred to engage with Christian Democratic leaders such as Radomiro Tomic, who was present at the conference, than with us. We met with "Humberto" in a private room at the conference site. It turned sour almost as soon as it started. Basically, Humberto berated us, accusing us of being Pinochet's pawns.

I responded, "You do not have any idea of what is truly going on in Chile. People reject violence; the majority needed to defeat Pinochet has become alienated from armed struggle."

Ricardo Nuñez, the leader of our group, added, "It is you and your friends in Chile who are playing Pinochet's game."

"You guys support kidnappings of innocent civilians," my colleague Jaime Estévez chimed in. After Jaime's accusation, a fistfight almost broke out.

We wanted the Cubans to understand that their support for the Patriotic Front and the MIR would not hasten Pinochet's downfall by as much as a minute—that in fact it was counterproductive. But they turned a deaf ear to us; nothing positive came out of this encounter. (I can't help adding a postscript: some years later, as it happened, this same Humberto was arrested in Havana for his participation in a scheme to sell pornographic videos featuring children in Miami.)

Later in the conference, all Chileans were invited to a private session with Fidel Castro. About twenty-five or thirty of us attended. Castro was better informed about Chile and his analysis was considerably more sophisticated than Humberto's; he spoke to us for about an hour about issues ranging from globalization to Pinochet. We, the "renovated" Socialists, were in the minority there and we decided not to take the floor. Those who did, including several Christian Democrats, did so to thank Fidel and a few, embarrassingly for us and, I suspect, for the Cuban leader, to lavishly praise him.

On September 17, ten days after "Operation Twentieth Century," the Christian Democrats sent a letter to the Communist leadership: "The relationship of the Communist Party with violence and terrorism and the maintenance by you of military and paramilitary structures is the principal obstacle to a coordinated and ascending mobilization. The discovery of the arsenals, the attack on Pinochet and its sequel of deaths, have aggravated the militarization of Chilean politics."

Around that same time, in October 1986, President Raúl Alfonsín of Argentina visited Cuba and asked Fidel Castro to stop supporting armed struggle in Chile. Alfonsín feared that the U.S. administration's policy, which was now more sympathetic to the Chilean democratic opposition, could recoil, and that a growing armed rebellion against Pinochet could eventually affect Argentina's political process. The Argentine president also spoke about the issue with Mikhail Gorbachev, who claimed he had nothing to do with the armed movement in Chile. Castro admitted that FPMR fighters had been training in Cuba to put an end to the Pinochet dictatorship, but facilitated a contact between the Chilean Communist leadership and Argentine government officials that contributed to a reassessment of the Communist strategy regarding armed struggle.

The failure of the Pinochet ambush provoked a strong internal debate between the political commission of the Communist Party and the top commanders of the FPMR. The political commission criticized the inadequate training of some of the combatants, who were less than expert in the use of their weapons, as well as the absence of a previous rehearsal on the actual ground of the ambush.

The first combatant to be captured was Juan Moreno Ávila, who had left traces of his fingerprints on a soft-drink bottle recovered from the La Obra house. ("It was conventional detective work that caught some of us," Bunster later told me.) The police quickly located Moreno's mother and sister, who, after being brutally beaten up, gave up his address. His arrest led to the detention of four more combatants. Others were arrested in different circumstances. In the last days of the dictatorship, in January 1990, Moreno escaped from prison, along with practically all the fellow combatants with whom he had been jailed and with other political prisoners. He stayed in Chile, living under a false identity, for more than ten years, working alongside retired army personnel and policemen at a private security company. Interviewed in September 2006 he declared, "I have built a life under another name; what do I gain by legalizing my situation now? I lose more than I gain by becoming Juan Moreno Ávila again."

Fabiola, the only woman who participated in the attack, was never caught; she remained in Chile, carefully preserving her anonymity. Seven other fighters were transported out of Chile a few days after the attack for military training in Hanoi, via Buenos Aires and Moscow. Most of them ended up fighting against the "Contras" in Nicaragua, and a few, after returning clandestinely to Chile for a period, settled in Havana. César Bunster, the operation's logistics man, stayed underground for some time, then abandoned Chile but later returned to live under an assumed identity for eighteen years. Bunster worked as an interpreter; ironically, he translated for Lord Norman Lamont, Pinochet's most ardent British supporter, when Lamont visited Chile to meet with Pinochet Foundation delegates. In 2004, the Chilean courts declared that the arrest warrant against Bunster had lapsed, and he now resides in Chile. "I never thought Pinochet would escape alive. My only doubt was how many lives of combatants would be lost," he told me on a hot summer evening in Santiago twenty years after the assault on Pinochet.

In June 1987 the CNI mounted "Operation Albania," a fake confrontation in which several FPMR militants, including José Valenzuela Levy, a.k.a. Commander Ernesto, who had directed the attack on Pinochet's motorcade, and six other FPMR militants were assassinated in cold blood after having been arrested several days before. Commander Ernesto was shot seven times in the head and received nine bullets in his body (the assassins were tried and convicted when democracy returned to Chile). Also assassinated, under different circumstances, were the combatants Julio Guerra and Cecilia Magni (Commander Tamara). Mauricio Arenas, a.k.a. Joaquín, head of Unit 504, the rearguard unit, was gravely wounded in a shootout with the CNI but survived, escaped from jail in January 1990, returned later to Chile to resume armed struggle, and died of lung cancer in Argentina. Mauricio Hernández (Ramiro), head of Unit 503, on the hillside, who handled one of the LAW rocket launchers, continued leading violent actions well into the democratic era, was jailed in 1992, escaped in 1996, and wound up in prison in Brazil for kidnapping a Brazilian businessman.

Rodrigo Rodríguez Otero, a.k.a. Tarzan, remained in hiding in Chile. He was shot in one arm in another military operation of the FPMR, and owing to the seriousness of the wound he was transferred to Havana for proper medical treatment. Tarzan returned to Chile, but he eventually abandoned armed struggle and settled in Spain. Víctor Díaz, a.k.a. Enzo, whose father had been tortured to death and made to disappear, escaped from jail in January 1990 and ended up residing in Paris, where he works as a cameraman and set technician for a TV production company. Other combatants also wound up living in Europe.

The failure of the Pinochet ambush, the adverse political fallout it caused, and the capture or killings of so many combatants convinced the CCP to exercise more direct control over the FPMR. Raúl Pellegrin resented his removal as commander and created an "autonomous" faction of the front, to which he attracted a substantial majority of the militants, including most of the Pinochet attackers. Pellegrin's breakaway group undertook many violent actions over the years, among them the kidnapping of the deputy director of the army's weapons factory, Colonel Carlos Carreño. Pellegrin was murdered in October 1988, after being captured and tortured, together with his partner, Commander Tamara (Cecilia Magni), in the area of the Tinguiririca River, about a hundred miles south of Santiago, where he and other members of the "autonomous" wing of the FPMR had hoped to launch a "National Patriotic War."

AT THE TIME of the 1986 ambush in Cajón del Maipo, Pinochet was already setting his sights on holding the planned 1988 plebiscite. In a speech in the southern town of Santa Juana, Pinochet had hinted that he would be the candidate, although the junta had to vote on it. "We will not hand over the power for the fun of it," Pinochet had declared. The junta favored the "projection of the regime" into the future, but not necessarily with General Pinochet at its helm. Admiral Merino and Air Force Commander Matthei backed the idea of holding a competitive election. Later, General Matthei went even further: the "ideal" candidate, he said, in either a plebiscite or a competitive election, should be a civilian.

At a meeting of the Central Committee of the Socialist Party in late September 1986, one of its members, José Joaquin Brunner, presented a document, "Notes for Discussion," in which he offered a thumbnail analysis of the present political moment and the coming challenges.

The strategy of social mobilization through protests and strikes was becoming increasingly weak, fragmented, and improvised, he wrote. Moreover, Pinochet's effort to portray the opposition as an armed minority, rather than the overwhelming majority of the country, was succeeding, especially in the wake of the failed ambush. Pinochet had "redefined the national situation, once again, in terms of a scenario of war," while simultaneously accentuating the "personalist" trait of the regime as opposed to the "institutional" ideal favored by the junta commanders. Brunner ended on a pragmatic note, concluding that if we were to find a workable way out of Pinochet's tyranny, we would have to work within the confines of the 1980 constitution, using it to demand the expression of popular sovereignty in whatever form was available, whether via elections or a plebiscite. Our priority should be to press for the dictation of the transition laws; to register to vote whenever voter rolls would be opened; and to be ready to negotiate with the armed forces while also pressuring the Communist Party into abandoning its armed operations.

Brunner's remarks sparked an intense discussion. I still have the notes I scribbled while it was going on. I took the floor to agree that our protests had been losing their resolve; even so, demobilization would be far more demoralizing. As the ambush on Pinochet receded into the past, the contradictions within the regime would sharpen once again, I added. I agreed, though, that we needed a new message— we should mobilize to demand free elections instead of a plebiscite in '88. Nobody said it clearly and openly, but we were all thinking the same thing: to succeed, we were going to have to play Pinochet's game. The biggest question was whether Pinochet would allow us to compete on anything remotely resembling "a level playing field." The day the voter rolls were finally opened, almost fifteen years after they were destroyed (the 1978 *Consulta* motivated by the UN human rights condemnation of the Pinochet regime and the 1980 constitutional referendum had been conducted without voter rolls), the first person to sign up—as citizen number 1, in the voter registry number 1, on voting table number 1—was General Augusto Pinochet. The first step toward the plebiscite had been taken.

After the Chilean summer, the country prepared itself for its first papal visit. Pope John Paul II landed in Chile on April 1, 1987, and his visit was controversial from the start. Speaking to reporters aboard the plane carrying him throughout South America, Pope John Paul had bluntly characterized Pinochet's government as "dictatorial," and defended the efforts of the Chilean Catholic Church to restore democracy. Pinochet had stated sarcastically that "it would be better if [bishops and priests] spent 90 percent of their time praying." The Pope's response was unambiguous: "There are those who tell us, 'Stay in the sacristy and do nothing else; yes, do nothing else.' Because they say it is politics, but it is not politics. This is what we are."

When the Pope visited Pinochet at La Moneda, the general invited him to go through what looked like a door but actually was a floor-to-ceiling window leading to a small balcony that overlooked an awaiting crowd of government employees and other guests summoned by the regime. This salute, not contemplated in the program, was a serious breach of protocol, but Pinochet calculated that being seen with the Pope was worth it and would win him a lot of points. The Pope did not flinch; with Pinochet by his side, he plastered a smile across his face and saluted the people. Afterward the two met privately for more than forty minutes. Nothing was known about their dialogue until 2007, when Cardinal Stanislao Dziwisz, Karol Wojtyla's private secretary since 1966, revealed that the Pope, mincing no words, told Pinochet that the time had come to transfer power to civilian authorities. A few hours later, the Pope met with a group of opposition leaders—a clear gesture of support toward the democratic movement.

Though the plebiscite was still a year away, Pinochet began to prepare for it by introducing changes in the government's team. In July 1987, he rewarded the loyalty of his former interior minister, Sergio Fernández, by reappointing him to the same cabinet seat. Hernán Büchi was confirmed as minister of finance, and Sergio Melnick became minister of planning. It was the cabinet of the "projection" of the regime, one that would press for the plebiscite and ensure Pinochet's nomination.

Minister Melnick, a clever commercial engineer, intended to bring new ideas and dynamism to his ministry. Most important for Pinochet was the fact that this was a lucky man; just a few months earlier, on March 20, he had been the only one of nine passengers to survive a deadly crash of a Beechcraft passenger plane. After the ambush, Pinochet's well-known inclination to the superstitious and esoteric had become more marked. One of his former aides, Press Secretary Federico Willoughby, said of Pinochet in 1989, "I don't think he is afraid of sickness or death. He is much more afraid of bad omens, curses, and humiliation. . . . Every Tuesday the thirteenth [a traditionally unlucky day in many Spanish-speaking cultures] he seems worried. He will not walk under a ladder. There are colors that displease him. . . . He is interested in horoscopes, astrology and those things." Pinochet was confident about the outcome of the coming election, but he probably felt a bit of extra luck would not hurt.

We in the opposition opted to reject the plebiscite and demand free and competitive elections immediately. Though the National Accord was no longer politically relevant, in 1987 its leader, a former Frei

Montalva minister, Sergio Molina, organized a Committee for Free Elections (Comité de Elecciones Libres, CEL), whose fourteen-member board included noted writers, scientists, diplomats, and businessmen, among them Eduardo Frei Ruiz-Tagle who, years later, would become president of Chile.

In an open letter to Interior Minister Ricardo García the CEL explained its objections to a plebiscite. A plebiscite "does not allow a choice among alternatives, and that is why democracies do not use this procedure for selecting political authorities. Plebiscites or referendums are utilized to solve differences of opinion on fundamental matters." Then they listed the minimum requirements of a fair election: freedom of expression, freedom of assembly and political association, judicial appeals, nonintervention by sitting authorities, adequate control of the electoral act, and so forth. On March 17, 1987, through an unprecedented joint declaration of its Nuñez and Almeyda wings, the Socialist Party supported the committee's call for free elections.

The process of convergence between the two main sectors of the Socialist Party had been spurred by Almeyda's dramatic return to Chile from a stint in the Dawson Island prison camp. Fifteen years earlier he had been forced into exile when spurious charges of misusing public money had been brought against him. Then, in March 1987 he had crossed the Andes from Argentina on a mule, making his way to Chile through snow-covered mountains and crossing the border about four hundred miles north of Santiago. He had surprised the Pinochet regime by turning himself over to a Santiago criminal court, which found no merit to the charges that the Pinochet government had lodged against him fifteen years before. But Pinochet had Almeyda arrested anyway and sent him on internal exile, or "relegation," to Patagonia. Even so, it became increasingly difficult for Pinochet to enforce his exile policy as more Chileans attempted to force their way back into the country.

In order to draw the left toward a peaceful mobilization campaign for free elections, a Committee of the Left for Free Elections (Comité de Izquierda por las Elecciones Libres, CIEL) was created. Women's movements and student organizations for free elections sprang up throughout Chile.

Pinochet rejected the possibility of elections because, supposedly, the opposition "lacked political projects and had no definitions on substantive matters," which would make any election "an expression of demagogy and a return to the old habits of political deal-making." Defending the plebiscite, Pinochet argued in his message to the nation of September 11, 1987: "What more freedom than to be able to choose freely between extending the progress achieved thus far or to destroy the country, going backward."

Many felt we needed a Plan B. If Pinochet and his followers continued to reject the demand for free elections, we had to decide whether or not to participate in the plebiscite.

Pinochet's position was becoming ever clearer. In July 1987, in a meeting with the newly born Renovación Nacional Party (an amalgamation of three right-wing groups, including the UDI Party), Minister of the Interior Sergio Fernández went far to dispel any remaining doubts: "I am here to win the plebiscite with General Pinochet leading us," he said. "I know the debate going on within your group, but I reject any change of the system. Besides, we have to end once and for all the confusion among supporters of the military regime. We cannot continue wasting time!"

Many conservatives preferred a competitive election to a plebiscite, even if they could live with a Pinochet candidacy. In a plebiscite, it was argued, Pinochet's name alone on the ballot would be like a lightning rod for dissent, whereas in a competitive election the logic of faults and merits is distributed among several candidates. Another reason for conservatives to support competitive elections was that the drive for free elections was straining the democratic forces: if we succeeded in canceling the plebiscite, we in the opposition still had to form a coalition, develop a program, and find a candidate. In short, the plebiscite united us; competitive elections could divide us.

Rightists who didn't favor Pinochet were still divided on who would be the ideal candidate. Admiral Merino had declared that it should be "a civilian, fifty-two or fifty-three years old, center-rightist." Air Force General Matthei had also favored "a civilian, since the armed forces should not be judge and plaintiff." Right-wing politicians such as Sergio Onofre Jarpa and Francisco Bulnes also favored a civilian.

Our main concern in the opposition was to mobilize the people to register to vote. This was a fundamental step, whether we got free elections or had to settle for the plebiscite. The Socialist Party and the CIEL began to organize groups of volunteers to go neighborhood by neighborhood, block by block, house by house, delivering information on where to register to vote, offering to take photos for free so ID cards could be quickly obtained, and establishing local committees for free elections. We traveled extensively throughout metropolitan areas and into the rural regions to mobilize people. "We are asking you to register, to tell your friends and family to do the same, to create pluralist committees for free elections. That way we will have enough strength to break Pinochet's institutional design or, at worst, to defeat him in the plebiscite," I said in a speech in late 1987.

We also began to coordinate our efforts with the National Workers Command, an ad-hoc organization of labor unions that demanded free elections. Only free elections would allow legitimate social demands to be satisfied, we argued.

In May 1987, the National Democratic Institute (NDI)—a nonprofit organization linked to the U.S. Democratic Party, dedicated to expanding and strengthening democracy worldwide—invited me to join an international delegation to observe the first congressional elections to be held under the democratic government of President Corazón Aquino in the Philippines. It was a great opportunity to study firsthand the National Movement for Free Elections (NAMFREL), a nonpartisan organization that had done much to guard against fraud in the "snap elections" of 1986 that led to the fall of Ferdinand Marcos. Four Chileans, each representing a different political sector, were invited to be part of the delegation: Andres Allamand, the maverick rightist who favored free elections (though he ended up voting for Pinochet in the 1988 plebiscite); José Miguel Barros, an independent representing the CEL; Carlos Figueroa, representing the Christian Democratic Party; and me, representing the Socialist Party and the CIEL.

As Election Day drew near, we were dispersed to different parts of the Philippines. I ended up in the city of Tuguegarao, in the Cagayan region by the North China Sea. On Election Day we mobilized ourselves in a "Jeepney," a small, beat-up colorfully painted bus, and drove from one polling site to another. There were NAMFREL observers at every polling place, and an atmosphere of tranquillity and order prevailed. The only sign of trouble came at about 6 P.M., when we were told by radio that armed guerrillas had interrupted voting at a village not far from our location. From our local team, only Larry Garber, an NDI official, and I dared to go take a look. After driving along a narrow dirt road and emerging into a breathtakingly beautiful valley filled with rice paddies and palm trees on the horizon, we entered a picturesque village.

Though there were guerrillas in the region, the report about the attack on the voting site, a modest schoolhouse, turned out to be false. Actually, since it was becoming dark, the problem they were having was the lack of electricity. All of the registered voters had completed their civic duty; now local electoral officials were counting ballots by candlelight, while NAMFREL observers looked on. It was admirable and inspiring. This is what we need in Chile, I concluded; committed volunteers, ready to overcome any obstacle.

But our situation in Chile was different. Our movement for free elections had to continue to articulate a clear antidictatorial stand and be accompanied by social mobilization. But the lesson of NAMFREL that was transferable was the importance of having well-trained poll watchers to impede fraud.

Pinochet continued his unannounced campaign throughout 1987, traveling around the country to open new housing projects, announcing minimum wage increases, and meeting with his key generals, who acted like virtual campaign chiefs.

On the right, those who wanted elections began to believe that the plebiscite was inevitable. But it was not inevitable that Pinochet should be the candidate. For shrewd conservatives, the "projection of the regime," or the economic model, was more important than Pinochet's staying in power. Around November 1987, Patricio Aylwin, president of the Christian Democratic Party, expressed his conviction that the opposition had to participate in the plebiscite, on the platform of saying "no" to the dictatorship's candidate. Some electoral experts counseled against participating in the plebiscite: too many factors militated against the possibility of winning a clear victory.

An intense period of internal discussion within the Socialist Party began. To have poll watchers defend our vote in the plebiscite, we needed to be a registered political party. Pinochet's constitution prohibited the registration of any Socialist organization, so we couldn't register in our own name. In the CIEL we discussed the idea of creating a political party comprising all the opposition.

The Communist Party continued to reject the movement for free elections and, even more decisively, the "no" campaign—quixotically insisting that the only elections it would participate in were general elections without Pinochet and his 1980 constitution.

On October 1, 1987, the top underground leadership of the Communist Party requested a meeting with us Socialists. We decided to hold it in my townhouse on Reina Victoria Street. It was the last townhouse in a gated community of six houses, and its backyard abutted the Canal San Ramón (one of the waterways that brings the snowmelt down from the Andes into Santiago), which made it harder to ambush and at the same time easier to escape from. The Communists sent Manuel Cantero and Jorge Insunza; our side was represented by Ricardo Lagos, Ricardo Nuñez, Erich Schnake—who had been allowed back in the country from exile—and me.

That night, I arrived late from an intense day of political work to find Jorge Insunza sitting in my living room. He was disguised in a way that seemed odd and almost funny for those of us who remembered him as a public figure from the Allende period. A bald man, he was wearing a blond wig, had lightened his dark mustache, and was dressed like a hippie of the late-sixties era. I had to contain a chuckle when I saw him. Manuel Cantero arrived soon after; as usual, the Socialists arrived last and late.

As we began to eat and talk, Lagos posed an awkward question to Cantero: "Are you Manuel Cantero?" he asked. No names had been given before the agreed meeting, and Cantero, like Insunza, was in disguise. After a tense moment Cantero responded, "No, I am not Manuel Cantero." Of course he was, and we just pretended that nothing had been said and continued our conversation.

They weren't just being paranoid. Five Communist militants had recently been kidnapped by the CNI and made to disappear. It was the usual cowardly response of the secret police to FPMR actions, this time to the kidnapping of an army colonel, Carlos Carreño, deputy director of the Army Weapons Production Company (Fábricas y Maestranzas del Ejército, FAMAE), who eventually was released unharmed. Cantero and Insunza confirmed that the five disappeared militants, who were never found again, were members of their party. Their main objective, they said, was to impede Pinochet from staying in power until 1997 and for that they were willing to make concessions—including publicly reconsidering their negative view on our voter registration drive and joining the campaign for free elections. Their commitment could be "loyal and effective," Cantero and Insunza said. But they had two conditions: one, rejection of the plebiscite, and two, a wide political agreement of the opposition through a mechanism to be discussed.

Our response was that so long as Pinochet persisted in the idea of the plebiscite then we should strive to defeat him at his own game. As regards the second point, we suggested that we could ask the Catholic Church to call on all political parties to support a peaceful drive for voter registration and free elections. The Communist Party could accept the call and abide by it. Our Communist interlocutors told us that within a few days they would attempt to begin a conversation with the Christian Democratic leadership. The CCP was feeling the pressure, as several emblematic Communist figures, such as the actress Maria Maluenda and a former party spokesman, Patricio Hales, had already parted with the official line and joined the voter registration drive and the movement for free elections.

Ricardo Lagos and I had witnessed that rank-and-file Communists were in favor of voter registration. On August 15, 1987, we went to a *población* in working-class Renca borough, accompanied by an American political scientist, Arturo Valenzuela, and the *Washington Post* journalist Pamela Constable, knocking on doors to ask people to register. A Communist leader who had recently returned from exile confronted us and, accompanied by a couple of activists, yelled, "Inscripción igual traición!" ("Registering to vote equals treason!") An animated dialogue ensued, and an old Communist member from the neighborhood interjected, "I am with Mr. Lagos on this," and told his party leader that he should listen to the views of the common people.

On November 3, 1987, in a meeting of the Central Committee of the Socialist Party, I supported a proposal to create a Party for Democracy. Some argued that such an idea was the equivalent of "entering Pinochet's system," but the majority disagreed. This party would be "a tactical instrument, pluralist, and unitary in the sense of incorporating all those—individuals or groups—who reject Pinochet's institutions and seek a political solution to the country's crisis," I said. We agreed that we should begin the process of registering the Party for Democracy by gathering one hundred signatures from as wide a political spectrum possible.

This ideal scenario was obviated when the Christian Democratic Party decided to register as a legal entity, eliminating the possibility of our having one umbrella party for the whole opposition. So the Socialist Party would have to shoulder the creation of the new organization for the rest of the opposition. There were daunting logistical problems, too: the date for the plebiscite had not been set—like the good military tactician that he was, Pinochet would fix it at the time that would be the most convenient for his offensive. But assuming it would be on September 11, 1988 (in fact it would be held on October 5), we had to register our new party and train our poll watchers by no later than March 15, 1988. In short, at the height of the Southern Hemisphere summer, when everybody was on vacation, we would have to gather tens of thousands of signatures and then create an organization out of whole cloth. To make things worse, we didn't just have Pinochet to contend with—our colleagues from the Almeyda sector of the Socialist Party and the Communists remained staunchly opposed to our approach. But many independents, Communist dissidents, and democratic conservatives were on our side.

In the end, we took the chance. On Tuesday, November 20, at the Spanish Circle Club, before a notary public, we signed the documents founding the party. I was one of the hundred initial signatories and was elected to its first Council of Directors. On December 15, 1987, the Central Committee of our Socialist Party ratified the decision to create the Party for Democracy (Partido por la Democracia, PPD), designating Ricardo Lagos as its first chairman. Now, we had to go out and get thirty-five thousand signatures so we could become legal.

When we evaluated our results two weeks later, on January 30, they were truly dismal; nationwide we had gathered only three thousand names. Then, someone had a brilliant idea: Why don't we take to the streets? We didn't have much to lose. The Socialist Youth set up portable tables on the sidewalks of busy downtown streets; several of us adults went out with them. To our delighted amazement, passersby began to sign on! It took courage to do it, since the affiliation form required them to give, in addition to their signature, their full name, address, place and date of birth, ID number, and electoral registration data. Even so, our first day out we signed up as many as we had in the two previous weeks. The Pinochet-designated mayor of Santiago quickly threw a monkey wrench into the works—he decided that we needed municipal permits to set up tables on city streets, and of course he wasn't willing to grant them. Then Ricardo Lagos remembered the cigarette girls at old-fashioned nightclubs, who carried their wares in hanging trays. So as not to place tables on the actual street surface we equipped our volunteers with hanging desks.

By then, most of the opposition had come around to our point of view—they realized there was no alternative but to participate in the plebiscite. On February 2, 1988, sixteen opposition parties, some of them just tiny groups or individuals heading "virtual" organizations, formed the "Comando de Partidos por el 'No'" (Coalition of Parties for "No") and endorsed a formal document to that effect. We would beat Pinochet at his own game. Nineteen eighty-eight was going to be the "decisive year," not 1986, as the Communists had proclaimed before they attempted to kill the dictator.

Abraham Lowenthal, a distinguished professor and friend, invited me to teach a graduate course on U.S.–Latin American relations at the School of International Affairs of the University of Southern California, from February to April 1988. I realized how much interest in Chile there was in the States when the actor Christopher Reeve showed up at a roundtable discussion at USC and the actress Daryl Hannah sent us a letter expressing her support for the cause of democracy. Reeve, known worldwide for his *Superman* movies, had been in Chile in November 1987 to express his solidarity with Chilean actors involved in pro-democracy activities who had been receiving anonymous death threats.

The *Los Angeles Times* invited me to write an op-ed on the situation in Chile. My article, published on March 21, 1988, was entitled "Beating Pinochet at His Own Game." I argued that the Communists' assumption that dictatorships do not lose plebiscites ran up against the evidence from Uruguay and Poland, where dictatorial regimes had lost referendums, in 1980 and 1987, respectively. I asserted that if our drive to register a minimum of 6.5 million voters succeeded and we were able to safeguard the polling against fraud, we had a chance of winning. The United States could help by supporting our demand for essential freedoms. In any case, I concluded, it was up to us Chileans to defeat Pinochet.

A couple of weeks later, shortly before returning to Chile, I was invited to give a lecture at the University of California at San Diego. A student in the audience condemned my *Los Angeles Times* op-ed in the harshest terms. At best, he said, I was naïve; at worst, a collaborator. I didn't feel the least bit embarrassed by his criticism—I could justify my stance on ethical and political grounds. Besides, I would soon be returning to the front lines, while my critic remained safe and sound in sunny California. In fact, I was back in Santiago before the end of the month, working in the newly created PPD and in the Comando de Partidos por el "No." I was elected vice president of the party for the Santiago metropolitan region, specifically in charge of training almost ten thousand poll watchers of the twenty thousand total we needed nationwide. In May 1988, the voting law was passed by the junta, allowing registered political parties to oversee the vote through poll watchers.

The course to train monitors, who in turn would train poll watchers, took about three hours. I taught all day Saturdays and Sundays, mornings and afternoons, at the PPD headquarters, located in Dominica Street, in the bohemian Bellavista neighborhood in Santiago. During the week I went to different boroughs in the evenings to teach—especially to distant rural ones, where volunteers were harder to find. I no longer had a moment to myself, but I was encouraged that people were showing up to volunteer, in numbers that way exceeded our expectations.

I still have my handwritten notes for a speech I gave to commemorate the graduation of the poll watchers in Providencia borough from their training. "This is a step to beat Pinochet," I said. "We don't know yet the exact date of the plebiscite, but we have already achieved small victories. We have registered six and half million people to vote; we have legalized the PPD as an instrument to defeat fraud; and now we are well on our way to training all twenty thousand poll watchers the PPD needs to control the vote nationally. You, here in Providencia, are an example to follow, just like the small and isolated community of Isla Mocha, where we needed four poll watchers; well, we already have them!" We have to "stand up to the dictator, to tell him NO!" I stated. The group's next tasks, I said, were to organize an electoral team, to choose a general supervisor for the borough, and select messengers to take the voting summaries to the data center for the metropolitan region.

In retrospect, the decisive moment of the campaign occurred when Ricardo Lagos rocked the nation on the live TV program *De Cara al País* (Face the Nation), the first political program to air on Chilean television since 1973. Only registered political parties could participate in it. The Party for Democracy was represented by Lagos; Carolina Tohá, a young woman whose father, Allende minister José Tohá, was tortured and died in captivity; the lawyer Jorge Schaulsohn; and the former conservative congressman Armando Jaramillo. They were interrogated by a team of journalists. Before he went on the air, Lagos attended a special training session with media consultants, who taught him tricks of the trade.

The program aired on April 25, 1988. The streets were deserted that night, since everybody was home watching this show, a real novelty in Pinochet's Chile. At one point during the live broadcast, Lagos turned to the camera and addressed Pinochet directly, pointing his index finger at him. He accused him of reneging on his 1980 promise not to run in 1989; he showed a press clipping in which Pinochet stated that he would not be a candidate. "And now, you promise the country eight more years, with torture, assassinations and violation of human rights. To me, it seems incomprehensible that a Chilean would be so power hungry as to presume to hold on to it for twenty-five years."

The moderator attempted to cut him off, but Lagos pushed on:

"Chile has never been like nowadays. And you [Pinochet] will have to respond."

"What the country wishes to know—" the journalist tried to interject.

"You will excuse me," Lagos continued. "I speak after fifteen years of silence and I believe it is essential that the country know it is at a crossroad. And our best chance to move forward is through the victory of the 'no.'"

But Lagos was still not finished. He showed a graph that demonstrated that most Chileans were poorer in 1988 than in 1970, proving that the Chicago model had benefited only the few. "These are Central Bank and Institute of National Statistics figures," he added. "I invite any minister to debate this with me, here or in another program."

Lagos had jump-started the incipient "no" campaign with electric force. Pinochet watched in disbelief. He called his advisers to instruct them to send troops into the streets, but they convinced him that that would be an overreaction. The following morning, lawyers of the Interior Ministry were ordered to sift through Lagos's words and charge him with something, but they could not find anything that justified taking him to court.

Admiral Merino opined that Lagos's attack on Pinochet would backfire and actually help the "yes" campaign. Lagos responded that if that was the case, then the government should rebroadcast his interview. They didn't take up his suggestion.

We did not grasp the impact of the broadcast until a few days later, when Lagos, Carlos Ominami, Luis Alvarado, and I went to the May Day rally at O'Higgins Park. Lagos suggested that we take the metro so we wouldn't have to deal with parking. When we entered the park, people tried to touch him and hug him. Overnight, Lagos had become a celebrity. Ominami, Alvarado, and I did our best as his improvised bodyguards, but by the time we got to the stage our shirts had been pulled out of our pants, buttons were missing, and we were soaked in sweat. When Lagos's presence was announced over the public address system, he received a deafening ovation. Ricardo Lagos had not only given the decisive impulse to the "no" campaign; he had become a national leader.

Needless to say, he had also become Pinochet's nemesis. Though he didn't mention him by name, everyone knew who Pinochet was talking about when, on June 9, he declared, "I say to those bad Chileans who insult us on television because they know we are in a democracy and we are not going to do anything to them: be careful, because patience has a limit and this limit can be felt." Then, sounding half like a gangster, half like a politician, he added, "As we approach the plebiscite we are going to show this minority, which shouts and vociferates . . . we are going to wipe them off the map." Pinochet was so angered with Lagos that one day he could not resist saying: "There is a bandit called Froilán going around . . ." referring to Lagos's unusual and generally unknown middle name.

In 1987 Lagos had traveled to Washington to meet with members of Congress, State Department officials, and opinion leaders. The 1988 American presidential election was in full swing, and he asked me whether I could arrange an interview with the Democratic contender,

Michael Dukakis. "Impossible," I said. "No presidential candidate will meet with a Chilean opposition leader during a campaign." I made the contact, however, for Lagos to meet with Dukakis's top foreign policy adviser, Madeleine K. Albright, at her Georgetown residence. When Lagos returned to Santiago he told me, "I saw Dukakis!"

"What do you mean you saw Dukakis?" I inquired, surprised.

"Well, I was at Capitol Hill on my way to a meeting with a senator and a crowd of journalists approached with Dukakis in the middle. He said 'hello' as if I were a voter, and continued on. So, I can say I saw Dukakis!"

After that visit, one of Lagos's conservative friends told him that Pinochet had said, "Why does Lagos travel to Washington and not to Moscow? He is a Communist. He has to go to Moscow!" Remembering the "Froilán" episode, Lagos told his right-wing friend, "Tell Pinochet to change the date of the plebiscite, because he is going to lose." When the friend asked why, Lagos replied, "October 5 is St. Froilán's day."

In the meantime, the Americans sent high-level messengers to Santiago to talk to Pinochet about the merits of a peaceful road to democracy. The powerful congressman Henry Hyde, the highest-ranking Republican on the House Select Committee on Intelligence, visited Pinochet on July 21, 1988, and congratulated him on the country's economic performance; he also attempted to convince Pinochet—he later told me—that even though military men had many talents, governing should be left in the hands of civilians.

"What about General Eisenhower. Wasn't he president of your country?" replied an annoyed Pinochet.

"Yes, he was, but he was elected and at the time he was a retired general," countered Hyde.

In July 1988 I was named joint representative of the Socialist Party and the PPD in the executive committee of the "no" campaign. The committee was composed of Belisario Velasco and Gutenberg Martínez for the Christian Democrats, Ricardo Solari for the "Almeyda Socialists," and me for the "Nuñez Socialists" and the PPD. The executive director was Genaro Arriagada, a Christian Democrat. Occasionally, other leaders such as Carlos Montes, Luciano Valle, Edgardo Boeninger, or Patricio Rojas would attend the executive meetings. Enrique Correa directed a press and political analysis team composed of the sociologists Manuel Antonio Garretón, Angel Flisfisch, Eugenio Tironi, and Carlos Vergara, and the political scientists Carlos Huneeus and Ignacio Walker.

One of our main tasks was to decide the direction of the campaign. Touring the country and organizing rallies was a key element. Rallies in provincial towns were usually large; others, in isolated neighborhoods or rural villages, were smaller, but participants were almost always enthusiastic. One time Eduardo Frei Ruiz-Tagle and I gave speeches in a vacant lot in a housing development of the rural town of Melipilla to an enthusiastic audience of about two hundred people. I discovered that our campaign was drawing world attention when the small rally was filmed by a PBS crew led by a distinguished American journalist. As we moved throughout the country we perceived enthusiasm and organization even in the smallest and most geographically isolated places. Somewhat later, as the campaign wound up in September 1988, I was one of two speakers at the town of Talagante, west of Santiago, before at least eight thousand people—a record crowd for a small town.

On August 30, 1988, in a unanimous decision, the junta designated Pinochet as the candidate for the plebiscite. In a speech in Viña del Mar, Pinochet had already framed the question of the plebiscite as "whether the people want or do not want President Pinochet to continue."

Pinochet, the bulldog-faced man in uniform and dark sunglasses that the people had feared for so long, was suddenly replaced by a smiling man in light-colored civilian clothes with a pearl tie clasp, the very image of a kind, silver-haired, grandfatherly figure who cared about the welfare of all Chileans, but also knew when to apply discipline. Pinochet's campaign was predicated on fear; in speech after speech he insisted that the plebiscite offered a choice between him or chaos. A veiled threat by the commander of the army's special forces, the "black berets," in which Pinochet was offered "steely daggers to defend the beloved Chilean people," framed the electoral campaign as war.

In January 1988, Pinochet had complained about the public's apathetic attitude about the coming plebiscite. "I have been saying for quite a while that we are at war. People do not understand this. We are at war between democrats and totalitarian Communists. This is a war to the death." A few weeks later, in March 1988, responding to opposition criticism, Pinochet defined his regime as "a democratic government. We do not oppose ideas," he said. "Ideas are respected. What we oppose is that ideas be spread or that some may attempt to apply them here in the country." Clearly, our campaign was not going to be easy.

UNDISCOURAGED, OUR VOLUNTEERS went door to door throughout the entire country. A pamphlet we prepared set ground rules for our canvassers: they were to respect mealtimes and not disturb people too early or too late in the day. They should dress cleanly and appropriately; identify themselves by name; and always be courteous, even if the person they were addressing was sympathetic to Pinochet. No visit should last more than ten minutes.

Though we were a massive presence in the streets, we did not have access to television, which the regime tightly controlled. To give a semblance of fairness in the run-up to the plebiscite, the government decided that both the "yes" and the "no" campaigns would be allowed fifteen minutes daily to present their views. Pinochet did not assign much importance to these mini-programs, as they were aired late at night. He made a big mistake.

The "No" TV programs were creative and upbeat, with excellent production values. Though we on the executive committee were kept apprised of their themes, their specific contents were left to a team of Chilean professionals advised by some American campaign experts. The "no" was a difficult sell; we were selling a negative and leaving the future as an open question. But the country had been force-fed nothing but official television for fifteen years, and Chileans were eager to see something different, even if they had to stay up late at night to do it. Our first broadcast was widely viewed.

Patricio Bañados, who had been fired from the University of Chile's Channel 11 eight years before for refusing to read insulting sentences about former president Frei, was the telegenic news anchor of the program, a mixture of Dan Rather and Peter Jennings. Behind him, a painted rainbow symbolized the colors of the opposition. The past divided Chile, so our communications advisers concluded that we had to speak about the future; the campaign's theme song, "Chile, la alegría ya viene" (Chile, happiness is on the way), provided a catchy soundtrack that symbolized hope with lively video images of people of all ages and from all walks of life, from taxi drivers to sports stars, saying "no" with a gesture, a song, or in words. Humor was an important component of the programs, each of which ended with the same powerful slogan: "Without hatred, without fear, vote no."

Pinochet's supporters urged him to improve the quality of his own propagandistic and boring "Yes" programs. But instead, his broadcasts just became more strident, painting the opposition as Marxists and terrorists. The "no" vote was portrayed as the return of the Allende period. The programs reached their nadir when Ricardo Lagos's former wife was put on the air, rather confusedly attacking her ex-husband. That sordid episode backfired, turning off many "yes" supporters.

On September 1, 1988, Chile's exile policy was rescinded and hundreds of expatriates returned home. When Volodia Teitelboim, the former senator and Communist Party leader, arrived, the "yes" television program made sure to quote an apologetic declaration he made regarding violence. The "yes" programs had little to say about the return of Hortensia "Tencha" Bussi de Allende, President Allende's widow. I, along with dozens of friends and supporters, greeted her at the airport and I drove the vehicle just ahead of hers in the long motorcade that escorted her to a temporary place of residence. The route was mobbed by excited well-wishers; my car was dented and scuffed as dozens of people tried to climb over it to see or attempt to touch Tencha.

On October 1, 1988, I accompanied her and some of her relatives to the Pan-American Highway South, for the last "no" rally before the vote. Close to a million people turned out. A group of us formed a wedge with Tencha inside, and pushed, shoved, and elbowed our way to the stage. I actually had to bodily lift Panchita and Ramón Huidobro, the mother and stepfather of the writer Isabel Allende (a relative of Salvador Allende's, not his daughter Isabel—currently a congresswoman) over a fence so that they could get into the reserved-seating section. There was a feeling of victory in the air, enhanced by the mild spring weather and the presence of so many former exiles on the stage. But there were still dangerous obstacles to overcome before the October 5 plebiscite.

On Sunday, October 2, Lagos called me to an urgent meeting. He and the Christian Democratic leader, Patricio Alywin, had received information from a high source in the Carabineros that several Mercedes-Benz buses similar to those used by the Carabineros had been stolen; their intelligence unit feared that they might be used in terrorist operations. Such information was particularly worrisome in light of an assertion by Undersecretary of the Interior Alberto Cardemil to CEL leaders that the government had uncovered an extremist plot, to be carried out by common criminals, to disrupt the October 5 referendum. Moreover, Mónica Jiménez, a civic education leader, had been told by Army General Jorge Zincke, commander of the Santiago garrison, that he had received intelligence that acts of violence would be committed on the day of the plebiscite, starting at 5 P.M. An unexplained blackout that took place on the night of Saturday October 1 lent weight to these rumors.

Lagos secretly met with a distant relative of his, Air Force General
Fernando Silva, at a tennis court in La Reina, both of them dressed in
shorts and carrying tennis rackets. Lagos told General Silva about the
rumors he'd been hearing. He had checked with the Communists and
was convinced that they were not involved in any of the conspiracies.
Silva agreed to talk to Air Force Commander in Chief Matthei immediately. General Matthei already knew about the plan, and sent a message to Lagos that he would oppose any attempt to tamper with the
plebiscite results. Lagos, Aylwin, and the opposition leader, Alejandro
Hales, met with General Rodolfo Stange, director general of the
Carabineros. He confirmed that buses had been stolen and added that
all regular police buses had been painted with numbers on their roofs
to readily identify them as police vehicles. Stange assured them that
any attempt at disguise would backfire, as his officers would be on the
lookout for incorrectly numbered buses and would shoot at them
from helicopters if necessary.

That same Sunday, while Enrique Correa, a Socialist Party member,
was sent to meet with senior officials of the Catholic Church, Lagos
asked me to meet with U.S. Ambassador Harry Barnes and as many
influential European ambassadors as I could and inform them of
these developments. When I couldn't reach the ambassador through
one of his aides, I called him at home. He invited me to drop by
right away. I drove to his mansion through long motorcades of
pro-Pinochet demonstrators in their final campaign effort. Some
of them glared at me because I did not beep my horn for "yes."

Barnes told me that he, too, had heard rumors about schemes to
disrupt the voting, and that he took the detailed information I
brought him, all of it confirmed by government sources, very seriously. Many years later, Ambassador Marilyn McAffee, Barnes's cultural attaché at the time, told me that as soon as I left, Barnes called
the State Department to urge them to release an official statement
warning Pinochet about the dire consequences for bilateral relations
if his regime disrupted the plebiscite. Barnes's superiors replied that
they could only make an official response to an actual event. So
Barnes instructed McAffee to leak the information I'd given him to a
UPI correspondent. The reporter spoke to Mónica Jiménez and me,
got the green light from his Miami editor, and published the story
within twenty-four hours.

Meanwhile, that same Sunday, the Chilean ambassador to the
United States, Hernán Felipe Errázuriz, was summoned to the State
Department in Washington, D.C., for a meeting with the acting secre-

tary of state, John Whitehead, Assistant Secretary for Inter-American Affairs Elliot Abrams, Deputy Assistant Secretary Michael Skol, and others. Whitehead told the ambassador that he had received multiple reports of a military plan to interrupt the plebiscite and negate its results if it became clear that the "no" vote would carry the day. Any such effort, Whitehead said, "would have grave consequences."

I have seen the cable Ambassador Errázuriz sent to his superiors after this conversation; in it he reported that he denied everything. Whitehead's "information . . . was not serious," he had told the Americans. Furthermore, such "rumors had been floated by the opposition for some time." On the contrary, Errázuriz asserted, "it is the opposition that has declared that it will not acknowledge the result if the 'no' is defeated." Errázuriz added that "opinion polls show that the government is ahead" and that, therefore, "interrupting the plebiscite would go against the interests of the government." What Ambassador Errázuriz did not know, or did not want to admit, was that the most recent poll conducted by the Centro de Estudios Públicos (CEP), a conservative-leaning institution that did serious public opinion research, predicted that the "no" would win with 52 percent of the vote, against 32 percent for the "yes," and 16 percent undecided.

On the Saturday prior to the plebiscite, scheduled for Wednesday, the CEP opinion poll was privately presented to a group of rightist politicians and government officials at the home of Oscar Godoy, a political scientist. "Our information is different," replied Foreign Minister Ricardo García. But García was worried, and he went to his car to phone Pinochet with the information he had just heard. When he came back he said, "I just spoke to Pinochet and he is utterly confident. If he knows we are going to lose he must be a Sir Laurence Olivier!" True, Skopus, a polling company close to the government, had predicted different results: 55.3 percent "yes" and 46.1 percent "no." But the fact that their numbers added up to 101.4—and that there were no undecideds—suggested that their conclusions were perhaps best taken with a grain of salt. Maybe Pinochet was so confident because his favorite fortune-teller, María Eugenia Pirzio-Biroli, whom he had named mayor of the village of Puerto Cisnes, had predicted that he would win the plebiscite.

On Monday, October 3, during the U.S. State Department's noon briefing in Washington, a reporter asked about the UPI newswire that had just appeared regarding plots to cancel the plebiscite or nullify its results. Phyllis Oakley, the spokesperson, responded that Acting Secretary

Whitehead had already transmitted the U.S.'s "serious concern" to the Chilean ambassador. In his Monday-evening briefing papers, President Reagan was apprised of the State Department's warnings to Pinochet as well. It was a busy day—that morning I met with the ambassador of Great Britain and shared our concerns with him.

It was increasingly clear that official ties between Pinochet's government and the United States were fraying. New developments in the Letelier case had not helped matters at all. Since the DINA's dissolution, an army major named Armando Fernández Larios who had been part of the Letelier murder plot had been disappointed with the bureaucratic chores the army had assigned him. Revelations about his role in mass executions, including the infamous 1973 "Caravan of Death," had left him feeling vulnerable as well. He told his superiors that he wanted to go to the United States to clear his name. He was summoned to the Defense Ministry building, where Pinochet himself attempted to change his mind: "Be a good soldier, be firm, and this problem will have a happy ending," he assured him. But Fernández Larios defied his commander in chief. He departed for the States, leaving behind a letter in which he stated that he hoped that in the future, "no junior officer is blamed for the actions of the Army's high command." In February 1987, "overwhelmed by guilt," as he declared, he appeared before a federal court in Washington D.C. to confess his part in the Letelier assassination. It was a big blow to Pinochet, who was heard to say, "For me, Fernández Larios is a deserter." In August 1987, Robert Gelbard, assistant secretary of state for Inter-American Affairs, told Ambassador Errázuriz that the status of the Letelier case was "clearly unsatisfactory," and that the Reagan administration could no longer accept that the Pinochet government "would ignore its commitment to investigate and explain" the crime.

Americans did not limit themselves to verbal expressions of displeasure with the regime; they also gave active assistance to the opposition. American consultants recruited by the NDI worked with our professionals to produce our "no" TV programs and commercials and to develop an independent polling capability; they also helped us design and implement the computer programs we needed for "D-Day." The U.S. Congress budgeted $1 million for use by the National Endowment for Democracy to support civic education efforts, to help voters register and acquire the photographs they needed for ID cards, and to subsidize get-out-the-vote initiatives in poor neighborhoods. In contrast to the U.S. covert actions in 1973, this cooperation was overt, above board, and explicitly for the cause of democracy.

Rounding up the circle from the Nixon-Kissinger destabilization-of-democracy era, in 1988 former presidents Gerald Ford and Jimmy Carter co-chaired a "Committee to Support Free Elections in Chile," organized jointly by Senator Edward Kennedy (D-Massachusetts) and Senator Richard Lugar (R-Indiana). This bipartisan group was about to witness a very different outcome from the one promoted by the U.S. government that ushered General Pinochet into power.

As "D-Day" approached, we made every effort to keep the opposition unified. Patricio Aylwin, president of the Christian Democratic Party and the spokesman and coordinator of the "no" campaign, put me in charge of a team whose job was to remain in constant contact with the underground leadership of the Communist Party during the lead-up to and especially on the day of the plebiscite. Keeping the Communists on a peaceful track, duly informed and coordinated with the Comando de Partidos por el "No," was an important responsibility—especially if things went wrong. The Communist Party had lost much of its military capacity to the "autonomous" faction of the FPMR (which had declared a "unilateral truce" for the plebiscite period), but we had to insist on preventing any recourse to violence during those days. My fellow teammates were Enrique Krauss, a former Christian Democratic congressman who would become minister of the Interior under President Aylwin, and a member of the Radical Party, Mario Astorga, who had been minister of education under President Allende. Our first encounter with the Communists, just to touch bases, was on September 27, 1988.

The next day, the executive committee of the Comando de Partidos por el "No" met with the top leaders of its constituent parties. I drafted the final instructions for the day of the plebiscite on the basis of the discussions we held that day; I still have the original manuscript. The PPD would be based at the Hotel Galerías in downtown Santiago; this was where Lagos would be, after he finished voting. At the headquarters of the Comando, a few blocks away, only the executive committee and the analysis team would be present. Eduardo Engel, a distinguished Yale economist, had set up a "quick-count" computerized projection system at the CEL headquarters that would process data from 2,220 carefully selected polling sites. At the Comando de Partidos por el "No," the economist Gonzalo Martner was in charge of a parallel vote-counting system based on two lines of tallying, one from Christian Democratic experts and the other from the PPD. Both groups would fax actual tabulations from polling sites to various posts and they would then be sent on to be entered into the central computer. The key to avoiding fraud, Glenn Cowan of the NDI had counseled us, was to protect the votes at their source, that is, at the voting tables themselves. About two hundred voters were registered to each table. Votes would be cast secretly in booths and deposited in a ballot box corresponding to each table. The number of tables in each voting site, generally schools or sports arenas, would vary from a few dozen up to one hundred. Voting tables would be managed by voters selected at random by the Electoral Service (an autonomous entity in charge of organizing, controlling, and supervising all elections), and the counting would be public for anybody to watch. The key to our tally was that the actual counting of each voting table would be witnessed.

Hundreds of foreign journalists were in Chile to cover the elections; I gave dozens of interviews to foreign media and participated in several television debates. Many delegations of international observers were present as well, but the Pinochet regime refused to grant them any formal status. Pinochet had declared in June 1988 that observers "come to say there is fraud. More than three hundred marionettes are coming; yes, they are marionettes." Pinochet also attacked the World Council of Churches as "a front organization of the Communist Party. [It] also talks about fraud. But what if there is fraud at the last minute? What are they going to say? That I leave? The heck I will leave! But I am just talking hypothetically; do not take it seriously," Pinochet added, in his characteristically sarcastic style.

On the morning of October 5, 1988, I voted at my old high school, the Liceo de Aplicación, on Ricardo Cumming Avenue, one block from Alameda Avenue. Ricardo Lagos and I went together, since we voted in the same place. When we arrived many voters recognized and applauded him; a few hissed. Then it was over and everyone went back quietly to the all-important business of the day. At my table my identity was checked, my name was found on the voter registration book, I was handed a paper ballot and a pencil, and I was invited to enter the voting booth. The ballot read, "Plebiscite, President of the Republic, Augusto Pinochet Ugarte." Below his name were two short horizontal lines, one followed by the word "yes" and another by the word "no." This is what we meant by defeating Pinochet with a pencil, I thought, as I made an X on the "no" line. It was the first time I had voted since the spring of 1973, more than fifteen years before.

After I voted, I greeted the PPD poll watchers, who told me the situation had been normal so far. It was about 9:45 A.M. and almost all the voting tables set up at the school had opened. I was impressed by the long lines of voters waiting to cast their ballots. Then I separated from Lagos and went on a tour of voting sites throughout the metropolitan region. I began in Maipú, a suburb west of Santiago, where the only problem I encountered was at a single polling station where about a half-dozen people who wanted to vote did not appear in the rolls. Then I drove to a couple of working-class boroughs south of Santiago, where the lines of voters were much longer because some of the voting tables had opened late. Still, by and large the situation seemed satisfactory, according to what I saw and what our PPD poll watchers told me.

At noon I went along with my colleagues Enrique Krauss and Mario Astorga to our scheduled meeting with the Communist representatives. We met in a vacant office in a building on MacIver Street and exchanged information about the opening of voting tables throughout the country and about the electoral process in general. We agreed that the main problem thus far were the number of voting tables that had opened late. Turnout was massive; I recall saying that I thought we might get as many as 7 million voters, rather than the 6.5 million we had initially hoped for.

We became worried at 11:30 A.M., when Undersecretary of the Interior Cardemil announced on television that only 75 percent of the voting tables were operative, when the Comando's figure was more like 89 percent. Was the government attempting to discourage people so that they would stay home to avoid long lines?

Our second meeting with the Communists was in the afternoon, at around 4:30 P.M., at an apartment building on Seminario Avenue. This time, our mutual concern was a television interview with a retired navy officer who owned an agency called Gallup-Chile. He claimed that his company's exit polls gave the "yes" option a clear advantage. "If the right-wing television stations continue with so-called news and projections saying that the 'yes' won," our Communist contacts observed, "then Pinochet backers will be celebrating victory up and down affluent neighborhoods. The plebiscite will be over before the votes are even counted."

We became increasingly concerned as the state television network began reporting ludicrous isolated results. Channel 13 of the Catholic University followed the public tally vote by vote at the Instituto Nacional, where Pinochet himself and many government officials had cast their ballots. Not surprisingly, the results favored the "yes."

Genaro Arriagada, the executive director of the "no" campaign, had already called General Jorge Zincke, commander of the Santiago

Garrison, to complain about the huge lines of people waiting outside voting sites, because the military was impeding people from going inside. Zincke argued that the measures had been taken to avoid excessive crowds around the tables and booths. Our fear was that potential voters would get tired of waiting and go home before they cast their ballots—or that the tables would close before everyone in line had an opportunity to vote. The director of the Electoral Service, Juan Ignacio García, had told the Christian Democratic Party leader, Gutenberg Martínez, that the tables could not close, no matter how late the hour, as long as potential voters were waiting in line.

Pinochet, wearing civilian clothes, had voted and returned to La Moneda, where he spoke briefly to the press. "Just in case," he said, "there are twenty-five thousand troops ready to act." Then he withdrew to the fortified bunker he had ordered built beneath Constitution Square. As the evening set in, the streets of Santiago began to empty out as people returned to their homes to watch TV or listen to their radios for early election returns. At the Comando headquarters we continued to receive troubling signals—now there were rumors of a massive military search taking place in the poor neighborhood of La Victoria. Patricio Aylwin called General Zincke to express his concern. The general clarified that it had been a limited search of an unoccupied house, where explosives and some weapons had been found.

By early evening the CEL quick-count was already projecting a comfortable victory for the "no," but this information had not yet been publicized. It was well past seven o'clock when Undersecretary of the Interior Cardemil reported the first official counts: The "yes" had received 57.3 percent of the vote and the "no" only 40.5 percent. It was unbelievable! Those results came from seventy-nine tables— 15,800 votes, a mere three tenths of a percent of the total universe of Chilean voters.

We were outraged. We had promised not to announce our parallel tally until we'd counted 500,000 votes. Ricardo Lagos called Genaro Arriagada and urged him to release our available results immediately, before the Pinochet regime's distortions took hold—or worse, they halted the counting and imposed a blackout on communications. But Arriagada wanted to stick to the original plan. "If you do not announce the tally of the Comando by 9:30 P.M.," a furious Lagos promised, "I will deliver the results gathered by the PPD tabulation line of the Comando." Patricio Aylwin, the leader of the Christian Democrats and "no" spokesman, agreed with Lagos and instructed Arriagada to release what we had.

By then, commanders of the navy, air force, and Carabineros were receiving informal reports that the "no" vote was well ahead. A scheduled 8 P.M. meeting of Pinochet with the junta was postponed for one hour. At around 8:45, Pinochet emerged from his bunker and faced the press. "I have been informed that the 'yes' is winning," he said. Then, he abruptly changed the subject: "I have received some disquieting information. Some individuals wearing ski masks and carrying weapons have been spotted." In fact, there had been some ominous developments. A police bus with false identification numbers had been sighted; also, near the former La Bandera slum the police had exchanged fire with some suspicious vehicles. One of them turned out to be carrying armed CNI agents.

At around 9 P.M., Arriagada read the results that were currently available to the Comando: with 188,000 votes counted, the "no" had 58.7 percent, the "yes," 41.3 percent. The packed room of "no" staff and observers and national and international journalists erupted in cheers. The second official tally was supposed to have been released at 8:30 P.M., but it had been postponed till ten.

At "no" headquarters a phone call came through from Radio Nacional de España, in Madrid; they wanted to interview one of us live. I was chosen. As I spoke, I looked out the second-floor window and saw that the streets outside were completely deserted; there were no signs of the policemen who had been guarding our building all day. If pro-Pinochet thugs or the CNI had chosen that moment to attack us, they could have done so with impunity. When I got off the phone, I told my fellow Comando members that we seemed to be defenseless; Arriagada, who had just returned from the press center, confirmed that we were alone and added that there were no police in sight for several blocks in any direction. We tried to communicate with the high command of Carabineros but were only able to reach a lower-raking officer, who gave us a laughable explanation: the police, he told us, had gone on a break for a bite to eat, all at the same time, and at the most tense moment of the key night of that critical year.

Some twenty minutes later, as in a dream, Bianca Jagger walked into our headquarters, followed by Adolfo Suárez, the former president of Spain; Pierre Mauroy, a former French prime minister; and a number of other distinguished international observers. They had come to be our "human shields." As it turned out, police forces had redeployed several blocks east and west, along Alameda Avenue, and some blocks north and south, to better isolate the area. Still, it was a very suspicious-looking situation.

At 10 P.M. Cardemil released the government's second tally, this time with 677 tables counted: 51.3 percent for the "yes," 46.5 percent for the "no." The "no" vote was much larger this time and the regime's implausible advantage of seventeen points had been reduced by two thirds, but the numbers were just as ridiculous as before. The undersecretary promised a third report at 11:15 P.M.

At the Comando, Aylwin had been joined by Lagos, who had moved to our headquarters. After the official tally announcement, we decided to contact the commanders in chief of the armed forces and the head of the Carabineros and inform them of the true results—the Comando's. They thanked us for the information and confessed that they already knew that we had won.

At 10:45 P.M. the right-wing leader Sergio Onofre Jarpa called his old friend and former colleague, Undersecretary Cardemil. "Hey, Alberto, you are not going to do anything foolish, are you?"

"You know me, Don Sergio," Cardemil replied. "I will not lend my name to anything foolish."

"All right. That's what I imagined," added Jarpa. "I never took you for a fool." Both men spoke in the deceptively curt phrases of the southern Chilean countryside where they came from.

At the press center, Arriagada read the latest Comando data, based on 2 million ballots: "no" votes, 57.8 percent; "yes" votes, 40.2 percent.

Aylwin and Jarpa were appearing together on a live TV show. Both were old foxes of Chilean politics; both had opposed President Allende. An aide handed Aylwin a piece of paper with the results that Arriagada had just reported; after looking it over, he passed it to Jarpa. The leader of the right-wing Renovación Nacional party acknowledged on the air that the "no" vote was decisively ahead.

At La Moneda, Pinochet roared, "It's a big lie, a big lie. Here there are only traitors and liars!" First he ordered his interior minister to stop releasing results, and then he summoned the junta members to La Moneda. Before they arrived, Pinochet demanded the resignations of every minister in his cabinet. Some of them were crying; others looked pale and shocked.

At 1 A.M. Pinochet decided to meet with a few key ministers and just the commanders in chief of the armed forces, not the full junta. The commanders agreed among themselves to meet first at the Defense Ministry and then walk from there over to La Moneda. "I will snap the pin off the grenade," said Air Force Commander Matthei, meaning that he would tell the truth about the plebiscite results. As the commanders entered the palace, journalists rushed to get a statement from them. "I am very clear that the 'no' won, but we are calm," the air force commander said. At the Comando we were elated by this official recognition of our victory. Arriagada went to fetch some champagne. Shortly afterward, the Comando released further results. With over 4.5 million votes counted, the "no" was clearly and irreversibly triumphant.

At La Moneda, Pinochet banged on a table. His humor worsened when General Matthei told him he had already acknowledged the triumph of the "no."

"You see, you inform yourselves with the enemy, leaving the government as a fool," Pinochet complained.

Interior Minister Fernández attempted to introduce some order and a note of cheer to the gathering. "The results are negative . . . but the government should feel satisfied," he declared. "The votes obtained by President Pinochet have been extraordinary, noteworthy."

"Very well, where is the champagne then?" General Matthei sarcastically interrupted him. He added that it was an insult to the commanders in chief to deliver a victory speech when they had so clearly lost. As tensions rose, General Sergio Valenzuela, minister secretary-general of the presidency, fainted and collapsed to the ground. He had to be carried out of the room.

At one point, the ministers left to attend the brief ceremony that went along with their collective resignations; Pinochet remained alone with the commanders in chief of the armed forces and the police. What transpired has been the subject of some controversy.

According to credible versions, including Air Force Commander Matthei's, Pinochet asked his colleagues to grant him special expanded powers; he presented them with a decree he had drafted to empower him to deal with the emergency that the "no" victory posed to his regime. It was like a coup within the 9/11 coup. But Matthei, Admiral Merino, and General Stange all refused to sign the document. The constitution should be strictly adhered to, they asserted. The old general insisted, arguing that the unity of the armed forces would be endangered, but Admiral Merino closed the discussion by stating that they had all sworn to respect the constitution and that they had no other choice.

"All right!" Pinochet conceded irritably. "Do whatever you want!"

Pinochet was not the all-powerful dictator that he wished to be. He was constrained by the legality he had built into the constitution to legitimize his rule, and by the influence of civilian leaders such as Jarpa and the power of the rest of the armed forces and the Carabineros. As the commanders left the palace some time after 2:00 A.M., Santiago Sinclair, the army vice commander in chief, came in.

"My general, your army is ready for whatever you decide."

Pinochet looked at him silently for a few seconds. "We follow the constitution, Mr. Vice Commander in Chief," he finally said. That was it.

Several pages of Pinochet's memoirs exude bitterness about that night; he complains about, among others, Ambassador Barnes, international observers, the Catholic Church, and even his own people. "We gave the final vote count that night, with some delay, but we did deliver it," wrote Pinochet. Only a few reporters were present when Undersecretary Cardemil read his last report. With 71.7 percent of the tables counted, the "yes" had gotten 44.3 percent of the votes and the "no," 53.5 percent. We cheered at the Comando because this was the final official confirmation of our victory. When all 7.2 million ballots had been counted, 54.7 percent were for the "no," 43 percent for the "yes." We had won by a landslide.

Outside our headquarters a few hundred campaign volunteers celebrated, many of them with defiant fists in the air, singing the national anthem. The Carabineros dispersed them with threats of violence. Inside, our security measures had collapsed; about two hundred people had rushed in to celebrate. I saw one of the Communists we had met regularly with, who had always been skeptical about the plebiscite, hugging people and cheering as if he were celebrating the triumph of a strategy that he had advocated all along. Aylwin said a few brief words; then he and Ricardo Lagos embraced, foreshadowing the new coalition that would rule Chile in the not-too-distant future. A sad chapter of Chile's—and the world's—history was coming to a close.

Seven

GOVERNING WITH
THE ENEMY

The morning after the plebiscite, the opposition newspaper *Fortín Mapocho*, published by my friend Alberto "Gato" Gamboa, hit the stands with an enormous banner headline: "He Ran Alone and Came In Second!" The government newspaper, *La Nación*, it was later discovered, had had a front page already laid out and mocked up to announce a fraud; not only did it proclaim the victory of the "yes," it even provided concrete election returns.

Practically all of the media in the world reacted. A *New York Times* editorial entitled "In Chile: Positively No" captured the giddy sense of triumph: "Fifteen years ago a near-war between the two largest democratic forces, the Christian Democrats and Socialists, opened the way to rule by General Pinochet and an era of terror. Learning from past mistakes those same forces worked together this time to defeat the dictator. Two weeks ago, spring once again burst upon the magnificent Andean landscape. Now, after 15 hard and bleak years it has returned to the human spirit of Chile as well."

October 6 was celebration time. Thousands of people walked down Alameda Avenue singing, "Chile, happiness is coming," blowing on plastic horns, and throwing confetti and leaflets. As the numbers of marchers grew, they inundated the whole avenue, bringing traffic to a standstill. Though most policemen simply observed the festivities tolerantly, one officer detained half a dozen or so young revelers and locked them up in a bus, causing tension in the crowd.

For some reason that I cannot recall, I was in the Comando de Partidos por el "No" headquarters at the time. Around noon, the

phone rang and the caller asked to speak to someone in charge. I was
the only member of the executive committee on the premises and the
call was transferred to me. Army General Sergio Badiola, chief administrator of Santiago, was on the other end.

"Look, you have to move all those people out of Alameda Avenue,"
the general said. "You have twenty minutes. Then, I start using force."

"Wait just a moment," I responded. "These people are celebrating
peacefully because of what happened last night. You can't use force
against them."

"Well, I am sorry, but there is a traffic mess here downtown and
they have to go," General Badiola insisted.

"First, tell the Carabineros to release a busload of kids they arrested for no apparent reason, and then I'll do what I can," I said.

"All right," Badiola said, "but you've got just twenty minutes."

From our second-floor window we saw the marchers being released from the bus. Then, Andrés Palma, a young Christian Democratic leader who years later would become minister of planning,
saved my skin by grabbing a bullhorn and addressing the crowds below from an open window: "*Compañeros, camaradas, amigos,* everybody go now to Parque Forestal. The celebration continues there!"
He spoke with such humor and conviction that thousands of people
began marching toward the park. We had successfully averted our
first post-plebiscite conflict with the Pinochet government.

In the afternoon, crowds gathered around La Moneda and began
shouting for Pinochet to resign. Repression followed: dozens were detained, and there were beatings and attacks on journalists. That same
night, as massive "no" caravans paraded throughout the city, Pinochet
appeared on television dressed in his army uniform, the candidate's
mufti back in the closet. With huge bags under his eyes and a tired but
stern expression on his face, he delivered an unyielding speech. Then,
he left for a ten-day vacation.

The "no" campaign issued an official statement the night of the
plebiscite. The Chilean people had roundly rejected Pinochet's intention "to remain in power eight more years," we said. Our victory was
not "a defeat of the armed forces and the national police," we added,
but of Pinochet, who had "been the obstacle to consensus and understanding among Chileans." A few days later, on October 14, the sixteen signatories of the Comando de Partidos por el "No" circulated
a second declaration, proposing to commence a dialogue with the
government toward a "National Agreement for Democracy and Constitutional Consensus." Several constitutional modifications were proposed, including the immediate repeal of Article 8, which outlawed

groups that advocated violence, as well as doctrines or any concepts "that offend the family" or "are based on class conflict"—and the direct election of future Congresses.

If Pinochet was resistant to change, his hard-line interior minister, Sergio Fernández, went even further than his boss. Fernández came up with a baffling argument, stressing that 43 percent of the country had voted directly for Pinochet; therefore the seemingly impressive 55 percent that the opposition had garnered should actually be divided by sixteen, the number of political parties in the "no" coalition. It was an odd calculation and the first signal that Pinochet might be a candidate in the December 1989 elections after all.

When Pinochet returned from his vacation he was in full force. Addressing a meeting of pro-regime women, he spoke his mind. "Remember that in world history there was another plebiscite, in which Christ and Barabbas were judged, and the people voted for Barabbas," he said, blasphemously comparing himself to Jesus Christ.

Pinochet was deeply saddened. He had lost decisively in all but two of the thirteen regions of the country, including his beloved northern city of Iquique. "Iquique also!" he had exclaimed incredulously, when he was informed of the voting trends on election night. Pinochet and his economic team had trusted that Chile's undeniable economic growth would win them the election. But the new prosperity benefited only a small portion of society. Pinochet had created two Chiles: one entrepreneurial and modern, characterized by the construction of new high-rises and by burgeoning exports of grapes, kiwis, salmon, and wood products; the other, economically stagnant and left behind. The clearest expression of this socioeconomic apartheid was the fact that Pinochet lost in boom cities and towns such as Copiapó and Curicó, which, because of their recent export-driven prosperity, had been thought to be government strongholds.

Pinochet also lost because he had taken it for granted that an ideologically rigid opposition would refuse to confront him at his own game. Instead, the plebiscite provided us with the opportunity to mobilize a wide arc of political forces whose sole common denominator was the desire to defeat the dictator. Pinochet and his advisers had not anticipated that we would be able to mount a sophisticated and highly efficient vote-counting control system, rendering fraud a virtual impossibility.

The opposition had used its daily fifteen-minute allotment of air time to present a forward-looking, agile, and professionally made TV program, whereas the "yes" faction had sought to frighten the public with grim forebodings of the chaos that had characterized the Allende period—forgetting that 40 percent of the electorate was composed of young people who had not experienced the Allende years firsthand. Most important, Chileans had grown tired of repression and violence.

In bitter symbolism, less than three weeks after the plebiscite, the top leaders of the "autonomous" FPMR, who had dismissed the referendum as an anticipated Pinochet fraud, were captured and assassinated after they had attacked and briefly seized the village of Los Queñes, about a hundred miles from Santiago, where they had hoped to begin a new stage of their military strategy against Pinochet. With the death of Commanders José Miguel (Raúl Pellegrin) and Tamara (Cecilia Magni), and the detention of other militants, armed struggle also died as a relevant option to end the dictatorship.

Pinochet's extreme intransigence was his alone. Renovación Nacional declared itself in favor of modifying the constitution; even the UDI held that Pinochet was constitutionally enjoined from running for election in 1989 and that he should designate and campaign for his successor instead. Generals Stange and Matthei, members of the junta, also publicly conceded that constitutional reforms were necessary. However congenial Interior Minister Fernández's hard line might have been to Pinochet, it clashed with the mood of the country; on October 21, 1988, Fernández was replaced by Carlos Cáceres, an attorney who had been Pinochet's finance minister. Not that Pinochet really expected Cáceres to make changes. He told him he would have only a little room to amend the constitution—a tiny space he indicated by almost touching his index finger to his thumb.

Given the fact that I had correctly predicted the triumph of a strategy that many believed unlikely to beat Pinochet, the *Los Angeles Times* asked me to write a follow-up op-ed. In my new piece, titled "Cold Reality Dawns in Chile: Democratization Must Be Negotiated with Pinochet's Camp," I indicated that "the mood of the country" favored "negotiation and agreement." Since Pinochet continued being the obstacle, I argued, we would have to attempt to isolate him politically while throwing our support to those "in favor of introducing changes in the constitution in order to open the door to a full transition to democracy." It would not be easy, I warned; it would require our loose "no" coalition to transform itself into a unified alliance for the 1989 election, with a program to govern and a candidate that we could all get behind.

As we prepared to discuss reforms to the constitution, a major crisis erupted in U.S.-Chile relations in March 1989, when the Food and Drug Administration (FDA) discovered an insignificant amount of cyanide in three grapes of a shipment that had entered through Philadelphia. The FDA banned Chilean fruits from American supermarket shelves, arguing safety reasons. The Pinochet regime reacted with outrage and so did political forces across the political spectrum. Eventually, Chilean fruits returned to U.S. supermarkets, but Pinochet theorized that the measure had been politically motivated by the State Department and was aimed at dissuading him from backtracking on the transition process.

Soon after Cáceres was installed as interior minister we began to negotiate with the government. Pinochet immediately warned that certain laws were sacrosanct, including the repressive Article 8 of the constitution, the mechanism of constitutional reform, and the composition of the Senate (some of whose members were to be "designated" by the regime rather than elected). Even so, by early 1989 we were making significant progress. But in April 1989 Pinochet confronted Cáceres about several of the reforms we had been discussing. As Cáceres recalled it later, Pinochet was almost incoherent with rage, pacing up and down the room sputtering, "This reform no, this other one no, that one also no." Given Pinochet's agitated state, Cáceres diplomatically suggested that perhaps they should "choose another moment to discuss the problem." Pinochet agreed and set up a meeting for the following morning. But when Cáceres arrived the next day, Pinochet demanded his resignation. At the next cabinet meeting, when Cáceres's departure was announced, many of his fellow ministers also resigned in sympathy—the beginnings of a potential mutiny that showed up Pinochet's weakness. One minister who was present at the cabinet session told me, "Pinochet fired Cáceres as if he were a house maid. I had never seen such mistreatment. But at that point, Pinochet had little power left. We simply refused to accept Cáceres's removal. Pinochet was no longer in full command." After a series of conversations with his cabinet and the junta, Pinochet reinstated the interior minister, allowing the dialogue with the opposition to proceed. On May 31 we formally agreed to a series of reforms.

The changes in the constitution were modest, but they included the elimination of the hated Article 8; an increase in the number of elected senators to reduce the weight of the designated ones that the democratic opposition had been unable to eliminate; some minor changes in the provisions of the National Security Council so as to increase the number of its civilian members; the revocation of the president's power to dissolve the Lower House of Congress once during each session; and the reduction of the presidential term of office from eight to four years. We were far from satisfied, but the changes represented real progress. The reforms were approved in a new national plebiscite in July 1989.

As the right-wing parties and the democratic forces began to prepare for the presidential and congressional elections of December 1989, Pinochet steadily lost power. The political philosopher Giovanni Sartori had once observed that the Achilles heel of any authoritarian regime is the question of succession; the dependence of the dictatorship on a now defeated Pinochet was leading to the regime's collapse. For many of Pinochet's former supporters, what mattered now was *Pinochetismo,* not Pinochet. The key was to preserve at least the economic model instituted by Pinochet. In the meantime, Pinochet, like Franco, sabotaged his successor government by placing in its way as many roadblocks and impediments as he could. For example, the number of judges on the Supreme Court was increased at the same time that a one time bonus was offered to sitting judges who resigned, allowing Pinochet to personally designate nine of the sixteen members of the tribunal. In addition, numerous state enterprises in the transportation, telecommunications, insurance, and energy sectors were hurriedly and shadily privatized.

In the meantime, the opposition turned its attention to internal issues that had been put on the back burner so that we could concentrate on winning the plebiscite.

We needed an alliance to govern Chile in the post-Pinochet era. It was common sense that the "no" coalition should transform itself into the Concertación de Partidos por la Democracia, which it did. The leading participating parties were the Christian Democrats, the Radical Party, the Socialist Party (both the Nuñez and Almeyda wings), the Party for Democracy, and a few other groups and factions, some of which dissolved later on. The Chilean Communist Party (CCP) was not part of the Concertación.

I had written in my *Los Angeles Times* op-ed on October 18, 1988, that we would probably have to choose "a centrist candidate" to represent the opposition in the December 1989 presidential elections. Ricardo Lagos, a leftist, was the most popular and brilliant figure of the opposition, but we knew that his name would polarize at a time when we needed a moderate figure. That person was Patricio Aylwin, the coordinator of the "no" campaign and the president of the Christian Democratic Party. After an internal struggle within the Christian Democrats, Aylwin became the candidate of the Concertación in May 1989. We now had a coalition prepared to govern, and a candidate.

The right had its own problems choosing its candidate. Pinochet and his closest cronies continued to promote his name, but most conservatives, including those in the business sector, preferred a civilian. Pinochet was told that he could be the candidate if he became a civilian—exactly as had been suggested to him before the plebiscite. He refused to consider the proposal now as he had then because he realized that his army post not only protected him but was the sole source of his dwindling power. The hard-line nationalists hoped that Pinochet would opt for a Plan B: either Lucía Hiriart de Pinochet would be the candidate, as suggested in May 1989 by an Acción Nacional (National Action) group, or, more likely, the lawyer Pablo Rodríguez (the former leader of the ultraright Patria y Libertad movement) would become the presidential candidate. But Jaime Guzmán, the UDI leader, a close ally of the Chicago Boys, convinced Pinochet that the ideal candidate was Finance Minister Hernán Büchi.

Büchi was also the preference of the business sector. He resigned his ministerial post in April 1989. But only hours before facing Aylwin on a televised debate, in June, he abruptly declined the candidature, asserting he could not overcome his profound, "vital, personal reservation" about entering electoral politics. After a month of further persuasion, he changed his mind again and became the official candidate of *Pinochetismo*. Called "Prince Valiant" by Pinochet because of his haircut (a reference to an iconic fifties film), Büchi had won the general's trust; he was a former radical left student at the University of Chile, a jogger, and overall a truly unconventional figure. Aylwin was the opposite: now over seventy, he was a traditional politician, conservative in his thinking and dress. The French pollster and campaign expert Jacques Séguéla commented at the time that Aylwin looked every bit like a candidate of the right, whereas the young technocrat Büchi looked like a standard-bearer of the left-center opposition.

In December 1989 Aylwin won the presidency with 55.2 percent of the votes, against 29.4 percent for Büchi and 15.4 percent for a populist third candidate, businessman Francisco Javier Errázuriz. Once again, Pinochet had been soundly defeated. The Concertación coalition got 72 out of 120 members of the Lower House, and 22 of the 38 elected Senators. However, the presence of the nine nonelected senators prevented the Concertación from achieving the majority.

The electoral results of the Chilean Communist Party were poor, as it was unable to elect any representative to Congress. The CCP had ratified a political strategy that was ambiguous toward the role of military action. At an event in April, it had reaffirmed the importance of "the military component as a permanent component of the revolutionary line of the Communists," though it had "lamented the separation of a group [the FPMR] which has a militarist view." Soon after, a significant number of disillusioned activists abandoned the ranks of the party.

A certain tension had developed between the Party for Democracy (Partido por la Democracia, PPD), the instrumental party created principally by Socialists, and the Socialist Party itself, which did not enjoy legal status. The PPD had been so successful that it made no sense to consider discarding it. The interim solution was for the Socialist Party to consider the PPD a "movement" in which Socialists participated. It wasn't until after the presidential and congressional elections, on December 29, 1989, that the Almeyda and Arrate wings of the Socialist Party, joined by other smaller factions, were formally reunited at an emotional ceremony at the Hotel Tupahue in downtown Santiago.

I played two roles during the presidential and congressional campaigns. As vice president of the International Commission of the Concertación, I worked with Juan Somavía and a team of experts from different parties of the coalition to develop the presidential candidate's foreign policy platform; we also wrote briefs for our candidate's television debates and conferences. Most of my time was spent as the campaign chief for Ricardo Lagos's senatorial bid. The joy we felt for Aylwin's victory was tempered for many of us with profound sadness at Lagos's loss.

According to the baroquely complicated binominal system imposed by Pinochet, two Senate candidates were elected from each district, although voters could only cast their ballot for one of them. It was possible for a coalition to seat two candidates, but only if between them they received at least double the votes of the candidates from the second most voted list (in this case the pro-Pinochet parties). In such a system, the Communist lists did not stand a chance. If our coalition did not "double," the leading candidate of the second most voted list would gain a seat, even if he or she had received fewer votes than the second person in the most voted list. Andrés Zaldívar, Lagos's coalition partner, received 8,500 more votes than Lagos. Lagos in turn got 175,323 votes more than the third-place candidate, the rightist Jaime Guzmán; but since Lagos and Zaldívar together had failed to double Guzmán and his partner's total, the binominal system, favoring the runner-up list, allowed Guzmán to take a seat in the Senate.

But Lagos and I later came to realize that his loss was a "blessed defeat." If elected, he would have become the most outspokenly pro-democratic senator, confirming his reputation as a confrontational, "radical" politician. Instead, he cultivated a more statesmanlike profile as Aylwin's minister of education.

During the transitional period after the Aylwin election, most of our activities centered on the configuration of the new government and the inauguration ceremonies, to take place on March 11, 1990. Pinochet kept himself busy tying up the loose ends of matters that he did not want Aylwin to have a say in; the CNI did not halt its dirty work either. On September 4, 1989, the MIR leader, Jecar Neghme, was assassinated in a downtown Santiago street as he was leaving a political meeting, reminding us all that we were still living under a dictatorship.

I had been elected president of the metropolitan chapter of the PPD and everyone believed I would be a candidate for Congress. I wielded a great deal of power and it was assumed that I would run in a "sure district." But I was not interested in serving in Congress. If Aylwin so decided, he could name me to an executive post, I said. One of my top choices was to become ambassador to the Organization of American States (OAS), in Washington, D.C. But first I needed a vacation. Pamela and I rented a cabin on the Pacific shore where there was only one telephone, at the reception desk. It was there that I was eventually located, after Minister-designate Enrique Correa had patiently waited on the one telephone line to tell me that the president had decided to name me ambassador to the OAS. Given the option to wait for a direct connection with Aylwin, I decided to accept right away to avoid a phone mishap.

On December 21, 1989, Carlos Cáceres, Pinochet's interior minister, convinced him to invite President-elect Aylwin to La Moneda to initiate the transition process. Pinochet asked Aylwin for tea. The president-elect arrived accompanied by his designated interior minister, Enrique Krauss (one of my partners in our secret conversations with the Communist Party during the plebiscite). With Pinochet were Cáceres and Pinochet's key aide, General Jorge Ballerino.

Minister Cáceres received Aylwin at the door of La Moneda and led him to the Carrera Room, where Pinochet awaited him. It was the first time that Aylwin had set foot in the presidential palace since 1973. He did not smile when he shook Pinochet's hand. Then they moved to Pinochet's office.

Aylwin got straight to the point: "General, though you have the right to continue for eight more years, it would be better for Chile, for the army, and for the government that you leave the post of commander in chief," he said.

Pinochet, moving comfortably in his seat, responded, "So, you want to throw me out. . . . You are mistaken, the best defense you will have during your administration is if I remain as commander in chief." There were younger army officers who could be a problem for democracy, Pinochet said, but he could control them. "My people are nervous. Nobody will take better care of you than me," he said.

The reason Aylwin demanded Pinochet's resignation from the army before he formally assumed office was that he could not risk the possibility of Pinochet's refusing to let go of his military power base once Aylwin assumed the presidency. This would be tantamount to Pinochet's rebuffing the civilian authority over the military. Aylwin left the palace without even sharing a cup of tea with the dictator.

On March 11, 1990, Pinochet's motorcade drove through the streets of Valparaíso to the Congress in Santiago, where the inauguration of President Aylwin was to take place. As Pinochet's vehicle approached, angry bystanders pelted it with tomatoes and eggs, shouting, "Assassin, assassin!"

While hundreds of journalists from throughout the world and dozens of presidents, prime ministers, and other distinguished guests looked on, Pinochet handed over the presidential sash. But the ceremony contained an important detail. Senate President Gabriel Valdés, the legal symbol of the new democracy, received the sash from Pinochet. Then he placed it across Aylwin's chest. Later that day, at the presidential summer residence in Viña del Mar, Army Commander in Chief Pinochet, accompanied by his five highest-ranking generals, formally presented his respects to President Aylwin. Then the former president but still active army commander attended a luncheon in his honor at an army cavalry institution in nearby Quillota. A musical group sang one of Pinochet's favorite songs, "El Rey" (The King): "With money or without it, I always do whatever I want, because I am still the king!"

I missed part of the inauguration ceremonies because some foreign heads of state had deliberately planned their arrivals to take place after the new government had assumed office, so they would not have to pay the courtesy call on Pinochet that protocol would have required if they arrived before the transfer of power. The foreign minister and the deputy foreign minister had to attend all of the official ceremonies, so I was instructed to welcome, among others, President Felipe González of Spain and President Daniel Ortega of Nicaragua at a reception at the Club Español. The following day I participated in a moving ceremony that Aylwin presided over at the National Stadium. It was a kind of "exorcism" of the evils perpetrated at that place. A rider mounted on a white horse galloped across the field and then a huge Chilean flag was unrolled across it. In a corner of the field, the mother of a disappeared political prisoner danced a *cueca sola,* the national folk dance, but alone instead of with a partner, to symbolize the missing. Eighty thousand people applauded President Aylwin and the foreign leaders who were present, from president Alan García of Peru to Senator Ted Kennedy, who was a member of the U.S. delegation, led by Vice President Dan Quayle, who had arrived before the inauguration to meet with Pinochet and attend all official ceremonies.

President Aylwin's problems with Pinochet began soon after. In 1989, Pinochet had told the journalists Raquel Correa and Elizabeth Subercaseaux that he had refused to resign from his post as army commander because "my people could be humiliated." Referring to the possibility of eventual trials, Pinochet warned, "What I say is that my people will not be touched."

Moreover, Pinochet kept on talking as if he were still a politician. After Aylwin's election, Pinochet declared, "With the passing years people are going to be asking for me to come back. I will be looking at what happens in Chile, not as a vulture, but with a desire of helping the country to move forward." It was the continuation of a famous combination threat and prediction Pinochet had made a few months before: "When Rome was under siege, they went to search for Cincinnatus to serve the homeland. The messengers found him plowing his land. He was a man of simple tastes. He put on the uniform and defeated the enemy. He was given honors. Then he went back to his fields. There is a second part. Rome again was under siege. Once more they went looking for Cincinnatus. But this second part I'd better not tell." Lucius Quintus Cincinnatus was twice dictator of Rome, in 458 and then again in 439 BC Pinochet was counting on President Aylwin to fail.

About a week after Aylwin's inauguration, Pinochet asked him for an audience. The general expressed that he owed obedience to the president, but not to his defense minister. President Aylwin, a well-versed jurist, reached for a copy of the constitution on his desk. "Look, General," he said, "your constitution says that the armed forces are under the authority of the Ministry of Defense. The army is under the authority of the Ministry of Defense. Hence, you, as chief of the army, are under the defense minister. It is crystal clear and we are not going to keep on discussing the issue, General, because this is a constitutional norm."

Pinochet was caught and did not say another word. But he was upset. Patricio Rojas, the new defense minister, had alienated Pinochet even before assuming his post when he had rejected his predecessor's recommendations for undersecretaries, culled from lists of top officers from the armed forces and police. Pinochet never met with Minister Rojas. Whenever he was summoned, he sent the vice commander in chief in his stead. Moreover, Pinochet decreed the creation of an Advisory Committee of the Commander in Chief (Comité Asesor, CAS), led by General Ballerino, and dictated a set of rules for its operation that the Aylwin government considered illegal. After a failed dialogue on the issue, Aylwin requested a formal opinion from the Comptroller General's Office, which authorized the establishment of the committee but found that some of its attributes were indeed illegal. Pinochet also attempted to keep the army involved in internal security, but the Aylwin administration made it clear to him that that was a function of the Carabineros and Investigaciones.

In the meantime, workers at Exxon's La Disputada copper mine, near Santiago, discovered the buried bodies of three men, on a site that had belonged to the army. They were identified as three Communist leaders who had been kidnapped by the DINA in 1976. Even more shocking for the nation was the discovery of twenty-one buried bodies in the northern Atacama Desert, near a former prison camp in Pisagua. The dry desert conditions had kept the bodies well preserved; it was clear that they had been tied up and blindfolded before execution; expressions of horror and despair could still be discerned on some of their faces. The bodies were quickly identified because ID cards and personal letters to family members were found in their clothing. Under the new democratic administration, people dared to talk. Similar discoveries were made in other parts of the country. Pinochet was unmoved. When two or more unidentified bodies were exhumed from a single grave, he took sarcastic note of the killers' "good economy."

Anticipating the public outcry for prosecution of the perpetrators of these crimes, President Aylwin decided to create a Truth and Reconciliation Commission to gather evidence on those believed to have disappeared or been killed during the Pinochet years. The army rejected the commission, arguing that only a judicial tribunal would have the authority to investigate. Pinochet loyalists revived rumors about "Plan Z," Allende's alleged plot to wipe out the high command of the armed forces, a blatantly propagandistic and discredited specimen of disinformation, and spun elaborate versions of Chile's situation before the coup, which presumably were supposed to justify the atrocities that were committed afterward.

The day Aylwin announced the formation of the Truth and Reconciliation Commission, also known as the Rettig Commission after the jurist who headed it, Raúl Rettig, Pinochet tried to reach the president by phone to express his disapproval. Aylwin decided not to return the general's insistent calls. But in order to loosen things up, the president organized a luncheon with the commanders in chief and the Carabineros director on May 4, 1990, which Pinochet declined to attend, sending a replacement. The day before the luncheon, Aylwin had finally granted Pinochet an audience. The general had protested that the president was on a witch hunt against the armed forces and his regime. Aylwin calmly responded that the armed forces would not be on trial, but that the truth about what had happened during the last seventeen years would have to come out.

A few weeks later, when the official decree that set up the commission was issued, Pinochet released a statement to the press that accused the Rettig Commission of being a subterfuge for a vendetta against the army and its commander in chief. An angry Aylwin summoned Pinochet to La Moneda on May 28. Pinochet's fleet of bullet-proof Mercedes-Benzes (actually, the vehicles belonged to the presidency; Aylwin used a regular unarmored car, while Pinochet had kept the entire presidential motor pool for his own use) was denied access to the palace's underground parking garage. Accompanied by a dozen bodyguards, the old general was forced to walk through a gauntlet of demonstrators to the main gate. It didn't get any better inside the palace. Aylwin reprimanded Pinochet for presuming to question or even discuss publicly his presidential decisions. He demanded that Pinochet dissolve the CNI secret police; moreover, he ordered Pinochet to cooperate with the Rettig Commission's investigations.

All in all, it was a humiliating experience for Pinochet, who keenly felt the loss of the symbols of his power. The fact that he no longer had access to the palace's underground parking garage galled him, as did the insults he'd had to endure from the demonstrators outside the palace—who'd shouted "Assassin!" at him as he walked by. Pinochet complained to Aylwin about it. "No problem," Aylwin told him. "Whenever you need to tell me something, come to my private residence at 8 A.M. Nobody has to know." After that, communications between the two men improved.

Aylwin confided to me in an interview that Pinochet, "a cunning old man," always attempted to gain a little ground at his expense.

Pinochet, who "detests Carabineros, told me that I was badly protected. He offered to place the president's security in the hands of the army. He wanted to make me a sort of prisoner," Aylwin asserted. "It was one of his little devilish tricks." Aylwin declined the offer.

One day, Pinochet's wife, Lucía, made very aggressive political declarations to a magazine. Aylwin summoned Pinochet to La Moneda and told him sternly that his wife's words were "absolutely unacceptable for the wife of an army commander in chief."

"Please don't tell me, Mr. President. Forty years! Forty years I have been married!" Pinochet responded, lifting his arms in the air in a gesture of utter helplessness.

"The only thing left for me to do was to console him!" Aylwin bemusedly recalled. "I can still vividly remember the image of Pinochet posing as his wife's victim." As a dissimulator, Pinochet was "an artist," he added.

Pinochet feared, above all, that Aylwin would try to alter the Prussian traditions of the Chilean Army. In September 1990, during a party at a private club, the general bitterly attacked the West German Army, saying that postwar reforms had turned it into an army of "marihuana smokers, homosexuals, long-haired individuals, and trade unionists." Aylwin rebuked Pinochet for potentially jeopardizing Chile's relations with Germany.

On September 4, I attended the official state burial of Salvador Allende. It was very emotional. His body was removed from an unmarked grave in Viña del Mar and taken to the General Cemetery in Santiago. Accompanying Tencha Bussi de Allende were numerous foreign dignitaries. Pinochet dismissed the burial ceremony as a political stunt and flatly refused to allow the army to render military honors befitting a deceased president.

During the traditional military parade on Army Day, September 19, President Aylwin and his cabinet were booed by the public in the reviewing stand, mostly relatives of the marching troops. Afterward, in another act of insubordination, General Carlos Parera did not request Aylwin's permission to carry on with the parade, as was customary. Following this incident, President Aylwin refused to promote Parera to a higher grade within the rank of general. Pinochet took the general's side and the impasse had to be resolved by the Comptroller General's office, which ruled in favor of the government.

That same day, in Washington, D.C., in my position as ambassador to the OAS, I attended a cocktail party at the Chilean Army mission, which was headed by General Ramón Castro. Castro was the trusted Pinochet aide who as army secretary-general had purchased the El Melocotón estate for his boss on suspiciously convenient terms. General Castro delivered a speech lauding Pinochet and strongly criticizing democracy. I was outraged, and left without staying for the champagne. That evening, I also cut short my presence at the Army Day reception at Fort McNair. General Castro and his wife courteously accompanied me and Pamela to the door of the reception room. I could not resist and, as our wives chatted, I took the general aside and told him I had found his morning's intervention wholly "inappropriate and unacceptable. You and I are never going to agree about our country's past, for sure. But we should be able to work together for the common future," I added.

General Castro lowered his head slightly and folded his hands behind him, as if he were bowing to a superior officer, and apologized. "It was not my intention to offend or to cause a problem for you or for the government," he said. I never again had a problem with General Castro, nor did I ever hear him speak another word of criticism toward the democratic government or its authorities, even after President Aylwin vetoed his promotion. Tensions between Pinochet and the democratic government reached their peak in December 1990, when a congressional investigation uncovered questionable payments to Pinochet's eldest son. Augusto Pinochet Jr. had received checks totaling $3 million in 1989 when the army purchased a small rifle company, Valmoval, even though he was not one of the company's owners. According to the conservative leader, Andrés Allamand, the military in its congressional testimony gave "partial, contradictory and in some cases unbelievable" explanations for the payments. General Pinochet had been involved in at least some phases of the transaction. The scandal, known as the "Pinocheques," swiftly devolved into a call for Pinochet's resignation.

General Ballerino then suggested that Pinochet could be willing to shorten his term as army commander. To avoid any confusion, it was decided that Pinochet and Aylwin should talk face-to-face about the delicate matter.

The conservative politician Sergio Onofre Jarpa arranged a meeting between Pinochet and President Aylwin alone, but in the Byzantine dialogue that took place on that occasion neither side ever touched on the issue. In a later conversation, Jarpa told Aylwin that Pinochet had confided to him, Jarpa, that the president had not given him "the angle in the conversation to pose the early retirement question." Apparently neither of them wanted to be the first to raise it. It was possible that Pinochet was ready to leave, and not only because he felt burdened by the "Pinocheques" case. He had lost control over the other branches of the armed forces and the police. High-ranking army officers, including CNI officials, had organized an illegal money racket that was publicly denounced in the wake of the murder of an investor who had demanded his money back. To top things off, the son of the former DINA chief, General Manuel Contreras, had killed a high-ranking CNI official during an argument at a scandalous party.

But if Pinochet was tired, he was not beaten. He would only leave on his own terms.

On the morning of December 19, 1990, during a meeting with the CAS chief, General Ballerino, Defense Minister Patricio Rojas asked him about Pinochet's early retirement. Ballerino replied that Pinochet would consider leaving after Aylwin's presidential term, provided he received certain guarantees from the government, including the right to designate his successor as commander in chief of the army. Rojas thought that this date was too far away, but agreed to talk again. However, General Ballerino interpreted the conversation to mean that Pinochet was being pressured to resign by Defense Secretary Rojas. General Guillermo Garín, the former vice commander in chief of the army, told me that Pinochet's perception was that the defense minister was bent on removing him. But in the version narrated to me by Enrique Correa, the minister secretary-general of government, it was clear that the whole idea of shortening Pinochet's period at the helm of the army had been raised by Ballerino, not by the defense minister.

That same day, Aylwin had followed Pinochet's advice and invited recent graduates of the army high command course to bring their wives to a celebratory luncheon at La Moneda. It was the first and only time that President Aylwin and his wife, Leonor, got together with General Pinochet and his wife, Lucía. It was a somewhat awkward gathering, but pleasant enough. That evening Aylwin was scheduled to attend the graduation of Carabineros officers at their school.

The luncheon ended at around 3 P.M. When the general left he learned from the headlines in an afternoon newspaper, *La Segunda,* that the State Defense Council, an independent organ charged with representing, defending, and advising the state regarding its interests, had decided to press charges against his son. Around the same time, Defense Minister Rojas met again with General Ballerino and expressed his position on Pinochet's retirement: he should leave no later than April 15, 1991, and he would not be allowed to name his successor. Rojas added that he expected to hear the general's response first thing the next morning.

Pinochet reacted by ordering an "Alert 1" mobilization of the army: within two hours, fifty-seven thousand army troops and officers had to be at their posts. The army called it an "exercise of coordination and liaison," and justified it with a reference to an obscure section of the army's rules of procedure. But it was a brutal show of force, and its real meaning was unmistakable. Defense Minister Rojas called Pinochet and demanded an explanation.

"If I am pressured, I act," was his laconic response.

President Aylwin was about to go to the Carabineros graduation ceremony when he learned about the military movement. He was advised to cancel his plans, but he decided to attend. Pinochet, who was scheduled to participate, did not arrive. Aylwin informed the president of the lower house of Congress, the Socialist José Antonio Viera-Gallo, also present at the ceremony, about the military situation. Viera-Gallo took refuge in gallows humor. "Does that mean that we civilian authorities here are all under arrest now?" he asked dryly. "We were quite scared," Aylwin acknowledged in an interview I had with him years later.

However, it was only an army move, it wasn't joined by any of the other branches of the military or the Carabineros. The next day, Aylwin summoned all of the commanders in chief and met with them individually.

"By what right do you do things that cause enormous damage to the nation, to the prestige of the country abroad?" he shouted at Pinochet. Pinochet responded with bureaucratic explanations, downplaying his show of force. The other commanders expressed their full support of the constitutional order.

Toward late January 1991 the congressional investigation of the "Pinocheques" ended anticlimactically, with a watered-down report that avoided mentioning Pinochet or pointing the finger at his son. It was a sad moment, but two key Aylwin ministers, Enrique Correa and Edgardo Boeninger, minister secretary-general of the presidency, had pushed for an outcome that would safeguard the transition to democracy. To this day, Correa suspects that Pinochet, as a brilliant tactician, followed a double-pronged approach to kill the "Pinocheques" affair: floating the idea that he was willing to leave the army post early and also exerting pressure via the liaison exercise.

In February 1991 the Rettig Commission delivered its report on human rights abuses during the Pinochet period. The document shocked public opinion with its initial census of 2,115 people assassinated by state agents and 164 killed as victims of political violence, as well as its graphic descriptions of killings and torture by the Pinochet security authorities. Predictably, it was bitterly attacked by Pinochet as a one-sided version of history that did not examine the root causes of the military action—this despite the fact that his former minister of education, Gonzalo Vial, had drafted the section of the document that dealt with historical context. Through legislation in Congress, a package of moral and material reparations was provided to the families of victims. In addition, the Corporation for Reparation and Reconciliation was created to investigate new cases of disappeared and assassinated people as they were discovered, completing the work of the Rettig Commission. The Nelson Mandela government in South Africa received direct advisory support from the Chilean authorities when it replicated Chile's Truth and Reconciliation Commission in 1995.

The report was very critical of the Chilean judiciary under the Pinochet regime, as President Aylwin had been when, in a letter to the Supreme Court, he expressed his view that the 1978 amnesty law—which pardoned all individuals who committed crimes during the period of the State of Siege, from September 11, 1973, to March 3, 1978—could not be applied until the crimes it covered had been thoroughly investigated. In 1992 the Supreme Court, guided by the views of lower courts, particularly by Judge Juan Guzmán, resolved that the disappeared political prisoners had been subjected to "kidnapping"; consequently, since kidnapping is an ongoing crime so long as the death of the victim cannot be certified, the amnesty did not apply to its perpetrators. Judicial investigations should proceed. As a result, high military officers, including generals, began to be charged and prosecuted for various human rights crimes. At the same time, the Supreme Court ordered that the Letelier case be reopened. Special Magistrate Adolfo Bañados was assigned to oversee the case. Bañados tried Manuel Contreras, the former DINA chief, and the DINA operations director, Colonel Pedro Espinoza, and later, in 1993, condemned them to seven and six years in prison, respectively. "I will not go to jail," Contreras said defiantly, when he was notified of his sentence. He was ready to resist justice.

As HEALTH ISSUES sapped some of Pinochet's rebellious energy (he had a pacemaker installed for a heart ailment), he slowly began getting used to the idea that he was a subordinate of the president. Increasingly, Pinochet and his entourage fought to secure his historical legacy. He sought to minimize or justify the record of his bloody reign of terror; mostly he wanted to make sure that history books would remember him as the man who had brought order and modernity to Chile.

In September 1991, General Pinochet formally invited me to participate in a defense policy seminar to be held at the Army War Academy. I accepted, and on September 5 I delivered a lecture on the relationship between defense policy and foreign policy. I never expected Pinochet to be there, but he arrived punctually and took a seat specially reserved for him.

I was very frank in my presentation. I questioned the argument that the only requirements for an effective defense were material and human resources. What about democracy? I asked. What about the prestige or cohesion of a nation? The coercive capacities of the military had to be enhanced with soft-power factors, from economic strength to social cohesion. I attacked the notion held by many military officers that "foreign ideas" represented some sort of a threat. What are foreign ideas? I asked. In Chile's struggle for independence, our forefathers drew on European ideas. The universal notions of freedom and equality were born in Paris, but now belong to the world commons. Democracy was born in Greece; nationalism emerged in nineteenth-century Europe. In recent years our country received ideas from Chicago, I added. In a global world, ideas are transnational—the challenge is to adapt them to local realities. My audience, mostly army officers in uniform, acknowledged my talk with a desultory round of polite applause.

During the coffee break we were ushered into a private room and I noticed that Pinochet was headed my way; apparently he intended to greet me. I could not bring myself to shake his hand. As a diplomat, and for state reasons, I have had to deal with any number of unsavory people. This time, however, I turned my back and struck up a conversation with a high-ranking military officer. Out of the corner of my eye, I saw Pinochet walking away. That was my closest brush with the man who had had such a baleful influence on my life—and on the lives of a whole generation of Chileans. Sometime later, Pinochet sent me a letter, signed personally, on his "Captain General, Commander in Chief of the Army" stationery: "I wish to express my appreciation for your valuable participation in the seminar about 'Defense Policy.'. . . Captain General Augusto Pinochet wishes to reiterate his thanks for your important professional contribution, taking this opportunity to transmit his highest regard toward you personally."

As weary as he was, as marginal as he was becoming, Pinochet continued his games of brinksmanship. He never openly defied the civilian authorities, but he took advantage of whatever opportunities he had to remind the democratic government that he still had power and that he answered mainly to himself.

Toward the end of 1992 a huge scandal blew up: Pinochet's Advisory Committee of the Commander in Chief, the CAS, was systematically spying on the political elite, both in the government and in the moderate right-wing opposition.

The Army Telecommunications Command in Peñalolen, in the Andes foothills, had been taping private telephone conversations and delivering the reports to General Ballerino, the head of the CAS. Before its dissolution, the CNI had carried on such extensive wiretapping operations that it had an officer working at the main local telephone company. Since the secret police's dissolution, a new spying unit had been created that answered directly to the CAS. One of its first operations was mounted to spoil the emerging presidential campaign of Sebastián Piñera, a businessman and moderate rightist.

On Sunday, August 23, Piñera was a guest on a political television program. Ricardo Claro, the owner of the television station, unexpectedly appeared on camera and, to everyone's astonishment, played a tape recording of a conversation between Piñera and a close adviser and supporter in which they discussed plans to ensure that a journalist friend on the program would put pressure on Piñera's political rival, Evelyn Matthei, when it was her turn to be interviewed. This was a major scandal. Piñera admitted that the taped conversation had taken place; after he suspended his fledgling presidential campaign he dedicated himself full-time to finding out who was behind the plot to bring him down.

Everyone suspected the army because it had the technology to tap phone calls; another prime suspect was Evelyn Matthei herself, who initially denied any involvement. But several months later, she admitted that she had obtained the tape from Army Captain Fernando Diez. The army sought to present the case as the isolated responsibility of Captain Diez, who after acknowledging his role was prosecuted by the army but did not receive any punishment, and was later forced into retirement. The auditor general, Fernando Torres Silva, instructed all the other military personnel involved to deny that they ever taped civilian conversations or that they knew what Captain Diez was up to.

But the operation against Piñera was just a part of a wider eaves-dropping operation, as an investigation by *Qué Pasa* magazine demon-strated fifteen years later. Every day the CAS received reports on bugging and wiretaps signed by Captain Diez, who was actually in charge of the so-called Fourth Electronic War Company. He had served in the DINA and the CNI, and had even served directly under Pinochet. His wiretapping job, according to a quoted source, was "to provide Pinochet with all the elements and criteria to address the military-civilian relationship." When President Aylwin demanded to have access to all the documentation pertaining to the internal army investigation of the case, Pinochet blandly told him that it had been incinerated.

In May 1993, the last year of Aylwin's mandate, the president traveled to Sweden on an official visit. The balance of Aylwin's four years of democratic rule had been excellent: inflation had been re-duced from 32 percent in 1989 to 12 percent in 1993, unemployment had declined to 6 percent, and economic growth was above 7 percent annually, with real wages growing about 15 percent. A *New York Times* editorial entitled "Encouraging Success in Chile" stressed that Presi-dent Aylwin's administration had "restored union rights, increased social expenditures and promised compensation to victims of repres-sion. Meanwhile, the new government has skillfully managed rela-tions with the military and kept inflation down. This sensible course has built support for market policies and kept faith with the poor." The editorial comment ended with an assertion that "Chile today stands out as a notable success in a bleak neighborhood."

Some argued that Chile was managing its economy efficiently, but that its democracy was feeble, that the democratic government made the "trains run on time," but it was a democracy "under tute-lage." The main criticism was that, although Pinochet had been re-moved from the presidency, he still held democracy hostage from his key post as commander in chief of the army. The pending matter of the "Pinocheques," in the hands of the independent State Defense Council, demonstrated just how disruptive Pinochet could still be.

The Council had decided to press charges against the general's son, Augusto Pinochet Jr. At first the case attracted scant public atten-tion and proceeded quietly. But then, on May 28, 1993, the govern-ment newspaper, *La Nación,* ran a front-page headline: "Case of Pinochet's Son's Checks Is Reopened: Eight Generals Summoned to

Testify." Pinochet was apoplectic. About three dozen generals joined the commander in chief at the armed forces building, and troops in combat gear, including Special Forces wearing their black berets, were mobilized. The episode became known as the *boinazo* (the "berets mobilization"). From Sweden, Aylwin authorized Vice President Enrique Krauss to negotiate with Pinochet.

At the home of General Ballerino a meeting was held where Pinochet delivered to the government a long and disorderly list of demands, among them a new and complete amnesty for human rights violations, beyond that of 1978; a commitment by the government to leave the Organic Law of the Armed Forces intact; special discretion in court citations of military officers and special jails for those condemned; wage increases; and resolution on various decrees and military requests held up by the government. Conversations took place between Vice President Krauss and Minister Secretary-General Correa, on the government side, and Generals Pinochet and Ballerino, on the army side. On May 31 they agreed to set up a commission to study the pending issues. At the last minute, Pinochet demanded even more, the removal of Defense Minister Rojas and Army Undersecretary Marcos Sánchez (Aylwin told me that Pinochet would greet the undersecretary by squeezing his hand so hard as to cause him pain). Krauss did not need to consult with President Aylwin to flatly reject Pinochet's request regarding Minister Rojas. On June 1, the *boinazo* mobilization ended.

On June 5, President Aylwin returned to Chile and summoned Pinochet to a tense meeting. "Your actions do not have any justification whatsoever. They are not a personal affront. They damage the country," Aylwin said. As usual, Pinochet downplayed the significance of the army's show of force. "I believe Pinochet wanted to show his political muscle, forcing me to cut short my visit to Sweden and return immediately to Chile," Aylwin told me years later.

Aylwin reflected on the two shows of military force by Pinochet, the 1990 "liaison exercise" and the *boinazo*. "Pinochet did not have any way of continuing the pressure after the 'liaison exercise' because only his family interests were at stake," Aylwin said, "but on the *boinazo* he had dozens of army officers summoned and tried by the courts for human rights crimes. . . . Thus, he institutionalized the checks scandal, surrounding it with matters affecting many high officers." This is why in 1993 Pinochet got some of what he wanted. The "Pinocheques" case was transferred to a less dynamic court, where it quickly got bogged down; Aylwin agreed not to change the Organic

Law of the Armed Forces, and the undersecretary of the army was transferred to an equivalent post in the Justice Ministry. But after the spying scandal, almost as if to vitiate Pinochet's small victories, the CAS began to fall apart.

Pinochet had been betting that the first Concertación government would fail and that he would be called back by popular demand. But in December 1993 the Christian Democrat Eduardo Frei Ruiz-Tagle was elected president, defeating Arturo Alessandri, the candidate of the right-wing opposition. On March 11, 1994, Aylwin handed over the presidential sash to Frei Ruiz-Tagle at a formal inauguration ceremony in Congress that I attended. As Aylwin departed, he received a standing ovation. Pinochet joined in the applause, but unlike Aylwin, he was staying in his post. President Aylwin later compared his situation with Pinochet to that of the first elected president of Spain if Franco had still been alive and commanding the army.

As PINOCHET'S POWER slowly dwindled, the Chicago economic model was gaining ground beyond Chile's borders. The demonstration effect of the Pinochet experience influenced countries as diverse as Peru and the Russian Federation. In Peru, President Alberto Fujimori adopted many of the market-oriented economic reforms implemented by Pinochet and increasingly enacted authoritarian and antidemocratic measures along with them, such that he earned the nickname "Chinochet" (he used to be referred to as "Chino" because of his Asian origin). Eventually, Fujimori was pressured into leaving office, but his successors continued the free-market reform path inspired by the Chilean model.

As the fall of the Berlin Wall, the disintegration of the Soviet Union, and the collapse of Communist regimes in Eastern Europe opened the way for new economic strategies, increased attention was focused on the Pinochet regime's economic policies. The new Czechoslovak and Polish authorities contacted Hernán Büchi, Pinochet's last finance minister, to seek his advice on privatization and on ways to deal with bankrupt state banks. The conservative institute Libertad y Desarrollo (Liberty and Development) hosted two dozen economists from the former Soviet Union at a 1992 conference.

Pinochet's rule, which combined authoritarian politics with liberal, market-oriented economic policies, was held up as a paradigm. In the late 1990s, the prime minister of the Russian Federation, Sergei Stepashin, a former general, was heard to declare, "Some have compared me to Pinochet. No, I am not General Pinochet." Another popular political figure in Russian politics in the mid-nineties was

Aleksandr Lebed, also a former general, who, according to the *New York Times*, "called for a restoration of order in his chaotic country, citing the example of General Augusto Pinochet in Chile." In fact, an organization was established in Moscow calling itself "Pinochet for Russia," which, according to Pinochet's daughter Lucía, regularly solicited books and other materials from the Pinochet Foundation archives.

Though the rightist parties were increasingly reconciled to the fading away of the old soldier, they wanted above all to preserve and enhance the economic model identified with him. Most Latin American military dictatorships in the 1970s had run disastrous economies. Despite its ups and downs, under Pinochet, Chile's economy had been lifted out of the doldrums and had been placed on track to sustained economic growth.

One of the most exported components of the Pinochet model was its pensions system of individual capitalization. Due largely to its tireless promoter, José Piñera (minister of labor under Pinochet), the private pensions system was adopted by countries as diverse as Peru, Mexico, and Slovakia. George W. Bush, an enthusiastic backer of the Chilean pensions model, invited Piñera to dinner at the Texas governor's mansion in Austin to discuss the privatization of Social Security. According to a conversation I had with Piñera, Bush said that changing the pension system in the U.S. from Social Security's pay-as-you-go model to a system of privately funded individual retirement accounts was "the most important issue facing the nation."

When Bush ran for president in 1999 he listed private investment accounts in Social Security as one of his top objectives. Bush called the Chilean system "a great example," adding that the United States could "take some lessons from Chile." Once elected president, he appointed a commission to come up with specific proposals. The 9/11 terrorist attacks and the Iraq War, widespread opposition to the idea of privatization, not to mention the manifold shortcomings of the Chilean system (which forced the Michelle Bachelet administration to successfully undertake a major reform of it), pushed the issue to the back burner.

The Chilean economic experience became the foundation of the so-called "Washington Consensus," a package of ten free-market policy ideas conceived by the British economist John Williamson, and since adopted by the main multilateral financial institutions, to guide the development of nations emerging from authoritarian rule and state-controlled economies. When I was in Washington in 1992 as

Chile's ambassador to the OAS, I attended a seminar at the Inter-American Development Bank. Several economists asked whether the Chilean experience could be replicated elsewhere without the benefit of Pinochet's iron hand. A heated debate ensued in which I argued that the fact that Chile's economic performance under a democratic regime was much better than it had been under Pinochet suggested that it could.

Furthermore, I argued that while the Concertación government in Chile agreed that it was important to develop a strong "market economy," it would never agree to letting loose a "market society." Neoliberalism assumed that the state had to be reduced to prevent it from having the capability of interfering with the free interplay of the marketplace. But the evidence is that, on the contrary, we needed a strong state to pursue well-focused social policies to create opportunities for all, particularly in education and health. Inequality deepened by orthodox Chicago policies was as big an obstacle to sustained economic growth as incomplete basic economic reforms, I added.

So how successful was Pinochet's economic model, the inspiration of the Washington Consensus?

That model in place during Pinochet's seventeen years in power had two clear phases. The first was from 1975 to 1980, when, after Admiral Merino convinced Pinochet that the Chicago orthodoxy could solve Chile's problems, privatizations and market reforms were implemented to the fullest extent. The second phase was from 1985 to 1989. It took place under Finance Minister Büchi's guidance, when the free-market model was resumed, with a second wave of privatizations and an export-driven boom (of products from fresh fruits to wood and paper), but tempered with a considerable dose of Keynesian pragmatism, including the nonorthodox maintenance of high tariffs in some sectors, price guarantees for selective products, subsidies to exports, subsidies to debtors in dollars, debt conversions with special exchange rates, and other measures.

A study by the economist Andrés Sanfuentes demonstrated that between 1973 and 1989 the average annual growth of GDP reached an average of 3.5 percent, but per capita GDP growth remained under 2 percent, well below historical rates of growth in Chile. A comparison by the economists Patricio Meller, Sergio Lehmann, and Rodrigo Cifuentes of economic and social indicators under Pinochet and Aylwin revealed that Pinochet's 3.5 percent GDP growth pales in comparison to Aylwin's 6.3 percent between 1990 and 1993. The domestic investment rate during Pinochet's reign (1974 to 1989) reached

18.7 percent, compared to Aylwin's 24.8 percent. Unemployment was relatively high during the Pinochet years, only improving toward the late eighties. Inflation, which reached a rate of 32 percent in the last year of the dictatorship, was never brought under full control. Poverty affected about 39 percent of the population in the last year of the dictatorship. Inequality in 1990 was much deeper than in 1970, as economic reforms led to an enlargement of the preexisting gap between rich and poor. In sum, Sanfuentes concluded, "The economic results of 17 years of dictatorship were mediocre, clearly nonexportable."

What *were* the merits of the Chilean model, then?

First, it changed prevailing values. An entrepreneurial spirit emerged; Chileans began to produce and export nontraditional goods and services as never before. The profit motive became legitimized in Chilean society, as did, perhaps to excess, the consumption drive. Second, though Pinochet could not bring inflation down to single-digit figures, it was dramatically reduced and hyperinflation became a thing of the past. Third, the export-driven growth of the late 1980s was sustainable and led to a balance-of-payments surplus. Fourth, the restoration and development of market mechanisms made the economy more resilient and adaptable.

But the real Chilean economic miracle actually occurred under democracy, when the foundations laid in the Pinochet period were developed with full respect for the rule of law, with a critical free press, with a functioning Congress, with free labor unions, and with active political parties and NGOs. In December 2000 the United States and Chile initiated negotiations for a bilateral free trade agreement—the first such talks undertaken by Washington since the 1993 NAFTA (North American Free Trade Association) accord—which would have been unthinkable under the Pinochet regime. The agreement was signed in June 2003, during the Ricardo Lagos administration, and led to a substantial expansion of bilateral trade and investment. Similar trade accords were reached with, among others, the European Union, Japan, China, India, and several Latin American partners.

In 2003 John Williamson revised his Washington Consensus, arguing that to resume economic growth countries had "to complete and complement the reforms that were initially introduced in the late 1980s and early 1990s." Williamson stressed the need "to reduce vulnerability to crises, complete liberalization . . . and include income distribution concerns in their policy packages." Again, Chile, whose growth record was at the time the best in the region, "ought to be more of a reference point for Latin America," said Williamson. In

2004, Chile, according to the World Competitiveness Report, had tripled the size of its economy in twenty years, growing three times more than Argentina, Brazil, or Mexico. The poverty rate, which reached almost 40 percent in 1990, had been reduced to 18 percent in 2004. Public debt had fallen from 100 percent of GDP in 1986 to only 12 percent in 2004.

Some, particularly Pinochet supporters, feared—or cynically hoped—that democracy would bring back irresponsible economic policies, resulting in diminished foreign investment and domestic savings, which would in turn prompt the sorts of ill-considered populist socioeconomic measures that would lead inexorably to hyperinflation and instability. Quite the opposite occurred. The democratic governments of Presidents Patricio Aylwin, Eduardo Frei Ruiz-Tagle, and Ricardo Lagos improved the nation's economic performance overall, while promoting strong social policies to tackle poverty and inequality.

But Chile's critics were right about one thing. If Chile was managing its economy efficiently, its democracy was still feeble. Though Pinochet had been removed from the presidency and his dictatorship had ended, the general still remained as commander in chief of the army, a position that enabled him to make considerable mischief.

The weakened Pinochet who was scheduled to retire in March 1998 got along relatively well with President Eduardo Frei Ruiz-Tagle, who assumed office in March 1994. Pinochet had begun to accept that it would be politically impossible to interfere with trials against high military officers when a democratically elected government was in place, never mind to dictate a new amnesty. But his main concern continued to be damage control, first for himself and his family, then for his men.

The main civil-military problem during this period emerged from the Supreme Court's decision on the sentences handed down in the Letelier case, otherwise known as the "false passports case." On May 30, 1995, the Supreme Court confirmed a lower-court decision that condemned Manuel Contreras to seven years in prison and Colonel Pedro Espinoza to six years. For Pinochet it was unacceptable that high-ranking army officers should be confined in common jails, but the Frei government would not allow Contreras and Espinoza to serve out their sentences inside military bases.

President Frei, in consultation with his political ministers and the defense minister, Edmundo Pérez Yoma, decided that the solution would be to build a special prison for former military officers condemned for human rights crimes. The place chosen was Punta Peuco, north of Santiago. The only problem was that Ricardo Lagos, minister of public works and leader of the leftist parties of the government coalition, was not consulted; he was merely asked to stamp his signature on the decree to build the prison. Lagos refused, citing ethical concerns. Condemned military officers should serve in regular prisons under rules common to every other prisoner, he argued. A crisis ensued, with the defense minister asserting that Lagos should leave the cabinet. But Socialist and PPD leaders responded that if he was removed all the Socialist and PPD ministers would resign, which would create a major earthquake in the governing alliance.

Finally, the impasse was resolved through the preparation of a special decree that contained an ingenious loophole. According to this new document, military officers would serve their sentences in regular prisons as determined by the National Prisons Service—which was allowed to build new jails to accommodate them, if necessary. The jail in Punta Peuco was constructed in record time.

But Contreras declared that he would not go "to any jail so long as there is no real justice," and proceeded to repair to his farm estate in southern Chile. The courts ordered that the prison term imposed on Contreras should be executed. Contreras moved from his farm to the Sangra Regiment barracks in Puerto Montt, then to the Arauco Regiment barracks in Osorno, and then to the navy hospital in the southern port of Talcahuano. After a veritable soap opera's worth of concatenating events that raised the collective blood pressure of the entire country, Contreras was transferred by helicopter from Talcahuano to Santiago and, at 2 A.M. on October 21, 1995, entered the Punta Peuco prison to serve his sentence.

Throughout this episode Pinochet played his usual pragmatic, middle-of-the-road game. He publicly complained that Contreras had faced "a fabricated tribunal similar to Nuremberg, for political reasons." Pinochet claimed to believe that Contreras was innocent. But at the same time he insisted that the army could not impede or delay Supreme Court decisions. During the toughest moments of the crisis, Pinochet traveled abroad on official business.

The "Pinocheques" case was dormant but not dead. In mid-1995, the State Defense Council decided to request that it be reopened so that charges could be brought against those involved, including Pinochet Jr. On July 14 the court denied the State Defense Council's request, and dictated a temporary stay of the case, whereupon the State Defense Council announced that it would appeal to a higher court. Pinochet's reaction was instantaneous. On July 22, with Pinochet's authorization, more than a thousand military officers and soldiers on active duty, accompanied by their families, gathered in front of the Punta Peuco prison. The *Peucazo,* as the protest would come to be called, was a good way for Pinochet to kill two birds with one stone: to show displeasure with the reactivation of the "Pinocheques" case and indirectly to express his solidarity with General Contreras.

Frei did not want to confront two crises involving Pinochet at the same time. The administration's priority was to ensure that Contreras would go to jail as ordered by the Supreme Court. Hence, President Frei called the acting president of the State Defense Council and, in his characteristically blunt style, told him that an appeal in the "Pinocheques" case had the potential to endanger democracy. While recognizing and respecting the independence of the council, Frei requested that it let the lower Santiago court's decision stand.

Again, a negotiation ensued between Pinochet and the defense minister. The general reiterated the army's desire to seek an end to the human rights prosecutions involving military officers; he requested that the president pardon Contreras and Espinoza when they completed half of their jail sentences; again he demanded that former high-ranking military officers serve their sentences in military custody; and he requested an improvement in institutional salaries. The government agreed to the salary increase; both sides also agreed that officers could serve their sentences in prisons jointly run by the army and the National Prisons Services.

The Frei government tried to shift the focus of its relationship with Pinochet and the army to professional matters. I personally participated in 1996 in an unprecedented and stimulating meeting of the minds between high-ranking officers of all the branches of the armed forces and key civilians, led by the defense minister, the results of which were formally delivered to President Frei as the first *White Book of the National Defense of Chile*. It was my first experience of fruitful and genuine dialogue between civilian authorities and high-ranking military officers. Other countries in South America followed Chile's example. Along the same lines, efforts were made to reduce and modernize the army and to develop infrastructure connections to isolated regions, particularly in Patagonia, a geopolitical issue of special interest for Pinochet.

The Frei presidency also initiated an important roundtable dialogue—called *Mesa de Diálogo*—among representatives of the commanders in chief of the armed forces, human rights lawyers, religious figures, and independent opinion leaders to tackle the issue of the disappeared political prisoners: to establish what had happened to them, and where their bodies were, and thus move toward national reconciliation. It was successful in facilitating a genuine convergence and exchange of views between the military and the human rights community, but it was largely discredited when much of the information that was gathered under its auspices about the locations of human remains proved to be inexact.

During this period a strange phenomenon occurred. Pinochet sought out Socialist politicians to talk with them about national security and various other matters. According to several sources, he seemed to hold an attitude of hate-admiration for Socialists. "The general would make a point of saying in public that he was reading Antonio Gramsci to understand the Socialists better, since Pinochet believed that all Socialists had shifted from 'Marxism' to 'Gramcianism,'" I was told by Socialist Senator Jaime Gazmuri, who, as a member of the Defense Committee of the Senate, had regular contact with the army chief.

On May 30, 1996, a group of top military officers, duly authorized by Pinochet and led by General Juan Emilio Cheyre, attended a seminar about "Armed Forces and Political Transitions," organized by the Ortega y Gasset Institute in El Escorial, Spain, whose main purpose was to establish a dialogue between the army and Socialist leaders such as Ricardo Lagos, Camilo Escalona, Jaime Gazmuri, and Enrique Correa. Back in Chile, the officers briefed Pinochet on the discussions of the seminar; Pinochet, "in a semi-ironic tone, commented about 'our Socialist friends,'" General Carlos Molina, who participated in the event, told me.

Pinochet yearned for legitimacy and he knew that he could get it only from his former enemies, not from rightists, who had always backed him, and not even from Christian Democrats. "Pinochet needed to close a circle of history: he had ordered the killing of Socialist leaders—some of whom had considered the general a friend—and now he coveted our respect," reflected Senator Gazmuri in a conversation we had. It was an unrealistic aspiration, given Pinochet's total lack of repentance about the human rights crimes committed under his watch.

Like President Aylwin before him, President Frei frequently would receive Pinochet at his residence to talk about delicate matters. President Frei told me, "Pinochet always carried a college notebook during those conversations. If he did not get what he wanted, he would cross out the issue in his notebook, saying, 'That was never on the agenda.'" Slowly and carefully, the Frei administration began to discuss with Pinochet the date of his retirement. An agreement was reached in principle; he would leave in December 1997, even though the constitution permitted him to remain as army commander until March 1998. Then he would become a senator for life. His successor as commander in chief of the army, Frei and Pinochet agreed, would be General Ricardo Izurieta, a highly competent officer from an army family with no human rights stains on his record. In addition, Pinochet had promised Frei to take along with him into retirement all the "questionable generals," from a human rights perspective.

But as the date of his retirement approached, members of Congress and human rights organizations bitterly criticized Pinochet's new status in Congress. The date of his retirement was pushed back to January 27; in the midst of the Chilean summer vacations, Pinochet's retirement and the assumption of his role as senator-for-life would have less impact, it was believed. But the attacks against him continued. The general responded in his own inimitable style, stating that he had intelligence concerning some of his critics that he could divulge. Pinochet's threat poured oil on the fire. A group of Christian Democratic congressmen filed a political impeachment against Pinochet for having failed to execute his duties as army commander from 1990 to 1998. The accusation did not mention a word about the dictatorship; it was eventually defeated in Congress. Furious, Pinochet announced that he would stay in his job until the very last day of his term, which he did. On March 10, 1998, Pinochet handed over the commander-in-chief post that he had occupied since Allende appointed him to it almost a quarter of a century before. General Izurieta received the command baton from President Frei, and from Pinochet, a replica of the sword of Bernardo O'Higgins. The old soldier's voice broke a couple of times as he turned a page of history and began a new stage of his life. Outside, street battles raged between anti-Pinochet protesters and some of the old general's loyalists. Even as he retired, Pinochet continued to divide Chile.

At his retirement, the eighty-two-year-old general was the oldest military man in the world on active duty, having served sixty-five years in the army. Pinochet was named army commander emeritus for life and was provided with a sizable contingent of military bodyguards, vehicles, and even an ambulance. The next day, Pinochet entered the Senate as a civilian, escorted by a kind of Praetorian Guard of right-wing parliamentarians who had served his regime in different roles. It was an embarrassing scene. Socialist, PPD, and Radical Party senators

placed photographs of Allende, Letelier, General Prats, and other victims of the dictatorship over their desks. Then, members of the
Lower House came in wearing black armbands and carrying pictures
of disappeared political prisoners. Soon total chaos reigned, as insults
were shouted back and forth across the aisles, with pushing and shoving, screams from the gallery, the bell of the president of the Senate
calling for order, and Pinochet quietly sitting in the last row of the
Senate seats, with a scornful smile. Outside the Congress, protesters
thronged the streets. The next day the world press published pictures
of Pinochet's tough reception.

The senator-for-life was interested in the legal immunity that
came along with his new position, not in being a legislator. He attended very few sessions, spending more of his time at the Augusto
Pinochet Foundation, a surprise gift to him from a group of businessmen and former aides, where he had a staff and an office that contained an exact duplicate of the presidential desk at La Moneda. But
Pinochet was deeply concerned about the respect he received from
his peers. He had established September 11 as a national holiday com-
memorating the coup, and it held great significance for him and his
supporters. But as September 11, 1998, approached, a debate took
place in Congress about the elimination of the national holiday. The
vote was still tied at the end of the day. Pinochet was worried because
one of the nonelected senators who supported retaining the holiday
had intimated that he might reverse his vote to break the deadlock the
next morning.

Pinochet went to talk to Senate President Andrés Zaldívar. "I
want to make a deal with you," Pinochet told him. "Why don't we,
within a couple of weeks, cosponsor a bill that eliminates 9/11 as a
holiday in exchange for a day of national unity?" Zaldívar refused to
delay two weeks, and they agreed to draft a bill to be adopted within
twenty-four hours.

When the session was about to start the next day, Pinochet did
not appear. Zaldívar opened the draft agreement for cosponsorship
signatures; meanwhile, a Senate page sent to look for Pinochet found
him at the congressional restaurant, eating a sandwich. He returned
to the Senate chamber at the last minute to make sure he would be
the last one to endorse the bill; he signed it with a smile, and then he
approached the presidential podium with the paper in hand. President
Zaldívar stood up and came forward to receive the document, but
Pinochet followed him back and, in an unexpected theatrical gesture,
took a seat at the head table as the process of the bill's formal adop-

tion began. The next day, newspaper photos showed Pinochet seated next to the Senate president, appearing as a statesman-politician who had enabled an important accord to eliminate a holiday that divided Chileans.

In September 1992 Pinochet had declared he would celebrate the 9/11 date "until the day I die." But in 1998 the situation was different. "I was going to lose anyhow," he admitted in an interview. "I had established the holiday and I wanted to be the one to annul it." Not long afterward, Pinochet decided to visit London. He loved to travel, and London was his favorite city in the world. That would soon change.

Eight

LOST IN
LONDON

I t was Pinochet's worst nightmare. On October 16, 1998, the
heavily sedated former dictator was sleeping soundly in suite 801
on the eighth floor of the London Clinic, recuperating from back
surgery. Suddenly he was awakened by a nurse as twelve policemen,
led by two detectives, Andrew Hewett and Sergeant David Jones,
from the extradition group in the Organized Crime Division of Scotland Yard, crowded into his room. Pinochet sat up in bed as Sergeant
Jones showed him his badge.

A police translator introduced the detectives. When she finished,
Sergeant Jones served Pinochet with a "priority red warrant." "You
are under arrest," he said. Then he read Pinochet his rights.

"I have come here on a secret mission!" Pinochet reacted, with all
the authority he could muster.

"What kind of mission is that?" inquired the detective.

"I have a diplomatic passport and immunity," Pinochet sputtered.
"You cannot arrest me! This is humiliating and unacceptable. It is
shameful that I could be subjected to this kind of treatment!"

Jones proceeded to read the arrest warrant, which mentioned the
murders perpetrated in Chile since September 11, 1973.

"This is absolutely illegal!" cried Pinochet. "I know who is behind
this: it is that bastard Communist Garcés!"

The policemen were fully in charge. Pinochet's security escort,
Captain Juan Gana, was instructed to wait outside the clinic.
Pinochet's phone was disconnected and his television was taken out
of his room.

242

Captain Gana called the head of Pinochet's security detail to communicate the bad news. He in turn notified the army attaché to the Chilean embassy in London, General Oscar Izurieta, who rushed to the clinic. Ambassador Mario Artaza, Chile's envoy to Great Britain, was watching television, ready to go to bed, when General Izurieta called him with the news. Artaza phoned Foreign Minister José Miguel Insulza in Santiago, who was about to appear on a television program. There was no tension in the conversation; it was "a matter-of-fact" dialogue, as the ambassador described it to me years later. Insulza instructed Artaza to learn what he could and to get in touch with Deputy Foreign Minister Mariano Fernández, who was accompanying President Eduardo Frei on a visit to Portugal. Artaza promised to call again as soon as he had more information.

After Artaza got off the phone, he put on his street clothes. He could hardly believe what was happening; at the same time, he realized that he had seen signs on the horizon concerning Pinochet for a while. A week earlier he'd received an urgent call from two Chilean ministers in Santiago who'd heard a rumor that Pinochet had died on the operating table. As he made his way across London, Artaza—a long time friend and close colleague of mine—reflected on the ironies of life. He was a member of the Socialist Party, had been kicked out of the Foreign Service shortly after the 1973 coup and had been reinstated seventeen years later, when democracy returned to Chile, and had close relatives who had been victims of Pinochet's rule of terror. And yet it was he who was riding to the dictator's rescue.

It was raining hard when he arrived at the clinic. Outside the entrance, protected from the rain by construction scaffolds that had been erected in front of the building, were General Izurieta, the Chilean navy attaché, and Pinochet's personal physician. The ambassador rang the bell and a Scotland Yard policeman opened the door. Artaza asked to see Pinochet and was refused, as the others had been before him. Through the duty officer at the Foreign Office, the ambassador got connected by phone with Henry Hogger, the director for Latin America, who in turn called the detective in charge at the clinic. Minutes later Artaza was walking down a dimly lit corridor, on his way to Pinochet's suite. Pinochet seemed to be sleeping when they entered the room. A nurse said, "Let him sleep."

"No, wait a minute. I have to talk to him," Artaza insisted.

Artaza touched Pinochet's shoulder and asked, "Senator, do you recognize me?" He had met Pinochet at the airport on his previous visits to London, and had invited him for tea at the Savoy just a few days earlier. "I am Ambassador Artaza."

"Yes, Ambassador," Pinochet replied.

"Do you understand what has happened to you?"

Pinochet remained silent.

"You are under arrest by order of a Spanish judge, who is asking for your extradition. Do you understand?"

Pinochet replied with his usual asperity. "Ambassador, I came to this country on a diplomatic passport, as I have many other times before. I have not entered here as if I were a bandit!"

Artaza left the suite and convinced the detective in charge to let Pinochet's personal doctor examine him. Then he briefed the attachés and returned to his residence to call Foreign Minister Insulza and Deputy Minister Fernández. Not long afterward, the Scotland Yard detectives left the clinic, leaving uniformed policemen in charge. Sergeant Jones wondered who Garcés was, whom Pinochet had blamed for his arrest.

Joan Garcés was the lawyer and political scientist who had been President Allende's closest adviser, and who had been with him at La Moneda on September 11, 1973. Born in Valencia, he had studied law in Spain and obtained a doctoral degree in political science at the Sorbonne in Paris during the 1960s. There he developed an academic interest in Chilean politics. After teaching in Colombia, Garcés moved to Chile (his brother Vicente would also do so). Allende read one of Garcés's essays on the electoral prospects of the left with great interest; when he became president in 1970, he invited Garcés to be his adviser.

The day of the coup Allende had charged Garcés to tell Chile's story to the world. Garcés escaped from the palace during the siege and eventually made contact with his brother. The Garcés brothers found refuge at the Spanish embassy and eventually made their way to Madrid.

Joan Garcés established the Salvador Allende Foundation in Madrid and in 1976 published a book about the Chilean road to socialism. A relatively short man with a white mustache, a full head of dark hair, and thick-rimmed glasses, from 1973 on his main objective in life was to denounce and punish Pinochet for his human rights crimes. According to one friend, "Garcés spiritually died at La Moneda, the day of the coup." In July 1996, Central Tribunal 6 of Spain admitted a suit against Pinochet for the crimes of genocide, terrorism, and torture. It was the long-sought outcome of collaboration between Garcés and the Progressive Union of Public Defenders. The Union, led by Carlos Castresana, had filed a suit on behalf of the victims of the Argentine dictatorship, mentioning thirty-five disappeared Spanish citizens. Garcés contacted Castresana and asked if the Argentine suit could be extended to include victims of the Pinochet regime. In March 1998 Garcés requested that Judge Castellón issue a provisional arrest warrant without bail and an international search order through Interpol against Pinochet and thirty-eight of his collaborators.

At first García-Castellón did not accept Garcés's request. In Spanish official circles there was great uneasiness about the course of events. The attorney general's office felt that trials against South American ex-dictators were a waste of time and money, not to mention that they raised the thorny legal issue of jurisdiction. But when García-Castellón asked a superior court to relieve him of the Pinochet matter, it ruled that he either had to declare himself incompetent to carry on with the case or continue to investigate it. On May 10, 1998, Joan Garcés filed a new suit against Pinochet, on behalf of the Chilean Group of Families of Disappeared Political Prisoners and the Communist Party of Chile, before Judge Baltasar Garzón's Central Tribunal 5. The new suit cited "Operation Condor," the conspiracy among South American dictatorships to eliminate dissidents worldwide. Garzón, who was already deeply involved in the Argentine investigations, felt that the international scope of the Condor operations played in favor of Spanish jurisdiction. Joan Garcés finally had a strong ally in the Spanish judiciary.

PINOCHET LOVED LONDON. In contrast to his experience in other cities, where protesters would organize to heckle him and disturb his sightseeing, he always felt safe and welcome there, he said. London had a special meaning for him, too. Chile's national independence hero, Bernardo O'Higgins, had lived in London in the 1790s. There, O'Higgins had regularly visited with Francisco de Miranda, the Venezuelan pioneer of the Latin American independence movement. Also in London, in Westminster Abbey, lay the remains of Admiral Thomas A. Cochrane, the Scottish sailor who was considered the founder of the Chilean Navy. And the great British Antarctic explorer Sir Ernest Shackleton and the crew of his ship, *Endurance,* had been rescued by the Chilean crew of the steamer *Yelcho* in 1916, adding to the almost mythical ties between Great Britain and Chile. A book published in London in 1899, entitled *Temperate Chile,* has a first chapter with the title "The Chilenos: The English of the Pacific." More important, Pinochet had friends in high places in Britain. One of them was former prime minister Margaret Thatcher, who had received him warmly every time he visited London.

His first visit to Great Britain had been in April 1991, when he was a guest of Royal Ordnance, which was partnering with FAMAE, the Chilean Army weapons manufacturer, to produce a multirocket launcher called Rayo. The rocket launcher proved a dud, but the deal cemented Pinochet's relations with the British firm. A first sign of trouble for the former dictator occurred when a Chilean human rights organization called a rally in front of British Aerospace headquarters in London. But Pinochet returned to Chile without any problems.

In February 1994 Pinochet traveled again to London, this time on vacation. A month after he returned to Chile, he attended a reception for Margaret Thatcher at the British embassy when her book tour—she had just published her memoirs—took her to Santiago. This is when the two of them first met. Later, she joined Pinochet and his former economic ministers for a private dinner.

In June 1994 Pinochet visited Royal Ordnance again to check on the Rayo rocket launcher project (which formally began the following year). On that occasion he received another negative signal when Amnesty International, through the human rights lawyer Geoffrey Bindman, asked the British attorney general to arrest Pinochet in accordance with the provisions of the UN Convention against Torture, signed and ratified by Great Britain in 1988. The British police began an investigation, but Pinochet returned to Chile before it could get anywhere. Pinochet traveled to the English capital again in 1997. Margaret Thatcher invited him to her Chester Square home in Belgravia for tea; he reciprocated her hospitality by sending her flowers and chocolates on her birthday.

When Pinochet made his next trip to London, the British political landscape had changed considerably. Conservative Prime Minister John Major was out of office. The Labor Party was in power and the new government, led by Prime Minister Tony Blair, belonged to a generation that had demonstrated on Trafalgar Square against the overthrow of Salvador Allende. Pinochet had also hoped to visit Napoleon's tomb in France on this trip, but the French government denied him a visa.

He arrived at London's Gatwick Airport on September 22, 1998, after a twenty-six-hour flight with a stopover in Frankfurt, and checked into the five-star InterContinental Hotel on Park Lane. During his stay he dined at a number of top restaurants, including White's, an exclusive club south of Piccadilly, at 37–38 St. James's Street, where he was the honored guest of Peter Schaad, a right-wing businessman and admirer. He did not return to the fashionable River Café, in Hammersmith—the last time he was there, Ruth Rogers, its owner, had donated his party's £500 ($800) bill to Amnesty International when she learned for whom she'd been cooking. Pinochet had come to London for a vacation, but also for medical reasons. His doctors in Chile had recommended that he undergo back surgery at the Military Hospital. Pinochet sought a second opinion from a renowned London specialist, Dr. Farhad Afshar, who agreed with the Chilean doctors' diagnosis. Against his family's and his aides' advice, Pinochet decided to extend his stay in London so that Dr. Afshar could do the surgery himself, on October 9. Pinochet also rejected the option that the London physician travel to Chile to perform the operation.

In the meantime, Pinochet went browsing for books, mainly biographies and encyclopedias. At a shop called Books etc, on Piccadilly, he bought a biography of Adolf Hitler. At Foyle's, on Charing Cross Road, he purchased a volume on Napoleon. While dining at the restaurant at Fortnum and Mason, Pinochet was recognized by one of the waiters, a son of former Chilean exiles, who notified Amnesty International that the ex-dictator was in London. The wheels of the human rights machinery began to turn. Amnesty International lawyers in London called their colleagues in Madrid, who notified Joan Garcés.

Oblivious of these developments, Pinochet visited Madame Tussaud's wax museum and the British National Army Museum; just like a normal tourist, he went shopping at Burberry's. He completed an interview with the journalist Jon Lee Anderson for *The New Yorker* that he had begun in Chile, part of a public relations effort that his daughter Lucía had launched to transform his image into that of an elder statesman. Pinochet told Anderson that he had only been "an aspiring dictator"; then he added with an ironic smile, "History teaches you that dictators never end up well." Later Pinochet's entourage accused Anderson of being a part of the alleged international conspiracy against Pinochet, since the interview, published while he was in London, confirmed to the world his whereabouts.

Baroness Thatcher invited Pinochet for tea on Monday, October 5. They had a pleasant conversation about the current Chilean situation, especially the approaching presidential elections in 1999. Referring to Ricardo Lagos, Pinochet told Thatcher that opinion polls indicated that Chile could have "its first Socialist president since 1973."

"What a disaster," the Iron Lady observed.

Storm clouds were gathering on the horizon. On October 6 the British press reported that Pinochet had been denied a visa to enter France. On October 8, Pinochet was hospitalized in preparation for his surgery the following day. The surgery went well, but the next day, on October 10, *The Guardian,* under the headline "Former Chilean

Dictator Operated On," reported that the Foreign Office had confirmed Pinochet's presence in London.

Judge Garzón decided to interrogate Pinochet. He had intended
to send the former dictator merely a written questionnaire; he hadn't
planned to have him arrested. But first the British police and then Interpol told him that as preparations were under way for Pinochet's
swift return to Chile, they couldn't guarantee that he would remain in
London unless he was in custody. The Spanish magistrate had a key
ally in the British embassy in Madrid: Chargé d'affaires John Drew.
The two had become friends after Garzón complained about England's failure to cooperate during an investigation into drug trafficking and money laundering in Gibraltar. Drew had apologized and
offered his good services for future situations. Judge Garzón had
called the British diplomat on the morning of Thursday, October 15,
and cashed in his chips.

"I have been informed that Pinochet may leave England as soon
as this weekend," he said. "The British police are asking me if I intend
to issue an arrest warrant. I have not made up my mind. Before I decide what to do, I need to know if I can count on the cooperation of
the Home Office."

Drew was not surprised to hear from Garzón, as he had been
reading press reports about Pinochet's presence in London. He promised to do what he could. That same afternoon, he sent a message to
the Foreign Office, informing them that Judge Garzón needed to execute his request to interrogate Pinochet immediately.

On Thursday, October 15, the journalist Hugh O'Shaughnessy
published an opinion piece in *The Guardian* entitled "A Murderer
Among Us," in which he asserted that Pinochet was "hiding some-
where in London," supposedly at the London Clinic, and he called on
British authorities to arrest him for the torture and murder of Chilean
and British nationals. Meanwhile, Jeremy Corbyn, a Labour MP, addressed a letter to Prime Minister Blair demanding that Spanish judicial authorities be permitted to interrogate Pinochet with a view to
extradition, and lamenting that the former dictator had been allowed
"free and secret entry into the country."

Garzón still doubted whether he had enough substance to obtain
an arrest warrant. On the morning of Friday, October 16, Joan Garcés,
accompanied by another lawyer, Enrique de Santiago, came to see
Garzón to solicit the urgent questioning of Pinochet; they expanded
the charges against him to include crimes against humanity, genocide,
terrorism, and torture. In their new suit they named two specific dis-

appeared Chileans who had been arrested in the context of Operation Condor.

At last Garzón resolved to issue an order for the "international search and capture with the purpose of extradition" of the former Chilean dictator. Interpol had already told Garzón what was needed for the warrant: Pinochet's personal data, a description of the crimes he was wanted for, the victims' data, and the articles of the Spanish penal code that Pinochet's actions had violated. Garzón did the best he could with what he had on hand. But there was a problem. It was Friday afternoon and Garzón's tribunal was deserted; practically all of its personnel had already gone home for the weekend. Garzón intercepted a clerk on his way out the door and told him that he had an emergency resolution for him to prepare. The clerk turned pale when he realized the contents of the resolution. A few moments later they faxed the document to London. The judged issued a second arrest warrant against Pinochet on Sunday, October 18, 1998, expanding on the original one. Garzón telephoned the Interpol office in Madrid and told them to warn their London colleagues that the order was on its way. Garzón went to pick up his wife, Rosario, to drive to Jaen, in southern Spain.

The judge and his wife were on their way to Jaen to see Garzón's favorite bullfighter, Curro Romero, in one of his last appearances before he retired, when the British chargé d'affaires rang his cell phone. John Drew told the judge that the Home Office would cooperate if he sent an arrest order. Garzón replied that he already had, and asked to be kept posted.

In London, things were moving quickly. The Foreign Office had already given its opinion in a memo. Pinochet was not protected by diplomatic immunity because he was not on a "special mission." London Interpol sent Inspector Hewett of Scotland Yard copies of the arrest warrant in English and Spanish. Now all he needed was a court order from a magistrate from the Bow Street Penal Tribunal in charge of extraditions. It was 5 P.M. London time. Detective Hewett and Sergeant David Jones tried to contact the magistrate on call, Nicholas Evans, but he had gone home. The detectives, along with a Bow Street official, drove to the Evans residence, north of London. With the help of the Bow Street official, the magistrate transferred the arrest order to a form for signatories of the European Extradition Treaty and the British Law on Extradition. At 9 P.M. Hewett reported to his chief that he had the order and both the Foreign Office and the Home Office were duly informed.

Not long after Garzón and his wife returned to their hotel from the bullfight, his cell phone rang again. "The arrest warrant is ready," John Drew told him.

Garzón was confused. "Yes, as I told you, I signed the order and sent it over to London."

"No," Drew interrupted. "I mean the British magistrate has signed Pinochet's arrest order. He will be detained any minute now at the clinic where he is staying."

"Well, let me know," the Spanish judge said. "No matter how late it may be, let me know."

Garzón told his wife what was going on while he waited to receive confirmation of the arrest. "And now what are we going to do?" he wondered. He hadn't realized until that moment that he was making history.

IN SANTIAGO, I had become foreign policy adviser in my friend Ricardo Lagos's presidential campaign, after having resigned from my post as ambassador of Chile to Brazil. On that climactic Friday evening, I was in Buenos Aires with Yoko Ono.

Lagos described himself as the candidate with the greatest commitment to the arts and culture, and he had dispatched me to the Argentine capital to convince Yoko to visit Santiago. That Friday evening she agreed to come to Chile, a trip she had contemplated merely as a hypothesis until then. Saturday morning we were flying to Santiago. On the plane I briefed her about Chile's recent political history and about Ricardo Lagos's role in the restoration of democracy. She was talkative and interested; she told me that John Lennon and she had deeply lamented Allende's overthrow and the bloodshed that followed the military coup in September 1973. We talked about art, our respective families, and the snow capped Andes beneath us.

When we landed I was surprised to see Lagos's chief of staff, "Cacho" Rubio, waiting for us on the tarmac, with a VIP van. I had anticipated we would go through international police and customs as normal passengers. But when we descended, Rubio pulled me aside and told me, "Look, major crap has hit the fan. Last night they arrested Pinochet in London. The big story today is not Yoko but Pinochet. We have to take her through the VIP so that journalists don't ask her about Pinochet's arrest. Otherwise, her whole visit will become 'Pinochetized.'"

The presidential suite had been reserved for her at the Hotel Carrera. I left her there so she could get some rest and have a light lunch and went to see Lagos. "This is unbelievable," he said. "Pinochet never goes away. I'd been looking forward to programmatic debates about Chile's future; now the presidential campaign will become polarized around Pinochet. And what are we to do about my press conference with Yoko Ono this afternoon?"

I suggested that all the journalists at the press conference should be from the arts and culture sections of their papers. No political journalist should be allowed in. "Yoko will not appreciate having to answer any questions about Pinochet," I said. Lagos agreed.

I went ahead to inform Yoko about Pinochet's arrest in London and she became nervous and uneasy about the press conference. But when Lagos arrived she calmed down noticeably; they got along well together and she was pleased with the arrangements he'd made for the rest of her visit.

The questions at the press conference dealt with Yoko's influence on John Lennon's music, the release of a new compilation of Lennon's work, Yoko's vanguard work in the Fluxus movement, etc. Not a word was said about Pinochet. Lagos described what Yoko would be doing in Chile, the artists she would meet, the museums she would visit, the importance of her visit for Chilean culture. The whole thing took about half an hour.

After the photo-ops, Yoko went upstairs to her room and Ricardo Lagos faced the dozens of TV, radio, and newspaper reporters who were now clamoring for his reaction to Pinochet's arrest. Lagos was concise and cautious: "General Pinochet's detention is a consequence of the indignation aroused in Chile and throughout the world by his regime's violations of human rights. His arrest is a strictly judicial matter; the Chilean nation should not be dragged in—there is no reason why we should shoulder the consequences of actions and facts that are the exclusive responsibility of Mr. Pinochet."

The government of President Eduardo Frei Ruiz-Tagle also reacted that day. Unlike Lagos, they viewed the arrest as a threat to Chile's sovereign rights, declaring that, regardless of the ex-dictator's past actions, his detention violated the principle of diplomatic immunity that he enjoyed as a senator-for-life and the principle of territorial jurisdiction, whereby it is the exclusive right of a state to adjudicate crimes committed in its own national territory. For all that, the protest that Foreign Minister José Miguel Insulza presented to the British government was mildly worded.

The Chilean Foreign Ministry argued that Pinochet's diplomatic passport stated that he had gone on a "special mission" to Britain, though the nature of the mission had not been communicated to the British embassy in Santiago. The British replied that they could not have formally authorized the mission if they didn't know what it was. Later, the Chilean government stated that Pinochet's special mission was to pay a visit to Royal Ordnance, the arms company. But the greatest damage to Pinochet's immunity claim had in fact been done the year before, in October 1997, by General Fernando Torres Silva, auditor general of the Chilean Army. He had secretly traveled to Madrid, supposedly on vacation, to meet with the Spanish judicial authorities, hoping to forestall his boss's prosecution.

The general had not just spoken to the Spanish officials; he had provided them with supposedly exculpatory documents. By doing so he had implicitly recognized the competence of a foreign judge to evaluate documents in Pinochet's defense. Belatedly realizing the error, the Chilean Army stated that General Torres's mission to Spain had been undertaken as a "personal initiative." But Joan Garcés declared that, from then on, "neither General Fernando Torres nor Pinochet can claim absence of defense in the development of the penal process"

The news of Pinochet's arrest fell like a cluster bomb of hate and polarization in Chile; it became the hardest test yet for the country's already complex transition to democracy. Within hours, some two thousand people poured into the streets of downtown Santiago, dancing and chanting, "It's a carnival, the dictator's in jail." Right-wing politicians denounced the arrest and militants of the Unión Demócrata Independiente (UDI) and Renovación Nacional (RN) parties blocked traffic in the streets of the affluent Santiago borough of Las Condes. A delegation of UDI and RN congressmen rushed to London to lend their personal support to the ex-dictator.

As days went by and it became clear that Pinochet would not be released quickly, the polarization within Chile intensified. Violent protests erupted in front of the Spanish and British embassies in Santiago and demonstrators pelted the residences of both ambassadors with rocks and eggs. "English pirates, return our granddad!" they yelled. The daily newspaper *La Tercera* reported that "astonishingly, this time the protesters throwing rocks were not students or militants of some leftist party, but ladies with high heels and handbags" who had come to express their support for the general. As the level of violence escalated, the police used water cannons and made some arrests. Observers noted that the police exercised much more restraint with the pro-Pinochet demonstrators than they did with their opposites.

Chile's main business association announced that it had initiated contacts with English and Spanish business partners to garner support for a quick solution to Pinochet's problems. Congresswoman Pía Guzmán called for a boycott of the 83 percent English-owned Chilean Tobacco Co."and, obviously," she said, "of whisky." There were calls to cancel a major purchase of military equipment from a Spanish-French consortium, a proposal that the government rejected. The right-wing parties demanded that Chile break off diplomatic relations with Great Britain and Spain, without even reflecting on the impact that such a measure would have on official bilateral efforts to seek a solution to the impasse.

Cristián Labbé, a former army colonel who had been in charge of Pinochet's security and who was now the mayor of Providencia borough, an affluent sector of Santiago, declared a "municipal war" against the Spanish embassy, which was located in the borough: its reserved parking spaces were taken away and its trash collection services were canceled. Labbé also closed the offices of the British Cultural Council and fined CTC, a Spanish telecommunications company, both also located in his borough.

When garbage began piling up in front of the Spanish mission, Cristina Girardi, the leftist mayor of Cerro Navia, a working-class borough in western Santiago, sent a truck across town to collect the garbage. The truck carried a huge banner that read, "We pick up your garbage because you are already picking up ours." Another left-wing mayor, the Socialist Johnny Carrasco of Pudahuel borough, offered the Spanish and the British the use of all of his municipality's facilities. It was as if a civil war had broken out.

From London, where he had traveled with other conservative leaders to offer the dictator his assistance, Pablo Longueira, president of the far-right UDI, opined that the general's arrest had been part of a "conspiracy organized by international Chilean, Spanish, and English Socialists." His UDI colleague Senator Andrés Chadwick agreed: "The Spanish judge is Socialist, the English government is Socialist, and the main people in Chile who have applauded the arrest are Socialists, headed by Ricardo Lagos." Tony Blair's spokesman responded with typical English dry humor: "I'd like to hear what José María Aznar [the conservative president of the Spanish government] says when he is accused of being part of an international Socialist conspiracy."

The Economist editorialized in favor of Pinochet's extradition to Spain, arguing that "former dictators are not immune." The conservative Spanish newspaper *ABC* also supported Pinochet's extradition, asserting that such a petition did not reflect "a non-existent neo-colonial inclination," but only the desire "to inquire about 3,196 lives."

The fallout from the arrest was worldwide. UN Secretary-General Kofi Annan applauded the detention, stressing that international humanitarian law was gaining momentum, and that there were increasingly few places in the world where alleged violators of human rights could hide. Lionel Jospin, the prime minister of France, fully supported the arrest, whereas Fidel Castro's posture was more nuanced: Pinochet's arrest, he said, was "morally just, juridically dubious, and politically complicated for Chile." Argentine president Carlos Menem backed his Chilean colleague, Eduardo Frei. At a Latin American summit in Brasilia on October 26 he suggested that a letter be sent to Tony Blair condemning Pinochet's arrest and underlining the principle of nonintervention in domestic affairs—an idea that was vehemently opposed by the immense majority of the Latin American leaders present at the meeting. Felipe González, a former president of Spain, warned that judging Pinochet in Spain "could give us great satisfaction now and lead to repenting later."

Bill Clinton's administration walked a fine line on the Pinochet drama. Secretary of State Madeleine Albright declared that, although the United States supported bringing criminals to justice, Chile as a democratic state was "wrestling with a very difficult problem of how to balance the needs of justice with the requirements of reconciliation." She asked for respect for Chile's position, without actually supporting it. In December 1998, a State Department spokesperson, James Rubin, responding to a question about the issue, asserted that the administration was "not yet prepared to give an opinion about the legal value" of the Pinochet extradition case.

Clearly there was a debate within the Clinton administration regarding Pinochet. After Pinochet's arrest, Joan Garcés had traveled to Washington to seek advice from the legal team that had acted in the prosecution of the Letelier case, and to pressure the United States to cooperate, including releasing classified documents relevant to Pinochet's extradition to Spain (the White House complied, declassifying thousands of documents). A Justice Department spokesperson, John Russell, told reporters in early November 1998 that the possibility was being considered at high levels of the administration of asking for Pinochet's extradition to the United States for the murder of Orlando Letelier, if he were to get immunity in Britain. The State Department and the White House objected to Russell's comments and the Justice Department issued a retraction. But a few months later, in January 1999, Attorney General Janet Reno confirmed that her department was reviewing whether Pinochet could be tried in the United States for the Letelier-Moffit murders. At about the same time, the British Foreign Office denied a press report that Secretary Albright had urged London to return Pinochet to Chile.

Former president George H. W. Bush called the charges against Pinochet "a travesty of justice" and urged the British government to send Pinochet back to Chile "as soon as possible." The question of what to do with Pinochet was debated in all corners of the United States. Editorials supporting Pinochet's arrest were published in the *Dallas Morning News*, the *San Francisco Chronicle*, the *Denver Post*, the *Philadelphia Inquirer*, the *Los Angeles Times*, the *Washington Post*, the *Chicago Tribune*, and the *New York Times*. On the opposite side, the *Washington Times* editorialized that the arrest would "go down as a classic example of fool-hardy intervention" and that Pinochet, despite having been a dictator, had "prevented a Communist revolution . . . and [had] correctly [seen] in free markets the best hope for Chilean progress." Similarly, the *Wall Street Journal* wondered why, if Britain could arrest General Pinochet at Spain's request, Spain did not arrest Fidel Castro when he visited, adding that Castro's human rights violations dwarfed "the most exaggerated accusations against General Pinochet."

The right in the United States misinterpreted the Chilean government's position regarding Pinochet's detention. At the time, John Bolton, a neoconservative advocate whom I would get to know superficially at the UN when he and I were ambassadors for our respective countries, contacted the Chilean envoy to Washington, Ambassador Genaro Arriagada, to let him know that as far as defending Pinochet was concerned, he and the Chilean diplomat were "partners."

"I don't think you understand the issue," Arriagada told Bolton. "The Chilean government is not defending Pinochet. It is upholding international law and, specifically, the territoriality of jurisdiction. Pinochet is not above the law."

As the months went by, Pinochet's legal proceedings took unexpected twists and turns. Immediately after Pinochet was arrested, Eduardo Fungairiño, Spain's chief prosecutor, challenged Judge Garzón's case, arguing that Spain could not try crimes that were not committed on or by its own citizens; he added that the crimes enumerated in the Pinochet warrant fit neither the United Nations' nor Spain's definitions of genocide, and that the charge of terrorism was inapplicable. Moreover, Fungairiño argued, the offenses attributed to

Pinochet were subject to an amnesty; technically, they had already been dealt with by the Chilean courts. But on November 5, 1998, the eleven members of the Penal Chamber of the Audiencia Nacional, the National Court of Spain, confirmed unanimously that Spain was entitled to investigate crimes of genocide, terrorism, and torture committed by the military governments of Chile and Argentina against their own people. The ruling was celebrated worldwide by human rights defenders.

Four days after Pinochet's detention, Judge Manuel García-Castellón turned over his case files to Judge Garzón to consolidate and simplify the legal and diplomatic actions necessary for Pinochet's extradition. On December 10, 1998, Judge Garzón combined the findings of the Chilean and Argentine investigations and indicted Pinochet for genocide, terrorism, and torture. The new charges added the names of more than 120 Chileans killed or disappeared after the coup.

There was no longer any way to avoid the judicial hearings in London; they would proceed as planned. Pinochet's defense was conducted by the prestigious and expensive firm of Kingsley & Napley. The original arrest warrant issued by the London magistrate under the UK Extradition Act on October 16 was followed by another provisional warrant on October 22, based on five new charges tailored to British laws. Most of the alleged offenses, from torture to hostage taking and conspiracy to commit murder, had been perpetrated in Chile.

On October 28, the High Court, with Lord Chief Justice Thomas Bringham presiding, heard the charges and the evidence from the Crown Prosecution Service, acting on behalf of the government of Spain. The court overturned the first warrant on the grounds that murders of nationals in other nations were not extraditable crimes under British law. As regards the second warrant, Lord Bringham ruled that Pinochet had "sovereign immunity" as a former head of state for acts carried out as part of his official duties. It wasn't "diplomatic" immunity, but a modern formulation of the ancient concept of the "divine right of kings."

Pinochet supporters celebrated in the streets of Santiago. A Gulfstream III air force jet, sent four days earlier to London in anticipation of a favorable ruling, hastened preparations to fly Pinochet home. But the High Court allowed the Crown Prosecution Service to appeal the decision before Britain's supreme tribunal, the judicial committee of the House of Lords.

Pinochet was moved from the London Clinic, in the exclusive Harley Street neighborhood, to the Grovelands Priory Hospital, a private psychiatric rehabilitation center in Southgate, North London. Pinochet supporters felt optimistic. Two days before the High Court pronouncement, Pinochet had released a message to the public: "Tell my friends to get me out of here!" After the October 28 ruling Pinochet declared, "The [court's decision] caused me happiness, gave me strength and faith in justice."

Meanwhile, Spain submitted its formal request for extradition, greatly expanding on the list of offenses. The Swiss and French governments also submitted formal extradition requests on November 11 and 13, respectively.

The hearings of the House of Lords, which ran from November 4 to 13, were broadcast live on Chilean TV; extracts were shown on CNN, the BBC, and other worldwide networks. Outside the Gothic Houses of Parliament hundreds of journalists, Pinochet supporters who had flown in from Chile, Chilean former exiles, and human rights activists from all over the world stood vigil.

The day before the High Court ruling, the English government recommended that its citizens not travel to Chile except for "essential reasons." Two days earlier, a Santiago-bound British Airways plane had been delayed for several hours because of a false bomb threat.

On November 25 the judicial committee of the House of Lords announced that they were ready to render their decision as to whether Pinochet should enjoy immunity in Britain for actions committed when he was head of state. CNN, the BBC, Fox, and other networks covered the proceedings live. All of the major Chilean TV networks transmitted direct via satellite with their own correspondents; Chileans rushed to their televisions, as if the national team were competing in a World Cup tournament. Each of the five judges voted, one by one. At one point the result was a tie: two for immunity, two against. When the last Lord voted, against, there were a few boos but mostly loud cheers across Chile. Outside Parliament the anti-Pinochet crowd burst into applause; the families of victims began to read their names aloud. The right was astounded. Pinochet's friend Peter Schaad recounted that the general's entourage was so confident about a positive outcome that all his bags were packed and ready for the trip back to Chile. To make things worse, the adverse ruling came on Pinochet's birthday. The Lords had rejected the notion that kidnapping, torture, and murder could be considered official functions of a head of state and thus merit immunity.

Pinochet moved from the Grovelands Priory Hospital to a private residence next to a golf course in Virginia Water, Surrey, whose rent was ten thousand pounds a month. The house was guarded by a team of fifteen Scotland Yard agents, and its rooms were filled with state-of-the-art security cameras and microphones. Pinochet's daily routine included morning exercises, lunch with family members, afternoon screenings of movies brought from Spain, tea time, and then meetings with visitors. Accompanied by his family and guards, Pinochet used to sing a Carlos Gardel tango, "El Ladrillo" (The Brick), about the troubles of a man in jail.

General Juan Emilio Cheyre, who visited Pinochet in London, told me in an interview that the old man "felt vulnerable, though not scared." His "entourage made up of family, political aides, and doctors made it very difficult for the army to influence him on key decisions." Pinochet "seemed lost and confused by the tales and recommendations that various actors brought to him."

Pinochet was taken before a British judge on the afternoon of December 11, amid tight security. Because of the pro- and anti-Pinochet demonstrations that were raging, Magistrate Graham Parkinson decided that he should appear at Belmarsh Magistrates' Court, in Woolwich, southeast London, instead of Bow Street Court, in central London. Pinochet's lawyer, Fernando Barros, urged him to enter the courtroom in a wheelchair. "It is important to convey an image that will generate compassion," he said.

"Well, I don't like the idea of compassion. I should stand like a soldier," Pinochet countered. He was determined to make his entrance on his own two feet. Finally, the lawyers and his family got through to him, when they explained that a wheelchair would not fit into the cubicle where the accused were supposed to sit. Instead, in a wheelchair he would be seated next to his defense team.

Pinochet's caravan of vehicles entered the court building through the garage to avoid photographers. He was pushed into the courtroom in the wheelchair by his son Marco Antonio and was positioned next to the defense lawyers, as planned.

The court secretary asked the defendant to identify himself.

"I am Augusto Pinochet Ugarte," said the general. "I am the commander in chief of the Chilean Army." He corrected himself. "I *was* the commander in chief, president of Chile, captain general of Chile, and I am senator of the Republic," he concluded, speaking slowly and distinctly for the sake of the translator.

"Thanks," said Judge Parkinson, and he proceeded to read the legal details of the extradition case. James Lewis, representing the Crown, and Clive Nicholls, for the defense, discussed possible dates for the formal hearings on the extradition.

Nicholls took advantage of the opportunity to ask the court whether the general could be allowed to go outside the house to exercise in the garden. Lewis had no objection and Judge Parkinson concurred that it would be "inhumane" to impede Pinochet to walk in the garden of his Virginia Water residence. Then, the date for the hearing was fixed for January 18. The proceeding was over, but Nicholls asked the magistrate if the general could make a statement. It was highly unusual, but the magistrate allowed it.

"With all due respect, I do not recognize jurisdiction of any court other than one from my own country to judge me for the lies posed by the gentlemen [señores] from Spain." Pinochet had been reading from a prepared text, but he improvised the attack on the Spanish magistrates. His voice was dripping with scorn when he pronounced the word "señores," which he used sarcastically when referring to politicians, leftists, Russians, or any other category of beings he despised.

"Is that all?" asked the judge.

Nicholls stood up and, very nervously, intervened to clarify that Pinochet had meant no disrespect.

"I don't interpret it that way," said the judge.

"The senator recognizes the jurisdiction of this court," added the defense lawyer.

"I heard what he said," Parkinson answered sternly. "My duty is to carry on these proceedings according to the Extradition Law in force in England, and I will do so."

The court procedure was over. But a few days later, the rollercoaster case took another turn. Pinochet's defense lodged a petition to the Law Lords to overturn their decision on the grounds that one of the judges who had voted against Pinochet, Lord Hoffman, had undisclosed connections to Amnesty International, a participant in the case, along with other human rights organizations. On December 17, in a ruling that was unprecedented in British legal history, a panel presided over by Lord Nicholas Browne-Wilkinson ruled unanimously that it "reluctantly felt bound to set aside" the previous ruling and called for a new hearing before a different panel of judges. This time, it was the Pinochet group's turn to celebrate. It was like a tie game going into half time.

The appeal would be heard all over again, this time before a set of seven magistrates. The same interveners were allowed to participate, but this time the government of Chile joined the defense, arguing that state immunity should be upheld. The Frei government was in a difficult position. It wanted justice for the disappeared prisoners and other human rights crimes committed under Pinochet's rule, but it felt it had to defend Chile's sovereign rights, too. "I defend principles, not concrete individuals," said President Frei. Foreign Minister Insulza suggested that there might be "humanitarian motives" to release Pinochet.

David Aaronovitch, a columnist for *The Independent,* responded to the "humanitarian" appeal: "Your beloved general is safe with us. He will not be tortured, stabbed or shot, or have electrodes attached to his genitals. We will not drop him from a helicopter into the sea, kidnap his grandchildren, break his hands or gouge his eyes." British Home Secretary Jack Straw said that if his office had a final ruling on Pinochet, he might consider releasing him on "compassionate grounds."

The hearings by the new Law Lords panel began on January 18, 1999, and lasted two weeks. Again, world public opinion followed the case. Judgment was rendered on March 24, 1999. This time the seven-magistrate panel agreed six to one that Pinochet was not entitled to state immunity. Now the pro-extradition forces rejoiced.

But the Law Lords limited the number of charges on which the ex-dictator could be extradited, centering the case on the crime of torture and the extraterritoriality provisions of the UN Convention against Torture. Those torture crimes had to be recognized as crimes in the UK at the time they were committed; that is, British courts could exert jurisdiction only for crimes committed after September 29, 1988, when the UK enacted legislation making torture an extraterritorial offense. Consequently, Judge Garzón attached fifty-three new torture cases to the extradition request, all dating from between October 1988 and March 1990, when democracy returned to Chile. It was a mixed ruling, but it allowed for the extradition process to proceed. On April 14, 1999, Home Secretary Straw issued his second "authority to proceed" in a document addressed to the Chief Metropolitan Stipendiary Magistrate at Bow Street Court.

A Chilean Air Force Boeing 707 had been waiting at Brize North base in Oxfordshire to transport Pinochet to Chile in case of a favorable outcome. It flew back across the Atlantic without its passenger. Straw's decision was applauded by Labour backbenchers and the human rights community, but it provoked new right-wing protests in Santiago and indignation among some powerful international figures close to the old general.

Baroness Margaret Thatcher led the pro-Pinochet offensive, describing Straw's decision to proceed with the extradition process as "a grave mistake." This was not the first time Thatcher had defended

Pinochet. On October 21, 1998, less than a week after his arrest, *The Times* published a letter in which she credited Pinochet for saving "many British lives" during the Malvinas (Falklands) War. Taking up Pinochet's view of his dictatorship as an ongoing struggle against a violent insurgency, she conceded that "there were indeed abuses of human rights in Chile," but insisted that the violence had been "on both sides of the political divide." She called upon the United Kingdom to respect "the delicate balances" of the Chilean transition to democracy, "with which we interfere at our peril." Thatcher concluded by asserting that "General Pinochet must be allowed to return to his country forthwith."

Because of the Pinochet affair, Thatcher distanced herself from Tony Blair, whom she had often praised before the general's arrest. The day after her letter was published in *The Times*, Prime Minister Blair called a cabinet meeting. It was decided that Home Secretary Jack Straw would assume a quasi-judicial role in the case, and that the Pinochet situation would not be debated by cabinet members. Blair would counter Baroness Thatcher's political approach with a strictly juridical stand.

But Thatcher's campaign only intensified. On a sunny day on March 29, 1999, she visited Pinochet's residence in Surrey, taking along a television crew. Pinochet, with his wife, Lucía, at his side, played the gracious host, smiling as he invited the Iron Lady into his "simple and small house."

Referring to the Malvinas (Falklands) War, she thanked Pinochet "for the information you gave us, and also the refuge you gave to any of our armed forces who were able, if they were shipwrecked, to make their way to Chile.

"I am also very much aware that it is you who brought democracy to Chile," Thatcher effused. "You set up a constitution suitable for democracy, you put it into effect, elections were held and then, in accordance with the result, you stepped down," she added.

Clutching his cane and smiling, Pinochet thanked Thatcher for all her "kindness."

Thatcher's first speech in three years in the House of Lords, in July 1999, was in defense of the ex-dictator. In a grave voice, she described the circumstances of Pinochet's detention, attributing it to "the organized international left," which, she said, was bent on revenge because Pinochet "had saved Chile when Communism was advancing throughout the Hemisphere." She praised free enterprise in Chile, which, she suggested, was imperiled by Pinochet's detention, and ominously warned that "a Pandora's box" had been opened, and "unless Senator Pinochet returns to Chile without delay, there will be no hope of closing it." The baroness had been given four minutes to speak, but she exceeded her allotted time. "Very seldom do I exhaust my time," she protested when she was interrupted. Raising her voice, she continued her speech.

The indirect ties between Thatcher and Pinochet dated back to the late 1970s. Thatcher's economic adviser, Sir Alan Walters, had traveled to Chile and returned with good things to say about Pinochet's economic policies, especially the privatization process and pension reform. Repression under Pinochet was ignored by Thatcher's advisers. The British Conservative author and journalist Robin Harris—of whom Baroness Thatcher had said he was her "indispensable sherpa in the enterprise of writing" her book *The Downing Street Years*— wrote that Allende "must not be allowed this posthumous revenge against the man who stopped Chile from becoming another Cuba and who then turned Chile into Latin America's most successful capitalist economy."

When Thatcher became prime minister in 1979, her first official act regarding Chile was to reestablish diplomatic relations at the ambassadorial level, downgraded since 1976 after Dr. Sheila Cassidy, a British physician, was jailed and tortured for having treated a wounded fugitive leader of the MIR. In late 1979 and early 1980 several loans guaranteed by the British were made to Chilean banks. Official high-level visits to Chile by Thatcher officials became common. More important, in July 1980 Thatcher decided to lift the arms embargo imposed by the Labor government of Prime Minister Harold Wilson. This decision motivated strong criticisms and the Conservative government was forced to clarify its policy. Even though Chile would no longer be subject to "a special limitation," London would discourage the sale to Chile of "light weapons which could be used for repressive actions." Soon after, the Chilean Navy bought several warships from English companies. Great Britain also led a group of countries that sought to put an end to the UN mandate for a special rapporteur to investigate the human rights situation in Chile.

It did not come as a surprise, then, that Margaret Thatcher would lead a full-bore lobbying campaign on Pinochet's behalf. The executive role in this effort was played by Lord Norman Lamont, former conservative chancellor of the exchequer (whose claim to fame was the withdrawal under his watch of the pound from the European Exchange Rate Mechanism, and the accusation that he had used taxpayers' money to evict a "sex therapist" known as Miss Whiplash from a flat he owned). Lamont visited Pinochet on several occasions, appeared on TV programs and in press interviews to defend him, and traveled to Chile to coordinate his efforts with those of the Pinochet Foundation. His efforts on Pinochet's behalf were so tireless and unstinting that the Pinochet Foundation decorated him with the Star for Merit medal, in a ceremony in Santiago in December 2000.

THE DEBATE ABOUT the juridical ramifications of Pinochet's arrest intensified worldwide. But the polemic over the Pinochet case was far from strictly juridical. Pinochet was a political hot potato. For the Blair government there was always the risk that Pinochet could die in captivity and that the damage to its relations with Chile, a traditional ally, could open a flank for Conservative criticism. President Frei told me that at the time it was very difficult for him to get through to Blair. "But after Pinochet suffered a minor stroke, it was Blair who phoned me," said Frei. "If Pinochet dies in England it will be your problem; if he dies in Chile it will not be," Frei remarked to the British prime minister. On the other hand, the Blair administration could not simply let Pinochet go when Labor had for years criticized its Conservative predecessors for allowing Pinochet to travel freely in Great Britain.

For the rightist Spanish government, Pinochet's detention not only caused a strain in its relations with Chile but brought unwelcome attention to its own domestic contradiction, since none of the members of the Franco dictatorship had even been taken to court on human rights charges.

And of course the situation created a tangle of problems for Chile's political players. The Chilean right could not abandon its "godfather," but it knew that its presidential candidate, Joaquin Lavín, of the right-wing UDI, who for some time had sought to position himself in the center of the political spectrum, would lose points if he and his comrades appeared to be too close to Pinochet. As for the Lagos campaign, Pinochet's arrest had distracted attention from our proposals to encourage economic growth while ensuring equal access to the opportunities of progress. Our program for the future was being overwhelmed by arguments about the past. Lagos's strictly judicial response to Pinochet's case was fine, but insufficient. Moreover, some on the left—a minority, but vocal—were willing to pay the price that a trial of Pinochet in Spain could exact on Lagos's presidential bid. The positive aspect of the Pinochet detention was that it had once again placed on the national agenda the issue of human rights justice, which some preferred to leave in the painful past.

In late January 1999 I accompanied Lagos to Stockholm and then to the World Economic Forum in Davos, Switzerland. By then we had accepted an invitation from Moisés Naim, the editor of *Foreign Policy*, to write a joint essay on the Pinochet case for the journal. During the trip from Stockholm to Davos we talked about what we would write. I reminded Lagos of a wonderful exchange between Sir Thomas More and his interlocutor, William Roper, in Robert Bolt's play *A Man for All Seasons*, where More tells Roper that he knows only "the law . . . what's legal, not what's right." Roper disagrees, saying that to go after the devil he would "cut a great road though the law in England." More responds, "Oh? And when the last law was down and the Devil turned round on you, where would you hide, Roper, the laws all being flat? This country's planted thick with laws from coast to coast—Man's laws, not God's—and if you cut them . . . d'you really think you could stand upright in the winds that would blow then?"

Though Pinochet should not be above the law, he could not be denied its full benefits. The rule of law had to be defended.

We continued our discussion in Davos and produced a first draft of our piece. In the meantime we met with numerous prime ministers and political and economic leaders. Unavoidably, Pinochet was one of the main topics of conversation. Shortly before we left for Europe, Lagos had stated that any initiative to take Pinochet back to Chile should be premised on a political willingness to judge him there. Using soccer language, Lagos argued that the world community had shown Chile a "yellow card"—a warning—because though we had advanced in making justice and building democracy, our democracy was "incomplete." Isabel Chadwick, the wife of a disappeared political prisoner, who had searched for her young husband for years after 1973, suffering humiliation and deceit in the process, wrote in the Spanish issue of *Newsweek* a column that reflected the view of a majority of Chileans: "We would prefer that Chileans be in charge of judging the horrendous past of this man [Pinochet]. If that is not possible, we will accept justice in any form that it may come."

Our article, "The Pinochet Dilemma," appeared in the spring 1999 issue of *Foreign Policy* magazine. We wrote that transnational law had "eroded national borders to the point where former heads of state are not guaranteed immunity" and that, therefore, there was an urgent need to "reach consensus on how such laws should be implemented." We pointed to the fact that war criminals from Rwanda and the former Yugoslavia were being tried by international courts set up by the UN, and that the Nuremberg war crimes tribunal had been an international court. The question we posed was, "Who should handle international justice in a globalized world?" We said that "the country where the violations took place should be the first preference, so long as justice can be carried out." We had to avoid a situation where only the big powers could "pick and choose at their discretion which ex-dictators to bring to justice." Although today it may be a widely repudiated former dictator being put on trial, "tomorrow it could be a more dubious case."

We concluded that the International Criminal Court was the instrument best suited to meet the dual purpose of curtailing impunity from serious human rights violations while ensuring just and fair processes under clear rules. The greatest merit of *l'affaire* Pinochet, we said, was that it had catalyzed serious discussions about the international juridical order.

The world was becoming a smaller place for former, current, and aspiring tyrants. Soon after Pinochet's arrest, Lawrence Kabila, president of Democratic Republic of Congo, who was preparing to travel to France, requested formal assurances of diplomatic immunity. He was told that, unlike Pinochet, he enjoyed the "benefits from immunity accorded to chiefs of state while in office." When Khieu Samphan and Noun Chen, two of the top leaders of the Khmer Rouge, turned themselves in to the Phnom Penh government in late December 1998 and apologized publicly for the crimes committed in their name, the prime minister declined to prosecute them for the sake of national reconciliation. But, he added, he could not guarantee their immunity outside of Cambodia. Later, other heads of state accused of human rights crimes actually had to face justice: the former Peruvian President Alberto Fujimori was extradited from Chile, where he had sought refuge; Charles Taylor, the former president of Liberia, was charged with war crimes and crimes against humanity and was handed over to Sierra Leone's Special Court by Nigeria. Fallen dictators could no longer "count on a comfortable haven abroad, safe from extradition," one newspaper reflected.

For Lagos and me, the Pinochet case demonstrated that a country in transition to democracy had to confront all pending troublesome issues and not "sweep them under the rug." True, many transitions from dictatorship to democracy had occurred through painstaking processes of political bargaining; this was the case in Brazil, Portugal, South Africa, Uruguay, and Spain. But unlike Brazil and Spain—

former dictatorships that had become full democracies—Chile still had not regained its full popular sovereignty because Pinochet had left behind authoritarian enclaves, such as the nonelected senators and a military-influenced National Security Council.

It seemed to us at the time that some rightists preferred to leave Pinochet in London, out of sight and out of mind, rather than negotiate the uprooting of those authoritarian enclaves and the complete transition to democracy. We concluded that if Pinochet did not return to Chile to be judged, we Chileans would feel that much less acutely "the urgency to create conditions for justice" in our own country, and would "lose an opportunity to right some of the wrongs of the Chilean transition."

In the meantime the extradition process wended its way through the British courts. After Jack Straw gave the order to proceed on April 15, 1999, Pinochet's defense unsuccessfully attempted to appeal the home secretary's decision. Hearings for the next stage of the process commenced on June 27.

By late July a medical evaluation of the former dictator, requested by the Chilean government, indicated that his health had "gravely deteriorated," lending weight to the supposition that Pinochet would be released on humanitarian grounds. But as Santiago lobbied the governments of Great Britain and Spain to drop the case against the eighty-three-year-old former dictator because of his advanced age and ill health, Pinochet kicked the legs out from under the negotiating table. As defiant as ever, the old general broke his months-long silence and gave an exclusive interview to *The Telegraph* in which he claimed that he was "Britain's only political prisoner." Denying any responsibility for the torture or killings of Chilean dissidents under his regime, he insisted that he had been "kidnapped" by Scotland Yard. The Chilean government was furious. Juan Gabriel Valdés, Chile's new foreign minister, said that "making political declarations" is not the best way to present an image that "might be regarded sympathetically from a humanitarian viewpoint."

At last it was announced that Magistrate Ronald David Bartle of the Bow Street Court would announce his verdict on the Kingdom of Spain's extradition request on October 8, 1999. Magistrate Bartle was a former Tory candidate for Parliament and member of the Royal Society of St. George, whose vice president was Baroness Thatcher. Magistrate Bartle had excused Pinochet from appearing at the court hearing because he had suffered two minor strokes. Pinochet's prospects for avoiding extradition seemed promising.

It was time for Pinochet's defenders to unleash their heaviest artillery. On October 6, 1999, two days before Magistrate Bartle would issue his verdict, Margaret Thatcher, who had been attending the Conservative Party Conference at Blackpool, stood up to raise her voice for Pinochet. The only problem was that the Conservative leader, William Hague, had wanted the Blackpool event to give a new impetus to the party, and a Thatcher speech on Pinochet would focus attention on the ex-dictator and away from the forward-looking Conservative program. She was forced to move her speech to a nearby location, which turned out to be a rather run-down movie theater with about a thousand seats. Chilean Pinochet supporters, mostly members of Congress from the UDI, arrived with banners and posters emblazoned with slogans such as "Free Pinochet" and "The Only Political Prisoner of Great Britain." Outside the theater other Chileans had arrived, who had traveled to Blackpool to chant anti-Pinochet slogans such as "The Best Decision, Extradition."

Inside the theater, Chilean and British orators took to the stage and delivered their speeches, which mostly consisted of reheated rhetoric from the cold war. One Pinochet supporter, the Chilean senator Marcos Cariola, misspoke: "General *Allende* saved Chile from a civil war," he thundered. Thatcher opened her speech dramatically: "Today I break my self-denying ordinance. And for a very good reason: to express my outrage at the callous and unjust treatment of Senator Pinochet." Returning to the Malvinas/Falklands theme, Thatcher said that on Pinochet's "express instructions, and at great risk, Chile provided enormously valuable assistance." In an indiscreet passage, she revealed that "during the Falklands War, the Chilean Air Force gave us early warning of Argentine air attacks, which allowed the task force to take decisive action. The value of this intelligence was proved by what happened when it stopped—Argentine planes attacked and destroyed the *Sir Galahad* and *Sir Tristram* landing ships, with heavy casualties. Without President Pinochet, there would certainly have been many more."

Also attending the Blackpool meeting was right-wing Chilean senator Evelyn Matthei, who confirmed that Chilean Air Force radar gathered intelligence and informed the Royal Air Force about imminent Argentine attacks. Now, she concluded, it was the turn of the British to return the favor. Such revelations led to a formal condemnation of Pinochet's actions by the Argentine Senate, which declared that, in violating Chile's official neutrality, the former dictator had betrayed the common struggle of the heroes of the two countries' struggle for independence, Bernardo O'Higgins and José de San Martín.

Thatcher ominously predicted that Pinochet's arrest could have devastating consequences for Chile, empowering the "small minority of Communists who once nearly wrecked the country under Allende to overturn the prosperous, democratic order that Pinochet and his successors built. Make no mistake," she continued, "revenge by the left, not justice for the victims, is what the Pinochet case is all about."

Outside, the anti-Pinochet protesters yelled, *"Asesinos, asesinos!* Assassins, assassins!" as the British and Chilean right-wingers left the theater. "Go back to Chile!" and "We will lynch you!" Conservative activists shouted back.

Pinochet's supporters were flabbergasted when Magistrate Bartle upheld the Spanish request to extradite Pinochet for the "mental torture" of the families of more than a thousand disappeared prisoners, conspiracy to commit torture from September 11, 1973, through March 11, 1990, and the torture of thirty-five persons perpetrated between July 8, 1988, and March 11, 1999.

The Chilean government saw no other option but to file an official request with Jack Straw to return Pinochet to Chile on "humanitarian grounds." Weeks before, following Spain's rejection of a proposal for international mediation to decide who had jurisdiction in the Pinochet case, the Frei administration had canceled an arbitration pact with Spain dating back to 1927 and recalled its ambassador from Madrid. In September, at the UN General Assembly, Foreign Minister Valdés denounced "foreign judges" who claimed jurisdiction over matters pertaining to Chilean tribunals, and countries that had "selective and sometimes paternalistic" attitudes regarding human rights in other nations.

In early November 1999, the Home Office asked General Pinochet to undergo medical tests after a third stroke made it seem likely that he was unfit for extradition. On January 5, 2000, Pinochet was examined by a team of medical experts at Northwick Park Hospital, in Harrow, near London. A Home Office spokesman said the doctor's report would not be published. Still, the High Court proceedings went on and Pinochet lawyers were notified that an appeal from the defense would be heard on March 20, 2000.

On December 4, 1999, Ricardo Lagos had won a razor-thin victory in the presidential election over the conservative candidate, Joaquín Lavín, forcing a second round of balloting on January 16. The Pinochet case had poisoned the political climate, awakening the ghosts of the past. Caught between leftist forces that espoused an uncompromising hard line on the Pinochet case and a distrustful centrist electorate, Lagos had lost about four percentage points on the left to a combination of Communist and green presidential candidates and had been unable to convince many centrist voters who had abstained or even voted for Lavín. Pinochet's arrest had helped Lavín: it had galvanized the right yet left him free to campaign for change unencumbered by the burden of the general's presence.

In London the signals became increasingly clear. On January 11, Jack Straw said that he was "minded" to release Pinochet after viewing the results of the medical exams. The Home Office declared the "unequivocal and unanimous" conclusion of the medical team that Pinochet was "unfit to stand trial, and that no change to that position [could] be expected." Hence, "no purpose would be served by continuing the present extradition proceeding." Baroness Thatcher, who three months earlier, in Blackpool, had blasted Straw for being partial and for having "visited Chile as a young left-wing activist," now said that she trusted the home secretary's judgment.

Then a new and unexpected twist occurred in the case. Belgium and six human rights groups filed an appeal in the British High Court seeking to prevent Pinochet from leaving the UK pending a judicial review of Straw's handling of the general's medical reports. France and Switzerland joined Belgium in the challenge.

Joan Garcés and Judge Garzón requested that Madrid join the legal objection to Straw's decision and that a new medical examination be conducted by professionals designated by the Spanish tribunals. However, citing a political commitment to the Chilean government, Spain's foreign minister, Abel Matutes, refused to pass along Garzón's appeal request to British lawyers representing Spain, though he agreed that there should be a new medical examination.

On January 31, 2000, the British justice Maurice Kay ruled against the judicial review appeal. But, in another surprise turn, on February 15 a three-member High Court appeals panel reversed Kay's decision, ruling that Straw's refusal to hand over Pinochet's medical records was unlawful, and requested that the home secretary deliver the medical records to the four countries concerned. The next day the Spanish press published extracts from Pinochet's confidential medical record, which reported that he had suffered brain damage that could impair his capacity to respond to questions in a trial. On February 22, after medical experts from the four countries criticized the methodology used by the British doctors, Spain, Belgium, France, and Switzerland formally requested a new medical examination to determine Pinochet's mental capacity to stand trial.

Meanwhile, Ricardo Lagos had been elected president of Chile in the runoff election, held on Sunday, January 16, 2000. At the Hotel Carrera, where we established our campaign headquarters for that day, we embraced in jubilation when we learned the final results—51.3 percent had voted for Lagos, against 48.6 for Lavín. It had been a record-high turnout. More voters had gone to the polls than in the first round. Pinochet had watched the returns thanks to the satellite dish installed in his Surrey residence, but he had gone to bed before hearing of Lagos's victory.

It was as if we had closed a historical circle: a Socialist would again be in La Moneda palace, almost twenty-seven years after Allende's death in the same building. And Pinochet was under arrest in London. Sixty thousand supporters had gathered outside the hotel, on the Plaza de la Constitución, across from La Moneda. Lagos addressed them late in the evening. He said that he would be the "president of all the Chileans. We will have a Chile that grows, creates jobs, and defeats unemployment. Behind these purposes all Chileans are united." Suddenly, the crowd of cheering supporters began yelling, *"Juicio a Pinochet, Juicio a Pinochet!* Put Pinochet on trial!" Lagos interrupted his speech and responded sternly, "Under my government trials will be resolved by the courts, and as president I will respect what the courts decide!" The crowd quieted down.

After the speech some journalists asked Lagos about Pinochet's detention. The president-elect responded, "Pinochet is the past. Chileans have better things to think about."

Lagos offered me the post of ambassador to the United States, which I declined. Pamela, my daughter Paloma, and I did not want to leave Chile after two successive postings abroad (at the Organization of American States in Washington and in Brazil). He then asked me to become deputy foreign minister, a post I accepted after thinking it over for forty-eight hours. The next day, at the campaign headquarters on Providencia Avenue, he called me over to his office.

"I have a first task for you as deputy foreign minister-designate," he said. "Augusto Pinochet Jr. has requested an interview with me. I will not receive him but I have told him that you will," he said.

I protested, but Lagos said that I should just listen to Pinochet's eldest son.

To keep the appointment with Pinochet Jr. a secret from the press, I received him at 8 A.M. at campaign headquarters. Augusto Pinochet Hiriart came accompanied by someone he identified as a lawyer. Pinochet Jr. bore an uncanny resemblance to his father when he was at the height of his power. After some small talk about books of mine that he had supposedly read, and about his business plans in Iquique and about South American integration, I asked him bluntly what I could do for him.

In a humble tone of voice that sounded like a defeated General Pinochet, he said, "I have come to ask that Don Ricardo Lagos intervene in favor of my father so that he can be returned to Chile on humanitarian grounds. He has influence with the Blair government, even more so now that he has been elected president of Chile. They will listen to him. My father is a very sick man and his family wants him back in his homeland."

"You know the president-elect's position on the matter," I replied. "The key issue here is that if your father returns to Chile, he must confront justice. No one can be above the law in a democracy." I ended the meeting with the promise that I would convey our conversation to President-elect Lagos.

Chilean and British conservatives had repeatedly lobbied Lagos to use his influence with European social democratic leaders on Pinochet's behalf, as I personally witnessed. Lagos's position was clear. He would favor Pinochet's return on the condition that he would face a court of law in Chile without any obstructions.

As the world braced itself for another surprise in the Pinochet case, on Thursday, March 2, 2000, Home Secretary Straw announced his final decision: Britain would drop the extradition proceedings against Pinochet; to do otherwise, he said, would violate the European Convention on Human Rights. Straw said he had considered the legal challenges to the medical reports but found them unjustified. This time, Belgium, Spain, France, and Switzerland would not appeal.

Pinochet and his team learned about Straw's decision from a live TV broadcast by a Chilean journalist, Mónica Pérez, at around 8:30 A.M. As he filled a briefcase with selected papers, his entourage packed the rest of his things. Moving quickly was of the essence, because British tribunals opened at 10 A.M. and Pinochet's lawyers feared there would be another last-minute challenge to Straw's decision.

At 9:45 A.M., after seventeen months in London, Pinochet and his entourage left in a caravan of vehicles for Waddington Air Base in Lincolnshire, where a Chilean Air Force jet was waiting. There were hospital facilities in the rear of the plane, which also contained a private bedroom for Pinochet. His departure was momentarily delayed when his defense lawyer, Michael Kaplan, came on board to present Pinochet with a gift from Margaret Thatcher, a reproduction of a silver plate that was made in 1588 to commemorate Sir Francis Drake's victory over the Spanish Armada. The symbolism was duly appreciated, but the Iron Lady probably did not know that, in Chile, Drake is remembered not so much as a British naval hero but as the common pirate who in 1578 pillaged Valparaíso—the birthplace of her departing friend.

Once airborne, one of Pinochet's lawyers opened a champagne bottle to celebrate. It would be smooth sailing all the way to Chile—except for a few tense moments when the plane landed for refueling in Asuncion, a British island territory in the middle of the Atlantic Ocean. "Is the air force plane considered Chilean territory?" a nervous lawyer asked. Near the end of the journey the plane had to change course because the Argentine government would not authorize it to fly over Argentina.

Once Pinochet's plane crossed into Chilean territory, it was escorted by Chilean Air Force fighter planes. Pinochet arrived in Santiago on Friday, March 3, at around 10:30 A.M. on a sunny day. All four commanders in chief of the armed forces and Carabineros were on the receiving line, along with family members, miscellaneous army generals, right-wing politicians, directors of the Pinochet Foundation, and a marching band playing the general's favorite tunes: "Erika" and "Lili Marlene."

Sitting in a wheelchair, General Pinochet was lowered down a yellow ramp. He wore a dark blue suit with a purple tie. When the wheelchair was on the ground, Pinochet rose up as if by a miracle and embraced General Ricardo Izurieta, the army commander in chief. Pinochet was all smiles; he seemed surprisingly strong for a man of his age, especially after such a long, exhausting trip, not to mention his supposed grave medical condition. After walking with a firm pace down the receiving line, Pinochet raised his cane with his right arm, saluting the public and journalists. Then, escorted by heavily armed Special Forces troops in combat gear, he boarded a Puma helicopter, which took him to the Military Hospital for a checkup.

All in all, it had been a hero's welcome. President-elect Lagos was furious: "The interests of the nation demanded prudence," he said. "What we have seen today on television certainly does not help Chile." Le Monde's editorial on the subject was entitled "La Mascarade Pinochet." Street protesters in Santiago staged a parody of the reception in front of the armed forces building, where they awarded a symbolic Oscar to Pinochet for his role as "the English patient."

Six months later and thousands of miles away, in Jakarta, Indonesia, a court dismissed a corruption and human rights abuses case presented by the government against former president Suharto, after a team of doctors declared him "unfit to stand trial." Suharto, seventy-nine, had been under house arrest for more than four months during the judicial proceedings. Every time he had to appear before the court, his health worsened and he had to be rushed to the hospital. Hundreds protested in the streets, yelling, "He's not sick. He is pretending, just like Pinochet." Suharto died in 2008, having escaped justice.

An article in the January 2006 issue of the *British Medical Journal* proposed a new term for the medical lexicon: "Pinochet Syndrome." Its defining features are: "(1) Ill health, which is (2) cited as a reason to delay or stop extradition and judicial investigations into crimes against humanity by (3) a deposed or former national leader." The article referred to various instances when Pinochet and other ex-dictators were "regularly hospitalized just before important court decisions." The cases of Pinochet syndrome showed an upward trend, the author argued; he concluded that "if the medical and legal professions can develop more effective tools for managing it, the duration of symptoms in a case will, we hope, shorten."

Safe and sound in Santiago in March 2000, Pinochet may have thought he'd pulled off a hairbreadth escape. In fact his troubles were just beginning.

Nine

REVERSALS
OF FORTUNE

W hen the dust settled after Pinochet's triumphant return to Chile, the wheels of justice began to grind again. More than seventy-nine judicial suits were lodged against Pinochet in Chilean tribunals. Actually, the first criminal complaint against him—for the kidnapping and assassination of the members of the clandestine directorate of the Communist Party—had been presented in court on January 12, 1998, before he even left for England. Since Pinochet was a senator, the case had to be placed in the hands of a special magistrate. Judge Juan Guzmán was designated to undertake this task.

A soft-spoken, well-read, and generally conservative jurist, Judge Guzmán came from an affluent family who had celebrated Allende's overthrow. During the Pinochet regime there was "complicity between judges and the military" Guzmán wrote in his memoirs; the magistrates wanted revenge for the mistreatment they had experienced during the Allende era, he wrote, and they rejected habeas corpus petitions by simply filling out a form letter created for such purpose. But twenty-five years later, appalled by the horrors committed by Pinochet's secret police, Judge Guzmán had changed; he was determined to bring the former dictator and his collaborators to justice. His investigations were primarily focused on the so-called Caravan of Death, a squad of army officers that traveled by helicopter throughout Chile directing the killing of political prisoners held in different Chilean army garrisons. The action was ordered by Pinochet and carried out by General Sergio Arellano between September 30 and October 22, 1973, after the coup. Guzmán tirelessly interrogated witnesses, including General Arellano, and conducted forensic exams. While

Pinochet was still under arrest in London, Judge Guzmán sent him a questionnaire containing seventy-five queries.

The old general had only been on Chilean soil for a few hours when Guzmán formally requested the Santiago Court of Appeals to lift the immunity that Pinochet was entitled to as a senator-for-life. Pinochet's lawyers reacted immediately, demanding new medical exams. The Court of Appeals ruled that medical tests did not have to be carried out before the immunity issue was decided, and in May 2000, in a landmark decision, Pinochet's immunity was suspended, with thirteen votes in favor, nine against. Pinochet's lawyers appealed to the Supreme Court, supporting their plea with the British government's medical records, but it upheld the Court of Appeals rulings in August.

The right mobilized once again for Pinochet, as sixty politicians and retired military officers gathered around the general at his mansion in La Dehesa (a wealthy Santiago neighborhood) to offer their support, in an event carefully choreographed for domestic television. Smiling and balancing himself with a cane, Pinochet appeared surrounded by the politicians at the entrance of his house. He spoke for about ten minutes, promising that he would defend his honor and announcing a "letter to the Chilean people" that would justify his role in history. Pinochet's wife, Lucía, joined the offensive, criticizing the indictment as "entirely political, unjust, and cowardly."

The Supreme Court ruling directly implicated Pinochet as the perpetrator of the crimes committed by the Caravan of Death. Pinochet could not claim that he lacked legal authority over the Caravan's activities—all of its members were soldiers on active duty. Nor could he claim ignorance. When General Joaquín Lagos, commander of the First Army Division in Antofagasta, informed Pinochet of what the Caravan had been up to in his region, Pinochet not only didn't take any measures against the executioners, he promoted a number of them. A colonel testified that General Arellano had told him beforehand that executions would be carried out in several cities, which strongly suggested that he had been authorized by his superior, Army Commander in Chief Pinochet. Moreover Paragraph 7 of the Supreme Court ruling made explicit reference to the Chilean Army doctrine of "verticality of command" by quoting Pinochet's book *Política, Politiquería y Demagogia* (Politics, Politicking, and Demagogy), published in 1983, in which he argued that command and obedience are the key constituents of military life: "He who does not know how to give orders is useless. And he who does not know how to obey is also useless."

The Letelier case also resurfaced. The Chilean Supreme Court had considered the case to be closed on May 30, 1995, when the former DINA chief Manuel Contreras and the former DINA operations chief Pedro Espinoza were sentenced. But after an affidavit came to light in which Espinoza directly implicated Pinochet in the assassination, a Washington, D.C., court sent a petition via the U.S. State Department to the Chilean Supreme Court requesting that forty-two former Pinochet officials be subpoenaed to respond to detailed questions prepared by U.S. investigators. The Chilean Court acted on the U.S. request less than two weeks after Pinochet's return to Chile. John Beasley, head of the Justice Department's team of investigators, recommended that General Pinochet be prosecuted as the intellectual author of the assassination, but the case eventually stagnated in Washington.

In Chile, however, the Caravan of Death case continued to move through the courts. On December 1, 2000, Judge Guzmán indicted Augusto Pinochet as perpetrator of the Caravan of Death's crimes and placed him under house arrest. A few days later the Court of Appeals reversed Guzmán's decision, ordering that Pinochet be subjected to medical tests and adding that the questionnaire that Judge Guzmán had sent to Pinochet in London, and which he had answered in writing, was insufficient; he had to testify before the judge in person.

The medical tests were conducted at the Military Hospital by psychiatrists, neurologists, and other experts within a matter of weeks. According to one of the doctors who examined Pinochet, the general showed "a great sense of humor, a unique wit, and an impressive spark." One of the doctors, the psychiatrist Luis Fornazzari, was from Iquique, Pinochet's favorite Chilean city.

"I know you," said Pinochet when he saw the physician. "I knew your aunts, they were pretty, and, by the way, you sure look like Joan Garcés," he added.

Dr. Fornazzari asked, "How should I interpret your idea that I resemble Joan Garcés?"

"Well, you are the psychiatrist. . . . "

The doctor concluded that Pinochet's "memory mechanisms [were] extraordinarily well conserved." He added, "Pinochet made a mental association between me and Garcés, being very clear that Joan Garcés, and not Judge Baltasar Garzón, had initiated the court proceedings against him."

The medical tests showed that, although Pinochet was lucid and remembered in detail information in the more remote past than that relating to the Caravan of Death, he suffered a "moderate subcortical dementia." He was not insane; rather, he suffered a mild illness related to his old age.

After the exams were completed, Judge Guzmán interrogated Pinochet. He concluded that the general was fit to face trial and prosecuted him six days later, a decision ratified by the Court of Appeals. Pinochet was held under house arrest at his Los Boldos estate near the Pacific Ocean (seventy-five miles southwest of Santiago) for forty-two days before he was granted bail. Then Pinochet's lawyers and political followers launched a new offensive before the courts and the government to declare Pinochet mentally incapacitated. On July 8, 2001, the Court of Appeals accepted the thesis that Pinochet's mental health did not allow for the due process of law. One year later, on July 1, 2002, the Supreme Court ratified the lower court's decision. The insanity verdict was criticized worldwide in human rights, judicial, and media circles—and also, oddly enough, by Pinochet's wife, Lucía. "You are not going to believe that stupidity that [Pinochet] is insane, are you?" she said to a journalist a few days after the Supreme Court's decision.

The president of the Senate, Andrés Zaldívar, contacted the army commander in chief, General Juan Emilio Cheyre, to tell him that if Pinochet was exempt from prosecution because of his mental illness, then neither should he return to the Senate. Cheyre talked to Pinochet, who was chiefly concerned about his retirement benefits. Once he was assured that he would receive a pension as a former president, Pinochet agreed to retire. He told Zaldívar to go and pick up his resignation, but the Senate president refused. The wrangling about protocol was solved when Cardinal Francisco Javier Errázuriz was chosen to receive Pinochet's voluntary resignation, effective on July 4, 2002.

Pinochet's dodging of prosecution for the Caravan of Death crimes extended to other judicial matters, including the assassination of General Prats in Argentina. But during 2003 Pinochet became careless. He attended the inauguration of a Mercedes-Benz dealership in May; he was spotted at one of his residences in Iquique wearing shorts and looking tanned and healthy; he met with retired generals and delivered political speeches. Pinochet was flaunting his freedom, irritating an army high command that was bent on resuming a strictly professional role.

When I was minister secretary general of the government, General Cheyre, the army commander in chief, told me that he had ordered Pinochet's army guards to empty the air out of the tires of his Mercedes-Benzes to prevent him from shopping and going out to restaurants. Pinochet's trip to Iquique in June 2003 was particularly annoying because Pinochet's bodyguards had violently detained a pair of fishermen that they accused of being potential assassins. Despite the fact that the army provided Pinochet with a substantial infrastructure and generous logistical support, the old general and his family distanced themselves from the new army leadership, whose fealty to the constitution and civilian rule they regarded with suspicion and hostility.

One day in January 2003, when almost everybody else was on vacation and I was the only minister at work at La Moneda palace, I received an urgent phone call from General Cheyre. Pinochet had suffered a stroke at his Los Boldos estate and was being transported by helicopter to Santiago's Military Hospital. Cheyre told me that Pinochet's family had not wanted Pinochet to be treated at the institutional hospital but that, as army commander in chief, he could not authorize them to take him anywhere else. The stroke turned out to be minor, but the incident revealed the growing mistrust between the former dictator and his family and close advisers and the new army high command.

Pinochet's high public profile worked against him when he gave a long interview to a Miami television station, in which he performed impressively well, without any signs of mental or physical debility. On May 28, 2004, the Court of Appeals judges voted fourteen to nine to revoke Pinochet's dementia status (and thus his immunity from prosecution; the Miami television interview—presented as evidence by the prosecution) had raised doubts about Pinochet's mental incapacity. In August 2004, the Supreme Court confirmed the Court of Appeals decision to strip Pinochet of his immunity from prosecution.

In December 2004 Judge Guzmán opened an "Operation Condor" file against Pinochet, this time prosecuting him as the intellectual perpetrator of nine kidnappings and a homicide within the framework of the transnational criminal network. New medical examinations by a court-appointed panel of psychiatrists concluded that the general was lucid and in optimal condition to stand trial. According to the plaintiffs' lawyer, Pinochet knew the names of his attorneys, relatives, and friends, knew what he was being questioned about, and understood the seriousness of the charges that had been lodged against him. It was only after a trip to the bathroom, accompanied by the defense psychiatrist, that he began to experience sudden difficulties in self-expression and claimed to be suffering from dizziness— a condition that the experts termed "exaggerated simulation of cognitive disturbance."

The criminal accusations against Pinochet multiplied. In 2005 Judge Víctor Montiglio slapped charges against him as coperpetrator of 6 of 119 kidnappings of political prisoners who were made to disappear between 1974 and 1975 in the DINA's Operation Colombo—prisoners that DINA later claimed had been killed in intraleft confrontations in Argentina. Pinochet was booked and spent his ninetieth birthday under house arrest. Also in 2005, Judge Alejandro Solís requested that Pinochet's presidential immunity be lifted so he could try him for his participation in the murders committed in the Villa Grimaldi torture center. The Court of Appeals acceded to his request. After Judge Solís interrogated Pinochet, he indicted him for thirty-six cases of kidnapping and twenty-three of torture and had him placed under house arrest. This was the first time that Pinochet was tried for the crime of torture.

Pinochet's immunity was lifted by the Supreme Court in September 2006 for the Villa Grimaldi case and, again, in October 2006, so that he could be prosecuted for the kidnapping of the DINA chemist Eugenio Berríos, who was found dead in Uruguay, and for the torture and killing of a priest, Antonio Llidó. Then the Caravan of Death case was reopened in November 2006, this time for the kidnapping and assassination of two additional victims, and Pinochet was duly prosecuted and placed under house arrest.

Pinochet's situation had become increasingly difficult since Lieutenant Ricardo Lawrence, a former DINA agent, testified that he had escorted Pinochet to the Villa Grimaldi torture center in 1976 to interrogate Víctor Díaz, a Communist Party leader who subsequently disappeared (he was the father of one of the commandos who ambushed Pinochet in 1986). The investigation also cited damning testimony from the DINA chief, General Manuel Contreras.

Pinochet decided to save himself. In a two-hour interrogation on Monday, November 14, 2006, conducted by Judge Víctor Montiglio, he stated repeatedly that he could not recall many of the episodes that the magistrate asked him about, but he detailed his relations with Contreras.

"Is it true that General Contreras reported exclusively to you about all DINA actions?" Judge Montiglio asked Pinochet.

"I don't remember, but oftentimes one had to yank information out of Contreras because he said little or he lied. But I don't remember," Pinochet responded.

"Is it true that DINA actions made Contreras's tenure at its helm untenable and that, therefore, the authorities at that time decided to dissolve that body and to replace it with the CNI?" inquired the judge.

"Manuel Contreras, in my view, wanted to take over the country, but I don't remember," said Pinochet. "I don't know if it was so, but this guy even blackmailed priests with pictures showing them with prostitutes. I fired Contreras because he was creating problems. He offered me some money deposits abroad and I fired him for that."

"Now, is it true what General Gustavo Leigh says, that the DINA chief went daily to pick you up so you could ride together to work, that you both received briefings about DINA actions over breakfast, and that there was a closed-circuit television connection between the Pinochet and Contreras offices?" continued the judge.

"That is a lie. Maybe Contreras came to pick me up some time. I don't remember. How can you imagine I would ride with the intelligence chief next to me?" Pinochet replied. But in an interview published posthumously in 2006, Pinochet said something different: "Sure I had breakfast with him [Contreras] so that he would tell me what was going on. But I did not ask him, 'Hey, who are you going to kill next?' . . . I didn't ask him, 'Hey, did you beat or torture someone?' That was his problem!"

Judge Montiglio pressed on with the interrogation. "Is it true what Contreras testified before the courts, that the president of the junta and later the president of the Republic was the direct chief of the DINA?"

Pinochet's reply was a jewel: "I don't remember, but it is not true. It is not true and if it was, then I don't remember. Contreras liked to cajole, wrap around his boss. Contreras gave the orders; it was he who managed the [DINA] institution."

Pinochet declared that everything he had done had been "for the sake of God, for Chile," and that he had "impeded the country from turning Communist and allowed it to progress up to this day." At the end of the interrogation, the judge asked Pinochet a moral question: "Are you sorry about the deaths that took place under your government?"

"I lament and suffer those losses," Pinochet responded. "But God makes things happen, and he will forgive me if on some occasion I committed an excess, which I do not believe I ever did."

Contreras was furious when he learned about Pinochet's testimony; through his lawyer, he demanded that he and Pinochet be cross-examined. A few days later, on November 18, Judge Montiglio complied.

"Mr. Contreras," asked the judge, "do you confirm that you were accountable exclusively to General Pinochet on the work of the DINA?"

"That is true," said Contreras. "I may add that when I speak of exclusively, what I mean is that I reported to him personally and in writing, through the daily bulletin. . . . Only on exceptional occasions did I report personally to the other members of the junta."

Then it was Pinochet's turn. "I don't remember well. But it seems that he [Contreras] reported to me personally and also to the members of the junta through the bulletin."

The judge went on. "Do you, Mr. Contreras, reaffirm your statement that the DINA never carried out any activity that was not ordered by or known in a proper and timely fashion to General Pinochet?"

"I reaffirm my assertions. Everything the DINA did and not just what is charged," responded the ex-DINA director.

Pinochet became emotional. "I say that General Contreras, as service director, is responsible for what was done by the DINA. How would I be responsible? I could only have an indirect responsibility because the chief could request something from the intelligence service, and how the service director obtained the information was his own business."

The atmosphere in the interrogation room became increasingly tense.

"Mr. Contreras, do you affirm your assertions that with regard to human rights violations, your superior has kept a permanent silence, refusing to defend the DINA?"

"I confirm all that I've said," Contreras replied.

"I would have had to devote all my time to the DINA!" Pinochet declared indignantly. "As far as defending the DINA, what was I going to defend it from if I didn't know? Who directed it was General Contreras," he added.

"I ordered what the president instructed me to do," Contreras responded directly to Pinochet.

The judge intervened, asking Contreras if he stood by his assertion that "Pinochet was responsible for any illicit action related to human rights violations as the responsible superior."

"I say that the president of the Republic, as the direct superior of the DINA, should have been accountable for all past and present accusations against the DINA," Contreras declared.

Then Pinochet backtracked on a serious accusation he had made against Contreras. "As far as the separation of General Contreras from his post of executive director of the DINA, I must rectify my statement, since I misspoke. I got confused; what I said does not reflect reality in the sense that I fired him because he offered me money deposits abroad; this is false and it is a slip of the mind because my memory is failing."

Contreras had made a serious miscalculation. He thought that because of all that he knew, Pinochet wouldn't dare to betray him, that he would defend him to the bitter end. But the reason the old general had remained on top for so long was because he was a skillful practitioner of realpolitik. In May 2006, Pinochet once more smeared Contreras in court testimony. "I believe Manuel Contreras is a liar, he shifted all the roles, his, mine, everybody's, and he appeared as an innocent little bird."

Contreras delivered documents to Judge Montiglio that demonstrated that he acted strictly on Pinochet's behalf, including a November 13, 1973, document that read: "The President of the Military Junta certifies that Lieutenant Colonel Manuel Contreras is his delegate to carry out duties before autonomous public and private organs, all of which must lend support and solve whatever he may request." Pinochet's testimony, Contreras said, constituted "the worst sign of disloyalty." Contending that he had become the scapegoat for human rights crimes for which General Pinochet should take responsibility, Contreras became increasingly outspoken, alleging even that the disgraced ex-dictator and his youngest son, Marco Antonio Pinochet, had obtained an illicit fortune from cocaine manufacturing and trafficking. According to this wild story, made public in July 2006, the drug production operation was overseen by Eugenio Berríos, a chemist working for the secret police, who had disappeared from Chile in 1991 (by order of Pinochet, according to judicial testimony of a Chilean Army general) when he faced questioning in the Letelier assassination case. He turned up dead in Uruguay in 1995.

Another strong Pinochet ally went to prison in 2005. In March of that year, a police dragnet turned up a former Nazi Luftwaffe medic named Paul Schäfer in Argentina and sent him back to Chile. Schäfer had led a bizarre and secretive paramilitary sect composed principally of young German émigrés at Colonia Dignidad, a huge estate in southern Chile, where he controlled every aspect of their lives—and, it was said, made free with the bodies of young boys. Among the estate's many amenities were dungeons, where Schäfer invited the DINA to deposit its political prisoners. Pinochet and his wife, Lucía, visited the Colonia Dignidad on more than one occasion, as did many of his ministers. Pinochet's ties to Schäfer were so close that the cult leader presented him with a Mercedes-Benz 600 Pullman limousine as a gift.

Schäfer escaped Chile in about 1995 and remained a fugitive for nearly a decade. As a result of his capture he was prosecuted for the assassination of a MIR leader, and government authorities recovered from the compound one of the largest caches of illegal weapons ever found, including rocket launchers, machine guns, and automatic rifles. The discovery led to the indictment for human rights crimes of more than ten other former cult members and several former secret police agents. Still unsolved is the case of Boris Weisfeiler, an American professor who vanished while hiking near the colony in 1985. Rumors abounded that Weisfeiler, a Jewish Russian émigré, had been executed on Paul Schäfer's orders.

According to official data, by mid-2007, 560 individuals, almost all of them former officials of the Chilean security forces, had been indicted or were under investigation for human rights crimes, including kidnappings and assassinations of political prisoners. One hundred forty-eight of them, including thirty-four former army generals, had been convicted. General Contreras accumulated 224 years of prison time; his last conviction, in September 2007, was for kidnapping, in connection with the Villa Grimaldi case.

PERHAPS THE ULTIMATE blow to the former dictator's reputation came in 2004, when the leader of the free world's struggle against "Communist terrorism" was brought down by the "war on terror" that began in the wake of America's own 9/11.

Between 1999 and 2001 the U.S. Senate Permanent Subcommittee on Investigations of the Committee on Government Affairs (now the Committee on Homeland Security and Governmental Affairs) investigated money laundering in the U.S. financial services sector. In 2003, at Senator Carl Levin's request, the Permanent Subcommittee initiated a follow-up investigation of the Riggs Bank of Washington, D.C., to evaluate the effectiveness of the anti-money-laundering provisions of the U.S. Patriot Act. The investigative staff reviewed more than one hundred boxes, folders, and compact discs containing hundreds of thousands of pages of documents. According to a July 15, 2004, report prepared by the minority staff of the Permanent Subcommittee, the evidence showed that since at least 1997 the Riggs Bank had "disregarded its anti-money laundering (AML) obligations, maintained a dysfunctional AML program despite frequent warning from the Office of the Comptroller of the Currency (OCC) regulations, and allowed or, at times, actively facilitated suspicious financial activity."

The documents also revealed that from 1994 until 2002 Riggs had opened at least six accounts and issued several certificates of deposit for Augusto Pinochet. According to the Senate report, "The aggregate deposits in the Pinochet accounts at Riggs ranged from $4 to 8 million at a time." Riggs accepted millions of dollars in deposits from him "with no serious inquiry into the source of his wealth"; set up off-shore shell corporations and opened accounts in the names of those corporations to disguise Pinochet's ownership of the funds; altered the names of his personal accounts to disguise ownership; secretly transferred $1.6 million from London to the United States while Pinochet was the target, in 1998, of a worldwide court order seeking to freeze his bank accounts; conducted transactions through Riggs's internal transactions settlement accounts to hide the general's cash transfers; and delivered over $1.9 million in four batches of cashiers checks to Pinochet in Chile. The Senate investigation also found that Riggs concealed the existence of the Pinochet accounts from OCC bank examiners for two years, resisted OCC requests for information, failed to identify or report suspicious account activity, and closed the Pinochet accounts only after a detailed OCC examination in 2002.

In a 1998 client profile, the bank described Pinochet as "a retired professional who achieved much success in his career and accumu-lated wealth during his lifetime in an orderly way," and estimated his personal net worth at $50 million to $100 million. When, in July 2000, pursuant to a routine anti-money-laundering examination, the OCC requested from the bank a list of accounts controlled by foreign polit-ical figures, Riggs omitted Pinochet's name from the list. In 2001, when a bank examiner asked about one of the two Bahamas-based shell corporations set up for Pinochet by Riggs—Ashburton Company Ltd. and Althorp Investment Company—the bank cagily responded that the owner was a public figure in Chile, and that his family mem-bers "were diplomats" and "landowners" with "vineyards."

The Permanent Subcommittee wasn't the first to discover the Pinochet-Riggs connection. But every time someone threatened to re-veal the existence of the accounts—for example, a 1999 Mexican newspaper article that reproduced a copy of one of Pinochet's Riggs Bank statements—Riggs promptly altered the accounts' official names or closed them and transferred the funds to new accounts. When con-fronted with evidence, Pinochet's lawyers simply lied. Marco Anto-nio, Pinochet's youngest son, referred to press reports about secret accounts in the Riggs Bank as "pure lies."

Pinochet and the Riggs Bank chairman and CEO, Joseph L. Allbritton, were close. Pinochet was Riggs's private banking depart-ment's fourth-largest customer. Allbritton received personal gifts from his Chilean friend and the banker intended to invite the former dictator to visit his horse farm in Virginia, according to draft letters discovered during the investigation—perhaps to reciprocate for the time that Allbritton and his wife, Barbara, had been Pinochet's guests at an army equestrian show at the Cavalry School of Quillota. A 1997 letter from Allbritton described Pinochet and their friendship in fulsome terms: "You have rid Chile from the totalitarian government and an archaic economic system based on state owned property and centralized planning. We in the United States and the rest of the Western Hemisphere owe you a tremendous debt of gratitude."

When the OCC investigators discovered the Pinochet accounts in the spring of 2002, they forced Riggs to close them. Nonetheless, the Riggs-Pinochet ties and the illegal acts of the bank secretly continued until the Permanent Subcommittee released its report in 2004. Riggs Bank pleaded guilty to felony charges for its failure to police international money laundering; ultimately it paid some $41 million in civil and criminal penalties. One federal judge branded Riggs Bank a greedy "henchman of dictators."

Riggs and the Allbritton family decided to cut their losses. In February 2005, as part of Judge Garzón's court-authorized deal to dismiss criminal charges against directors and officers of the bank and clear the way for its sale, the Riggs Bank and the controlling family made a $9 million payment to Joan Garcés's President Salvador Allende Foundation, which in turn divided it among 21,887 victims of Pinochet's regime. Just a few weeks later, Robert Allbritton resigned as the chairman and chief executive of Riggs National, the parent company of Riggs Bank, ending twenty-four years of Allbritton family control of the company. Once again, Pinochet had made world news, indirectly bringing down a 160-year-old bank in the process.

Riggs was just the tip of the iceberg when it came to Pinochet's illegal financial empire. Pinochet also had deposits in, among others, Citibank, Banco de Chile in the United States, Espirito Santo Bank of Miami, Coutts & Co. Bank of Miami, and the Atlantic Bank in Zurich and Gibraltar. Banco de Chile, the country's second-largest bank, agreed in early 2005 to pay $3 million in fines after the U.S. government determined that its Miami and New York branches failed to comply with anti-money-laundering rules.

Five days after the release of the U.S. Senate Permanent Subcommittee report on July 15, 2004, Chilean courts designated Judge Sergio Muñoz to open an investigation of Pinochet for tax evasion, money laundering, and misappropriation of government funds. On the evening of August 5 Judge Muñoz interrogated Pinochet at his residence on 3796 Los Flamencos Street in the exclusive La Dehesa neighborhood in Santiago. A few hours earlier the judge had ordered a freeze on all movements of Pinochet's monies. Pinochet, dressed in a sport jacket and wearing white sneakers, complained about his health, claimed that he had done much to improve the material well-being of the judicial branch, and announced that he had saved money from a young age. The judge warned Pinochet that his lawyers would have to fight to gain access to his now-frozen fortune amounting to "eight million *pesos* [about $16,000]." *Whaaattt?* Pinochet reacted, dumbfounded. "My mistake," Judge Muñoz corrected himself. "I meant eight million *dollars*." "Ahhh, okay," said Pinochet with a sigh of relief. Strangely, when asked about his financial adviser Oscar Aitken, with whom he had been consulting recently, Pinochet responded he could not remember if he knew such a person.

Backed by eight detectives, on January 6, 2005, Judge Sergio Muñoz searched Pinochet's Santiago offices and found four passports under false names. Pinochet's lawyers explained that they had been is-sued for security reasons and had never been used. But photocopies of three of them turned up among the documents that OCC examiners found at the Riggs Bank; Pinochet had used them to open accounts under assumed names. About sixty people who worked for Pinochet, from drivers to secretaries, were interrogated. The Chilean Congress also established a commission to determine whether Pinochet's Riggs accounts contained stolen government funds.

Pinochet's family and advisers could no longer deny the existence of foreign accounts. In March 2005, Pinochet's son Marco Antonio amended his earlier statements. "Now, having more information, I have realized that money went into Riggs from Citibank, Banco de Chile and Banco Atlántico . . . and maybe also from Espirito Santo [Bank]. The calculation I make is that adding the Riggs accounts, the total could add up to between $8.5 to $11 million between Riggs and Espirito Santo." Though several of the accounts were also in his own name, Marco Antonio insisted that his father was completely respon-sible for them.

Pinochet had always made much of his austere circumstances and cried poor. In a press interview with the journalist Raquel Correa on September 12, 1993, he was asked about his financial situation. "I'm short of money, as usual," he responded, as he was secretly socking away millions of dollars in accounts around the world, from the United States to Switzerland. When he was detained in London, wife, Lucía, complained that the large legal, medical, and housing bills would force the couple to "begin to sell the few things we have."

Caught in one lie after another, Pinochet's financial adviser, Oscar Aitken, admitted to the Chilean press that the general's fortune could add up to as much as $15 million—all of it accumulated legally through shrewd investing, he said. Aitken asserted that Riggs had "promised, and delivered, rates of return that doubled General Pinochet's capital every three years." A Riggs spokesperson responded that bank records showed that most of Pinochet's accounts had earned only 2 to 3 percent interest. Nicolás Eyzaquirre, Chile's finance minister, ridiculed Aitken's explanation of Pinochet's alleged earnings. "The only way to have achieved those high rates of return would have been if Pinochet himself and his children were financial geniuses, something which is very doubtful."

Among the names that Pinochet used to hide his assets were Augusto Ugarte, José Ramón Ugarte, Daniel López, and John Long. On November 22, 2005, Pinochet's defense attorneys admitted that Pinochet used the false name Daniel López for banking purposes; later, it was discovered that Mr. López had the same Chilean tax ID number as Pinochet's private secretary, Mónica Ananías. John Long, on the other hand, supposedly had been born in Miami on June 11, 1984, but disappeared from the earth in 1985. He opened a Riggs account with checks totaling $287,381 from the accounts of General Jorge Ballerino, Pinochet's aide, and General Ramón Castro, Pinochet's army secretary. Ultimately, $1.7 million passed through Mr. Long's account. Mr. Long in turn transferred money from Miami to Pinochet's son Augusto Jr., who was living at the time in Los Angeles. Before that money found its way to Augusto Jr., it passed through the account of the Chilean consul general in Los Angeles, a distant Pinochet relative.

In June 2005 an appeals court lifted Pinochet's immunity from prosecution on the tax fraud and corruption case, and in August, Pinochet's wife and his son Marco Antonio were summoned to the central headquarters of the Civilian Police. Unexpectedly, the judge had them indicted and arrested on the spot. When Doña Lucía realized she was under arrest, she swooned and had to be rushed to the Military Hospital. Her husband learned of the unfolding drama through a TV news report. Lucía was out on bail within a day, but Pinochet's youngest son was formally accused of being an accomplice in his father's tax fraud, and was arrested and held in jail as "a risk to society" for more than two weeks. In the midst of the political upheaval created by their arrest, Pinochet spoke: "If they want someone to arrest, putting Chile's history on trial, let it be me and not innocent people. I assume all responsibility."

His heartfelt declaration caused a further rift among his remaining followers. Whenever the courts touched his family, Pinochet took responsibility. But when his former political or military comrades were arrested for human rights violations perpetrated under his rule, Pinochet kept a judicious silence—or hung them out to dry.

A few weeks later the State Defense Council sued Pinochet for accepting kickbacks for various weapons deals. On October 25, 2005, the Supreme Court stripped Pinochet of his immunity from prosecution for corruption charges related to his multi-million-dollar bank accounts abroad. Pinochet's fortune was now estimated to be at least $27 million, probably more.

On November 8, 2005, Pinochet was questioned for three and a half hours at his private residence in La Dehesa by Judge Carlos Cerda, who succeeded Judge Sergio Muñoz after he was elected to the Supreme Court. He explained that he had received many "donations" and that his fortune was the result of "savings from a life of work." He acknowledged he had moved his money around several bank accounts because of the "permanent threat of [Spanish Judge Baltasar] Garzón and Joan Garcés who searched all over for my funds." Strangely, he claimed that he had been the victim of a robbery of half a million dollars while he was under arrest in London, money that had been given him by the army. Judge Cerda interrogated Pinochet again about the origins of his fortune on November 10. The contradictions in Pinochet's testimony were flagrant and sometimes amusing. When Judge Cerda asked him about a paper company he owned known as Trilateral International Trading, Pinochet responded: "I don't have any such society; if they opened one in my name, I don't know. Perhaps they made investments and made me a partner. It is unbelievable how one's name lends prestige abroad. When one says my name it's like putting a good label on a thing." As we know, however, Pinochet did not open accounts and register companies in tax havens with his own famous name that "would lend prestige" to partners, but in fact under false identities such as "Daniel López."

Judge Cerda questioned Pinochet again on November 15, and then held a fourth interrogation session on Thursday, November 17, 2005. It was then determined that Pinochet had received $6.8 million of "reserved funds"monies that state authorities can spend for official purposes only without accounting in detail how they are used during five trips abroad between 1974 and 1976. He had also received $5.5 million between 1995 and 1997—when he was only army commander in chief—during visits to England, Malaysia, Brazil, and China.

Pinochet admitted that it was "possible" he had been given those funds, but he could not recall exactly.

"What were the funds for?" the judge inquired. Pinochet explained that they were used to pay meeting expenses, meals, presents. Asked about the presents, he recalled buying "a set of fountain pens." What happened if there was any money left over after the trip? Pinochet explained that the remaining funds were "kept by the person." Further on in the interrogation, Pinochet changed the answer and said that the money "remained in the [military] command." "Generally the leftover funds were insignificant," he added.

"Yes, I used the identity Daniel López," Pinochet admitted, "but in the United States that is not a sin." Asked if he ever knew someone called John Long, Pinochet answered, "That name rings a bell." Pinochet admitted that "possibly" he owned bank accounts in the United States, England, the Bahamas, Gibraltar, and Switzerland. He could not recall having accounts in the Virgin Islands.

The judge stated for the record that during all his interrogations Pinochet "showed normal behavior. . . . He seemed sure about his responses." The month before the interrogation, court-appointed doctors had ruled, once again, that Pinochet was fit to stand trial.

On November 23, 2005, Pinochet was arrested on tax fraud and passport forgery charges arising from his foreign bank accounts maintained under false names, and held under house arrest. It was the first time Pinochet had been prosecuted and arrested on other than human rights counts. Some thought we were witnessing an "Al Capone–type" situation.

The Riggs case cost Pinochet much of his support from conservative politicians and businesspeople. In Chile, the least corrupt country in Latin America, stealing was regarded as a more serious crime than, say, being indirectly responsible for murdering political prisoners.

Many were surprised at Pinochet's corrupt accumulation of wealth. In a 1975 interview with the newspaper Las Ultimas Noticias, Pinochet had dismissed the idea that he would ever profit from his office. "When I have to leave I will go to a notary public and I will take an envelope with my assets, nothing more. It is likely that I will leave with less material possessions than I had when I assumed this post." Shortly after the coup, on September 21, 1973, Pinochet made a sworn statement before a notary public about his assets, which consisted, he said, of about $120,000 in savings from his service in Ecuador and other dollar deposits, a property in Santiago, a lot in Limache valued at $8,000, four cars, jewels, some furniture and antiques, books, and savings in Chilean currency. In 1989 Pinochet made a new voluntary sworn declaration, in which his funds from Ecuador and other dollar deposits had grown to about $470,000; he listed his El Melocotón estate, an apartment (no address), and more or less the same items described in 1973, adjusted in value. No accounts in Riggs or various other banks throughout the world were mentioned. Years later, when Judge Cerda asked Pinochet why a Banco Atlántico account in Zurich containing $2,658,604 had not been included in his sworn statement, Pinochet responded as follows: "I forgot. My glycemia was very high in those days."

In May 1999, while Pinochet was under house arrest in London and the Spanish judge Baltasar Garzón was seeking to freeze his assets, he and Lucía prudently dissolved their conjugal-common-assets regime and divided their property into two equal shares. Surprisingly, many of their holdings had not been mentioned in 1989. Moreover, the couple declared that this was a *partial* liquidation of assets; that is, not all of their assets were included in the division—left off the list, for example, were apartments in Santiago, Iquique, and Valparaíso. Some of the real estate that they did list was grossly undervalued. In the separation document, Pinochet's huge Los Boldos estate was valued at $45,000, whereas the courts fixed its value at more than $2.3 million.

There had been questions about Pinochet's honesty before. In 1984 a civil complaint was filed by a group of lawyers, including Patricio Aylwin, which charged that the general had acquired land for his El Melocotón weekend house at far less than the market price. First there were Pinochet-approved expropriations of neighboring properties; then they were purchased on Pinochet's behalf at ridiculously low prices (General Ramón Castro, whom I got to know in Washington, D.C., in the early 1990s, made the purchases on Pinochet's behalf). The judicial complaint never reached an investigation stage and the opposition leader, Jorge Lavandero, who publicly denounced the scandal, paid a high toll for his outspokenness: he was beaten up by agents of the security forces, an ordeal that left him with a partial hearing loss.

Also in 1984, former congressmen Carlos Dupré and José Monares petitioned the Comptroller General's Office to investigate Pinochet's sale of a lot in Limache to the National Defense Fund. The so-called Quinta Croce was a bad investment because it flooded during the rainy season; Pinochet got rid of it by selling it to a state agency, earning himself a 230 percent profit.

But for all his alleged petty chicaneries, few suspected that Pinochet had accumulated the tens of millions of dollars that he had. Where did this fortune come from? The judicial investigations suggest that one major source was the public funds that his cabinet-like military staff (the Casa Militar) managed. Pinochet's lawyers, Fernando Barros and Pablo Rodríguez, stated in April 2005 that $2.5 million of the general's fortune came from "reserved funds." These funds also financed the stays of Pinochet family members in the United States during the 1980s, according to court testimony by high-ranking army officers. The judicial investigations also revealed that public funds were used to improve three of Pinochet's properties, in the form of labor and materials provided by the Army Corps of Engineers.

According to the Chilean State Defense Council, another major source of Pinochet's fortune was the commissions he received for arms sales. Royal Ordnance, a subsidiary of BAE Systems, England's largest arms firm and a partner in the Chilean Army's Rayo rocket project, invited Pinochet to London on several occasions. After Pinochet retired as commander in chief, the army canceled the Rayo project because of its obsolete technology—writing off $80 million in the process. An investigation by *The Guardian* revealed in September 2005 that BAE secretly paid offshore firms controlled by Pinochet's financial adviser, Oscar Aitken, more than £1 million as commissions on arms deals. Pinochet's former son-in-law Roberto Thieme, once married to Lucía Pinochet, claimed that the Brazilian company Avibras had reached a monetary agreement in 1994 for Lucía to lobby her father and the army on its behalf to win the Rayo contract. The Brazilians were upset to learn that they had not been chosen given that their British competitor's bid of $300 million was double theirs.

In 1994, on the same day that the Chilean Air Force contracted to purchase twenty Belgian Mirage 5 fighter planes, money was deposited at the New York branch of the Banco de Chile in the account of one of the paper companies created by Pinochet's financial adviser, Mr. Aitken. BAE deposited funds into that account. So did the Belgian Air Force. In June 1998 the Chilean Army bought 202 Leopard I tanks for $80 million from RDM Technology, a Dutch company—which also deposited $600,000 into one of Pinochet's accounts in Banco de Chile, New York. Joep van den Nieuwenhuysen, the company's owner, admitted paying a total of $1.5 million to Aitken, Pinochet's money man.

A botched arms deal conducted by the army weapons company, FAMAE (Fábricas y Maestranzas del Ejército), to supply Croatia secretly with guns, mortars, surface-to-air missiles, and ammunition was also linked to Pinochet. A cargo plane carrying the weapons that left Chile in November 1991, ostensibly bound for Sri Lanka but actually heading for Croatia, never reached its destination because it was seized in Budapest, following a tip-off from the CIA. Colonel Gerardo Huber, a senior officer in FAMAE's Logistics Department, in 1991 was prepared to talk about the Croatian and other arms deals to investigators, but then his body turned up on the bank of a river outside Santiago in January 1992. His death was initially ruled a suicide, but in 2006 a judge concluded that he had been "neutralized" to prevent him from testifying. According to Colonel Huber's widow, her husband had been so upset about the improper activities that FAMAE was engaged in that he'd taken his concerns to Commander in Chief Pinochet. "You are mad. You need to go to the fifth floor of the Military Hospital [the psychiatric ward] and see a psychiatrist," Pinochet supposedly told him. In December 2007, the retired army general and former director of the Logistics Department, Carlos Krumm, testified in court that Pinochet had ordered the army to cooperate with the secret sale of weapons to Croatia.

Pinochet was said to have benefited from an arms deal that took place in the 1980s, during the Iraq-Iran War. Carlos Cardoen, a Chilean businessman and former arms manufacturer, had been selling cluster bombs to Saddam Hussein so successfully that he was asked by Saddam to set up a factory in Iraq. Pinochet wanted a piece of the action, too, so FAMAE copied Cardoen's cluster-bomb design and made a deal with the Iranians. Saddam Hussein was furious. But FAMAE's bombs were so poorly manufactured that the Iranians lost a Phantom fighter jet when the cluster bombs exploded in midair instead of on the ground. To compensate the Iranians, the Pinochet regime negotiated the sale, on convenient terms, of fifteen F-5 fighter jets, a deal that the Chilean Air Force opposed. Strangely, the person negotiating the deal was the head of FAMAE, Colonel Carlos Carreño, who was kidnapped in Santiago by the "autonomous" faction of the FPMR in September 1987 as he was about to travel to Teheran to close the transaction—which gave rise to speculation that the "autonomous" FPMR may have been infiltrated by a branch of the Chilean armed forces. (Carreño was released unharmed three months later in Sao Paulo, Brazil.) In any case, according to Cardoen, "Pinochet authorized the sale of weapons to Iran because there were economic incentives . . . commissions."

LUCÍA HIRIART DE Pinochet was a powerful woman, born into a political family (her father had been a Radical Party senator and interior minister). Every high military officer I interviewed while preparing this book, including General Guillermo Garín, the vice commander in chief of the army and a close Pinochet aide, underlined the power that Mrs. Pinochet wielded over her husband. Though Pinochet often ignored his wife's opinions about key political decisions (she opposed the removal of General Contreras as DINA chief, for example), she decisively influenced many of Pinochet's other subordinates' military careers. Lucía had once told her mother-in-law, Avelina, that she wanted to be an "Evita Perón." When Avelina replied that to achieve that status she would have to pass away, Lucía responded, "Then I want to be like Estela Perón" (known as "Isabelita"). Avelina countered, "For that you would have to kill my son." Lucía also spoke her mind. In April 1984 she stated, "If I were head of the government, I would be much tougher than my husband and I would keep all of Chile under a state of siege."

Several capable military officers saw their careers ruined because their personal lives did not comport with her high moral standards. Lucía took over the network Mothers' Centers (Centros de Madres, CEMA or CEMA-Chile), a national women's family association with fifty thousand members, and turned it into her fiefdom. CEMA's rules did not allow family members to work there, but somehow her son Augusto Jr. and daughter Verónica found their way onto its payroll. CEMA even donated $50,000 to its president, Lucía Hiriart de Pinochet, to pay for expenses she incurred during her husband's detention in London.

Since its founding in the 1950s, CEMA had traditionally been directed by the first lady. But when the military government ended, Pinochet was no longer president and Lucía Pinochet was no longer the first lady, but she refused to step down. President Aylwin recalled, "Unlike what happened between General Pinochet and me, where he formally delivered the transfer of the presidency, the same did not occur with the staff of the first lady. My wife had to start from zero. There was no transfer of any sort." Some of Lucía's reluctance to part with her CEMA responsibilities might have stemmed from the fact that, in accordance with a 1980 decree, the organization received 20 percent of the resources from the national lottery that were allotted for social assistance purposes, a subsidy that remained in force until 2005.

Marco Antonio, Pinochet's younger son, never finished college, though he was enrolled for a time at Dubuque University in Iowa, where he studied business administration. He used to present himself as a real estate developer and an importer of motor boats. During the Riggs Bank investigations, it became known that he also owned more than thirty companies worldwide, though his income tax declarations—which claimed a monthly income of about $2,000—made no mention of any of them. Perhaps that was because, as the Riggs inquiry discovered, he used a false passport under the name Marco A. Hiriart to deposit and withdraw funds from the account his father maintained at Riggs under the name José R. Ugarte. Lucía Hiriart and Marco Antonio were co-owners of many of the nearly hundred accounts that Pinochet had abroad.

In July 1975, when he was only sixteen years old, Marco Antonio wrecked a car on his way home from a party. Natalia Ducci, a passenger, was killed. Although he was too young to drive legally, Marco Antonio had a false license, not registered in any motor vehicle office in the county. DINA agents whisked him away from the scene, leaving Natalia's body lying in a gutter. Two years later, another girlfriend of his was gravely injured in a motorcycle accident. He was never prosecuted for either accident. Marco Antonio's apartment in Vitacura borough became famous among his friends for the wild parties held there. He sublet the apartment from a U.S. diplomat, who later discovered that Marco Antonio had completely transformed it, installing a Jacuzzi in the main room, adding wall-to-wall black carpeting, and putting disco lights on the ceiling. During his father's detention in London, a more mature and respectable Marco Antonio, married and in his forties, served as his father's chief spokesman.

The Pinochets' eldest daughter, Lucía, started her career as a secretary but swiftly rose to the helm of a company, Storil Limited, which enjoyed exclusive access to the insurance business of public companies managed by the State Insurance Institute—whose vice president, Mario Gutiérrez Ugarte, was one of General Pinochet's cousins. Lucía also ran a state-funded cultural foundation during the years of her father's regime. Later judicial investigations discovered that investments she made between 1994 and 2005 amounted to some $2,343,387. According to the U.S. Senate report on the Riggs Bank, she had multiple accounts at Citibank Miami and Citigroup Miami. She also had accounts at the Bank of America and Banco de Chile–New York; and her name appeared in several of the ghost companies created to hide Pinochet's fortune. Lucía lived for a few years in Fort Lauderdale, Florida, where she was a real estate agent and owned an antiques shop.

Augusto Jr. graduated from the Military Academy with mediocre grades, just like his father before him. Stationed in Punta Arenas, in an artillery exercise he missed the target and hit a flock of sheep. The owner was furious and to quiet things down Pinochet Jr.'s regiment ended up eating mutton for dinner for several weeks thereafter. After suffering a back injury in an accident in a military truck, he retired from the army and moved to Los Angeles, California, where he was an agent for the Chilean Army in the trade of vehicles and military matériel.

In the 1980s Pinochet Jr. embarked on a number of ill-starred business deals. Charges were brought against him for writing bad checks. With the sale of the rifle company Valmoval, in 1989, he finally struck gold. The "Pinocheques" scandal netted him some $3 million, with which he bought a mansion in Los Angeles. Soon after, his wife, Maria Verónica Molina, left him for a military guard who had been assigned to the family, and took possession of the California property. Pinochet Jr., contrary to the Chilean tradition, swiftly gained custody of their children. In 1992, in the midst of a violent quarrel, Maria Verónica shot her ex-husband in the ankle.

More business failures followed, and in 2004 Pinochet Jr. was prosecuted and condemned to 541 days in jail (not served) for state fraud, generated by the malicious use of tax receipts and falsification of license plates for stolen cars. That same year, the old general promised to buy him a house, so Augusto Jr. went ahead and rented one he liked near his parents' place in La Dehesa; eventually, he was evicted for nonpayment of rent. Augusto Jr. at one time trademarked his father's name for use on branded credit cards and on wines called "Capitán General" and "Don Augusto," and even sold used suits that had belonged to his father.

Verónica, Pinochet's second daughter, was much more discreet than her older sister, although she figured in the web of Pinochet accounts in Citigroup and Riggs Bank in Miami, and was a beneficiary of several of Pinochet's ghost companies. She also had four passports with different identities and different signatures on them. But her ex-husband, Julio Ponce Lerou, went from rags to riches during the Pinochet regime. Having graduated from the Forestry School at the age of thirty-two, he was swiftly named president of a state-owned cellulose company. A few years after that he became president of the state agency that supervised the privatization of all state-owned companies and was also designated the Pinochet government representative on the board of Soquimich, a company that he would acquire in 1988 and expand into hugely profitable new lines of businesses.

Pinochet's youngest daughter was his favorite: Jacqueline Marie. Although no properties were registered to her name, she once declared that she survived thanks to the rental income from the houses she owned. Like her brothers and sisters, Jacqueline had accounts at Espirito Santo Bank and Banco de Chile in Miami. Jacqueline also carried six different passports with six different names.

A quarrelsome lot, several of the Pinochet children were not on speaking terms with each other, but the family's scandals helped bring them closer together. In January 2006, Pinochet's wife and four of her children—Augusto, Marco Antonio, Verónica, and Jacqueline—were arrested on tax evasion and fraud charges. The fifth daughter, Lucía, failed to answer her subpoena and escaped the country, driving to Argentina and from there flying to Washington, D.C., where she sought political asylum. The U.S. authorities denied her request; instead they detained her for ten hours at the airport, canceled her visa, and then transferred her to an Arlington, Virginia, jail, where she remained for two days until she was returned to Chile. She blamed the Chilean government for her problems. The moment she landed in Santiago, Judge Cerda boarded the plane and arrested her.

Arrested along with the Pinochet family were Mónica Ananías, Pinochet's personal secretary; Oscar Aitken, the general's financial adviser and the former executor of his will; and Soledad Olave, Marco Antonio's wife, who was later freed after the charges against her were dismissed.

On his lawyers' advice, Pinochet paid almost $3 million in back taxes while he awaited trial. His two-pronged defense against the tax evasion charges was that, first, the courts were discriminating against him, and second, such crimes as he might have committed had lapsed under a statute of limitations. An official of Chile's Internal Revenue Service responded that if there was any discriminatory treatment it was in Pinochet's favor because he was "the only taxpayer whose declaration was taken at his home residence and in the presence of his attorneys." The State Defense Council representative argued that a statute of limitations could be upheld only after the investigation into the origins of Pinochet's fortune was concluded.

A strange episode occurred in mid-2006 when certificates of deposit for 9,600 kilos of gold in the care of the Hong Kong and Shanghai Bank that were supposedly owned by Pinochet came into the hands of Chilean authorities. The certificates were obvious forgeries. Pinochet backers took advantage of the "gold bars incident" to counterattack, arguing that Pinochet and his family were victims of a plot to persecute them and that all of the corruption charges lodged against them were as false as the certificates.

Despite such last-ditch efforts to restore the Pinochet name, the investigations and prosecutions had taken a steep toll. Pinochet had been hit at his weakest flank: his family. In the past he had ruthlessly abandoned even his most loyal allies to save himself, but he could not do the same to his wife and children. This was much worse than his long detention in London. This was the end. The right-wing political parties had abandoned him, businesspeople were putting a prudent distance between themselves and their former benefactor, and most of his unconditional supporters were now openly disappointed with him.

His ninety-first birthday festivities, celebrated while he was under house arrest, were confined to the house and a terrace, from where—smiling, dressed in an impeccable suit, and surrounded by friends and family—he saluted, with both arms raised in the air, about a hundred die-hard admirers gathered outside his house, who held up pictures of him. The absence of prominent right-wing politicians and members of Congress was noticeable and bitterly resented by his "true blue" followers.

Pinochet marked his birthday by releasing a statement, read by his wife, in which he assumed "political responsibility" for all the acts committed during his rule. "Today, close to the end of my days," he wrote, "I want to make clear that I harbor no rancor toward anybody . . . . If those who 30 years ago provoked chaos and confrontation have become renovated and reinserted themselves in the rule of law, it doesn't follow that those who averted chaos and conflict should be punished."

The purpose of Pinochet's letter—prepared with the assistance of a private media agency, supervised by Pinochet's attorneys, and masterminded by his daughter Lucía—was to make clear that he assumed only "political" and not any "judicial" responsibility, to repair his relations with his fellow retired army officers, and to emphasize the future rather than the past.

A week after the birthday party, on Sunday, December 3, 2006, Pinochet suffered a heart attack and underwent bypass surgery at the Military Hospital. According to medical sources, he was brought back from the brink of death. Only a handful of right-wing dignitaries showed up at the Military Hospital to visit. The head of the rightist UDI defensively declared that Pinochet's situation was a "medical matter, not a political act." Long before this episode, in May 2005, the right-wing presidential candidate, Joaquín Lavín, of UDI, had publicly expressed his "profound disaffection" with Pinochet in light of the reports on torture under his regime and especially the bank accounts scandal, which violated the "tradition that the presidents of Chile were persons who went home poorer than when they assumed the presidency." If such matters had been known in 1988, Lavín said, Pinochet could not have been the plebiscite's candidate.

Pinochet's last days were not only plagued by human rights trials and the Riggs Bank scandal; he also lived to see the constitution he had created fall apart as its authoritarian provisions were systematically rooted out. In August 2005 a reformed constitution signed by Ricardo Lagos (how painful it must have been for Pinochet that a Socialist head of state would sign it) eliminated unelected senators and senators-for-life; reduced the presidential term from six to four years; removed the armed forces as the "guarantors" of the institutional order of the Republic; changed the National Security Council so that it no longer met on its own initiative, but only when convened by the president; and granted the president of the Republic the power to fire the commanders of the armed forces. "Democratic at Last" was the title of the editorial in *The Economist* hailing Chile's new constitution. An article in the *New York Times* entitled "Chile, the Rich Kid on the Block (It Starts to Feel Lonely)," and an opinion piece by Jorge Castañeda in *Newsweek*, entitled "Why Chile Really Matters," underlined the dramatic post-Pinochet achievements of the democratic governments.

As Pinochet's trials ground on and his health steadily deteriorated, Michelle Bachelet, the first woman president in the history of Chile, was elected on January 15, 2006. Chile would now be ruled by a Socialist, agnostic, single mother, torture victim, and former political exile who was the daughter of Alberto Bachelet, an air force general who served under President Allende and died in prison in 1974. It was the greatest of ironies—the commanders of the Chilean armed forces would have to report to one of Pinochet's victims.

Chile had come full circle. Pinochet's coup had sought to eradicate Socialists, but a Socialist woman had risen from the torture chambers of the Villa Grimaldi detention center to become health minister, then defense minister, and now president of the Republic; she assumed office on March 11, 2006. I attended the moving ceremony in Congress where ex-President Lagos received a standing ovation and President Bachelet began to write a whole new page of history.

Nobody was thinking about General Pinochet anymore. He was the past.

Ten

PINOCHET'S
LONG SHADOW

Augusto Pinochet, one of the last surviving dictators of the twentieth century, left the stage of history on Sunday, December 10, 2006, as the world celebrated International Human Rights Day. In New York, as ambassador to the United Nations, I was struck that day by an odd presentiment; instead of watching European soccer, I had tuned in the TV to a Chilean cable channel. No sooner had I done so than I saw the news of Pinochet's passing. Pinochet, always superstitious, had believed the prediction of a Buddhist monk he'd met during a visit to the Chinese city of Xian in April 1993: "You will live one hundred years." He did not make it.

For years I had looked forward to this moment as a time to celebrate; to honor those who fought for democracy and were no longer with us; to revel in the feeling of sweet revenge after his dictatorship had inflicted so much pain on so many. But it was strange: his death did not bring me the joy I once expected, only quiet emotion.

We gathered that evening with some friends, Pinochet opponents all, at Pomaire, a Chilean restaurant on Manhattan's West Forty-sixth Street. Present were a photographer who had snapped the last picture of Orlando Letelier alive at a Madison Square Garden rally a few days before the terrorist bombing that took his life in Washington, D.C., and a former exile who had remained in the United States to become an official in the American labor movement. Alicia Bárcena, Under Secretary-General of the United Nations and a good Mexican friend of Chile, was coincidentally there and joined us, too. It was an intimate moment. We needed to be together to acknowledge our collective identity and to reflect on what we had experienced during our lives lived in the dictator's shadow.

Unlike the thousands of anti-Pinochet demonstrators who were celebrating in Santiago's Plaza Italia and in other capitals throughout the world, or like those well-to-do Chileans who, on September 11, 1973, had toasted the death of President Salvador Allende, we did not uncork any champagne bottles. I suspect that many other people close to Chile's drama felt a similar sensation of distance and ambivalence. Denic Catalán, the restaurant's owner, brought out a dusty bottle of wine produced by former political prisoners in Valparaíso that had been bottled and saved for just this occasion. But there were no cheers, only a quiet feeling of camaraderie among those of us who had endured a common tragedy that was finally coming to an end.

Part of the reason we were so subdued was because Pinochet had eluded justice. Though he had stood trial in Chile on numerous charges, had been stripped of his immunity, and at the time of his death was under house arrest, he had never been convicted of any of the crimes for which he stood accused. He'd taken full advantage of the rights guaranteed him by due process—rights that his victims were denied—and postponed his day of reckoning indefinitely. Moreover, my feelings of hate toward Pinochet and what he represented had waned through the years; instead, I felt a serene contempt for the man.

The news of Pinochet's death was reported worldwide; editorials were written about him in the *New York Times*, the *Washington Post*, the *Daily Independent* of Nigeria, the *Daily Mirror* of Sri Lanka, the *Folha de Sao Paulo* and *O Globo* of Brazil, the *Daily Telegraph* in London, *Le Monde* in Paris, *El País* in Spain, the *Yedioth Aharonot* in Israel, and the *Iran Daily* of Tehran, among others.

The White House had stated: "The Pinochet dictatorship represented one of the darkest periods of Chilean history. . . . Our thoughts are with the victims of his government, and their families." President Luiz Inácio "Lula" da Silva of Brazil said that Pinochet symbolized a dark period in the history of South America, "a long night where the lights of democracy disappeared." The French prime minister, Dominique de Villepin, lamented that Pinochet had died without a "court sentence that would have allowed those who suffered under his rule to close a chapter."

China's reaction was more measured. An official communiqué issued by the Chinese foreign minister in Beijing noted both the repression and the reforms that Pinochet had instituted and stated its hope

that "Chile could maintain its political stability, economic development and social progress." Vladimir Zhrinovski, vice president of the
Russian Duma, speculated that while "there were many victims" under Pinochet "the number would have been higher" under Allende.

Pinochet's family originally expressed the desire to have a "private family funeral," without army or government involvement, but
they soon changed their minds. President Bachelet, however, would
not authorize a state funeral or period of national mourning. Decades
before, Pinochet had refused to pay military honors to President Salvador Allende; Bachelet did not go that far, but granted Pinochet a funeral such as would be accorded to any other former commander in
chief of the army. The minister of defense attended the funeral, held
at the Military Academy, and flags on army bases were flown at half
mast (the right-wing parties Unión Demócrata Independiente and
Renovación Nacional also flew the national flag at half mast). At the
Army Military Academy, thousands filed past the former strongman's
coffin. Claques of Pinochet supporters shouted insults at indifferent
motorists, attacked foreign journalists covering the event, and insulted construction workers at a nearby site who'd shouted anti-
Pinochet slogans.

A solitary protest by a young man caught the attention of the media. After patiently waiting in line to view Pinochet, dressed in his full
military regalia, in his coffin, the young man spat on the glass that
covered the dead dictator's face. The young man was Francisco
Cuadrado Prats, the grandson of General Carlos Prats, who along
with his wife had been assassinated by the dictator's secret police in
Buenos Aires in 1974. Prats did not receive his military honors until
the democratic era.

At the Mass, the minister of defense was loudly booed and heck-
led by the participants. One of Pinochet's secretaries had placed a
presidential sash over the coffin, supposedly a request made by
Pinochet himself. In the middle of the Mass, flouting military regulations, Captain Augusto Pinochet Molina, one of Pinochet's grand-
sons, stood up and delivered a political speech defending the dictator
and his regime and denouncing all those who had supposedly persecuted him, including the courts of law. The following day, the army
commander in chief expelled him from the army.

Juan Emilio Cheyre, a former army commander in chief, told
me that he had spoken to Pinochet about his final wishes about a year
before he died. Fearing that his enemies would desecrate his tomb,
Pinochet had asked to be cremated. He wanted his eulogy to

acknowledge all the posts he'd held, along with the fact that he had willingly surrendered power after the plebiscite, that he had secured peace with Argentina when tensions flared up in the late 1970s, and that he had led the transformation of the Chilean economy. In sum, General Cheyre told me, "he did not want to enter history simply as a dictator."

After the Mass, Pinochet's body was transported by an army Puma helicopter to the Torquemada naval base, and from there to a cemetery in the beach community of Concón, where, true to his wishes, he was cremated. His ashes were placed in a bronze urn, which was then deposited in the chapel of Pinochet's Los Boldos estate, safely out of the reach of his enemies.

NOBODY WON WITH Pinochet's death. It was a draw. The courts did not sentence him and the remains of many prisoners who disappeared have still not been found (though his death seemingly broke the pact of silence among his military collaborators, as information emerged on the burial places of some victims); but Pinochet spent his last years on the defensive, a helpless witness to the destruction of his reputation.

Perhaps we did not celebrate on that Sunday when Pinochet passed away because, politically, Pinochet had died a long time before. A few days after his burial, the Pinochet Foundation publicized a posthumous letter by Pinochet entitled "Message to My Compatriots." The document had been written over two years before his death and placed in a sealed envelope. There was nothing new or newsworthy in it; it was simply the final salvo of the public relations campaign that had begun in London in 1999 with his "Letter to Chileans."

"I love my homeland; I love all of you," Pinochet stated. He reflected on the cold war and the 1973 military coup, arguing that "given the nature of the adversary, it was necessary to employ military control procedures like temporary detention, authorized exile, executions through military trials. In many deaths and in the disappearance of bodies it is very likely that it will never be known how or why they occurred." Pinochet repeated the threadbare argument that the left was plotting a civil war. Then he concluded: "I am proud of the enormous action that had to be done to prevent Marxism-Leninism from achieving total power, and also to enable my dear fatherland to become 'a great nation.'"

It was a feeble, self-serving, and incomplete historical analysis rather than a testament for posterity. Even right-wing leaders were disappointed. The Pinochet-inspired UDI party complained through its president, Senator Hernán Larraín: "He says nothing of what happened after 1974, when human rights violations, torture, and disappearances continued to occur." Other right-wing leaders went even further, flatly characterizing the farewell as "unsatisfactory." Pinochet never apologized for the crimes committed under his rule. "Apologize? About what?" he said in November 2003. When in 1984 he was asked about the large number of disappeared political prisoners, Pinochet callously responded, "Two thousand people are nothing," compared to the total population of Chile.

When the chief of Argentina's army, Martin Balza, courageously admitted in May 1995 that his military had perpetrated "grave errors" during the period of repression known as the "dirty war," Pinochet dismissed his comrade-in-arms' declarations, saying that they did not reflect Chilean reality. Unlike Pinochet, some of his followers expressed mea culpas for their obliviousness to human rights violations. Some military men also had the courage Pinochet lacked.

General Juan Emilio Cheyre, then army commander in chief, delivered a speech in November 2004 in which he abandoned the institutional policy of minimizing human rights violations as mere "excesses" and of arguing that there were only "individual" and not "institutional" responsibilities for their occurrence. General Cheyre's pronouncement was backed by a public declaration by eight former vice commanders in chief of the army. One month later, Cheyre manifested the army's "aspiration to accomplish more than a 'cleansing of historical memory,' but to guarantee that the acts we all condemn will never again be repeated, under any circumstances." He also announced concrete measures to introduce human rights considerations into the rules, teachings, and procedures of the army.

Many of these army reforms followed the release of the shocking report of the National Commission on Torture and Political Imprisonment, headed by Bishop Sergio Valech, which proved that torture was a deliberate policy of Pinochet's armed services. The commission, established by President Ricardo Lagos, registered more than 35,000 cases of torture and political imprisonment, and identified inhumane torture centers all over Chile, perpetrated in army regimental barracks, police precincts, clandestine buildings, prison camps, and on ships. The revelation that the detention and torture of thousands of Chileans had been carefully planned, and the admissions of public figures, from radio and TV personalities to athletes, that they, too, had been arrested and subjected to inhumane treatment, had a devastating impact. When he received the bishop's report, President Lagos put into words what so many Chileans were feeling: "How to explain so much horror? . . . How could we live thirty years in silence? How could we explain that ninety-four percent of those arrested were tortured or that of the three thousand four hundred women who testified, practically all were subjected to some sort of sexual violence?" Not all of the tortured or politically imprisoned testified, either. I did not, and neither did many of my friends. We were seeing only the tip of the proverbial iceberg.

The report directly impelled Congress to approve a reparations bill that provided monetary pensions to victims. The degrading and humiliating nature of torture encourages silence; people were daring finally to publicly acknowledge their intimate and lasting pain. The Lagos government felt an imperative to combat the amnesia that in so many other countries has permitted—or *encouraged*—the emergence of new monsters.

Though Pinochet exaggerated when he claimed that not even a leaf moved in the country without his knowing about it, he did in fact preside over one of the most hierarchical and disciplined regimes in the world. Yet he expected the world to swallow his claim that he never knew about the operations that his subordinates carried out to gun down, poison, slash the throats of, drown, and blow up dissidents in Chile, and in world capitals such as Washington, D.C., Buenos Aires, Rome, Mexico City, and Madrid. When the evidence proved so overwhelming that he could no longer deny it, he blamed everything on the DINA chief, General Manuel Contreras. Pinochet's civilian supporters looked the other way.

President Michelle Bachelet and her mother, Angela Jeria, were arrested on January 10, 1975, and taken to the Villa Grimaldi torture center, where they saw Contreras. Testifying before Judge Alejandro Solís in October 2006, Pinochet said that he did not even know of the existence of that facility—which his own daughter Lucía had visited. Before she became Chile's head of state, President Bachelet used to see one of her torturers in the elevators of the building where she lived. One day she said to him, "I know who you are; I have not forgotten." Although he didn't say anything, every time she saw him after that, the man looked down at his shoes. Times changed and the individual in the elevator was ultimately prosecuted and jailed.

But she wasn't vengeful; President Bachelet made a notable gesture of reconciliation in September 2006 during a ceremony marking the purchase of some fighter jets for the Chilean Air Force. Seeing that a former junta member, Air Force General Fernando Matthei, was present, she walked over to him and hugged him, calling him "Uncle Fernando," as he had been a close friend of her father, Air Force General Alberto Bachelet, who was tortured and died in prison during the Pinochet period. General Matthei was moved. Asked about Pinochet's failure to apologize for human rights violations, General Matthei responded, "That is his problem. . . . I personally asked for forgiveness the day the Rettig report was released. All other commanders in chief rejected it, except me as air force commander."

It was hard for Pinochet's subordinates to accept that their commander in chief—defiant to the end—not only denied responsibility for human rights violations but hid behind a dubious mental illness. But Pinochet was only being true to his nature. Intellectually and ethically limited, he had always been lacking in "grandeur."

Insensitive and sardonic to those below him, he was crafty, submissive, and obsequious with his betters. Though Pinochet was anti-Communist, his ideology was self-interest. To advance his career, before the coup he used to visit regularly with Letelier and his family, bringing presents for the children. Yet a few years later he gave the order to murder Letelier. In times of passionate commitments and causes, his policy was to be pragmatic and cautious, to appear neutral and cultivate the trust and friendship of those with power and authority.

The historian Cristián Gazmuri believes that Pinochet felt a deep resentment toward his more intelligent military comrades and toward politicians of all stripes who he suspected looked down on the military caste. Pinochet had always been second in command, second in line; he minimized his risks, hid his views, and took advantage of opportunities as they appeared. When he finally did reach the top, a lifetime of frustration and humiliation overflowed; the power that he had finally attained never made up for the resentment and mistrust that he'd accrued in its pursuit. This is why, perhaps, Pinochet was equally ruthless toward leftist dissidents, competing leaders within the armed forces, and politicians who wanted a brief duration of the military regime; he was an equal-opportunity hater of anyone who stood in his way, of anyone who might have held him in contempt. "Politicians are loafers and parasites; they are just a couple of alley cats trying to scrape together something," he said dismissively in 1987. Such a personality would use and discard his friends in the most Machiavellian manner.

For all his ethical and intellectual shortcomings, Pinochet possessed a remarkable power instinct. He was a master in the use of fear as a political weapon. Yet he was not an absolute dictator; he pragmatically recognized both his enormous power as well as its limitations. He was assertive and knew how to exercise authority. He was smart enough to rely on close advisers, whom he generally chose quite well, on matters such as economics, which he didn't really understand. Once he was asked how he had selected the Chicago Boys as his economic advisers. "I looked at their faces. I looked at them and listened to what they said. If there was anyone who had halfhearted ideas, he wouldn't do," Pinochet responded. He had many advisers, but he never fully trusted any of them. He withdrew authority as rapidly as he delegated it, particularly if he sensed that the group or person concerned was enjoying excessive influence.

HISTORIANS WILL BE arguing about Pinochet for a long time to come, just as they still hold passionate contending views about Julius Caesar or Napoleon. Pinochet personified a disturbing contradiction. He successfully promoted neoliberal economic reforms that Washington and international financial institutions recommended for emerging countries seeking to "put their houses in order." Most Latin American military dictatorships ran disastrous economies. Pinochet's was the exception. His dictatorship would have had far fewer defenders had it not been for his regime's economic reforms.

At first, Pinochet leaned toward nationalistic economic policies. It was Admiral José Toribio Merino who pressured Pinochet into accepting a new financial plan, just as he had pressured him into joining the coup in the days before 9/11. The plan had been prepared in the shadows by young technocrats close to the navy; though Pinochet was ignorant in economic matters, he adopted the so-called Chicago Boys' radical plans to overhaul the country's battered economy. Subsidies and price controls were scrapped, external tariffs were reduced, and a permissive foreign investment regime was put in place, while inflation was reduced through a Milton Friedman–inspired "shock treatment," which meant drastic public payroll and spending cuts, the return of nationalized and state-owned businesses to private hands, and the ruthless repression of labor unions. Also, banks were deregulated, interest rates freed, and foreign debt refinanced as abundant loans flowed from multilateral lending institutions and private banks. It was a hard slog—the economy shrank 13 percent in 1975—but a recovery followed as reforms were instituted that laid the foundations for the country's economic success.

Still, Chile was not yet out of the woods. The combination of a deregulated financial system to attract foreign capital coupled with a

pegged exchange rate and indexed wages led to a massive recession
that left more than a third of the workforce jobless. Pinochet had to
nationalize banks and industries on a scale unimagined by the Allende
government. Pinochet pulled away from the most dogmatic ideas of
the Chicago Boys, but, interestingly, without giving up on a market-
driven economy. Pragmatic policies restored economic growth as,
once again, Pinochet authorized a gradual reduction of the state's
role in the economy.

In the end, Pinochet won worldwide praise, though grudgingly in
some sectors, for having transformed the Chilean economy into the
most prosperous in Latin America, encouraging export growth, removing trade barriers, establishing an independent central bank able
to control interest and exchange rates, privatizing social security, and
reprivatizing companies in state hands. Chile became the model of an
IMF-compliant country, and Pinochet was hailed as the father of
Chilean modernization. A column in the *Los Angeles Times* by a conservative commentator, Jonah Goldberg, entitled "Iraq Needs a
Pinochet," stated, "[Pinochet's] list of sins—both venal and moral—is
long. But today Chile is a thriving, healthy democracy. Its economy is
the envy of Latin America. . . . An Iraqi Pinochet would provide order
and put the country on the path toward liberalism, democracy and
the rule of law." Another apologetic piece, with abundant use of the
word "but," appeared in the *Wall Street Journal*: "Pinochet probably
stashed millions in personal bank accounts," it read. "*But* he also supported the free-market reforms that have made Chile prosperous and
the envy of its neighbors. . . . Civil liberties were lost and opponents
tortured. *But* over time, with the return of private property, the rule
of law and the freer economy, democratic institutions also returned."

Some conservatives refuse to accept the premise that the general's economic record makes up for his "excesses." An editorial in *The
Economist*, suggestively titled "No Ifs or Buts," put it plainly: "Whatever the general did for the economy, he was a bad man. . . . He
presided over a viciously effective police state and came to personify a
whole era of the bloody despotism during the latter stages of the Cold
War. Even if history bothers to remember that he privatized the pension system, that should not wipe away the memory of the torture,
the 'disappeared' and the bodies dumped at sea." Along similar lines,
an article by John Londregan in the conservative newspaper the
Weekly Standard, published after Pinochet's death, argued that his
"embrace of economic reform seems unlikely to have sprung from a
commitment to freedom. . . . His free market reforms helped him to

garner support domestically on the right, and also among members of the international community." Londregan warned: "One must be careful not to fall into Pinochet's trap, accepting his brutal seizure of power and tyrannical rule as a natural accompaniment of free market reforms. . . . To this day we hear from Moscow that it takes a Pinochet to implement economic policies successfully."

The main problem for Pinochet's apologists was the brutality and corruption of their man. If only Pinochet had modernized Chile's economy to make it a model for the developing world without killing and torturing his opponents and getting caught with his hands in the cookie jar. Conservatives still feel obliged to defend the man and the regime that gave many of them access to riches and prosperity. The bottom line for Pinochet supporters is that, despite his sins, "he made the trains run on time," as Mussolini used to be praised.

They're not completely wrong. Chile's economic mentality changed under Pinochet. Economic policies that seemed bold at the time proved innovating and were incorporated in the policy mix by democratic governments, lending stability to the economy. A broad spectrum of players came to accept the idea that Chile needed to continue growing, and that private initiatives ought to be stimulated. Fiscal rigor and sound macroeconomic policies were a capital that did not belong exclusively to Pinochet, though he had given the green light to his economists to put those policies into practice. But it wasn't Pinochet's doing alone. The groundwork for Pinochet's economic modernization was laid by his predecessors. Land reform of the 1960s and early '70s broke up the inefficient semifeudal estates, allowing the military regime to stimulate the creation of agroindustry as a base for an export-driven economy. Chile's modernization really began around 1920 and had nothing to do with the Chicago Boys. By the time of the coup in 1973, thanks to the efforts of many previous governments, Chileans enjoyed a high level of education (illiteracy was less than 10 percent by 1970), and malnutrition and infant mortality had been declining for decades. Chilean universities were among the best in the Americas; there was an efficient transportation infrastructure; the Central Bank, the Internal Revenue Service, and the General Comptroller's Office, among others, were all solid state institutions. Chile's accumulated sociocultural capital were prerequisites for the success of the Pinochet government's economic reforms.

The key question is this: Was Pinochet necessary? Was the price paid for economic change under Pinochet worth it? Clearly it was not. To begin, systematic repression and violence against dissidents was not inevitable. Very likely, the economic reforms of the Pinochet regime would have been sternly opposed in a democratic context by labor unions, members of Congress, and political parties; but their implementation, even under authoritarian rule, did not require the murder of union leaders, the exile of thousands of dissidents, the torture and disappearance of political prisoners, the terrorist bombing of exiled leaders, and a permanent state of internal war. Mario Vargas Llosa has asserted that a Pinochet-type regime is not a necessary evil; no nation "needs to pass through dictatorship to modernize and reach well-being." Reforms imposed by a dictatorship "always have a price in atrocities and civic and ethical sequels that are infinitely costlier than [the] status quo." Besides, without freedom and the rule of law, public opinion may not be willing to accept the sacrifices required for economic reform to succeed and endure. In the end, economic liberty seldom thrives in the absence of political freedom.

Could Chile have reached its present level of prosperity without Pinochet? My answer is yes. Many Latin American countries that endured economic crises in the 1970s and '80s, such as Brazil and Peru, eventually chose to introduce tough economic reforms—not without vigorous opposition to them. Even Colombia, confronting domestic war, was able to implement economic reforms in a reasonably democratic context.

Moreover, the social costs of Pinochet's economic policies were huge. Pinochet did not build a single hospital in all his years of power and the country's infrastructure was left practically untouched until the return of democracy. In 1970, 20 percent of Chile's population had lived under the poverty line; by 1990, when Pinochet left office, the poor had doubled to 40 percent. Average salaries during the Pinochet years were lower than in 1970. The real Chilean economic miracle truly occurred during the sixteen years following the return of democracy, when the economy grew 5.6 percent, almost doubling the growth rates of the previous three decades. Chile is the Latin American country that grew the most from 1990 to 2006. The country's GDP, at purchasing-power parity, is now well above those of Argentina, Brazil, and Mexico. Between 1985 and 2005, Chile's GDP per capita rose from 24 to 40 percent of U.S. levels, a noticeable exception in comparison to the region's overall record of relative decline. Poverty fell from nearly 40 percent of the population in 1990 to 13.7 percent in 2006. Meat consumption increased from 36.6 kilos per capita annually in 1990 to 79 kilos in 2006. The percentage of Chilean homes owning refrigerators and washing machines jumped from 55 and 37 percent, respectively, in 1992, to 96 and 94 percent in 2006. In short, it took the return to democracy in 1990 to bestow legitimacy on Pinochet's reforms and to expand and improve the country's economic and social record.

Yet for many conservatives, and those who quietly profited under the dictator's rule, Pinochet remained a patriot who saved his country from Communism. Chile was surely polarized in 1973, and radical sectors within Allende's coalition, including my own Socialist Party, contributed to the climate of confrontation and insecurity. But the menace of leftist armed insurrection and the likelihood of imminent Communist takeover were highly exaggerated. The rapidity with which the perpetrators of the coup seized and held control of the country gainsays those myths. The violence that Pinochet unleashed was not a desperate expedient to save an imperiled country; it was a brutal power grab by what became a despotic regime.

Pinochet delivered order after a period of domestic instability and chaos, all of it exacerbated by the Nixon administration's covert and illegal efforts to remove President Allende. Allende was about to announce a plebiscite to resolve the nation's political impasse when the coup began; no matter how he would have fared in such an emergency referendum, his coalition had only the slimmest of chances of winning the 1976 presidential contest. Many of those who favored the coup wanted the armed forces to simply restore order and then immediately call for elections. But having seized power, Pinochet decided to keep it, eliminating democracy along with its defenders.

THE STORY OF Pinochet's rise and fall reflects the broader history of U.S. relations with Latin America and with what was once called the third world. Ferdinand Marcos in the Philippines, Saddam Hussein in Iraq, Manuel Noriega in Panama, and Anastasio Somoza in Nicaragua, to name just a few, were all at one time supported by the United States but were later abandoned or even outright opposed by the American government. The Pinochet dictatorship showed that the United States should beware of getting what it wishes for, because it may just come true. The Nixon administration embraced Pinochet after the coup that it had promoted since the very moment of President Allende's election. But the U.S. government, like a sorcerer's apprentice, helped to unleash forces that it could not control. Pinochet, believing he enjoyed unconditional support from his anti-Communist partner, went so far as to order a terrorist strike in the streets of the American capital, and then turned against Washington when Democratic and Republican administrations demanded justice in the Letelier murder case.

Pinochet was expendable. He never understood that, in an era of growing East-West détente, he no longer provided a necessary service; beyond that, libertarian values are too deeply ingrained in the American worldview to allow it to comport comfortably with a strongman for too long. This is why Pinochet's rule never found lasting friendship in Washington, even under an administration like that of Ronald Reagan.

In the first years of the George W. Bush administration, Secretary of State Colin Powell, during an appearance on Black Entertainment Television, when questioned by a student about the U.S. support for the Chilean coup and Pinochet, declared that that was "not a part of American history that we are proud of." When another student asked him a similar question in a different forum, he answered that he could "not justify or explain the actions and decisions that were made at that time."

Henry Kissinger's name became inextricably linked with Chile, first, because of the illegal attempts he and President Nixon sponsored to prevent Salvador Allende's democratic road to socialism from spreading, and, then, because of his unstinting support for Pinochet. In 2004, a heated debate broke out in the pages of the journal *Foreign Affairs* between Kenneth Maxwell, a British historian specializing in Latin America, and William D. Rogers, Kissinger's friend and partner, that ended with Maxwell's resignation as review editor of the journal. The issue at stake was the U.S. role in the downfall of Allende and the depth of American support for Pinochet's actions. In an article about the controversy in the *Washington Post,* Lynne Duke put matters in perspective: "Chile still reverberates along America's ideological divides over human rights and foreign policy, echoing the old realpolitik-versus-moralism debate heard during the Cold War, when Kissinger and people like him saw Chile as a domino about to fall. So, the battle over Chile goes on."

This controversy wasn't the only sign of the impact Pinochet had in the United States. President George W. Bush's ultimately frustrated reform of the United States' Social Security system had been inspired by the pension system that Pinochet imposed on Chile in 1980, which was later imitated in many other countries. Pinochet's Chile also served as the successful laboratory for the monetarist theories of the late Nobel laureate economist Milton Friedman. On a different ambit, Richard Helms was the first CIA director ever to be indicted, for failing to answer questions before the Senate about the operations to instigate a coup in Chile.

In 2007 the U.S ambassador to Chile, Craig Kelly, visited the former torture center of Villa Grimaldi and wrote in the memorial's guest book: "In the name of my country, I would like to express our profound sympathy to all the victims of torture. I hope this place can contribute to the spirit of 'never again' all over the world." It was a far cry from Kissinger's instructions to one of Kelly's predecessors, to "stop the political science lectures" to Pinochet on the need to respect human rights.

ACCORDING TO OPINION polls by the Centro de Estudios de la Realidad Contemporánea, Pinochet's image in Chile worsened over the years. In 1996, 63 percent of those polled said that history would remember Pinochet as a dictator. In 2006, that percentage had jumped to 82 percent—including 51 percent of those who identified themselves as voters of the far-right UDI and 69 percent of voters of the right-wing Renovación Nacional. But to take a Manichean view of Pinochet and his history is to miss much of his complexity. "I will die, the one who succeeds me will die, but there will be no elections in Chile," Pinochet asserted in 1975. But when he did finally lose the 1988 plebiscite, he handed over his presidency to the democratic opposition. True, he did not do so out of conviction; he relinquished power only reluctantly, when it became clear that the other commanders in chief would not join him in a second coup d'état. Pinochet's pragmatism allowed him to recognize that he had to relinquish part of his authority if he was going to retain any power at all. Few dictators make the choice that he did.

Without a doubt, Pinochet loved his homeland. He was truly committed to making Chile a great, powerful, and respected country. This commitment was part and parcel of his military upbringing. But ironically, he wanted to do so by excluding his compatriots whom he considered to be his political enemies—the majority of the country.

Confronted with a crisis with Argentina in 1978, Pinochet chose the road of negotiations instead of the temptation of armed conflict, which some of his comrades in arms favored. For all of his erratic conduct of the bilateral talks, peace prevailed, because Pinochet was always a realistic man and knew that war should be avoided.

Looking back, we can see that Pinochet was partly our own creation. The polarization of Chilean society, the unrealistic demands of the left for radical change from a government elected by a plurality, the ideologization and inflexibility of a formerly pragmatic political center, and the reaction of an uncompromising right that opposed change and defended its privileges—all contributed to the breakdown of Chilean democracy and the emergence of Pinochet.

Pinochet summed up the faults of a generation, though many still find it easier to exculpate their own errors by blaming him alone. With Pinochet's death, a part of all of us who have been linked to Chile in the last four decades also died. Part of a history that branded us in iron and blood passed away.

But Pinochet refuses to go away entirely. Ever distrustful, he, just like Franco, failed to create political institutions that could carry on his legacy. Yet he cannot be ignored or forgotten, for he has already become a historical benchmark. Chile and the world will have to learn to live with his legacy. In December 2007, one year after the dictator's death, his daughter Lucía announced that she might run for Congress and criticized those conservative politicians who had distanced themselves from the dictator. Earlier, a Chilean judge had ordered the arrest of twenty-three people, including Pinochet's widow and children, former military officers, and several Pinochet associates on corruption charges stemming from an investigation into money laundering and misappropriation of public funds. Although the Supreme Court threw out fifteen of the twenty-three indictments, the case was not closed.

In June 2007, I attended an exhibition at two art galleries in Manhattan's Chelsea neighborhood of eighteen young Chilean artists presenting works under the title "Daniel López Show" (Daniel López was a pseudonym used by Pinochet for his Riggs Bank accounts). Hundreds of New Yorkers attended the inauguration of the art display inspired by Pinochet. The exhibition brochure read: "The generation of artists shown here may not have had direct experience of Pinochet's bloody coup d'etat followed by decades of military regime . . . . This generation has instead experienced the aftermath of Pinochet's public trial ending with his death in a military hospital, December 2006, at age 91." The brochure concluded by explaining that the artists had "subverted Pinochet's pseudonym by making it the title of the exhibition, turning this name into an umbrella—a departure for a range of ideas associated with spinning off or relating directly to the morphing of identities, bending Daniel López into multiple and complex other directions."

Like all memorable characters in a drama, Pinochet touched the lives of countless people throughout the world. He influenced or was the target of the actions or policies of Baltasar Garzón, Margaret Thatcher, Henry Kissinger, Jimmy Carter, Fidel Castro, Ronald Reagan, Leonid Brezhnev, Milton Friedman, and many others. A whole generation was marked by Pinochet.

Like the various identities he used for his secret bank accounts, his memory conjures up different meanings for different individuals and sectors. Some will continue to underscore that he instituted visionary economic reforms that transformed Chile and influenced other nations. But when all is said and done, Pinochet will probably be remembered more as a notorious symbol of repression than as an economic reformer.

For those of us who fought Pinochet, his very name serves to remind us that, under his dictatorship, despite the odds against us, we made history. I have lived in peace with myself for what I did during Pinochet's times. We experienced a meaningful sense of place and purpose because we engaged in a costly but ultimately successful struggle for democracy and human rights that we will never forget. The Pinochet era is over, but the man continues to cast a long shadow.

ACKNOWLEDGMENTS

I DIDN'T PLAN TO WRITE this book. It was Bill Frucht, executive vice president of Basic Books, who came up with the idea that I tell the story of Augusto Pinochet's dictatorship and its legacy from my personal perspective. My first reaction was to decline the proposition, but after a period of reflection and Bill's capable persuasion, I took the challenge. I am glad I did.

I am also indebted to Bill Frucht for his constant encouragement and substantive advice throughout the writing process. Alix Sleight, assistant editor at Basic Books, helped reduce the book to a manageable size without doing harm to its substance, while also attending intensely and efficiently to the many details of the book's production. Joshua Berman supervised the editorial production to polish the manuscript into publishable form. Katherine Scott thoroughly copyedited the manuscript and came up with many useful suggestions. My literary agent and friend, Scott Mendel, went beyond the call of duty with his incisive suggestions and unstinting support for this project.

I am thankful to the several key players in the episodes narrated in this book who agreed to share their testimonies and insights. Among them: former presidents Patricio Aylwin and Eduardo Frei Ruiz-Tagle; ex-Army Commander in Chief Juan Emilio Cheyre and ex-Vice Commander in Chief Guillermo Garín; retired General Carlos Molina, former ministers Enrique Correa, Fernando Léniz, Sergio Melnick, and José Piñera; Senator Jaime Gazmuri; Chilean Ambassador Mario Artaza and U.S. Ambassador Marilyn McAfee; Judge Baltasar Garzón; the late former U.S. congressman Henry Hyde; the journalist Carlos Jorquera; the political scientist Oscar Godoy; retired U.S. Admiral Jonathan Howe; and Carlos Osorio, son of the deceased diplomat Guillermo Osorio.

My friend the former president Ricardo Lagos deserves a special note of appreciation. He supported me in this enterprise from the very beginning, read the entire manuscript, and helped me remember episodes we had lived through together, adding information as well as valuable comments and historical reflections.

I was privileged to have interviewed two actors central to the Pinochet assassination attempt of September 1986 but on opposite sides: Colonel Pedro Pablo Bustos, Pinochet's deputy security chief, and César Bunster, a key organizer of that attack. I thank them both for their assistance and candid reflections about that historical episode.

Joyce Horman, the widow of the murdered American citizen Charles Horman, allowed me access to the private files of Charles's father, Ed Horman, who had kept a meticulous record of his activities—including interviews and copies of all documents and correspondence—as he searched for his missing son and pursued his quest to bring Charles's murderers to justice. Joyce also sent me a photograph of Charles and his father to help illustrate these pages. I am also indebted to Angela Jeria, Congressman Tucapel Jiménez Jr., Ambassador Carmen Hertz, and Silvia Vera for furnishing or authorizing the use of photographs of their loved ones lost during the dictatorship.

The Chilean newspapers *El Mercurio* and *La Nación,* through the kind assistance of their editors Cristián Zegers and Rodrigo de Castro, respectively, generously allowed me to use photos from their archives to illustrate this volume. Likewise, the Fundación de Documentación y Archivo de la Vicaría de la Solidaridad supplied me with photographs of some victims of the Pinochet regime. The Ministry of Foreign Relations of Chile accorded me access to its historical files, where I discovered information heretofore unknown to the public.

María Isabel Seguel and Claudia Aguilar lent me a helpful hand, particularly throughout the initial stages of research and writing of this book.

As always, my main supporter and source of inspiration has been my wife, Pamela, who is a protagonist in many passages of this memoir of events in which she became entangled as a result of my political activity. She read the manuscript, criticized it with her usual sharp intellect, and offered many useful suggestions. This book could only be dedicated to her.

—*Heraldo Muñoz*
NEW YORK CITY, JUNE 2008

SOURCES

CHAPTER 1: A Different 9/11

Barra, Alfredo, *Las Dos Caras del Golpe* (Santiago: Editorial Puerto de Palos, 2005), pp. 23–24, 60–63, 68–74.

Cavallo, Ascanio, and Margarita Serrano, *Golpe: 11 de Septiembre de 1973* (Santiago: Aguilar 2005).

Garcés, Mario, and Sebastián Leiva, *El Golpe en La Legua* (Santiago: LOM ediciones, 2005), pp. 33–34, 49–63.

Guijón, Dr. Patricio, quoted in "Yo ví cuando Allende se disparó," *El Mercurio,* October 16, 2007, p. C3.

Jorquera, Carlos, interview with the author, Santiago, September 12, 2007.

Soto, Oscar, *El Ultimo Día de Salvador Allende* (Santiago: Aguilar, 1999), pp. 90–112.

CHAPTER 2: The Two Pinochets

Arancibia Clavel, Patricia, and Francisco Bulnes, *La Escuadra en Acción* (Santiago: Random House/Mondadori, 2004).

Bonnefoy, Pascale, *Terrorismo de Estadio* (Santiago: Ediciones Chile América/CESOC, 2005), pp. 119–122, 187–188, 198–199.

Caso Frei, "Ministro Indaga las Extrañas Coincidencias con Muerte del General Lutz," *La Segunda,* August 22, 2006, p. 17. See also "Investigación de TVN defiende tesis de asesinato de Frei Montalva," *La Tercera,* August 24, 2006, p. 7.

Constable, Pamela, and Arturo Valenzuela, *A Nation of Enemies* (New York: Norton, 1991).

Correa, Raquel, and Elizabeth Subercaseaux, *Ego Sum Pinochet* (Santiago: Zig Zag, 1989), pp. 39–42, 77, 110–113.

Garcés, Joan, *Desarrollo Político y Desarrollo Económico: Los Casos de Chile y Colombia* (Madrid: Editorial Tecnos, 1972), pp. 247–248, 267.

Gazmuri, Jaime (senator), interview in Patricia Arancibia Clavel, *Cita con la Historia* (Santiago: Biblioteca Americana, 2006), 427–428.

González, Mónica, *Chile: La Conjura* (Santiago: Ediciones B, 2000), pp. 167–168.

Guzmán, Nancy, *Romo: Confesiones de un Torturador* (Santiago: Planeta, 2000), pp. 108–115. See also "Osvaldo Romo, la Entrevista que Generó Intensa Polémica," *El Mercurio,* July 4, 2007.

Informe de la Comisión Nacional de Verdad y Reconciliación (Santiago: Ministerio Secretaria General de Gobierno, 1991).

Madariaga, Mónica, quoted in Sergio Marras, *Confesiones* (Santiago: Ediciones del Ornitorrinco, 1998), pp. 64–65.

Millas, Hernán, *Los Señores Censores* (Santiago: Editorial Antártica, 1985), pp. 15–23, 39–42.

Millas, Orlando, *Memorias, 1957–1991: Una Disgresión* (Santiago: Ediciones Chile-América/CESOC, 1996), pp. 354–358.

Oyarzún, Maria Eugenia, *Augusto Pinochet: Diálogos con su Historia* (Santiago: Editorial Sudamericana, 1999), pp. 211–213.

Palacios, Javier, quoted in "Cómo Palacios relató el 11 de Septiembre," El Mercurio .com, June 27, 2006.

Peña, Carlos, "Lady Macbeth en Chile," *El Mercurio,* August 14, 2005, p. D10.

Prats, Carlos, *Memorias: Testimonio de un Soldado* (Santiago: Pehuén Editores, 1985), pp. 456–457, 485–486.

Pinochet, Augusto, *Camino Recorrido: Biografía de un Soldado,* volume 1 (Santiago: Imprenta del Instituto Geográfico Militar, 1990), pp. 123–124, 196–197, 204–205, 261–262, 279.

Pinochet, Augusto, *Geopolítica* (Santiago: Instituto Geográfico Militar/Memorial del Ejército de Chile, 1968), pp. 238–239.

Pinochet, Augusto, *El Día Decisivo* (Santiago: Editorial Andrés Bello, 1980).

Pinochet, Augusto, interviewed by Patricia Arancibia and others, *La Tercera* (Reportajes), December 17, 2006, pp. R5, R9–R10.

Prose, Francine, "The Folklore of Exile," *New York Times,* July 9, 2006.

Teitelboim, Volodia, quoted in *El Mercurio,* August 13, 2006, p. R6.

Valenzuela, Arturo, *The Breakdown of Democratic Regimes: Chile* (Baltimore: Johns Hopkins University Press, 1978).

Vial, Gonzalo, *Pinochet: La Biografía* (Santiago: El Mercurio/Aguilar, 2002), volume 1, pp. 61–76, 101–120, 201–225.

Videla, Ernesto (general), interview in Patricia Arancibia Clavel, *Cita con la Historia* (Santiago: Biblioteca Americana, 2006), p. 160.

Villagrán, Fernando, and Marcelo, Mendoza, *La Muerte de Pinochet: Crónica de un Delirio* (Santiago: Planeta, 2003), pp. 40–56, 70–87.

CHAPTER 3: The Power to Dictate

Cavallo, Ascanio, Manuel Salazar, and Oscar Sepúlveda, *La Historia Oculta del Régimen Militar* (Santiago: Random House/Mondadori, 1997), pp. 81–94, 228–236, 304–319.

Fontaine, Arturo, *Los Economistas y el Presidente Pinochet* (Santiago: Zig Zag, 1988), pp. 17–20, 104.

Friedman, Milton, quoted in *La Tercera,* November 17, 2006, pp. 43–44, and in *El Mercurio,* November 17, pp. B4, B8.

Huneeus, Carlos, *The Pinochet Regime* (Boulder: Lynne Rienner, 2007), pp. 71–97.

Kelly, Roberto, cited in Patricia Arancibia Clavel, *Conversando con Roberto Kelly V.: Recuerdos de una Vida* (Santiago: Biblioteca Americana, 2005), pp. 164–165, 206–209, 212–219, 253–254.

"Las críticas y revelaciones de Sergio de Castro," *La Tercera,* June 10, 2007, pp. R6–R7.

Léniz, Fernando, former Pinochet minister of economy, interview with the author, Santiago, November 16, 2006.

Madariaga, Mónica, interview in *El Periodista,* November 10, 2006, pp. 18–19.

Muñoz, Heraldo, *La Política Exterior del Gobierno Militar Chileno* (Santiago: Ediciones del Ornitorrinco, 1986), pp. 155–163.

Villagrán, Fernando, and Marcelo Mendoza, *La Muerte de Pinochet: Crónica de un Delirio* (Santiago: Planeta, 2003), pp. 113–118, 186–194.

Vial, Gonzalo, *Pinochet: La Biografía* (Santiago: El Mercurio/Aguilar, 2002), volume 1, pp. 262–273.

CHAPTER 4: Pinochet's Global Reach

Barros, José Miguel, "Diplomacia Espiada," *Hoy,* October 5, 1986, pp. 12–13.

Bredemeier, Kenneth, "Townley Says He Acted as a 'Soldier,' Has No Regrets About Killing Letelier," *Washington Post,* January 23, 1979, p. A5.

Cavallo, Ascanio, Manuel Salazar, and Oscar Sepúlveda, *La Historia Oculta del Régimen Militar* (Santiago: Random House/Mondadori, 1997), pp. 146–147,186–187.

"Comunicados de Chile y EE.UU en Gestiones por el Caso Letelier," *El Mercurio,* March 11, 1978, p. 12.

Chilean Embassy (Washington, D.C.), coded messages directed to the Ministry of Foreign Relations, August 14, 1975; August 28, 1975; December 7, 1972; December 11, 1972; December 7, 1972; November 11, 1972; and December 1, 1972.

"Chilean Hailed on Return from U.S.," *New York Times,* September 10, 1977, p. 7.

Chilean Mission to the United Nations, coded messages directed to the Ministry of Foreign Relations, June 5, 1972; November 20, 1972.

Dallek, Robert, *Nixon and Kissinger: Partners in Power* (New York: HarperCollins, 2007), pp. 235–237.

Davis, Nathaniel, *The Last Two Years of Salvador Allende* (Ithaca: Cornell University Press, 1985), pp. 367–394.

DINA, "Primera Reunión de Trabajo de Inteligencia Nacional," Santiago, October 29, 1975 (unpublished document, in author's collection).

Dinges, John, *The Condor Years* (New York: New Press, 2004), pp. 75–77, 102–103, 127–133, 165.

Helms, Richard, *A Look over My Shoulder: A Life in the Central Intelligence Agency* (New York: Ballantine, 2003), pp. 394–404.

Howe, Jonathan (admiral), former special assistant for National Security Affairs to Vice President Nelson Rockefeller, interview with the author, Jacksonville, Florida, February 13, 2007.

Kissinger, Henry, *The White House Years* (Boston: Little, Brown, 1979).

Kissinger, Henry, *Years of Renewal* (New York: Simon & Schuster, 1999), pp. 750–759.

Kornbluh, Peter, *The Pinochet File* (New York: New Press, 2003), containing a summary and analysis of a declassified dossier of documents by U.S. government agencies on Chile, 1968 to 1991, released in November 2000. These documents were received by Heraldo Muñoz at the Ministry of Foreign Relations in 2000, were read at that time, and were researched for the preparation of the present book.

Lasky, Victor, *Turning Defeat into Victory: The Soviet Offensive Against Chile* (New York: American-Chilean Council, 1975).

Montero, Enrique (general), quoted in *La Segunda,* December 12, 2006, p. 18.

Montero, Admiral Raúl, interview, *La Época,* October 8, 1989, p. 10.

Muñoz, Heraldo, and Carlos Portales, *Elusive Friendship: A Survey of U.S.-Chilean Relations* (Boulder and London: Lynne Rienner, 1991), pp. 49–87.

Muñoz, Heraldo, *Las Relaciones Exteriores del Gobierno Militar Chileno* (Santiago: Ediciones del Ornitorrinco, 1986), pp. 51–54.

Nixon, Richard, *The Memoirs of Richard Nixon* (New York: Touchstone, 1990), pp. 489–490.

Osorio, Carlos, son of the mysteriously deceased career diplomat Guillermo Osorio, interview with the author, New York, July 7, 2007.

Pinochet, Augusto, *Camino Recorrido: Memorias de un Soldado,* volume 2 (Santiago: Imprenta del Instituto Geográfico Militar, 1991), pp. 73, 148–149, 237.

Pinochet, Augusto, *Camino Recorrido: Memorias de un Soldado,* volume 3, book 1 (Santiago: Imprenta del Instituto Geográfico Militar, 1993), pp. 22–23, 70–71, 234.

"Quiet Diplomacy, Deaf Chile," *New York Times,* April 15, 1982.

"67 minutos entre Carter y Pinochet," *El Mercurio,* September 7, 1977, p. A1.

U.S. Senate, *Covert Action in Chile: 1963–1973,* staff report of the Select Committee to Study Governmental Operations with Respect to Intelligence Activities (Washington, D.C.: U.S. Government Printing office, 1975).

Weiner, Tim, *Legacy of Ashes: The History of the CIA* (New York: Doubleday, 2007), pp. 311–313.

Whelan, James, *Out of the Ashes: Life, Death and Transfiguration of Democracy in Chile, 1833–1988* (Washington, D.C.: Regnery Gateway, 1989), chapter 9.

CHAPTER 5: Regime on the Ropes

De Castro, Sergio, interview in Patricia Arancibia Clavel, *Cita con la Historia* (Santiago: Biblioteca Americana, 2006), pp. 360–361, 366–368.

Foxley, Alejandro, *Latin American Experiments in Neo-Conservative Economics* (Berkeley: University of California Press, 1983), pp. 84–90.

Molina, Carlos (general), correspondence with the author, May 5 and 6, 2008.

Melnick, Sergio, minister of planning during the Pinochet regime, interview with the author, Santiago, November 17, 2006.

Spooner, Mary Helen, *Soldiers in a Narrow Land: The Pinochet Regime in Chile* (Berkeley: University of California Press, 1994), pp. 177–182.

Vial, Gonzalo, *Pinochet: La Biografía,* volume 2, (Santiago: *El Mercurio*/Aguilar, 2002), pp. 453–466, 474–495.

CHAPTER 6: To Kill Pinochet or Defeat Him with a Pencil

Alfonsín, Raúl, "Cuba Debe Decidir su Destino," *Clarín,* Buenos Aires, February 21, 2008, p. 23.

Álvarez, Rolando, "La Noche del Exilio? Los Origines de la Rebelión Popular en el Partido Comunista de Chile," in Verónica Valdivia, Rolando Álvarez, and Julio Pinto, *Su Revolución contra Nuestra Revolución* (Santiago: LOM Ediciones, 2006), pp. 135–152.

"Anatomía de una Emboscada," *Qué Pasa,* September 2006, pp. 26–31.

Andrew, Christopher, and Vasili Mitrokhin, *The World Was Going Our Way: The KGB and the Battle for the Third World* (New York: Basic Books, 2005), pp. 69–70, 86.

Arrate, Jorge, and Eduardo Rojas, *Memoria de la Izquierda Chilen—Volume 2 (1970–2000)* (Santiago: Ediciones B, 2003), pp. 393–421.

Bunster, César, interview with the author, Santiago, February 28, 2008.

Bustos, Pedro Pablo (colonel), deputy chief of Pinochet's security detail, interview with the author, Santiago, September 9, 2006.

Brunner, José J., "Notas para la Discusión," September 14, 1986 (unpublished manuscript, in author's collection).

Christian, Shirley, "As Chile Prepares to vote, U.S. Envoy Is Praised," *New York Times,* October 4, 1988.

Chilean embassy (Washington, D.C.), coded messages directed to the Ministry of Foreign Relations, numbers 133–138, August 25, 1987.

Chilean embassy (Washington, D.C.), secret messages directed to the Ministry of Foreign Relations, numbers 852–854, October 3, 1988, and numbers 868–873, October 5, 1988.

Communist Party of Chile, Central Committee, "Conferencia Nacional del Partido Comunista," official communiqué, of the Central Committee, Santiago, June 1984 (photocopy, in author's collection).

Communist Party of Chile, Central Committee, "Convocatoria al XV Congreso Nacional del Partido Comunista de Chile," Santiago, 1988 (photocopy, in author's collection) .

Communist Party of Chile, "Propuestas del Partido Comunista para una Salida Política," Santiago, February 1987 (unpublished document, in author's collection).

Correa, Raquel, and Elizabeth Subercaseaux, *Ego Sum Pinochet* (Santiago: Zig Zag, 1989), p. 145.

Corvalán, Luis, *Lo Internacional en la línea del P.C.* (Santiago: Editorial Austral, 1973), pp. 128–129.

Corvalán, Luis, interview in *Principios,* October 1982, pp. 39–40.

Corvalán, Luis, *Santiago-Moscú-Santiago: Apuntes del Exilio* (Dresden: Verlag Zeit in Bild, 1983), pp. 38–39.

"Declaración del Partido Comunista de Chile–Comisión Política," *La Época,* July 19, 1987, pp. 10–11.

Furci, Carmelo, *The Chilean Communist Party and the Road to Socialism* (London: Zed Books, 1984), pp. 46–60, 165–168.

Ganarekian, Barbara, "Washington Talk: How U.S. Political Pros Get Out the Vote in Chile," *New York Times,* November 18, 1988.

García Pinochet, Rodrigo, *Destino* (Santiago: Imprenta Nuevo Extremo, 2001), pp. 43–67.

Godoy, Oscar, interview with the author, New York, June 26, 2007.

Hyde, Henry J. (U.S. congressman), conversation with the author, New York City, March 27, 2006.

"In Chile: Positively No," *New York Times,* October 7, 1988.

"La Mujer del Atentado a Pinochet," *Punto Final,* September 2006, pp. 10–11.

Mayorga, Patricia, "Juan Pablo II Aconsejó a Pinochet que Entregara el Poder," *El Mercurio,* April 1, 2007, p. C4.

McAffee, Marilyn (U.S. ambassador), interview with the author, Jacksonville, Florida, February 13, 2007.

Muñoz, Heraldo, "Beating Pinochet at His Own Game," *Los Angeles Times,* March 21, 1988, p. 9.

"Nicaragua y Política Militar," *Principios,* no. 21, October 1981, pp. 53–54.

Peña, Cristóbal, *Los Fusileros: Crónica Secreta de una Guerrilla en Chile* (Santiago: Random House-Mondadori, 2007), pp. 120–139, 205, 289–290, 368–369.

Pinochet, Augusto, quoted in María Eugenia Oyarzún, *Augusto Pinochet: Diálogos con su Historia* (Santiago: Editorial Sudamericana), pp. 191–195.

Pinochet, Augusto, *Camino Recorrido: Memorias de un Soldado,* volume 3, book 2 (Santiago: Imprenta del Instituto Geográfico Militar, 1994), pp. 68–71, 143, 220–227.

Reagan, Ronald, *The Reagan Diaries*, edited by Douglas Brinkley (New York: Harper-Collins, 2007).

"Se Habría Descartado Expulsión de Ricardo Lagos," *La Segunda,* September 22, 1986. See also "Ex-Presidente de USA Intercede por Lagos," *La Tercera,* September 23, 1986.

Suro, Roberto, "Pope, on Latin trip, Attacks Pinochet Regime," *New York Times,* April 1, 1987; see also Larry Rohter, "Pinochet Foes Cheered by the Pope's Presence," *New York Times*, April 3, 1987.

U.S. State Department, "Noon briefing," Washington, D.C., October 3, 1988 (photocopy, in author's collection).

Vial, Gonzalo, *Pinochet: La Biografía,* volume 2, (Santiago: *El Mercurio*/Aguilar, 2002), pp. 545–548, 555–566, 573–582.

Verdugo, Patricia, and Carmen Hertz, *Operación Siglo XX* (Santiago: Ediciones Chile
   América/CESOC, 2002), pp. 79–82, 89–93, 127–148, 151–164, 167–194.
"Vietnam y Cuba: el destino de los fusileros," *La Tercera,* September 3, 2006.

CHAPTER 7: Governing with the Enemy
Aylwin, Patricio, in Margarita Serrano and Ascanio Cavallo, *El Poder de la Paradoja*
   (Santiago: Grupo Editorial Norma, 2006), pp. 146–161.
Aylwin, Patricio, interview with the author, Santiago, September 11, 2007.
Bush, George W., quoted in "Chile Proposes to Reform Pension System," *New York
   Times,* December 26, 2006, p. 22.
Cáceres, Carlos, interview in Patricia Arancibia Clavel, *Cita con la Historia* (Santiago:
   Biblioteca Americana, 2006), pp. 521–522.
Correa, Raquel, and Elizabeth Subercaseaux, *Ego Sum Pinochet* (Santiago: Zig Zag,
   1989), p. 141.
Cheyre, Juan Emilio (general, former commander in chief of the Chilean Army), in-
   terview with the author, Santiago, November 15, 2006.
"Encouraging Success in Chile," *New York Times,* March 19, 1991, p. A22.
Fuentes, Claudio, *La Transición de los Militares* (Santiago: LOM Ediciones, 2006), pp.
   66–84.
Gazmuri, Jaime (senator), interview with the author, New York City, May 3, 2008.
"Los Secretos del Espionaje Político en Democracia," *Qué Pasa,* no. 1852, October 7,
   2006, pp. 12–17.
Muñoz, Heraldo, "Cold Reality Dawns in Chile," *Los Angeles Times,* October 18, 1988, p. 7.
Meller, Patricio, Sergio Lehman, and Rodrigo Cifuentes, "Los Gobiernos de Aylwin y
   Pinochet: Comparación de Indicadores Económicos y Sociales," *Apuntes
   Cieplan,* no. 118, September 1993, pp. 7–9.
Molina, Carlos (general), correspondence with the author, May 5 and 6, 2008.
Pinochet, Augusto, interviewed in *El Mercurio,* Sunday, June 11, 1995.
Pinochet, Augusto, interviewed by Blanca Arthur, *El Mercurio*, Sunday, September 6,
   1998.
Pinochet, Augusto, *Camino Recorrido: Memorias de un Soldado,* volume 3, book 2 (San-
   tiago: Imprenta del Instituto Geográfico Militar, 1994), pp. 247–250.
Piñera, José, minister of labor and mining during Pinochet regime, conversation and
   electronic correspondence, April 6, 2005, and February 1, 2007.
Sanfuentes, Andrés, "La Herencia Económica de Pinochet," *Asuntos Públicos,* no. 585,
   December 28, 2006.
Williamson, John, "Latin America Needs to Modify, not Reverse, the Washington
   Consensus," press release, Washington D.C., May 12, 2003, p. 2.

CHAPTER 8: Lost in London
"Acto por el que se Decreta la Prisión Provisional Incondicional de Augusto Pinochet
   y se cursa Orden de Captura Internacional a Contar del Mismo," Juzgado de Instrucción Número 5, Audiencia Nacional, Madrid, October 16, 1998 (photocopy, in author's collection).
Afani, Paula, *La Nuera del General* (Santiago: Editorial Maye, 2006), pp. 77–78.
Albright, Madeleine, quoted in "Respect Chile on Pinochet, Albright says," *Los Angeles Times,* December 1, 1998, p. A8.
Anderson, Jon Lee, "The Dictator," *The New Yorker,* October 19, 1998, pp. 45–57; see
   also the Jon Lee Anderson interview at www.elhistoriador.com.ar/entrevistas
   /1/lee_anderson.php (in Spanish).

Artaza, Mario, (Chile's ambassador to the U.K.), conversation and electronic correspondence with the author, July 15, 2007.

Bachrach, Judy, "The Dictator and the Dead," *Vanity Fair,* June 1999, pp. 126–141.

Beckett, Andy, *Pinochet en Piccadilly* (Barcelona: Tusquets Editores, 2003), pp. 259–294.

Black, Mary E., "Diagnosing Pinochet Syndrome," *British Medical Journal,* January 21, 2006.

Chadwick, Isabel, "El Dolor por las Víctimas," *Newsweek en español,* December 9, 1998, p. 15.

Cheyre, Juan Emilio (general, former commander in chief of the Chilean Army), interview with author, Santiago, November 15, 2006.

Chile, Embassy of, "Representation on Behalf of Senator Augusto Pinochet to the United Kingdom Foreign and Commonwealth Office," no. 37, London, November 26, 1998 (photocopy, in author's collection).

"Chile's Chance," *Washington Post,* March 3, 2000.

"Diligencia Solicitando vía Interpol, la Declaración del General Pinochet," Juzgado Central de Instrucción Número 5, Audiencia Nacional, Madrid, Sumario 19/97 L, October 14, 1998.

Ekaizer, Ernesto, *Yo, Augusto* (Buenos Aires: Aguilar, 2003), pp. 519–538, 589–595.

"Felipe González sobre el Caso Pinochet," *El Mercurio,* December 16, 1998, p. C6.

"Frei Exigió Respeto por Soberanía," *El Mercurio,* December 29, 1998, pp. A1, A8.

Frei Ruiz-Tagle, Eduardo, interview with the author, New York, February 5, 2008.

García Pinochet, Rodrigo, *Destino* (Santiago: Imprenta Nuevo Extremo, 2001), pp. 103–116.

Garzón, Judge Baltasar, interviews with the author, New York City, October 23, 2005, and June 28, 2006.

Garzón, Baltasar, *Un Mundo sin Miedo* (Buenos Aires: Editorial Sudamericana, 2005), pp. 193–199.

Government of Chile, "Note on the Secretary of State's Discretion Under the Extradition Act of 1989," October 27, 1998 (photocopy, in author's collection).

"Homecoming for General Pinochet," editorial, *New York Times,* March 4, 2000.

Human Rights Watch, "When Tyrants Tremble," *Human Rights Watch Reports,* 1999.

"La Mascarade Pinochet," *Le Monde,* March 7, 2000, p. 15.

Lagos, Ricardo, and Heraldo Muñoz, "The Pinochet Dilemma," *Foreign Policy,* Spring 1999, pp. 26–39. Published in Spanish as "Pinochet y la Transición Incompleta," *El País,* February 24, 1999, pp. 15–16.

"Líderes Khmer Rouge Lamentan Crímenes," *El Mercurio,* December 30, 1998. See also "Se modifica el Escenario para los Dictadores," *La Hora,* November 26, 1998, p. 40.

O'Shaughnessy, Hugh, "A Murderer Among us," *The Guardian,* October 15, 1998, p. 18.

Romero, Simon, "Living in Exile Is Not What It Used to Be," *New York Times,* October 7, 2007, p. 10.

Sepúlveda, Alejandra, and Pablo Sapag, *Es la Prensa Estúpido, La Prensa!* (Santiago: Copygraph, 2001).

Sims, Calvin, "Jakarta Court Drops Charges Against Ailing Suharto," *New York Times,* September 29, 2000.

Smith, Anderson W., *Temperate Chile* (London: Adam & Charles Black, 1899).

Thatcher, Margaret, "Speech by Lady Thatcher to a Meeting in Blackpool Organized by the Chilean Reconciliation Movement," October 6, 1999; typescript available at Margaret Thatcher Foundation, London.

Thatcher, Margaret, quoted in "Pinochet 'Unfit to Face Trial'", *BBC News*, January 12, 2000, p. 2.

United Kingdom, Home Office, letter to Senator Augusto Pinochet, London, December 9, 1998 (photocopy, in author's collection).

United Kingdom, Home Office, letter to Senator Augusto Pinochet, London, April 15, 1999 (photocopy, in author's collection).

United Kingdom, Home Office, letter to Senator Augusto Pinochet c/o the Ambassador of Chile, January 11, 2000 (photocopy, in author's collection).

U.S. Opinion Round-up, "General Pinochet's Arrest Stirs Controversy," Federation of American Scientists website, www.fas.org/irp/news/1998/10/981020-chile.htm.

Valdés, Juan Gabriel, "Afirmaciones Finales sobre el 'Caso Pinochet,'" *El País*, March 9, 2000.

CHAPTER 9: Reversals of Fortune

Agnic, Ozren, *Pinochet S.A.: La Base de la Fortuna* (Santiago: RIL Editores, 2006), pp. 67–92.

Arancibia, Patricia, in Lilian Olivares, "Patricia Arancibia Relata su Entrevista 'Post Mortem' a Pinochet," *La Segunda*, December 11, 2006, p. 12.

Barría, Rodrigo, "La Doña," *El Mercurio*, August 14, 2005, p. D5.

Cardoen, Carlos, interview in *La Tercera*, Sunday, January 14, 2007, pp. 4–7.

Carvajal, Cynthia, "Defensa de Pinochet: 'Los Delitos Están Ultraprescritos,'" *El Mercurio*, March 16, 2006.

Carvajal, Cynthia, "Pinochet Declaró como Inculpado," *El Mercurio*, November 9, 2005.

Carvajal, Cynthia, "Riggs Donó a CEMA y Fundación Pinochet," *El Mercurio*, December 27, 2006.

Castillo, Benedicto, *Pinochet: El Gran Comisionista* (Santiago: Mare Nostrum, 2007), pp. 26–29.

"Caso Croacia: General Asegura que Pinochet Ordenó Colaborar en 'Exportación de Armas,'" *La Segunda*, December 11, 2007, p. 12.

Carvallo, Mauricio, "El Negocio de Armas de Pinochet," *El Mercurio*, October 23, 2005, p. D6.

"CDE: Fortuna de Pinochet proviene de gastos reservados y venta de armas," *El Mercurio*, October 13, 2005.

Contreras, Eduardo, *El Desaforado: Crónica del Juicio a Pinochet en Chile* (Santiago: El Periodista, 2003), pp. 41–57.

Contreras, Manuel, quoted in Cynthia Carvajal, "Es una Ofensa Gratuita (Decir que Miento), una Deslealtad," *El Mercurio*, May 23, 2006.

"Cuenta de Pinochet Recibió 1 Millón de Dólares en Abril," *El Mercurio*, Augusto 16, 2005.

Fornazzari, Luis, quoted in "A Pinochet Nadie le Había Hecho Preguntas tan Directas en su Vida," *El Mostrador*, January 20, 2001.

Gallardo, Eduardo, "Pinochet Stripped of Immunity on Corruption Charges," *Miami Herald*, October 20, 2005.

Garín, Guillermo (general, former vice commander in chief of the army), interviews with the author, Santiago, September 7, 2006, and November 16, 2006.

"Garín Acusó Motivos 'Políticos' Tras Versión de Pagar a Pinochet Derivados de Compras de Tanques," *La Tercera*, June 12, 2006.

Guzmán, Claudia, "La Palabra de un ex-DINA contra Schäfer," *El Mercurio*, Sunday, July 24, 2005.

Guzmán, Juan, *En el Borde del Mundo: Memorias del Juez que Procesó a Pinochet* (Barcelona: Editorial Anagrama, 2005).

Lavín, Joaquín, quoted in Mónica Guerra, "Fuerte Remezón por Llamado de Lavín a Hacer 'Mea Culpa,'" *El Mercurio,* September 14, 2006, p. C3. Also, "Lavín Profundiza su 'Desafección' con Pinochet," *El Mercurio,* May 9, 2005.

Leigh, David, and Robert Evans, "BAE's Secret £1M to Pinochet," *The Guardian,* September 15, 2005.

Molina, Jorge, "Riggs Paga US$ 9 Millones para que Retiren Demanda por Pinochet," *La Nación,* Santiago, July 7, 2006.

O'Brien, Timothy, and Larry Rother, "The Pinochet Money Trails," *New York Times,* December 13, 2004, p. A6.

O'Hara, Terence, "Drafts Show Allbritton's Pursuit of Pinochet," *Washington Post,* March 3, 2005, pp. E1E3.

O'Hara, Terence, "Robert Allbritton Resigns as CEO of Riggs Ahead of Merger," *Washington Post,* March 8, 2005, pp. E1, E4.

O'Hara, Terence, "The General and His Banker," *Washington Post,* March 21, 2005, p. 1.

Pinochet, Augusto, testimony before Chilean court, Santiago, November 17, 2005 (photocopy, in author's collection).

Pinochet, Augusto, interview by Raquel Correa, *El Mercurio,* September 12, 1993, p. D5.

Pinochet, Augusto, quoted in Hector Cossio, "Pinochet: 'Dios me Perdonará si Me Excedí Alguna vez, que no Creo,'" *La Tercera,* November 17, 2005.

Pinochet, Augusto, quoted in Carolina Valenzuela, "Pinochet Admite 'Caída de Mente' al Culpar a Contreras," *El Mercurio,* November 23, 2005.

Pinochet, Marco Antonio, interview in *La Tercera,* Sunday, March 20, 2005, pp. 12–13.

Pinochet Hiriart, Lucía, interview by Mauricio Carvallo, *El Mercurio,* Sunday, February 5, 2006, p. D4.

"Pinochet Defiende su Gobierno y Asume Responsabilidad Política 'por Todo lo Obrado,'" *La Tercera,* Sunday, November 26, 2006.

Rodríguez, Pablo, quoted in *El Mercurio,* December 31, 2005, p. C12.

Rohter, Larry, "Colonel's Death Gives Clues to Pinochet Army Deals," *New York Times,* June 19, 2006, p. A6.

Rohter, Larry, "Chile's Leader Attacks Amnesty for Pinochet-Era Crimes," *New York Times,* December 24, 2006, p. A2.

Salazar, Manuel, *Roberto Thieme: El Rebelde de Patria y Libertad* (Santiago: Mare Nostrum, 2007), pp. 212–216.

U.S. Senate, "Money Laundering: Enforcement and Effectiveness of the Patriot Act— Case Study Involving Riggs Bank," minority staff report of the Permanent Subcommittee on Investigations (Washington, D.C.: U.S. Senate, July 15, 2004), pp. 17–36.

Valenzuela, Carolina, "Corte Plantea que Pinochet Eludió Actuar a Favor de Religioso," *El Mercurio,* December 9, 2006.

Wehrhahn, Mónica, "Yo, Testigo de la Pinochet-Mafia," *El Mundo,* Madrid, August 14, 2005.

Zaldívar, Andrés, quoted in "Pinochet y Yo," *El Mercurio,* December 10, 2006, p. D5.

CHAPTER 10: Pinochet's Long Shadow

Castañeda, Jorge, "Why Chile Really Matters," *Newsweek,* March 27, 2006.

CERC, "Informe de Prensa-Encuesta Nacional," Santiago, August 2006, p. 7.

Cheyre, Juan Emilio (general), "Ejército de Chile: El Fin de una Visión," *La Tercera,* November 5, 2004.

Cheyre, Juan Emilio (general), "Discurso del Comandante en Jefe del Ejército en el Cierre del Seminario Ejército y Derechos Humanos para el Siglo XXI," photocopy in author's collection, Santiago, December 7, 2004, p. 2.

Declarations of foreign officials about Pinochet's death in www.emol.com, December 11, 2006; *El Mercurio*, December 12, 2006; *La Tercera*, December 12, 2006, and December 28, 2006.

"Democratic at Last," *The Economist*, September 16, 2005.

Dorfman, Ariel, "Spitting on the Dead Dictator," *Los Angeles Times*, December 17, 2006.

Duke, Lynne, "Plot Thickens: Three decades After Chile's Right-Wing Coup, Historians Have Yet to Dot All the i's. But One Thinks He May Have Crossed a K," *Washington Post*, February 27, 2005.

Goldberg, Jonah, "Iraq Needs a Pinochet," *Los Angeles Times*, December 14, 2006.

Larraín, Hernán, quoted in "Críticas y Alabanzas Provoca Carta Póstuma del General Pinochet," *El Mercurio*, December 25, 2006; see also *La Tercera*, December 25, 2006.

Londregan, John, "Don't Cry for Pinochet," *Weekly Standard*, December 25, 2006.

Maxwell, Kenneth, "The Case of the Missing Letter in *Foreign Affairs*: Kissinger, Pinochet and Operation Condor," *Working Papers on Latin America 4* (Cambridge, Mass.: Harvard University, David Rockefeller Center for Latin American Studies, 2005).

Navia, Patricio, *Las Grandes Alamedas: El Chile Post-Pinochet* (Santiago: La Tercera/Mondadori, 2004), pp. 17–39.

"No Ifs or Buts: Whatever the General Did for the Economy, He Was a Bad Man," *The Economist*, December 13, 2006.

Pinochet, Augusto, "Mensaje a Mis Compatriotas para ser Difundido a mi Fallecimiento," December 2006 (photocopy, in author's collection).

Powell, Colin (secretary of state), "Remarks and Question and Answer Session with Students," Washington, D.C., U.S. Department of State, January 31, 2003, transcript, p. 2.

Powell, Colin (secretary of state), "Interview on Black Entertainment Television's Youth Town Hall," U.S. Department of State, February 20, 2003, transcript, p. 2.

Rohter, Larry, "Chile, the Rich Kid on the Block (It Starts to Feel Lonely)," *New York Times*, April 28, 2004.

Prats, María Angélica, interview in *El País*, December 18, 2006.

Schemo, Diana Jean, "Kissinger Assailed in Debate on Chile," *New York Times*, June 5, 2004.

"The Pinochet Paradox," *Wall Street Journal*, December 12, 2006, p. A18.

"Un Funeral sui Géneris," editorial, *La Tercera*, December 13, 2006, p. 3.

Vargas Llosa, Mario, "Las Exequias de un Tirano," *El Comercio (Lima)*, December 17, 2006.

"Vaticinio que Impresionó a Pinochet," *La Segunda*, December 6, 2006.

INDEX